Applied Decision Analysis

Applied Decision Analysis

Edited by

Francisco Javier Girón
Real Academia de Ciencias
Madrid, Spain

with the assistance and collaboration of

M. Lina Martínez
Universidad de Málaga
Málaga, Spain

Kluwer Academic Publishers
Boston/Dordrecht/London

Distributors for North, Central and South America:
Kluwer Academic Publishers
101 Philip Drive
Assinippi Park
Norwell, Massachusetts 02061 USA
Telephone (781) 871-6600
Fax (781) 871-6528
E-Mail <kluwer@wkap.com>

Distributors for all other countries:
Kluwer Academic Publishers Group
Distribution Centre
Post Office Box 322
3300 AH Dordrecht, THE NETHERLANDS
Telephone 31 78 6392 392
Fax 31 78 6546 474
E-Mail <orderdept@wkap.nl>

Electronic Services <http://www.wkap.nl>

Library of Congress Cataloging-in-Publication Data

Applied decision analysis / edited by Francis Javier
Girón with the assistance and collaboration of M. Lina
Martinez.
p. cm.
Includes bibliographical references.
ISBN 0-7923-8250-1
1. Decision making. I. Girón, Francisco Javier.
II. Martinez, M. Lina.
HD30.23.A665 1998
658.4'03--dc21 98-29182
CIP

Printed on acid-free paper.

Printed in the United States of America

Table of Contents

III Economics and Finance

IV Educational Applications

V Miscellaneous Applications

VI Epilog

Contributing Authors

Ana Allueva Pinilla
Departamento de Matemática Aplicada. Facultad de Veterinaria
Universidad de Zaragoza
Zaragoza, Spain

M. del Mar Arenas
Departamento de Matemáticas
Universidad de Oviedo
Oviedo, Spain

Alejandro Balbás
Departamento de Economía de la Empresa
Universidad Carlos III de Madrid
Getafe (Madrid), Spain

Enrique Ballestero
Unidad de Economía
ETS Ingenieros de Montes
Madrid, Spain

José Miguel Bernardo
Departamento de Estadística e I.O. Facultad de Matemáticas
Universidad de Valencia
Burjassot (Valencia), Spain

Concha Bielza Lozoya
Departamento de Inteligencia Artificial. Facultad de Informática
Universidad Politécnica de Madrid
Boadilla del Monte (Madrid), Spain

Amelia Bilbao
Departamento de Matemáticas
Universidad de Oviedo
Oviedo, Spain

John Butler
MSIS Department. Graduate School of Business
University of Texas as Austin
Texas, USA

Rafael Caballero
Departamento de Economía Aplicada. Facultad de Ciencias Económicas
Universidad de Málaga
Málaga, Spain

S. Caballero
Servicio de Neonatología
Hospital General Universitario Gregorio Marañón
Madrid, Spain

Josep Conde
Departamento de Matemáticas
Universidad de Lleida
Lleida, Spain

James S. Dyer
MSIS Department. Graduate School of Business
University of Texas as Austin
Texas, USA

Thomas Edmunds
Lawrence Livermore National Laboratory
Livermore, USA

J. A. Fernández del Pozo
Departamento de Inteligencia Artificial. Facultad de Informática
Universidad Politécnica de Madrid
Madrid, Spain

Monique Florenzano
CNRS-CEPREMAP
Paris, France

Simon French
School of Informatics
University of Manchester
Manchester, United Kingdom

Eduardo Gallego Díaz
Departamento de Ingeniería Nuclear
E.T.S.I. Industriales
Madrid, Spain

Francisco Javier Girón
Departamento de Estadística e I. O. Facultad de Ciencias
Universidad de Málaga
Málaga, Spain

M. Gómez
Departamento de Inteligencia Artificial. Facultad de Informática
Universidad Politécnica de Madrid
Madrid, Spain

Trinidad Gómez
Departamento de Economía Aplicada. Facultad de Ciencias Económicas
Universidad de Málaga
Málaga, Spain

Mercedes González
Departamento de Economía Aplicada. Facultad de Ciencias Económicas
Universidad de Málaga
Málaga, Spain

Pascal Gourdel
CERMSEM
Université de Paris 1
Paris, France

Jianmin Jia
Department of Marketing
Chinese University of Hong Kong Shatin
Hong Kong, China

Mariano Jiménez
Departamento de Economía Aplicada
Universidad del País Vasco
Bilbao, Spain

Pedro Jiménez Guerra
Departamento de Matemáticas Fundamentales. Facultad de Ciencias. UNED
Real Academia de Ciencias
Madrid, Spain

Joseph B. Kadane
Department of Statistics
Carnegie-Mellon University
Pittsburgh (Pennsylvania), USA

Beatriz Lacruz Casaucau
Departamento de Métodos Estadísticos
Universidad de Zaragoza
Zaragoza, Spain

Pilar Lasala
Departamento de Métodos Estadísticos
Universidad de Zaragoza
Zaragoza, Spain

Alberto Lekuona
Departamento de Métodos Estadísticos
Universidad de Zaragoza
Zaragoza, Spain

Valeri Marakulin
Institute of Mathematics Russian Academy of Sciences
Novosibirsk, Russia

Jacinto Martín
Departamento de Inteligencia Artificial. Facultad de Informática
Universidad Politécnica de Madrid
Madrid, Spain

M. Lina Martínez García
Departamento de Estadística e I. O. Facultad de Ciencias
Universidad de Málaga
Málaga, Spain

M. Pilar Martínez García
Departamento de Métodos Cuantitativos para la Economía
Universidad de Murcia
Murcia, Spain

Alfonso Mateos Caballero
Departamento de Inteligencia Artificial. Facultad de Informática
Universidad Politécnica de Madrid
Madrid, Spain

Elías Moreno Bas
Departamento de Estadística. Facultad de Matemáticas
Universidad de Granada
Granada, Spain

Peter Müller
Institute of Statistics and Decision Sciences
Duke University
Durham, USA

M. José Muñoz Bouzo
Departamento de Economía
Universidad Carlos III de Madrid
Getafe (Madrid), Spain

J. Lynn Palmer
Department of Biomathematics
The University of Texas M.D. Anderson Cancer Center
Houston, USA

K. Nadia Papamichail
School of Informatics
University of Manchester
Manchester, United Kingdom

Lluis Miquel Plà Aragonés
R+D Center, Universitat de Lleida-IRTA
Lleida, Spain

J. Pomar
R+D Center, Universitat de Lleida-IRTA
Lleida, Spain

David C. Ranyard
School of Computer Studies
University of Leeds
Leeds, United Kingdom

Lourdes Rey
Departamento de Economía Aplicada. Facultad de Ciencias Económicas
Universidad de Málaga
Málaga, Spain

David Ríos Insua
Escuela de Ingeniería
Universidad Rey Juan Carlos
Madrid, Spain

Sixto Ríos Insua
Departamento de Inteligencia Artificial. Facultad de Informática
Universidad Politécnica de Madrid
Madrid, Spain

M. Victoria Rodríguez Uría
Departamento de Matemáticas
Universidad de Oviedo
Gijón, Spain

Carlos Romero
Unidad de Economía
ETS Ingenieros de Montes
Madrid, Spain

Francisco Ruiz de la Rua
Departamento de Economía Aplicada. Facultad de Ciencias Económicas
Universidad de Málaga
Málaga, Spain

K. A. Salewicz
IBM-Austria
Vienna, Austria

Manuel Sánchez Luna
Servicio de Neonatología
Hospital General Universitario Gregorio Marañón
Madrid, Spain

M. del Mar Sánchez de la Vega
Departamento de Métodos Cuantitativos para la Economía
Universidad de Murcia
Murcia, Spain

Rakesh Sarin
The Anderson School of Management at UCLA
Los Angeles, USA

Jim Q. Smith
Department of Statistics
University of Warwick
Coventry, United Kingdom

Ana Teruel Doñate
Departamento de Producción Animal y Ciencias de los Alimentos
Universidad de Zaragoza
Zaragoza, Spain

Pantelis Vlachos
Department of Statistics
Carnegie-Mellon University
Pittsburgh (Pennsylvania), USA

Andrés Weintraub
Departamento de Ingeniería Industrial. Facultad de Ciencias Físicas y Matemáticas
Universidad de Chile
Santiago, Chile

Samuel Wieand
National Surgical Adjuvant Breast and Bowel Program
University of Pittsburgh
Pittsburgh, USA

Preface

Taking advantage of the many specialists visiting Spain prior to the INFORMS Meeting in Barcelona, hold from July 14th to July 17th 1997, we organized a workshop on ***Decision Analysis Applications*** at the **Real Academia de Ciencias**, Madrid, Spain, from July 11th to 12th 1997, under the sponsorship of the **Instituto de España**. This workshop had a precedent in the International Conference ***Decision Making: Towards the 21st Century*** also held at the Real Academia de Ciencias in 1993.

The idea of organizing an event, this time devoted to applications of Decision Analysis, was due to Prof. Sixto Ríos, who some four years ago, sponsored and encouraged by the Royal Academy of Sciences, was the creator of an Interdisciplinary Working Group on Decision Analysis —formed with researchers from within and outside this Academy— which has been active since then, organizing periodical meetings, and whose last project has turned out into this Workshop. The workshop turned out to be an stimulating opportunity for communicating and discussing the enormous variety of applications of Decision Sciences.

In this volume we have included most of the invited papers and a selection of refereed contributed papers. Due to the varied nature of the applications, we have grouped them into five groups ending, as way of an epilog, with a paper by **Sarin** which contains important insights and reflections on the nature of Decision Analysis in public and private sectors.

The first part includes seven applications in **Natural Resources and Environmental Decision Making. French et al.** apply Bayesian methodology for handling uncertainty and multi-attribute utility methods to design a real-time on-line decision support system, RODOS, intended to be used throughout all phases of a nuclear accident.

The problem of ranking intervention strategies after contamination by radionuclides of an aquatic ecosystem is part of a large project, the MOIRA project, financed by the European Commission. **Gallego et al.** apply Multiattribute Decision Analysis methodology to develop a Decision Support System to select the optimal alternative. The interesting paper by **Martínez García and Vega** investigates the relation between environment and economic development in a growth model. They study the feasibility of sustained economic growth while, at the same time, mantaining environmental quality, by using optimal control theory.

Markov Decision Processes are applied, by **Plà et al.**, to develop a decision support system, running on a PC, to solve a dynamic sow model at farm level. **D. Ríos Insua et al.** describe developments in the methodology for reservoir operations and its implementation in an intelligent decision support system by using multiattribute utility theory, dynamic models and a new methodology which incorporates the ***management by exception principle***. The analysis of livestock production systems via their modelling by classical linear and compromise programming, in the context of either individual farms or the whole region of Jacetania (Spanish Pyrenees), is found in the paper by **Teruel and Allueva**.

Different computational systems for the management of forest industries in large Chilean forestry firms by using simulation, linear programming, mixed integer programming and heuristics are dealt with by **Weintraub**. These systems have been implemented and used for different levels of decision making.

The second part contains four papers devoted to **Medical Decision Making**. In **Girón et al.** the description of an automated decision diagnostic system for detecting breast cancer —based on a statistical logistic model and piecewise linear and quadratic loss functions—, using historical and semiologic data obtained from patients records and mammograms, is found.

By using recent advances in computation, **Kadane et al.** find optimal group-sequential strategies for each member of a monitoring committee of a clinical trial.

Müller and Palmer discuss expected utility optimization in the context of population models, which include several important models such as pharmacokinetic/pharmacodynamic models, growth curve models, and repeated measurement models. They focus on the problem of optimal design of apheresis schedules to collect blood stem cells from cancer patients. The methodology employed includes longitudinal data models and hierarchical prior models.

The multi-authored paper by **S. Ríos Insua et al.**, a team of decision-makers and members of a neonatology service, describes a decision support system, called IctNeo, for jaundice management in newborn babies, a complex problem daily faced by neonatology services. The basic tools for constructing the model are influence diagrams and multiattribute utility theory.

The third part, **Economics and Finance**, which constitutes an important area of applications, includes four papers. The first one by **Arenas et al.** uses fuzzy linear programming to solve a bank balance sheet problem, by computing the possibility distribution of the optimal value of the objective function when imprecise information or ambiguity is present.

A measure of the arbitrage opportunities in an intertemporal dynamic asset pricing model is introduced in the paper by **Balbás et al.**. Two interesting applications of this measure are considered. First, the measure of the cross-market arbitrage gives information about the integration between two or more financial markets. Second, dynamic asset pricing models with transaction costs can be analyzed.

Ballestero and Romero apply compromise programming and multiple criteria decision making to solve workers' enterprises models. These models are based upon a utility function with two arguments (leisure and income) which is optimised over the corresponding production feasibility frontier. In this way typical ***perverse behaviours*** are avoided.

The paper by **Florenzano et al.** is the most theoretical of the four in this part. Nevertheless, the authors prove an interesting result on the existence of finantial equilibrium on a two-period exchange model with bounded portfolios under very mild assumptions. They also characterize the asset trading that supports allocations, prices and finantial transfers at the limit when bounds are relaxed to infinity.

The fourth part, **Educational Applications**, contains two quite different applications. The first one by **Bernardo** refers to the problem, often encounter in education and in other contexts, of how to approach multiple-choice examinations. The author argues that answering this form of questions is a ***decision problem***, the solution of which depends on the examination rules and the candidates goals and their utility functions. He goes onto analysing two real situations often encountered in practice; namely, that of maximizing the expected score and that of maximizing the probability of obtaining the minimum grade required to pass. On the other hand, the paper by **Caballero et al.** addresses the important problem of determining the extra budget assignments of University Departments in order to balance their initial assignment by applying dynamic goal programming to obtain the best distribution of university resources to balance a usually initial unbalanced situation. They illustrate their approach with real data taken from the University of Málaga (Spain).

We have gathered under the name of **Miscellaneous Applications** two papers which did not fit properly in the former groups of applications, despite their interest. Thus, **Dyer et al.** apply multiattibute utility (MAU) theory to evaluate alternatives for disposition of surplus plutonium to prevent the proliferation of nuclear weapons, taking into account economical, technical, environmental and health and safety issues. **Lekuona et al.** propose a new approach to classical problems of maintenance and replacement based on the use of dynamic graphical models, a technique that has rarely been used to model temporal processes.

We hope that the wide and varied range of applications included in this volume can help those interested in real world applications in getting a glimpse of the possibilities of Decision Making in coping with complex problems.

FRANCISCO JAVIER GIRÓN
M. LINA MARTÍNEZ

Acknowledgements

The main sponsor of the Workshop was the **Instituto de España**, an all embracing Institution of the **Spanish Royal Academies**, which not only provided financial support but also helped in organizing the Workshop. My warmest gratitude to the President of the Instituto, Dr. Margarita Salas Falgueras, and to the Secretary Dr. Pedro García Barreno for his encouragement and kind disposition.

We want to thank the President of the **Real Academia de Ciencias**, Prof. Ángel Martín Municio who enthusistically supported the project, and its staff and that of the **Instituto de España** for their always efficient assistance. Special thanks are to be given to Prof. Sixto Ríos who encouraged and promoted the Workshop. The Scientific Committee, which includes Profs. Bernardo, French, G. Barreno, J. Guerra, Kadane, S. Ríos and Weintraub, helped in arranging the scientific contents of the Workshop.

The edition of the proceedings has been finantially supported by the project on *Complex Decision Making Problems* from Consejeria de Educacion y Cultura de la Comunidad de Madrid and a *Marroquí-Andaluz* project supported by the Consejería de Educación de la Junta de Andalucía.

I want to thank Zachary Rolnik, from Kluwer Academic Publisher, for the warm reception given to this volume, which may be regarded as a follow up of the preceding volume **Decision Theory and Decision Analysis: Trends and Challenges**, also published by Kluwer in 1994 and edited by Sixto Ríos.

Finally, I want to thank all anonymous referees who greatly helped the Editor in his task. And last but not least my deep gratitude to Prof. David Ríos for his disinterested help in the refereeing process and to the Associate editor M. L. Martínez for her assistance in the editorial and typesetting process.

Part I

Natural Resources and Environmental Decision Making

Design of a Decision Support System for use in the Event of a Nuclear Emergency

Simon French[1], K. Nadia Papamichail[1], David C. Ranyard[2] and Jim Q. Smith[3]

[1] School of Informatics, University of Manchester, Manchester M13 9PL, UK
[2] School of Computer Studies, University of Leeds, Leeds, LS2 9JT, UK
[3] Department of Statistics, University of Warwick, Coventry, CV4 7AL, UK

Abstract

Nuclear accidents such as that at Chernobyl in 1986 have emphasised the need for improving the emergency management of any accidental release of radio-activity. RODOS is a real-time on-line decision support system intended to be used throughout all phases of a nuclear accident. It follows a consistent Bayesian methodology for handling uncertainty and the effective communication of this to the decision makers. Evaluation is based upon multi-attribute value and utility methods with extensive provision of sensitivity analysis and automated explanations to the decision maker.

Keywords. Bayesian methods, belief networks, decision support systems, emergency response, multi-attribute value and utility models, RODOS, subjective probability

1 Introduction

Evaluation of the response to the Chernobyl nuclear accident has shown the importance of coherent, harmonised and sensitive emergency management extending both across many countries and many years into the future (International Chernobyl Report, 1991; Karaoglou, 1995). A means of supporting such a response is a common, comprehensive decision support system (DSS). The RODOS system (Real time Online DecisiOn Support) is being developed with this as its primary goal and is intended to be capable of finding broad application across Europe. The functionality offered by RODOS will include:

- prediction of atmospheric or hydrological dispersion and deposition from the near range to far distant areas;

- interpolation and contour mapping of contamination databases;
- predictions of the medical and other effects and the effectiveness of countermeasures in the short, medium and long term;
- support for the evaluation of countermeasure strategies including economic and social costs.

Data will be assimilated to update predictions on-line and provide estimates of the uncertainty associated with the predictions. Decision support can be provided at various levels: see Figure 1. RODOS is unique among emergency management DSS in that it will provide support at all levels, including level 3.

Level 0:	Acquisition, checking and presentation of radiological data, directly or with minimal analysis, and of geographic and demographic information.
Level 1:	Analysis and prediction of the current and future radiological situation based upon monitoring and meteorological data and models.
Level 2:	Simulation of potential countermeasures, e.g. sheltering, evacuation, issue of iodine tablets, food bans, and relocation; determination of their feasibility and quantification of their benefits and disadvantages.
Level 3:	Evaluation and ranking of alternative countermeasure strategies in the face of uncertainty by balancing their respective benefits and disadvantages.

Fig. 1. Levels of decision support for off-site emergency management. Support at higher levels includes that provided at lower levels

These are ambitious goals. Already the project consortium have developed a system (version PV3.0: see Ehrhardt et al. 1997) ready for operation in support of early phase, near range decisions, but that leaves many issues to be addressed, particularly relating to data assimilation and evaluation of strategies. This paper describes some of the issues faced and progress towards their resolution for later versions due by mid 1999.

2 The Context of Emergency Management

Nuclear emergency management raises many complex and difficult issues. There is great uncertainty about the likely development of an accident; yet difficult choices have to be made about the balance of risks to the public. The political processes involved are complicated: responsibility passes between several different groups of decision makers (DMs) of differing technical and political sophistication. Moreover, the process varies between countries. Thus we can only give an indication of the emergency management process here.

During the building and normal operation of nuclear plants, many preparations are made to deal with potential emergencies. For instance:

- demographic, geographic, agricultural and economic databases are established;
- evacuation routes and procedures are planned;
- exercises are held regularly to practise different accident scenarios.

Such preparations sensitise emergency management teams to the issues that they might face, but no accident ever goes "as planned". Emergency management is much more than the implementation of established rules.

When an accident threatens, plant managers will take engineering actions to avoid or reduce the risk of a release. The first decisions on protecting the public would be whether to take precautionary measures such as: issuing a warning, distribution of iodine tablets, and starting to evacuate some areas. If there is a release, decisions will be needed on: advice to take iodine tablets, advice on sheltering, and evacuation. In the following days decisions will be needed on such measures as: food bans; decontamination of livestock, agricultural produce and properties; and restrictions on business, leisure activities and access to the region. After several days or maybe weeks, there will be a need to consider longer term measures, e.g. permanent relocation (resettlement) and permanent changes to agricultural practice and local industry.

3 The conceptual software design of RODOS

The basic features and structure of RODOS are described in (Ehrhardt et al, 1993; Ehrhardt et al, 1997). Its conceptual architecture (not the physical software which includes, for instance, databases and user communication interfaces) consists of three types of subsystem:

- Analysing Subsystem (ASY) modules process incoming data and forecast the location and quantity of contamination including temporal variation.
- Countermeasure Subsystem (CSY) modules suggest possible countermeasures, check them for feasibility, and calculate their expected benefit in terms of a number of attributes.
- Evaluation Subsystem (ESY) modules rank countermeasure strategies according to their potential benefit and preference weights provided by the DMs.

These modules are imbedded in an operating system that provides temporal control, databases and a geographic information system (GSY), which displays demographic and geographic data as well as raw monitoring data.

It is possible to relate the levels to the ASY-CSY-ESY structure of RODOS: the GSY and ASY modules provide support at levels 0 and 1, the CSY modules provide support at level 2 and the ESY modules support at level 3: see Figure 2. However, this identification of level 3 decision support —i.e. prescriptive decision support— with the ESY modules of RODOS is a little too simplistic. The DMs need to make judgements in evaluation and the support of these judgement is provided by level 3 modules. But the DMs also need to address the uncertainty in all the information provided by RODOS. Although at first sight the modelling of uncertainty appears to be something external to the DMs, such a view is untenable at closer examination. The uncertainties for which RODOS must make allowances necessarily involve judgement.

Each phase of a nuclear accident has different types of information available and its own particular requirements. RODOS must recognise this temporal context

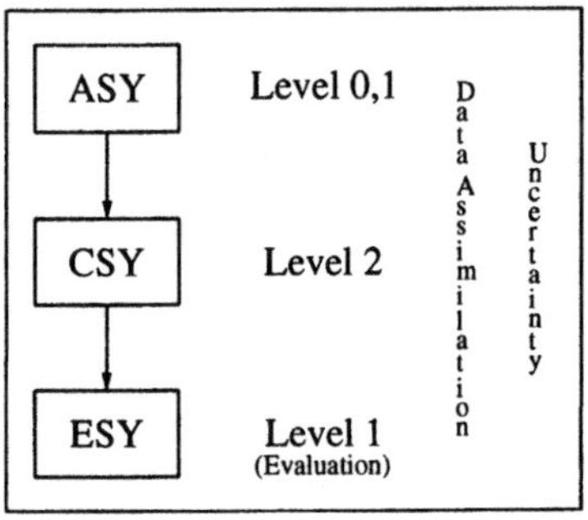

Fig. 2. Levels of decision support ad their relation to ASY, CSY and ESY subsystems

in order to support decision making throughout all phases. As time passes, RODOS will arrive at different decision points where it must select three modules to form an ASY, CSY, ESY chain appropriate to the context of the decision. The time intervals between two decision points may be a matter of minutes or hours early in an emergency situation and longer —days or weeks— at later phases.

4 The need to handle uncertainty in RODOS

A great deal of uncertainty is inherent in managing a nuclear accident. Techniques are being incorporated into RODOS to address the following issues:

- Will there be an accident, i.e. can a release be averted?
- What is the source term and its composition, its time behaviour, and its release co-ordinates and height(s)?
- How will the weather conditions develop?
- What observation errors are in any monitoring data?
- What is the quality of the meteorological, hydrological, agricultural, dose, health and economic models to be used?
- What will be the level of success in implementing any measure?
- What is the demography of the affected population?
- What is the accuracy of approximations used in calculations?

These uncertainties relate to the DMs' lack of knowledge of the evolving situation. Also they are often uncertain about their objectives and how to evaluate the consequences. How should they deal with such matters as "equity" or "public acceptability"? These uncertainties relate to value judgements. French (1996) has argued that such uncertainties can only be reduced by discussion and clear thought. One cannot derive values judgements from data analysis.

As an accident progresses, many types of data will become available, to reduce this uncertainty, including:

- Plant and engineering data —including expert judgement— suggesting the strength and composition of the source term;

- Meteorological data and forecasts, again incorporating expert judgement;
- On-site stack and periphery monitoring data: off-site fixed and mobile monitoring data;
- Hydrological data concerning both flow rates, depths, etc. and contamination;
- Population data concerning thc groups liable to be exposed;
- Agricultural, economic and land use data;
- Data on compliance with and effectiveness of countermeasures.

Note that some data arise from physical measurements, the characteristics of which are reasonably well understood, but others are derived from expert judgement, the characteristics of which are less clear and very different.

The client/server architecture of the system and the different categories of user expertise compelled the development of an integrated approach for handling and communicating uncertainty to DMs. RODOS follows a single, consistent mechanism for handling, modelling and representing uncertainty. This mechanism is provided by Bayesian probability techniques (French and Smith, 1997).

5 A data assimilation model chain

As we have noted, different modules will need to be brought together at different times to support decisions. Here we describe a sequence of modules which provide for data assimilation in the early phase and which have demonstrated the power of Bayesian belief nets to structure problems and develop algorithms for their solution.

The first module developed by NNC plc. and the Universities of Leeds and Manchester predicts possible source terms during the threat phase, based upon plant data. A prototype of this module has been implemented within the software package DXPRESS (Smedley et al, 1996). This module estimates the probabilities of various source terms categories given certain plant data: e.g., primary circuit integrity, availability of cooling circuits and core exit temperature. Based upon data from the plant's probability safety assessment, the belief net allows easy and repeated updating of the probabilities of the source term as data become available.

The probabilities from the belief net are used as prior information by a version of the RIMPUFF atmospheric dispersion code (Mikkelsen et al, 1984), which has been modified to update the predictions with incoming monitoring data (Smith and French, 1994, Ranyard and Smith, 1997). The current basis for the data assimilation here is an implementation of a dynamic Bayesian belief net (Smith et al, 1995). The monitoring data may come from on-site rings of monitors or from off-site monitoring.

Here we indicate the statistical modelling which underlies our Bayesian version of the RIMPUFF model. This module is designed to address the following questions.

- What is the likely spread of contamination?
- How can this prediction be updated in the light of monitoring data?
- What are the uncertainties in the predictions?

Until recently the atmospheric dispersion-deposition models used for this could not address the second and third questions directly. However, we have been able to combine Bayesian forecasting methodology with a puff model to address all three questions. The continuous release of airborne contaminants is approximated by a sequence of puffs that released at regular time intervals and then diffuse and disperse independently: see Figure 3. We have made use of the RIMPUFF model developed by (Mikkelsen et al, 1984).

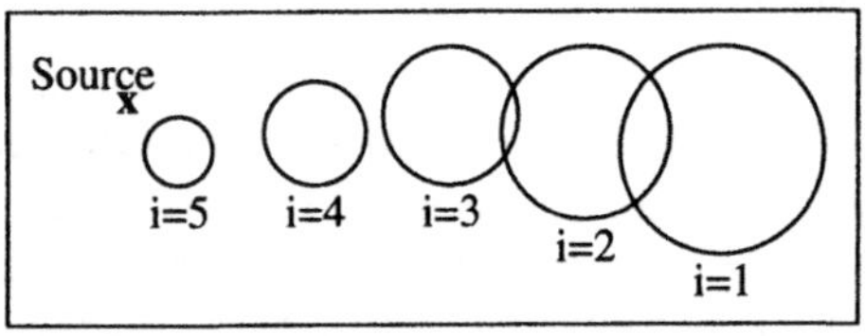

Fig. 3. A simple puff model

We index the puffs such that puff i is released at time $t = i$. Assume that the mass under puff i is q_i. We define $\boldsymbol{q}_t = (q_1, q_2, \ldots, q_t)^T$, which approximates the release profile of the source term. We use standard priors on the shape of the time profile —in statistical terms, time series— of the release (West and Harrison, 1989). Such priors can model uncertainty about the mass released and its duration. This gives a prior mean $\boldsymbol{\mu}_t$ (maybe via a hyperdistribution or an autoregressive time series). Moreover, if we have knowledge of some engineering activity that will lead to a sudden change in the scale of the release, we can intercede in the model and capture that (c.f. West and Harrison, 1989). Away from times when sudden changes in the release are expected, we can encode "smoothness" in the release profile through the covariances between the q_i.

Parameterising on masses under puffs:

- ⇒ time averaged or instantaneous concentrations at monitoring sites are *linear* functions of $\boldsymbol{q}_t$.
- ⇒ can use Kalman filtering and other linear techniques to assimilate monitoring data. We assume normality for simplicity, but the methods generalise (almost) straightforwardly.

Moreover, $\boldsymbol{q}_{t+1}$ is developed from $\boldsymbol{q}_t$ linearly: $\boldsymbol{q}_{t+1} \sim N(H_t \boldsymbol{q}_t, U_t)$. Here H_t encodes the transition that allows for the deposition and decay of some of the puffs' mass. Running this dynamic linear model will lead to estimates of the source term profile and predictions of the contamination spread ... if you believe the model. We can and do inflate the diagonal of U_t to allow somewhat for modelling error. However: there are omissions form the model which need addressing directly. The model clearly does not consider either uncertainty on release height or uncertainty on wind field.

Our solution to these problems is to run a mixed model. Specifically to deal with uncertainty on release height, we run three models at different release heights with probabilities: π_{h_1}, π_{h_2} π_{h_3} and $\sum_i \pi_{h_i} = 1$ (see Figure 4). We choose the π_{h_i} and the h_i to give a three point approximation to the prior on the release height (e.g.

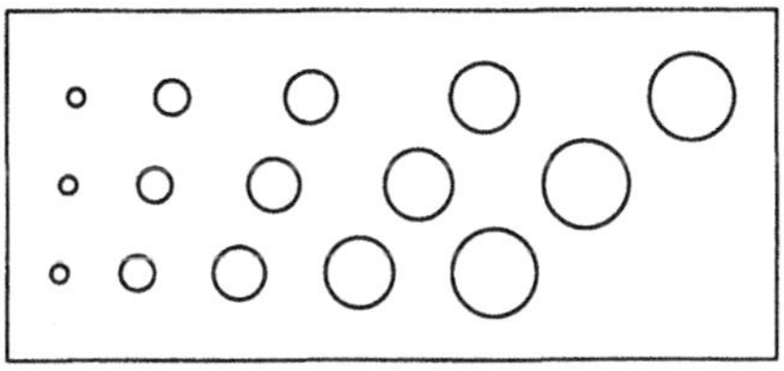

Fig. 4. Three puff models with different release heights

obtained by expert judgement from site engineers.) We then run this mixture of three models and update the π_{h_i} (i.e. update the distribution on the release height).

The uncertainty on the wind field is treated similarly. The wind field is non-uniform and reflects local topography. The wind field model can be rotated by $\pm\theta^0$ on the wind direction at the source. Thus, again, we run three models with probabilities: π_{ω_1}, π_{ω_2} π_{ω_3} and $\sum_i \pi_{\omega_i} = 1$. The π_{ω_i} and the θ_i are chosen to give a three point approximation to the prior on the wind direction at source (e.g. obtained by expert judgement from local meteorologists or staff on site) and a mixture of three models run to update the π_{ω_i} (i.e. update the distribution on the wind direction).

Thus the model as described so far estimates and provides distributions for: source term, release height and (gross changes in) wind direction. But what about:

- possibility of plume splitting (to branch around hills);
- puffs implying below ground spread (if using spherical puffs);
- local wind effects;
- shearing?

The RIMPUFF model allows puffs to pentify (see Figure 5). When a puff's diameter reaches a certain value, it pentifies in the horizontal plane. To model the possibility that the original puff was drifting away from its predicted trajectory, we introduce a random component associated with the distribution of mass between the siblings. Let the j-th puff pentify. We suppose:

$$\begin{pmatrix} q_{j_1} \\ q_{j_2} \\ q_{j_3} \\ q_{j_4} \\ q_{j_5} \end{pmatrix} = \begin{pmatrix} p_{j_1} \\ p_{j_2} \\ p_{j_3} \\ p_{j_4} \\ p_{j_5} \end{pmatrix} q_j + \boldsymbol{w}$$

where $\sum w_k = 1$ to conserve mass. This may be ensured by, say: $\boldsymbol{w} \sim N(\mathbf{0}, W)$, where, perhaps,

$$W = \begin{pmatrix} \zeta_1^2 & -{}^1\!/\!_2\zeta_1^2 & 0 & 0 & -{}^1\!/\!_2\zeta_1^2 \\ -{}^1\!/\!_2\zeta_1^2 & \zeta_1^2 & 0 & 0 & -{}^1\!/\!_2\zeta_1^2 \\ 0 & 0 & \zeta_2^2 & -{}^1\!/\!_2\zeta_2^2 & -{}^1\!/\!_2\zeta_2^2 \\ 0 & 0 & -{}^1\!/\!_2\zeta_2^2 & \zeta_2^2 & -{}^1\!/\!_2\zeta_2^2 \\ -{}^1\!/\!_2\zeta_1^2 & -{}^1\!/\!_2\zeta_1^2 & -{}^1\!/\!_2\zeta_2^2 & -{}^1\!/\!_2\zeta_2^2 & \zeta_1^2 + \zeta_2^2 \end{pmatrix}$$

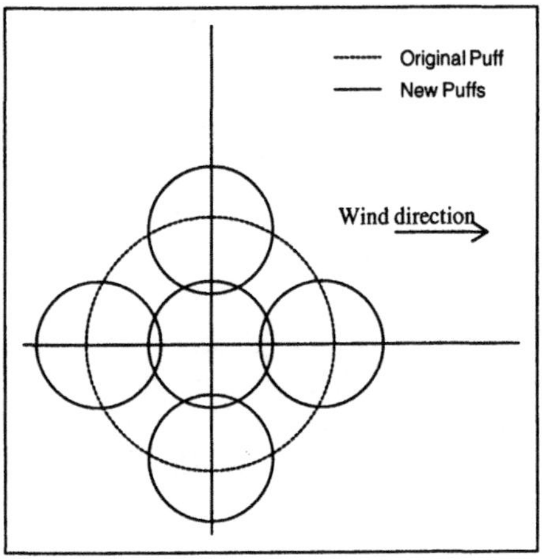

Fig. 5. Puff pentification

to represent different uncertainties in the local wind speed and wind direction: see Smith and French (1994).

Unfortunately, although the above model theoretically meets the requirements of the ASY module within RODOS, there is a practical requirement that we have to meet. Useable results are needed within a limited time. The covariance matrices within the model described above can become 100's×100's in dimension and computational efficiency thus declines dramatically.

Fortunately, this fragmenting puff model can be restructured as a dynamic junction tree (Smith et al, 1995). Denote by $j(\boldsymbol{l}) = j(t, l_1, l_2, \ldots, l_k)$ the puff fragment which is the l_k-th fragment of the l_{k-1}-th fragment of the $\ldots l_1$-th fragment of the puff released at time t. Let:

$Q(l)$ denote the mass of puff $j(\boldsymbol{l}).[Q(t) = Q((t))]$;

$\boldsymbol{Q}_c(l)$ denote the vector of masses of the children of puff $j(\boldsymbol{l})$;

$\boldsymbol{Q}(l) = (Q(l), \boldsymbol{Q}_c(l))^T$.

Let $\boldsymbol{Q}_t$ be the vector of masses of *all* puffs and puff fragments emitted on or before time t. Let $\boldsymbol{Y}(t, \boldsymbol{s})$ be the set of observations taken at time t at site(s) $\boldsymbol{s}$. Assume that $\boldsymbol{Y}(t, \boldsymbol{s}) \mid \theta(t, \boldsymbol{s})$ is independent of all other variables in the system, where

$$\theta(t, \boldsymbol{s}) = R(t, \boldsymbol{s})\boldsymbol{Q}_t + \varepsilon(t, \boldsymbol{s})$$

and $\varepsilon(t, \boldsymbol{s})$ is some error process —assumed normal with zero mean and independent components. The variance is assumed known and represents "observation + modelling" error.

The source emission process. We consider the simplest form: namely, constant emission.

$$Q(t) \sim N(Q(t-1), Z)$$

However, we can use any autoregression time series

The fragmentation process.

$$\boldsymbol{Q}_c(l) \sim N(\rho Q(l), W) \quad \text{where} \quad \rho = (\rho_1, \rho_2, \ldots, \rho_5)^T, \quad \sum \rho_k = 1.$$

This structure maps naturally onto a junction tree with cliques:

$C^*(t) = \{Q(t), Q(t+1)\}$	Adjacent puffs in emissions
$C(\boldsymbol{l}) = \{\boldsymbol{Q}(\boldsymbol{l})\}$	Parent and children puffs

Figure 6 illustrates a junction tree in which three puffs have been emitted by the source. The first puff has pentified to give clique $C(1)$. The fourth and fifth children within this clique have themselves pentified to give cliques $C(1,4)$ and $C(1,5)$ and the third child in $C(1,4)$ has, in turn, pentified. Similarly the second puff has pentified to give clique $C(2)$, and the third child within this clique pentified to give $C(2,3)$. Each pair of adjacent cliques in the tree shares a common puff, the separator. This implies that the joint distribution over the masses in all the puffs factorises into a very simple form that allows extremely efficient updating algorithms to be developed (Smith et al, 1995). Calculations may be chained up and down the dynamic (i.e. evolving) junction tree. This is straightforward when any single observation lies 'entirely' under any single clique; and we have developed good approximation schemes: e.g. divide observation into several in the ratio predicted by the current estimates of puff masses and then pretend each part is under a single clique. (Gargoum and Smith, 1993).

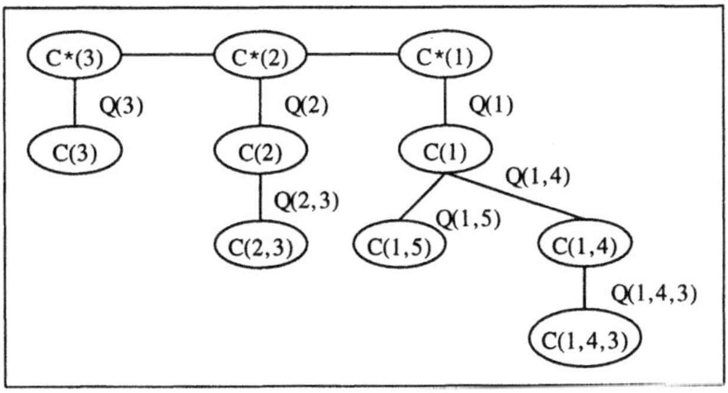

Fig. 6. Dynamic junction tree giving cliques and showing the 'separators' (i.e. masses of puffs lying in adjacent cliques)

Initial simulations have shown that the algorithm is fast enough to provide forecasts within the requirements of the RODOS decision support system. Indeed, the computational times of the algorithm are of the same order, although of course longer, as those for the algorithm without any updating for monitoring data. Moreover, the algorithm seems to behave sensibly in the manner it assimilates data.

We are now working with other groups in the RODOS consortium to develop data assimilation methods for hydrological models and for food-chains. We are also looking to Bayesian krigging and related methods to interpolate values for ground contamination within a GIS containing monitoring data.

6 Multi-attribute decision support within RODOS

The task of an ESY module is the evaluation of different countermeasure strategies. Issues that should be considered during the evaluation stage include feasibility, resources required, public acceptability, and social, psychological and political implications. Discussion of attributes which have been used or proposed for evaluating countermeasures may be found, *inter alia*, in French (1996), French, Halls and Ranyard (1997) and French, Harrison and Ranyard (1997). Whereas ASY and CSY modules may implement different models during the course of an accident depending on time, location and context, the ESY may be based upon the same software module with the attribute trees and weights changing over time.

The ESY will have the form of Figure 7. It is split into three further subsystems:

- a coarse expert system (CES) filter which rejects any strategies which are logically infeasible or do not satisfy some given constraints;
- a multi-attribute value and utility theory (MAV/UT) ranking module which takes the remaining list of strategies and ranks them according to their effectiveness against the attributes;
- a fine expert system filter (FES) which takes the top 10–15 strategies and produces a report detailing the pros and cons of each.

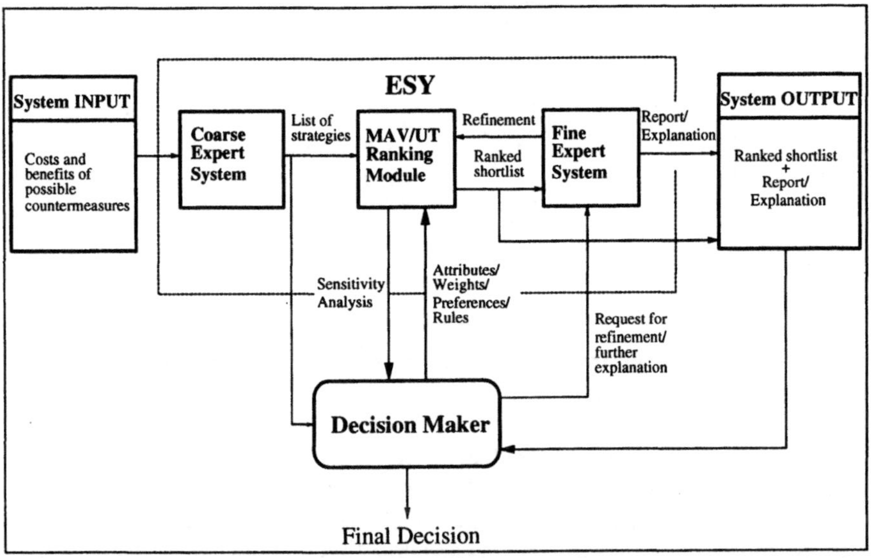

Fig. 7. The conceptual structure of the ESY module.

An ESY module has as input the costs and benefits of possible countermeasures which were identified and quantified by an appropriate CSY module. Thus, the consequences of applying countermeasures such as the issue of iodine tablets, sheltering, evacuation, temporary and permanent relocation, food bans, decontamination measures and changes in the agriculture to contaminated areas can be calculated. This means that the benefit of applying a particular countermeasure strategy or "portfolio" which specifies different countermeasures in various contaminated areas can be estimated.

The CES discards all strategies that do not follow some "coarse" feasibility rules or other constraints related to their acceptability. By decreasing the number of strategies the computational time needed to evaluate them is reduced. This is vital because the number of portfolios of countermeasures can grow exponentially. Those which satisfy the constraints are then passed to the MAV/UT module. Detailed description of the prototype CES module, which is based upon constraint satisfaction techniques, may be found in Papamichail and French (1997).

The ESY operates in interactive mode through graphical interfaces to communicate with a variety of DMs who may possess qualitatively different skills and perspectives. It presents the countermeasure strategies in a ranked short list together with the rules and preferences which determined the ranking. Intuitive justifications for choices and underlying uncertainties inherent in the predictions will also be provided. The ESY will assist DMs in modifying rules, weights and preferences and other model parameters as well as indicating the consequences of each change. Thus, the DMs can verify and correct the existing model as the ESY explains and refines its proposed short list. The ESY will also operate in reporting mode in order to generate reports which will give a detailed commentary on each proposed countermeasure strategy, explaining its strengths and weaknesses.

The MAV/UT ranking module makes heavy use of interactive sensitivity analysis to confirm that the strategies in the final ranked list are worthy of careful consideration. The sensitivity analysis used will be similar to the one in the VISA software package (see Belton, 1990). A prototype of the MAV/UT ranking module, HERESY, has been written. At present, HERESY evaluates alternatives by using a multi-attribute value function. Thus if does not explicitly allow for risk attitude. A modification which will enable the use of exponential multi-attribute utility functions is under development: French and Papamichail (1997). Such functions capture gross effects from risk aversion and are simple to elicit, explain and work with.

We recognise the complexity of the interactions that are needed with the DMs.

- They may not be convinced by the output of the MAV/UT ranking module and/or feel that there are some issues which need further explanation and clarification.
- Initial preferences, weights, attributes and rules will be encoded into the system. However, RODOS is designed to support decision making throughout all phases of a nuclear accident. Each phase has its own requirements and different types of decisions have to be taken each time. Thus there will be a need to adjust these parameters in an exploratory and informative manner.
- In a nuclear emergency, there will be a variety of DMs with qualitatively different

skills and perspectives such as plant managers and senior politicians, along with there advisers – but there may be no decision analyst available to explain the output of the model. The users may perceive decision theory as a black box and may not understand how information is elicited. Providing DMs with the facility of observing the step-by-step effect of a parameter would help them to assess and refine the parameters.

The sensitivity analysis within HERESY will address some of these issues. In addition, the final part of the ESY will be a fine expert system (FES). Our design of the FES is influenced by interpretative value analysis described in (Klein, 1994). This framework uses knowledge-based methods and heuristics to describe value-systems. It increases the transparency of multi-attribute theories by embedding them in a framework for explaining and refining value-based choices.

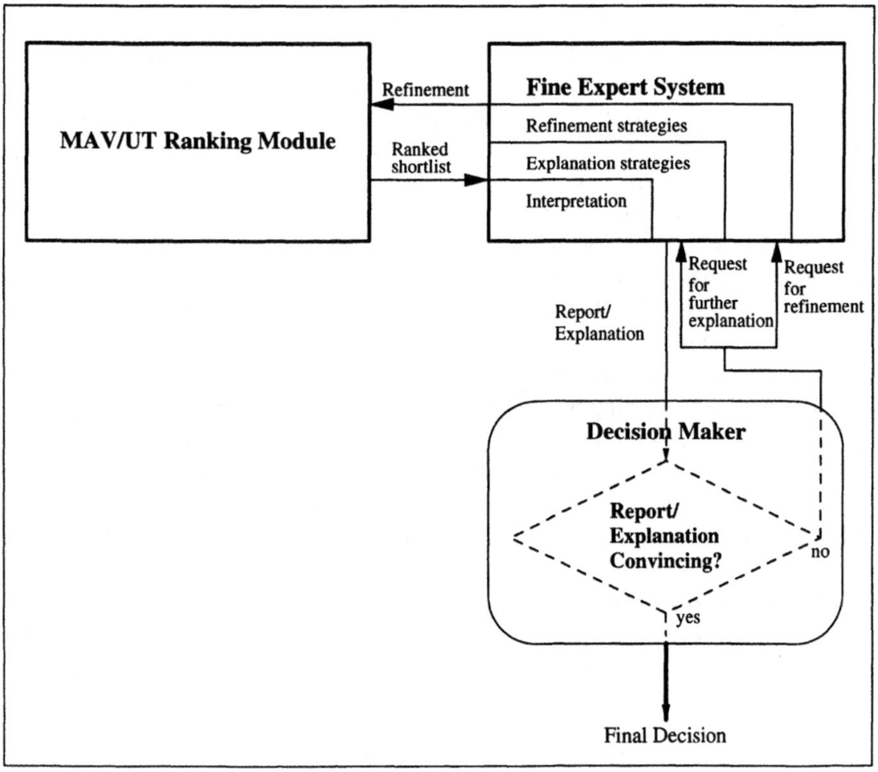

Fig. 8. The fine expert system.

The FES (see Figure 8) consists of:

- Interpretation which will analyse and interpret the model;
- Explanation strategies which will provide the user with sufficient insight into the system's operation by giving a critique of each strategy and justifying choices;

- Refinement strategies which will assist the user in identifying faulty parameters and correcting them.

The FES takes as input the ranked short list of the top 10–15 strategies. The small number of strategies allows a full set of explanations to be developed. If the DMs finds the explanation convincing then they are ready to take a final decision i.e. to choose the strategy to be applied. If not, they can either request further explanation from the fine expert system or refine the model in order to correct a suspicious component of the explanation. Refining the model means adjusting the judgemental model parameters such as attribute scores or weights in order to reflect the evolving preferences of the DMs. The FES operates in two modes. Interactive mode provides facilities for generating intuitive justifications for choices and assisting users in modifying model parameters. Reporting mode uses a combination of explanation strategies to generate intuitive reports about decisions.

7 Closing remarks

RODOS is the product of much research and development, of which we have only described a part. Moreover, the RODOS project involves many institutes and is truly a multi-disciplinary project: agricultural scientists, computer scientists, decision analysts, economists, meteorologists, radiation protection specialists, and statisticians, to name but a few disciplines, are all involved. This raises many issues in itself. Many have come to the problem of providing decision support for off-site emergency management from backgrounds in science. Scientists are trained to explain the past, to estimate parameters, and to develop and test models. Decision support requires the deployment of those models to predict the future and that requires a different emphasis and viewpoint. For instance, many talk of back-fitting or reconstructing the source term. In a sense this is reasonable: to predict the spread of the contamination one needs some knowledge of the source term. But the "best" estimate of the source term may not give the "best" prediction of the spread of health effects arising from the plume. It is not what goes up that matters so much as what comes down! Thinking of the plume: suppose that a puff model is used. Scientific estimation requires the use of sufficient puffs to capture the evolving shape of the plume. But decision making on evacuation simply requires (good!) predictions of its path, approximate time of arrival and strength. Sufficiently good assessments of these may be found from a model using fewer puffs. Moreover, using fewer puffs allows quicker calculation and hence many more "what-if" analyses.

Moreover, to provide support from the moment that an accident threatens through any release and into the long term, it is necessary that the output of any single analysis at one decision point not only supports the decision to be made then but also feeds as prior information into analyses designed to support subsequent decisions. Thus, the principles underpinning choice at one time should be compatible with those used at other times. To do otherwise invites inconsistency, risks confusing the DMs, and certainly requires extra calculations to convert the output of previous analyses into formats acceptable to subsequent ones. For example, we must ensure that not only do we analyse plant and engineering data to predict the source term during the threat stage, but if the release occurs we also use those data (and subsequent plant data) to combine with sparse monitoring data collected in order to predict the contamination spread by the plume. Later after the plume has passed, we should find a way of moving smoothly from the predictions of ground contamination coming from atmospheric dispersion-deposition models to interpolations in the growing set of ground monitoring measurements. We must continually balance that we have learnt from past data with the information inherent in incoming data. And at all times, we should ensure that the current estimates and descriptions of the uncertainty fit with and support the decisions to be made.

This need for coherence is well satisfied by the use of Bayesian methods, but the explicit subjectivity of Bayesian ideas in particular and decision analysis in general has not seemed natural to many of our colleagues. Fortunately, the success of Bayesian idea in delivering working algorithms such as NNC's source term belief net, Bayes-RIMPUFF and HERESY is a strong and winning argument. Ranyard and Smith (1997) discuss aspects of working with scientists to build prediction models.

Acknowledgements

The RODOS system is being developed by a consortium of nearly 40 institutes from across Europe and the Former Soviet Union; see http://rodos.fzk.de/ for a current list of the institutes and scientists involved. The authors are supported by a number of contracts under the EU's Framework research programmes: F14P-CT95-0007, F14C-CT96-0006 and IC15-CT96-0318. We are grateful to our many colleagues within the project for discussions and insights into decision support in emergency management. None the less, the views expressed here represent the authors views and do not necessarily represent the project's policy. We are also grateful to Tim Bedford and Roger Cooke for many discussions on risk analysis and belief nets. Many students have contributed to the project:, Ali Gargoum, Emma Halls, Miles Harrison, Douglas Vleeshhouwer and Shimon Young, in particular.

References

Belton, V. (1990). Multi Criteria Decision Analysis —practically the only way to choose. In L.C. Hendry and R.W. Englese (Eds.), *Operational Research Tutorial papers*, Birmingham: Operational Research Society. 53–101.

Ehrhardt, J., Päsler-Sauer, J., Schüle, O., Benz, G., Rafat, M. and Richter, J. (1993). Development of RODOS, a comprehensive decision support system for nuclear emergencies in Europe —an overview. *Radiation Protection Dosimetry* **50**, 195–203.

Ehrhardt, J., Brown, J., French, S., Kelly, G.N., Mikkelsen, T. and Müller, H. (1997). RODOS: decision making support for off-site emergency management after nuclear accidents. *Kerntechnik* **62**, 122–128.

French, S., Ranyard, D. and Smith, J. Q. (1995). Uncertainty in RODOS. *Research Report* **95.10**, School of Computer Studies, University of Leeds. Available by connecting to WWW at file://agora.leeds.ac.uk/scs/doc/reports/1995 or by anonymous ftp from agora.leeds.ac.uk of the file scs/doc/reports/ 1995/95_10.ps.Z. RODOS(B)-RP(94)05.

French, S. (1996). Multi-attribute decision support in the event of a nuclear accident. *Journal of Multi-Criteria Decision Analysis* **5**, 39–57.

French, S. and Papamichail, K. N. (1997). Further specification of RODOS-ESY. RODOS (WG5)-TN97-06. School of Informatics. University of Manchester.

French, S. and Smith, J. Q. (Eds.) (1997). *Bayesian Analysis in Practice*. Edward Arnold: London.

French, S., Halls, E. and Ranyard, D. C. (1997). Equity and MCDA in the event of a nuclear accident. In G. Fandal and T. Gal (Eds.) *Multiple Criteria Decision Making*. **LNEMS 448**, Springer Verlag: Berlin. 612–621.

French, S., Harrison, M. and Ranyard, D. C. (1997). Event conditional attribute modelling in decision making when there is a threat of a nuclear accident. In French and Smith (Eds.), *Bayesian Analysis in Practice*. Edward Arnold: London, 131–149.

Gargoum, A. S. and Smith, J. Q. (1993). Approximation schemes for efficient probability propagation in evolving high dimensional Gaussian processes. Dept. of Statistics, University of Warwick.

The International Chernobyl Project. (1991). Technical Report. IAEA Vienna.

Karaoglou, A., Desmet, G., Kelly, G. N. and Menzel, H. G. (Eds). (1995). *The Radiological Consequences of the Chernobyl Accident*. EUR 16544 EN. CEC, Luxembourg.

Klein, D. A. (1994). *Decision-Analytic Intelligent Systems —Automated Explanation and Knowledge Acquisition*. Lawrence Erlbaum Associates: New Jersey.

Mikkelsen, T. , Larsen, S. E. and Thykier-Nielsen, S. (1984). Description of the Risø puff diffusion model. *Nuclear Safety* **67**, 56–65.

Papamichail, K. N. and French, S. (1997). Screening strategies in nuclear emergencies. RODOS(WG5)-TN(97)-01. School of Informatics, University of Manchester.

Ranyard, D. C. and Smith, J. Q. (1997). Building a Bayesian model in a scientific environment: managing uncertainty after an accident. In French and Smith (Eds.), *Bayesian Analysis in Practice*. Edward Arnold: London, 245–258.

Smedley, C. , Grindon, E., Dutton, L. M. C. and Vleeshhouwer, D. B. (1996). Source term estimation based on plant status. RODOS(WG5)-TN(96)-02 (NNC, C5064 /TR002) NNC Ltd, Booth Hall, Knutsford WA16 8QZ.

Smith, J. Q. and French, S. (1994). Bayesian updating of atmospheric dispersion models for use after an accidental release of radioactivity. *The Statistician* **43**, 231–236.

Smith, J. Q., French, S. and Ranyard, D .C. (1995). An efficient graphical algorithm for updating the estimates of the dispersal of gaseous waste after an accidental release. In Gammerman, A. (Ed.) *Probabilistic Reasoning and Bayesian Belief Networks*. Alfred Waller: Henley on Thames, 125–144.

West, M. and Harrison, P. J. (1989). *Bayesian Forecasting and Dynamic Models*. Springer Verlag: New York.

Contaminated Aquatic Ecosystems Restoration: A Case Study

E. Gallego[1], S. Ríos-Insua[2], A. Mateos[2] and D. Ríos Insua[3]

[1] Dept. of Nuclear Engineering, Madrid Technical University, SPAIN
[2] Dept. of Artificial Intelligence, Madrid Technical University, SPAIN
[3] School of Engineering, University Rey Juan Carlos, Madrid, SPAIN

Abstract

We use Decision Analysis methods to rank intervention strategies after contamination by radionuclides of an aquatic ecosystem. We assume certainty since the validation of models used to quantify impacts of countermeasures suggest little uncertainty in policy effects. We construct a hierarchy of objectives, with attributes for lowest level objectives, and feasible countermeasures are then identified. Then, we model preferences over each consequence with component value functions, which we aggregate via a weighted sum, and rank alternatives. Finally, sensitivity analyses allow us to gain insight into the problem.

Keywords. Aquatic ecosystem, decision analysis, multiattribute value, radionuclide contamination, sensitivity analysis

1 Introduction

The main objective of the MOIRA project * is the development of a model-based Decision Support System (DSS) to select the optimal alternative in the event of radioactive contamination of aquatic ecosystems and their drainage areas. Intervention options are wide-ranging, from chemical treatment of water bodies to fishing bans

* MOIRA (A **MO**del-Based Computerised System for Management Support to **I**dentify **O**ptimal **R**emedial Strategies for Restoring Radionuclide Contaminated **A**quatic Ecosystems and Drainage Areas) is a project financed by the European Commission (Contract FI4P-CT96-0036). Participants in the project include ENEA (Italy, coordinator), KEMA (The Netherlands), Studsvik (Sweden), and the Universities of Uppsala (Sweden), Oslo (Norway) and Madrid Technical University.

or restrictions to the movement of communities. Potential actions can be broadly grouped into three categories, chemical, physical and social. In some cases, a combination of actions may be the optimal strategy. Yet another option would be not to take any remedial action.

The selection of the optimal strategy should be based on all relevant information, with the overall objective of minimizing the impact of contamination, not only from a radiological point of view, but also taking into account other important environmental, social and economic effects that the decision could entail. The MOIRA system incorporates a GIS (Geographical Information System) database together with a complete set of reliable, validated models to predict temporal behaviour of radionuclides in the freshwater environment and the ecological, social and economic impacts of the countermeasures as the basic pillars on which a decision must be based.

The site chosen to test the Multiattribute Decision Analysis (MDA) methodology in MOIRA is lake Øvre Heimdalsvatn, located in Oppland county (Norway). It is a small subalpine lake with mean depth of 4.7 m, maximum depth 13 m, surface area of .78 km^2, and catchment area of 23.6 km^2. The highest point of the catchment is 1843 m a.s.l., while the lake itself is at 1090 m a.s.l. The mean annual precipitation is 800 mm. This lake has been thoroughly studied, see Vik (1978). There is no permanent settlement within the catchment, but a scientific field station is installed in the lake, with an occupation of about 600 man-days per year. During summer, a herdsman looks after calves and sheep and there is some fishing activity, mainly for recreation. Scientists, the herdsman and anglers, as well as the animals, drink water from the lake, there being no other water demand.

After the Chernobyl accident, the lake was contaminated with a fallout of 130 kBq/m^2 of ^{137}Cs, which, in principle, required no countermeasures, given the low radiological impact that the low utilization of the lake by people implies. However, an evaluation of alternative strategies can be made with the objective of testing MOIRA. This paper presents the MDA methodology and its application to the lake Øvre Heimdalsvatn case.

The paper includes five more sections. In Section 2 we construct the objectives hierarchy. In Section 3, using the GIS and various models within the system, feasible countermeasures are identified, together with their impacts. In Section 4, preferences over each consequence are then modelled with component value functions, which are finally aggregated through a weighted sum, which allows us to rank the alternatives. In Section 5, sensitivity analyses provide additional insights on the problem. Finally, in Section 6, we provide conclusions.

2 A hierarchy of objectives

Once defined and characterized the contaminated site, the next step is the construction of a tree of objectives, which, for this specific case, must be a simplification of the more general hierarchy tree that the system will include. The three general objectives concerning environmental, social and economic impacts can be maintained for any given scenario. However, for each case, the three general objectives will be split in different branches of sub-objectives. In our case, the objectives hierarchy is in Figure 2.1.

The next step is the specification of attributes to measure the degree to which these objectives are met. In the case of lake Øvre Heimdalsvatn, given the low level of contamination, there would be no threats to the biota; hence, the environmental impact can be identified with the ecosystem health, which can be measured by the Lake Ecosystem Index, LEI (Håkanson, 1993). We shall consider both the *average improvement in LEI* (X_1) during the evaluated period and its *maximum point improvement in LEI* (X_2) at any time.

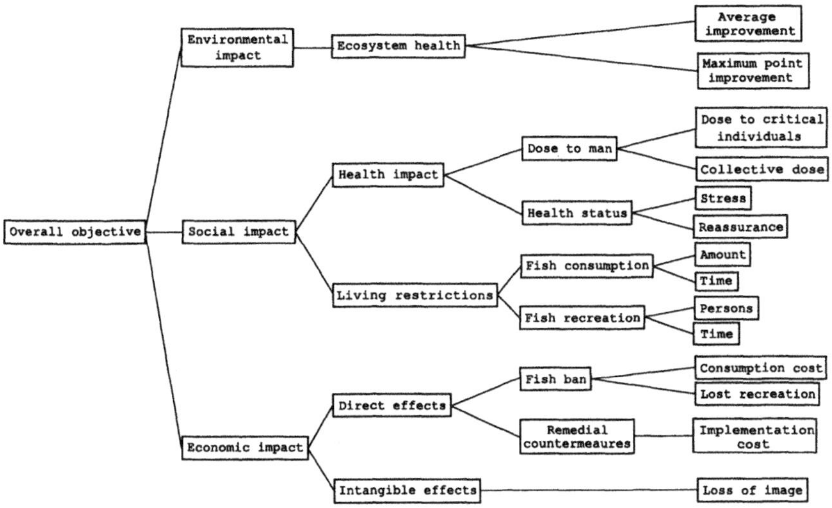

Fig. 2.1. Objectives hierarchy for lake Øvre Heimdalsvatn

As Social impact is concerned, there are two main objectives: minimizing impact on health and living conditions. The radiation dose is an obvious factor affecting health; in our case, we focus on *dose to critical individuals* (X_3), which should never receive levels above thresholds for early health effects, and *collective dose* (X_4), which induces a linear increase in the risk of developing serious latent effects, mainly cancer. Overall health status of people can also be affected by countermeasures, due to *stress* (X_5) and *reassurance* (X_6). In the "living restrictions" branch, the only action considered effective for this case is fish ban, which may reduce dose by ingestion. Related attributes would include *amount of fish banned for consumption* (X_7), *duration of ban on consumption* (*time*) (X_8), *number of persons disturbed* (X_9) and *duration of ban recreation* (*time*) (X_{10}), because of the prohibition to accessing the lake for fishing.

Finally, the economic impact will be decomposed into intangible effects, linked to the *loss of image* (X_{14}) and direct effects, more amenable to quantification, like those associated to a fish ban or the application of remedial chemical countermeasures. The economic impact of a fish ban will include the *cost of the fish banned for consumption* (X_{11}) and the subjective *cost of lost recreation* (X_{12}). For chemical countermeasures, the *implementation cost* (X_{13}) is well known and is a useful attribute.

The above objectives are listed in Table 2.1, with relevant ranges in our case. For all attributes except X_5, X_6 and X_{14}, we introduced natural scales. Constructed scales were all in the range 0 to 100. It was simple to check that, for all attributes except X_1, X_2 and X_6, less of an attribute was preferred to more. Hence, we list worst and best levels in the table below. The impact of selecting a particular countermeasure or strategy S_l can be characterized by the consequence $(x_1^l, \ldots, x_{14}^l)$, where x_i^l is the level in attribute X_i.

Attribute	Measure (units)	Level Worst	Level Best
X_1 : average improvement	%LEI	0.00	21.20
X_2 : maximum point improvement	%LEI	0.00	81.00
X_3 : dose to critical individuals	microSv	2470.00	1860.00
X_4 : collective dose	mSv×man	72.3	54.00
X_5 : stress effects	Const. scale	100.00	0.00
X_6 : reassurance effects	Const. scale	0.00	100.0
X_7 : amount of fish consumption	kg	445.00	0.00
X_8 : duration of fish ban	months	12.00	0.00
X_9 : persons affected by fish ban	n. of persons	30	0.00
X_{10} : duration of fish ban	months	12.00	0.00
X_{11} : fish consumption cost	kSEK	22.25	0.00
X_{12} : recreation lost	kSEK	120.00	0.00
X_{13} : implementation cost	kSEK	702.00	0.00
X_{14} : loss of image	Const. scale	100.00	0.00

kSEK=thousands of Swedish Crowns
mSv=.001 Sievert (1 Sv=1 Jul/kg)

Table 2.1. Attributes for evaluating countermeasures

3 Strategies and impacts

We then identify feasible strategies, including the no-action option, and describe their impacts in terms of each attribute. With that aim, a set of eight strategies has been analyzed, combining chemical countermeasures (addition of lime or potash at the beginning of July each year, with 40 tonnes the first year and 25 tonnes the next five; fertilisation of the lake with .1 tonnes of phosphorus per month from May to October during six years) with fish banning (during the first year after the accident). They are listed in Table 3.1, together with their impacts. Table 3.1 also summarizes the results of running the MOIRA submodels for each strategy:

- The MOIRA lake model, adapted from the VAMP model (Håkanson et al., 1996), used to obtain the ^{137}Cs concentrations in water and fish as a function of time. This model includes sub-models for the analyzed countermeasures (liming, potash treatment, fertilizing) as well as a model for assessing the Lake Ecosystem Index (Håkanson, 1997a).
- The MOIRA dose model (Jiménez and Gallego, 1996) to obtain individual and collective doses for each strategy.

For attributes 5 (stress), 6 (reassurance) and 14 (loss of image), values were directly elicited from experts in the MOIRA team. The social and economic impacts of a fish ban for 1 year (attributes 7 -amount of fish-, 9 -persons affected-, 11 -cost of fish consumption lost- and 12 -cost of lost recreation-) were quantified externally based on information about the site (database information). The implementation cost of chemical countermeasures was obtained directly from past experience (Håkanson, 1997b).

		Attributes						
Strat.	Description	X_1	X_2	X_3	X_4	X_5	X_6	X_7
S_1	No countermeas.	0	0	2470	72.3	50	0	0
S_2	Fish banning	0	0	2180	63.7	0	50	445
S_3	Lake liming	17.5	80.8	2340	68.3	100	50	0
S_4	Liming+Fish b.	17.5	80.8	2100	61.3	0	100	445
S_5	Potash treatment	15.7	17.2	2040	59.5	100	50	0
S_6	Potash+Fish b.	15.7	17.2	1860	54	0	100	445
S_7	Fertilizing	21.2	59.2	2450	71.5	100	50	0
S_8	Fertilizing+Fish b.	21.2	59.2	2160	63	0	100	445
Strat.	Description	X_8	X_9	X_{10}	X_{11}	X_{12}	X_{13}	X_{14}
S_1	No countermeas.	0	0	0	0	0	0	0
S_2	Fish banning	12	30	12	22	120	0	50
S_3	Lake liming	0	0	0	0	0	141	75
S_4	Liming+Fish b.	12	30	12	22	120	141	25
S_5	Potash treatment	0	0	0	0	0	702	75
S_6	Potash+Fish b.	12	30	12	22	120	702	25
S_7	Fertilizing	0	0	0	0	0	125	75
S_8	Fertilizing+Fish b.	12	30	12	22	120	125	25

Table 3.1. Matrix of countermeasure impacts

4 Ranking the alternatives

We rank the alternatives with a multiattribute value function, which combines multiple evaluation measures into a single measure or value for each strategy. The functional form used here, which we consider a valid approximation, see Raiffa (1982) and Stewart (1996), is additive:

$$v(S_l) = w_1 v_1 \left(x_1^l\right) + w_2 v_2 \left(x_2^l\right) + \cdots + w_{14} v_{14} \left(x_{14}^l\right) \tag{1}$$

where x_i^l is a specific level of X_i. To determine such function we need to specify: 1) Component value functions v_i for each evaluation measure; and 2) Weights or scaling constants w_i for each component value function. Next, we shall describe procedures to carry out the elicitations.

4.1 Elicitation of values

We present now a method to determine component value functions, based on the combination of two standard procedures **. Several authors, see e.g., Hershey et al. (1982), McCord and de Neufville (1986), Jaffray (1989), have suggested that, elicited value (or utility) functions are method dependent and bias and inconsistencies may be introduced in the elicitation process. To mitigate such problems, we use two methods jointly: the probability equivalent method (PE) and the certainty equivalent method (CE), Farquhar (1984). Furthermore, instead of assessing only one number in each probability question, as each method demands, we have assessed a class of value functions, von Nitzsch and Weber (1988) and Rios *et al.* (1994). This is less demanding, since we ask the expert to provide only incomplete preference statements by means of intervals, rather than unique numbers. Note that because of incomplete information, we obtain a class of value functions rather than a single value function for each one.

The system uses the PE-method known as *extreme gambles*, where the DM has to specify probability intervals $[p_t^L, p_t^U]$, such that

$$\begin{pmatrix} p_i & 1-p_i \\ x_i^* & x_{i*} \end{pmatrix} \sim x_i^t \quad \text{for all} \quad p_i \in [p_t^L, p_t^U],$$

where x_i^* and x_{i*} represent best and worst consequences for attribute X_i, and for some selected amounts $x_i^t \in [x_{i*}, x_i^*]$. We have taken three amounts, denoted $x_i^1 = \frac{1}{4}(x_{i*} + x_i^*)$, $x_i^2 = \frac{1}{2}(x_{i*} + x_i^*)$, $x_i^3 = \frac{3}{4}(x_{i*} + x_i^*)$, but some others could be chosen for comparison.

To obtain probability intervals with the PE-method, we used a computer program based on a graphical representation of probabilities for lotteries by means of colored sectors of a circle, to provide the probabilistic questions and guide the expert until an interval of indifference probabilities is obtained. Additional questions provided consistency checks.

The CE-method used in MOIRA is the *fractile method.* The DM is asked to provide certainty equivalent intervals or ranges of attributes for lotteries whose results are the extreme values x_i^* and x_{i*} and probabilities p^t and $1-p^t$, where, for example, we have taken $p^1 = .25$, $p^2 = .50$ and $p^3 = .75$. This means that the DM considers

$$\begin{pmatrix} p^t & 1-p^t \\ x_i^* & x_{i*} \end{pmatrix} \sim x_i^t, \quad \text{for all amounts} \quad x_i^t \in [x_{p^t}^L, x_{p^t}^U], \quad \text{for} \quad t = 1, 2, 3.$$

** With these procedures, we have assessed for each attribute a utility function instead of a value one. Recall, however, that each utility function is a value function, but not reciprocally.

The indicated computer program provides also a way to obtain, by means of the CE-method, the certainty equivalent intervals.

If the intersection of the two value ranges were empty in some range of the attribute, the DM would have inconsistent responses and we should reassess his given preferences. These reassessments finish once the DM provides a consistent range for the value function, which means that the intersection of both ranges is not empty along the whole the interval $[x_{i*}, x_i^*]$. Thus, the intersection will be the range for the DM's value functions. These ranges could be used later in sensitivity analysis to gain insight about the ranking of strategies and help the DM to discard certain strategies.

Once with the assessments, we build the component value functions v_i. We fit piecewise exponential functions, $a + be^{-cx}$, using least squares with the midpoints of value ranges, for values $x_{i*}, x_i^1, x_i^2, x_i^3, x_i^*$, in the X axis of each range of the class of value functions, obtained as the intersection of both ranges. Table 4.1 shows the fitted component value functions for all attribute.

Attributes	v_i	Range
X_1	$v_1(x_1) = 1.53 - 1.53\exp(-.04998x_1)$	$[0, 21.2]$
X_2	$v_2(x_2) = 1.198 - 1.198\exp(-.0222x_2)$	$[0, 81]$
X_3	$v_3(x_3) = .3847 + 60280\exp(-.006179x_3)$	$[1860, 2200]$
	$v_3(x_3) = .5876 - 5.027 \cdot 10^{-7}\exp(.00565x_3)$	$[2200, 2470]$
X_4	$v_4(x_4) = -1.95 + 10.01\exp(-.02262x_4)$	$[54, 72.3]$
X_5	$v_5(x_5) = -1.192 + 2.192\exp(-.00609x_5)$	$[0, 100]$
X_6	$v_6(x_6) = -2.638 + 2.638\exp(.003214x_6)$	$[0, 100]$
X_7	$v_7(x_7) = .2469 + .7531\exp(-.00464x_7)$	$[0, 225]$
	$v_7(x_7) = .7902 - .09563\exp(.004745x_7)$	$[225, 445]$
X_8	$v_8(x_8) = 1.516 - .5161\exp(.1175x_8)$	$[0, 7]$
	$v_8(x_8) = -.4072 + 1.757\exp(-.1218x_8)$	$[7, 12]$
X_9	$v_9(x_9) = .1232 + .8768\exp(-.04778x_9)$	$[0, 12.75]$
	$v_9(x_9) = 1.809 - .8976\exp(.02336x_9)$	$[12.75, 30]$
X_{10}	$v_{10}(x_{10}) = 1.397 - .3973\exp(.1523x_{10})$	$[0, 4]$
	$v_{10}(x_{10}) = -1.349 + 2.464\exp(-.0502x_{10})$	$[4, 12]$
X_{11}	$v_{11}(x_{11}) = -2.015 + 3.015\exp(-.01811x_{11})$	$[0, 22.25]$
X_{12}	$v_{12}(x_{12}) = 1.225 - .2252\exp(.01826x_{12})$	$[0, 70]$
	$v_{12}(x_{12}) = -.1608 + 3.459\exp(-.02557x_{12})$	$[70, 120]$
X_{13}	$v_{13}(x_{13}) = 2.192 - 1.192\exp(.000867x_{13})$	$[0, 702]$
X_{14}	$v_{14}(x_{14}) = 5.508 - 4.508\exp(.002003x_{14})$	$[0, 100]$

Table 4.1. The single-attribute value functions

4.2 Determining weights

We also need weights or scaling factors for each attribute in the lowest-level of the objectives hierarchy. Moreover, it will be useful to assess weights to higher level objectives to facilitate global sensitivity analyses. We shall start the procedure assessing attribute weights and, then, those of higher level objectives.

Let w_i^1 be the weight of attribute $X_i, i = 1, \ldots, 14$, level one, and more generally, w_i^j the weight of objective i in level j, where for $j = 4\,(i = 1,2,3), j = 3\,(i = 1,\ldots,5)$ and $j = 2$ $(i = 1,\ldots,6)$. For different levels of the hierarchy, we assess the weights based on tradeoffs among the corresponding attributes of lowest-level objectives stemming from the same objective. We begin with the lowest-level attributes and then continue the assessment in ascending order of the hierarchy. For lowest-level, we only obtain weights $w_i^1, i = 1,\ldots,12$, since $w_{13} = w_{14} = 1$. If x_i^m represents the average value of the range of X_i, we consider comparisons of the form

$$\left(\begin{array}{cc} \lambda_i^1 & 1-\lambda_i^1 \\ \left(x_{i_1}^*,\ldots,x_{i-1}^*,x_i^*,x_{i+1}^*,\ldots,x_{i_l}^*\right) & \left(x_{i_1*},\ldots,x_{(i-1)*},x_{i*},x_{(i+1)*},\ldots,x_{i_l*}\right) \end{array} \right)$$
$$\sim \left(x_{i_1*},\ldots,x_{(i-1)*},x_i^m,x_{(i+1)*},\ldots,x_{i_l*}\right) \qquad (2)$$

with attributes only arising from the same objective of the immediate upper level. Thus, we ask the DM to provide the λ_i^1, such that he is indifferent between the lottery and the sure consequence in (2).

As in the case of value assessment, we allow for imprecision since it may be more demanding for the DM to provide a unique value λ_i^1 instead of an interval. Then, from the properties of the value function, we have that $\lambda_i^{1L} = w_i^{1L} v_i(x_i^m)$, $\lambda_i^{1U} = w_i^{1U} v_i(x_i^m)$ and, hence, $w_i^{1L} = \lambda_i^{1L}/v_i(x_i^m)$, $w_i^{1U} = \lambda_i^{1U}/v_i(x_i^m)$. Table 4.2 shows the normalized average values

$$k_i^{1m} = \frac{w_i^{1L} + w_i^{1U}}{\sum\limits_{j=i_1}^{i_l} \left(w_j^{1L} + w_j^{1U}\right)}$$

for each interval, which will be used as scaling factors in the overall value v, as well as the normalized intervals, denoted $\left[k_i^{1L}, k_i^{1U}\right]$, where

$$k_i^{1L} = \frac{k_i^{1m} \cdot w_i^{1L}}{\left(w_i^{1L} + w_i^{1U}\right)/2} \quad \text{and} \quad k_i^{1U} = \frac{k_i^{1m} \cdot w_i^{1U}}{\left(w_i^{1L} + w_i^{1U}\right)/2}$$

Attribute	k_i^{1m}	$\left[k_i^{1L}, k_i^{1U}\right]$	Attribute	k_i^{1m}	$\left[k_i^{1L}, k_i^{1U}\right]$
X_1	.429	[.214, .644]	X_8	.621	[.518, .725]
X_2	.571	[.380, .761]	X_9	.372	[.278, .464]
X_3	.067	[0.0, .134]	X_{10}	.628	[.524, .733]
X_4	.933	[.861, 1.00]	X_{11}	.221	[.147, .294]
X_5	.452	[.258, .646]	X_{12}	.779	[.719, .839]
X_6	.548	[.365, .730]	X_{13}	1	[1, 1]
X_7	.379	[.284, .473]	X_{14}	1	[1, 1]

Table 4.2. Normalised average values and interval weights

We have applied the same procedure to assess weights for objectives of levels $j = 2, 3, 4$. Table 4.3 shows the normalized weights and intervals for all objectives in the hierarchy.

j	Objective	k_i^{jm}	$[k_i^{jL}, k_i^{jU}]$	j	Objective	k_i^{jm}	$[k_i^{jL}, k_i^{jU}]$
1	Environm. imp.	.173	[.115, .231]	2	Intangible eff.	.145	[.096, .193]
1	Social impact	.585	[.537, .631]	3	Dose to man	.656	[.524, .787]
1	Economic imp.	.242	[.217, .266]	3	Health status	.344	[.229, .458]
2	Ecosyst. health	1	[1, 1]	3	Fish consump.	.504	[.403, .605]
2	Health impact	.791	[.718, .862]	3	Fish recreat.	.496	[.396, .594]
2	Living restrict.	.209	[.139, .279]	3	Fish ban	.766	[.638, .893]
2	Direct eff.	.855	[.683, 1.0]	3	Remed. count.	.234	[.117, .351]

Table 4.3. Normalized weights and interval weights for objectives in level j

Now, for a strategy S_l with consequences $(x_1^l, \ldots, x_{14}^l)$, the overall value will be given by formula

$$\begin{aligned} v\left(x_1^l, \ldots, x_{14}^l\right) =& .074 v_1\left(x_1^l\right) + .098 v_2\left(x_2^l\right) + .022 v_3\left(x_3^l\right) + .283 v_4\left(x_4^l\right) \\ & + .072 v_5\left(x_5^l\right) + .087 v_6\left(x_6^l\right) + .023 v_7\left(x_7^l\right) + .038 v_8\left(x_8^l\right) \\ & + .023 v_9\left(x_9^l\right) + .038 v_{10}\left(x_{10}^l\right) + .036 v_{11}\left(x_{11}^l\right) \\ & + .123 v_{12}\left(x_{12}^l\right) + .048 v_{13}\left(x_{13}^l\right) + .035 v_{14}\left(x_{14}^l\right) \end{aligned} \quad (3)$$

where we obtain the estimated normalized weight ω_i of each value function v_i multiplying attribute weights by those of their respective upper level objectives. Using the data in Table 3.1, we compute the overall value of each strategy S_l from formula (3), as we show in Table 4.4. We therefore suggest as optimal alternative S_5.

Strategy	S_5	S_3	S_6	S_4	S_7	S_8	S_1	S_2
Value v	.6276	.5939	.5901	.5582	.5432	.5274	.3946	.3076

Table 4.4. Evaluation of countermeasures

5 Sensitivity analysis

The system evaluates a strategy S_l described by $(x_1^l, \ldots, x_{14}^l)$ and its value in each attribute, by means of value function (1). From the assessed weights, we obtain ranges $w_i \in [w_i^L, w_i^U]$, for $i = 1, \ldots, 14$, where

$$\begin{aligned} \left[w_1^L, w_1^U\right] &= \left[k_1^{4L} k_1^{3L} k_1^{1L}, k_1^{4U} k_1^{3U} k_1^{1U}\right] \\ \left[w_2^L, w_2^U\right] &= \left[k_1^{4L} k_2^{3L} k_2^{1L}, k_1^{4U} k_1^{3U} k_2^{1U}\right] \\ &\vdots \end{aligned}$$

Table 5.1 shows such interval weights. As we pointed out, these imprecise weights will be used in sensitivity analysis to gain insight and to help the DM to choose an strategy. The information summarized in constraints on ranges on the weights, may be used in computations described in Ríos Insua (1990) and Ríos Insua and French (1991), to eliminate strategies, mainly those which are dominated and/or non potentially optimal.

Attribute	$[w_i^L, w_i^U]$	Attribute	$[w_i^L, w_i^U]$	Attribute	$[w_i^L, w_i^U]$
X_1	[.024, .149]	X_6	[.032, .182]	X_{11}	[.013, .069]
X_2	[.043, .176]	X_7	[.008, .050]	X_{12}	[.067, .199]
X_3	[0.00, .057]	X_8	[.015, .077]	X_{13}	[.017, .093]
X_4	[.174, .428]	X_9	[.008, .048]	X_{14}	[.020, .051]
X_5	[.022, .161]	X_{10}	[.015, .076]		

Table 5.1. Interval weights for the overall value function

For that, let us rewrite $v(S_l) = v(S_l, \boldsymbol{w})$. If $(x_1^l, \ldots, x_{14}^l)$ is the consequence for strategy S_l and $(x_1^q, \ldots, x_{14}^q)$ is for S_q, we will check whether strategy S_q dominates S_l $(S_l \prec S_q)$, solving the optimization problem

$$[P_{lq}] : \left\{ \min_{w \in W} z_{lq} = v(S_q, \boldsymbol{w}) - v(S_l, \boldsymbol{w}) \right.$$

where we denote with $\boldsymbol{w} \in W$ the set of constraints $w_i \in [w_i^L, w_i^U]$, $i = 1, \ldots, 14$. If the optimal value $z_{lq}^* > 0$, then $S_l \prec S_q$ and we discard strategy S_l. Table 5.2 shows optimal values of those problems that need to be solved, a dash meaning that the problem needs not be solved. We see that the set of nondominated strategies is $\{S_1, S_3, S_4, S_5, S_6\}$, discarding the dominated strategies S_2, S_7 and S_8.

	S_3	S_6	S_4	S_7	S_8	S_1	S_2
S_5	−.114	−.330	−.337	−.084	−.316	−.033	−.063
S_3		−.504	−.327	.013	−.297	−.009	−.107
S_6			−.118	–	−.097	−.368	.066
S_4				–	.004	−.340	–
S_7					–	−.036	–
S_8						−.357	–

Table 5.2. Optimal values of $[P_{lq}]$ problems

These results imply that, for the assessed scenario, strategies like temporary fish ban, fertilisation of the lake, or a combination of both will never be optimal: The fish ban alternative S_2 is dominated by the chemical treatments S_6 (it can be shown that it is also dominated by S_4 and S_8, and even by fertilization S_7), while liming strategies S_3 and S_4, dominate the fertilization ones S_7 and S_8, respectively.

We can also determine the potentially optimal (p.o.) strategies among the non-dominated ones. To discover whether an strategy S_j is p.o., we consider the problem

$$[P_j] : \begin{cases} \min\limits_{w \in W} \; z_j \\ \text{s. t.} \quad v(S_j, w) - v(S_k, w) + z_j \geq 0, \quad \forall k \neq j. \end{cases}$$

If the optimal value $z_j^* \leq 0$, then S_j is p.o. Table 5.3. shows the optimal values of the problems solved. We see that all five strategies are p.o.

Strategy	S_1	S_3	S_4	S_5	S_6
Opt. value	$-.009$	$-.113$	$-.118$	$-.174$	$-.176$

Table 5.3. Optimal values of $[P_j]$

Next, we compute the adjacent potentially optimal (a.p.o.) alternatives, i.e., those that may share optimality with S_5. To find whether S_j is a.p.o. to S_5, we solve the problem

$$[P_j^*] : \begin{cases} \min\limits_{w \in W} \; z_{j5} = \left(v(S_j, w) - v(S_5, w)\right)^2 \\ \text{s. t.} \quad v(S_j, w) - v(S_5, w) \leq 0, \quad i = 1, 3, 4, 6. \end{cases}$$

Then, S_j is a.p.o. to S_5 if the optimal value $z_{j5}^* = 0$. Since the optimal values are $z_{j5}^* = 0$, $j = 1, 3, 4, 6$, all four alternatives are a.p.o. to S_5.

Finally, we compute the sensitivity index $r = \rho/\delta$, which gives us a relative measure of the insensitivity of S_5 to changes in w. The value $\rho = \min_j d_j$, where d_j is obtained solving the problem

$$[Pd_j] : \begin{cases} \min\limits_{w \in W} \; d_j = d(w, \omega) \\ \text{s. t.} \quad v(S_j, w) - v(S_5, w) = 0 \end{cases}$$

where ω, see (3), is the estimate of w and d is the Euclidean metric. δ is the solution of $\min_{w \in W} d(w, \omega)$. Then, we obtain that $\rho = d_6^* = .017$ and $\delta = .253$, the closest competitor to S_5 seems S_6. The sensitivity index is $r = .067$. Therefore, we have a very sensitive problem to changes in weights.

6 Conclusions

We have applied Decision Analysis methods to select the optimal strategy in the event of radioactive contamination of aquatic ecosystems and their drainage areas. We construct an overall rank by means of an additive value function, which represents the experts' preferences. To aid the DM to choose a final strategy, we apply some concepts which permit us to reduce the set of strategies of interest. A low sensitivity index, would suggest the need of an interactive DSS permitting easy changes on weights, to assess the robustness of the solution and, eventually, elicit additional information from the DM, see Ríos Insua (1990) for some ideas.

The methodology described is implemented in a PC based DSS which will allow the incorporation of all relevant information in the process, including imprecision on values.

Acknowledgments

This paper has been supported by EC project FIP-CT96-0036 and CICYT project TIC95-0028. The contribution of the following members of the MOIRA team is deeply acknowledged: Dr. John Brittain (Univ. Oslo) and Dr. Per Strand (Norvegian Radiation Protection Institute) who provided the definition of the scenario and descriptive data of lake Øvre Heimdalsvatn; Prof. Lars Håkanson and Mr. Otto Abrahamsson (Univ. Uppsala) who ran the lake model; and Mr. Fernando Jiménez, who ran the dose model.

References

Farquhar, P. H. (1984). Utility Assessment Methods. *Man. Sci.* **30**, 1283–1300.

Håkanson, L. (1993). A system for Lake Ecosystem Indices. *Journal of Aquatic Ecosystem Health* **2**, 165–184.

Håkanson, L., Brittain, J. E., Monte, L., Heling, R., Bergström, U. and Suolanen, V. (1996). Modelling of Radiocesium in Lakes - The VAMP Model. *J. Environ. Radioactivity* **33**, 255–308.

Håkanson, L. (1997a). The Application of the Lake Ecosystem Index. In *Multiattribute Decision Analysis in Radioecology (in preparison).*

Håkanson, L. (1997b). Personal communication.

Hershey, J. C., Kneunreuther, H. C. and Schoemaker, P. J. (1982). Sources of Bias in Assessments procedures for utility Functions. *Man. Sci.* **28**, 936–953.

Jaffray, J. Y. (1989). Some Experimental Findings on Decision Making under Risk and Their Implications. *E. J. O. R.* **38**, 301–306.

Jiménez, F. and Gallego, E. (1996). A Dose Model for Radionuclide Contaminated Water Bodies. Report CTN-12/96, Cátedra de Tecnología Nuclear. Universidad Politécnica de Madrid.

McCord, M. and de Neufville, R. (1986). "Lottery Equivalents": Reduction of the Certainty Effect Problem in Utility Assessment. *Man. Sci.* **32**, 56–61.

Raiffa, H. (1982). *The Art and Science of Negotiation.* Harvard University Press: Cambridge, Mass.

Ríos Insua, D. (1990). *Sensitivity Analysis in Multiobjective Decision Making.* LNEMS **347**. Springer: Berlin.

Ríos Insua, D. and French, S. (1991). A Framework for Sensitivity Analysis in Discrete Multi-Objective Decision-Making. *E. J. O. R.* **54**, 176–190.

Ríos, S., Ríos-Insua, S., Ríos Insua, D. and Pachón, J. G. (1994). Experiments in Robust Decision Making. In *Decision Theory and Decision Analysis: Trends and Challenges.* S. Ríos (Ed.), Kluwer: Boston.

Stewart, T. J. (1996). Robustness of Additive Value Function Methods in MCDM. *Journal of Multi-Criteria Decision Analysis* **5**, 301–309.

Belton, V. (1991). Multiple Criteria Decision Analysis, Practically the Only Way to Choose. In L. Hendry and R. Eglese (Eds.), *Operational Research Tutorial Papers.* Birmingham: Operational Research Society, 53–101.

Vik, R. (1978). The lake Øvre Heimdalsvatn, a Subalpine Freshwater Ecosystem. *Holartic Ecology* **1**, 81–320.

VISA for Windows (1995). V. Belton and Visual Thinking International Limited, V 4.10, Glasgow.

von Nitzsch, R. and Weber, M. (1988). Utility Function Assessment on a Micro-Computer: An Interactive Procedure. *Annals of Operations Research* **16**, 149–160.

Is Economic Growth Compatible with the Respect for the Environment?

M. Pilar Martínez García[1] and M. del Mar Sánchez de la Vega[1]

[1] Department of Quantitative Methods for Economics.
University of Murcia, SPAIN

Abstract

This paper investigates the relationship between environment and economic development in a growth model which takes into account an endogenous technological progress that allows more ecological production technologies. Using optimal control theory, the feasibility and optimality of a sustained economic growth that keeps constant environmental quality is studied.

Keywords. Endogenous growth, environmental quality, optimal control, sustainable development

1 Introduction

Economic growth has often been accused of causing serious environmental problems and endangering the development of future generations. Since the beginning of the 1970s the concern for a better environmental management, which takes into account not only the current generation's well-being but also our descendants' one, has been increasing. One of the most famous studies carried out in this field is the Meadows report: *The Limits of Growth* (1972), which maintains that there is an incompatibility between economic growth and the respect for the environment and the rights of future generations. *The Limits of Growth* asserts that the finite disposition of raw materials in nature as well as the limited regenerative capacity of the environment, impose physical limits to economic growth. However, human beings will always try to improve their living conditions, specially in developing countries where economic growth is necessary to overcome the unfair impoverished situation. Policies that boost the economic growth in these countries must be put into practise, but maybe, they should differ from traditional patterns based on an intensive use of the environment.

Technological progress that enables production technologies to use natural resources more efficiently seems to be the key to overcome the conflict between environment and economic growth. The *efficiency* in the use of natural resources will help us to achieve a *sustainable development* that *meets the needs of the present without compromising the ability of future generations to meet their own needs* (Brudland report: Hauff (1987)).

Authors like Gradus and Smulders (1993), Hung, Chang and Blackburn (1993), Bovenberg and Smulders (1995) among others, have studied the implications of environmental constraints and technological innovation for sustainability and growth. Since sustainable development is essentially an intertemporal optimization problem (Dasgupta (1993)), these papers have basically used optimal control theory. Building on these works, we present an economic growth model which incorporates a technological sector that investigates more ecological production technologies. Our model is similar to the Bovenberg and Smulders' one but they differ in the specification of technological knowledge production. Moreover, contrary to the previous papers, we have used general constant-to-scale production technologies.

The rest of the paper is organized as follows. The second section is devoted to describe the economy and define what is a socially optimal solution. Section three presents the necessary conditions for optimality. In the fourth section the feasibility and optimality of a sustained economic growth that maintains constant the environment is studied, and finally, section five displays the conclusions.

2 The Model

We study an economy with constant population where *natural environment, productive sectors* and *consumers' preferences have been taken into account.*

2.1 Natural Environment

In this model the natural environment is considered a renewable resource. It is assumed that there exists an index $N(t)$ that measures the level of environmental quality at any moment in time. There is another variable $p(t)$ that stands for the flow of polluting emissions derived from the production sectors of the economy. By *polluting emissions* we refer to emissions of pollutants or wastes, as well as to the exploitation of natural resource (wood cutting, exploitation of fisheries, etc.). It is done in this way because both activities are essentially equivalent. Dumping wastes or pollutants can be understood as exploiting a natural resource like water, air or land (depending on where the dumping is done).(see for instance Smulders (1995) and Dasgupta (1996) where this equivalence is explained in detail). The quality of the environment, $N(t)$, is supposed to depreciate due to the damaging effects of polluting emissions, $p(t)$, and increase owing to the absorption of pollution and the regenerative capacity of nature. Specially, we assume that $\dot{N} = E(N,p)$ such that $E \in C^2$ and $E_p < 0$, $E_{pp} < 0$, $E_{NN} < 0$, $E_{pN} > 0$, where the subindexes represent partial derivatives. We refer to Bovenberg and Smulders (1995) for a detailed explanation of this modelization of environmental quality. It is also assumed that for each level of emissions p, there exists a level of environmental quality $\overline{N}(p)$ for which the regenerative capacity of nature compensates for the damaging effects of pollution so that environmental quality remains constant over time: $E(\overline{N}(p),p) = 0$. Besides, it is supposed that $E_N(N,p) < 0$ in a neigbourhood of $\overline{N}(p)$. Consequently, $\overline{N}(p)$ is a locally stable equilibrium and represents the maximum sustainable level of environmental quality for a given level of emissions p. We are going to represent by $\varsigma(p)$ the elasticity of $\overline{N}(p)$ with respect to emissions, that is,

$$\varsigma(p) := \frac{d\overline{N}(p)}{dp}\frac{p}{\overline{N}} = -\frac{E_p}{E_N}\frac{p}{N} < 0.$$

Furthermore, it is assumed that the negative effect of an additional unit of emissions on the environment is negligible if the level of emissions is low, whereas if emissions approach a critical level, $p_{\max} > 0$, an additional unit will cause an extreme environmental damage. More precisely, for every fixed $N > 0$,

$$\lim_{p \to 0} E_p(N,p) = 0, \qquad \lim_{p \to p_{\max}} E_P(N,p) = -\infty. \tag{1}$$

2.2 Productive Sectors

It is considered an economy with two productive sectors. One of these sectors produce final output which can be either consumed or invested in accumulating physical capital. Consumption is represented by the letter c whereas the stock of physical capital is denoted by the letter k. The second sector, which is called the sector of technological research, or the sector of knowledge, produces knowledge devoted to improve the productivity of natural resources. The stock of accumulated knowledge in this field will be denoted by the letter h. This is a pure investment sector since its output is not consumed, it is only, as we shall see next, an intermediate good in final output production.

Final output production is described by the function $Y(N, k_Y, p_Y \in C^2$. Three different inputs are considered in the production of output: *environmental quality*, N, which has a positive impact on production (as an example we have that low-exploited soil and non-polluted air or water improves the productivity of capital in the agricultural sector); *physical capital* devoted to final output production, k_Y, which can be written as $k_Y = uk$ (where u is the fraction of physical capital invested in this sector); and finally, *effective emissions* derived from final output production, [1] p_Y. *Effective emissions* (those which are truly productive) are defined as $p_Y = hp$ (available

[1] In this model polluting emissions are considered as inputs. It is clear that natural resources like for instance fish or wood are inputs in production. However, considering pollutants like carbon dioxide or wastes as inputs is not so evident. Traditionally these ones have been modelled as non-desired by-products, derived necessarily from good production (Keeler, Spence, Zeckhauser (1971), Foster (1973)). However, this traditional way of modelling emissions rejects the important fact that it is possible to increase industrial production by increasing emissions.

Contrary to traditional view, modelling emissions as inputs in production (Brock (1977), Tahvonen and Kuuluvainen (1993), Bovenberg and Smulders (1995)), despite of being a simplification, it allows us to take into account the fact that an intensive use of the environment, keeping constant the rest of productive factors, increases output levels, as it is in the majority of the real problems.

technical knowledge multiplied by real emissions), which means that technological knowledge improves the productivity of emissions and makes the production sector use natural resources more efficiently. In addition, it is assumed that given N, k_Y and h there exists a level of real emissions, $\hat{p}$, such that:

$$\lim_{p \to \hat{p}} \frac{\partial Y}{\partial p}(N, k_Y, hp) = 0 \tag{2}$$

Whenever $p < \hat{p}(N, k_Y, h)$ function Y is strictly increasing with respect to all its arguments and linearly homogeneous with respect to k_Y and p_Y. Second order derivatives satisfy that $Y^2_{jj} < 0$ and $Y^2_{jk} > 0 \quad \forall j \neq k \quad j, k = N, k_Y, p_Y$. To guarantee certain interiority conditions, this function exhibits unbounded partial derivatives at the boundary, and all inputs are essential in the production process. More precisely,

$$\lim_{N \to 0} \frac{\partial Y}{\partial N} = +\infty, \qquad \lim_{k_Y \to 0} \frac{\partial Y}{\partial k_Y} = +\infty, \qquad \lim_{p_Y \to 0} \frac{\partial Y}{\partial p_Y} = +\infty. \tag{3}$$

$$Y(0, k_Y, p_Y) = Y(N, 0, p_Y) = Y(N, k_Y, 0) = 0 \tag{4}$$

Technological progress that enables production technologies to use natural resources more efficiently is characterized by the function $H(k_H, h) \in C^2$, which depends positively on *physical capital* invested in the technological knowledge sector, $k_H = (1 - u)k$, and on the level of available knowledge, h. The first input, k_H, shows the necessity of investing economic resources in Research & Development projects to improve the efficiency of natural resources and emissions. Second input, h, shows that the higher the level of knowledge, the easier it is to achieve a technological breakthrough. Function H is strictly increasing with respect to all its arguments and second derivatives are assumed to satisfy that $H^2_{jj} < 0$ and $H^2_{jk} > 0 \quad \forall j \neq k \quad j, k = k_H, h$. Finally, to guarantee interior solutions, the following properties must be satisfied

$$\lim_{k_H \to 0} \frac{\partial H}{\partial k_H} = +\infty, \qquad \lim_{h \to 0} \frac{\partial H}{\partial h} = +\infty. \tag{5}$$

$$H(0, h) = H(k_H, 0) = 0. \tag{6}$$

2.3 Preferences

It is assumed that there exists an instantaneous utility function $U(c, N) \in C^2$ strictly increasing and concave with respect to consumption and environmental quality. In addition, the following properties must be satisfied,[2]

[2] We could have supposed the existence of subsistence levels for consumption, $c_0 > 0$, and for environmental quality, $N_0 > 0$, such that nobody would accept lower levels. This could be represented by assuming that $\lim_{c \to c_0} \frac{\partial U}{\partial c}(c, N) = +\infty$ and $\lim_{N \to N_0} \frac{\partial U}{\partial N}(c, N) = +\infty$. But these are equivalent to conditions stated in Hauff and Volker (1987) if we take $c - c_0$ as consumption and $N - N_0$ as environmental quality.

$$\lim_{c \to 0} \frac{\partial U}{\partial c}(c, N) = +\infty, \ \lim_{N \to 0} \frac{\partial U}{\partial N}(c, N) = +\infty, \ \lim_{c \to \infty} \frac{\partial U}{\partial c}(c, N) = 0. \tag{7}$$

Once we have explained the economy, we shall focus on the social planner's problem, consisting on taking at any instant of time the proper decisions about consumption, emissions and investments in the productive sectors which maximize the flow of discounted utility along a sufficiently large time horizon.

Definition 1. *A socially optimal solution for the economy described above is a set of paths $N(t)$, $k(t)$, $h(t)$, $c(t)$, $p(t)$ and $u(t)$ that solve the following optimization problem:*

$$\max \int_0^\infty e^{-\rho t} \, U(c, N) \, dt \tag{8}$$

such that

$$\dot{N} = E(N, p) \tag{9}$$

$$\dot{k} = Y(N, uk, hp) - c - \eta k \tag{10}$$

$$\dot{h} = H((1-u)k, h) - \theta h \tag{11}$$

$$N(t) \in [0, N_{\max}], k(t) \geq 0, h(t) \geq 0, c \in [0, Y], u \in [0, 1], p \geq 0 \tag{12}$$

$$N(0) = N_0 > 0 \quad k(0) = k_0 > 0 \quad h(0) = h_0 > 0 \tag{13}$$

$$\liminf_{t \to \infty} N(t) \geq 0 \quad \liminf_{t \to \infty} k(t) \geq 0 \quad \liminf_{t \to \infty} h(t) \geq 0 \tag{14}$$

where $\rho > 0$ is the intertemporal discount rate, equation (10) describes the evolution of the stock of economy-wide physical capital, and equation (11) represents the motion law of technological knowledge. Parameters $\eta \geq 0$ and $\theta \geq 0$ are the respective depreciation rates. It is a deterministic optimal control problem with infinite horizon. We shall use the *catching-up* optimality criterium.

3 Necessary Conditions for Optimality

Condition (7) ensures that $c > 0$ on the optimal path, which together with condition (4) and the fact that $c \leq Y$, guarantees that $N(t)$, $k(t)$, $h(t)$, $u(t)$ and $p(t)$ are strictly positive on the optimal path. Applying Pontryagin Maximum Principle we obtain that control variables must satisfy the following conditions at any moment in time[3]:

[3] In order to simplify the exposition we have also assumed that $c < Y$ and $u < 1$ on the optimal path. In the next section we establish the existence of a unique optimal balanced path in which control variables are in the interior of the control set.

$$\frac{\partial U}{\partial c} - \mu_1 = 0 \tag{15}$$

$$\mu_1 \frac{\partial Y}{\partial k_Y} - \mu_2 \frac{\partial H}{\partial k_H} = 0 \tag{16}$$

$$\mu_1 h \frac{\partial Y}{\partial p_Y} + \mu_3 \frac{\partial E}{\partial p} = 0 \tag{17}$$

where μ_1, μ_2, and μ_3 are the shadow prices associated with state variables k, h and N, respectively.

Since functions U, Y and H are strictly increasing with respect to all their arguments and $\partial E/\partial p < 0$, equations (15–17) ensure that $\mu_1(t)$, $\mu_2(t)$ and $\mu_3(t)$ are strictly positive on the optimal path. Besides, coestate variables must satisfy the following differential equations:

$$\dot{\mu}_1 = \mu_1 \left(\rho - \frac{\partial Y}{\partial k_Y} + \eta \right) \tag{18}$$

$$\dot{\mu}_2 = \mu_2 \left(\rho - \frac{p\mu_1}{\mu_2} \frac{\partial Y}{\partial p_Y} - \frac{\partial H}{\partial h} + \theta \right) \tag{19}$$

$$\dot{\mu}_3 = \mu_3 \left(\rho - \frac{\partial E}{\partial N} \right) - \frac{\partial U}{\partial N} - \mu_1 \frac{\partial Y}{\partial N}. \tag{20}$$

It is easy to prove that $p(t) < \hat{p}(t)$ on the optimal path. If there was an instant t_0 such that $p(t_0) \geq \hat{p}(t_0)$, conditions (2) and (17) would imply that $\mu_3(t_0) = 0$, and by means of (20) we would have that $\dot{\mu}_3(t_0) < 0$ in a neighbourhood of t_0, which would contradict the fact that $\mu_3(t) > 0$ forall t on the optimal path. Therefore we can consider that function Y is strictly increasing with respect to all its arguments and linearly homogeneous with respect to k_Y and p_Y.

Denoting by $z = k/h$ and by $q_h = \mu_2/\mu_1$ and $q_N = \mu_3/\mu_1$ the shadow prices of technological knowledge and environmental quality relative to physical capital, we can establish the following lemma.

Lemma 1. *Equations (15)–(17) define control variables as differentiable implicit functions of state and coestate variables:* $c = c(\mu_1)$, $u = u(N, z, q_h, q_N/h)$ *and* $p = p(N, z, q_h, q_N/h)$. *Moreover,*

$$\frac{\partial c}{\partial \mu_1} < 0 \quad \frac{\partial p}{\partial q_h} < 0 \quad \frac{\partial p}{\partial (q_N/h)} < 0 \quad \frac{\partial p}{\partial N} > 0 \quad \frac{\partial p}{\partial z} > 0$$

$$\frac{\partial u}{\partial q_h} < 0 \quad \frac{\partial u}{\partial (q_N/h)} < 0 \quad \frac{\partial u}{\partial N} > 0 \quad \frac{\partial z_Y}{\partial z} > 0 \quad \frac{\partial z_H}{\partial z} > 0$$

where $z_Y = uz$ *and* $z_H = (1-u)z$.

Proof. Conditions (7) and the strict concavity of the utility function ensure the existence of a unique control c satisfying equation (15). Conditions (1), (3) and (5) together with the assumptions made on the second derivatives of the functions Y and H, and the linear homogeneity of the function Y, ensure that given state an coestate variables there are unique controls u and p which satisfy equations (16)–(17). Using the implicit function theorem we can establish that c, u and p are C^1 functions of the state and coestate variables. The signs of the derivatives are directly obtained by implicit derivation in (15)–(17). □

Using (18)–(20), the evolution of q_h and q_N is obtained,

$$\frac{\dot{q}_h}{q_h} = \frac{\partial Y}{\partial k_Y} - \frac{p}{q_h}\frac{\partial Y}{\partial p_Y} - \frac{\partial H}{\partial h} + \theta - \eta \tag{21}$$

$$\frac{\dot{q}_N}{q_N} = \frac{\partial Y}{\partial k_Y} - \frac{\partial E}{\partial N} - \frac{1}{q_N}\left(\frac{\partial U/\partial N}{\partial U/\partial c} + \frac{\partial Y}{\partial N}\right) - \eta \tag{22}$$

Taking logarithms in (15), deriving with respect time, and using (18) to eliminate μ_1 we obtain the growth rate of consumption on an optimal path:

$$\frac{\dot{c}}{c} = \sigma\left(\frac{\partial Y}{\partial k_Y} + \frac{\partial^2 U/\partial c \partial N}{\partial U/\partial c} E(N,p) - \rho - \eta\right) \tag{23}$$

where $\sigma = -\frac{\partial U/\partial c}{\partial^2 U/\partial c^2}\frac{1}{c}$ is the elasticity of intertemporal substitution which measures consumers' disposition to replace present consumption by future consumption. Empirical estimations show that σ is usually lower than 1 due to the fact that consumers always prefer smooth consumption paths.

Applying the same methodology to equations (16)–(17) we obtain:

$$\gamma\frac{\dot{N}}{N} + \left(\alpha + \beta\frac{u}{1-u}\right)\frac{\dot{u}}{u} + (\alpha - \beta)\left(\frac{\dot{k}}{k} - \frac{\dot{h}}{h}\right) - \alpha\frac{\dot{p}}{p} - \frac{\dot{q}_h}{q_h} = 0 \tag{24}$$

$$\left(\pi - \frac{E_{Np}\,N}{E_p}\right)\frac{\dot{N}}{N} - \varepsilon\left(\frac{\dot{u}}{u} + \frac{\dot{k}}{k} - \frac{\dot{h}}{h}\right) + \frac{\dot{h}}{h} + \left(\varepsilon - \frac{E_{pp}\,p}{E_p}\right)\frac{\dot{p}}{p} - \frac{\dot{q}_N}{q_N} = 0 \tag{25}$$

where $\gamma = \frac{\partial^2 Y}{\partial N \partial k_Y}\frac{N}{\partial Y/\partial k_Y}$, $\alpha = \frac{\partial^2 Y}{\partial k_Y^2}\frac{k_Y}{\partial Y/\partial k_Y}$, $\pi = \frac{\partial^2 Y}{\partial N \partial p_Y}\frac{N}{\partial Y/\partial p_Y}$, $\varepsilon = \frac{\partial^2 Y}{\partial p_Y^2}\frac{p_Y}{\partial Y/\partial p_Y}$ and $\beta = \frac{\partial^2 H}{\partial k_H^2}\frac{k_H}{\partial H/\partial k_H}$. Observe that these elasticities will be constant only in the case of Cobb-Douglas production functions.

4 Balanced Path

If technological research is removed from our model, we shall have the Brock's model, studied with great detail by Tahvonen and Kuuluvainen (1993). In the Brock's model a sustained economic growth that keeps constant environmental quality is infeasible. In this case the only possibility of protecting the environment from the economic activity is an stationary economy, without economic development. Tahvonen and Kuuluvainen (1993) study the steady state characteristics for this economy. In what follows we shall prove that, if some social and environmental conditions are satisfied, technological research allows an economic development that maintains constant environmental quality.

Definition 2. *A balanced path for the economy described above is a set of paths $N(t)$, $k(t)$, $h(t)$, $c(t)$, $u(t)$ and $p(t)$ such that $u(t)$ and the ratio Y/k are constant and $N(t)$, $k(t)$, $h(t)$ and $p(t)$ grow at constant rates. A socially optimal balanced path is a balanced path which is solution of the optimization problem (8)–(14) for some initial conditions N_0, k_0 and h_0.*

Because of the existence of a maximum level for environmental quality, $N_{\max}$, this one cannot grow continuously at a strictly positive constant growth rate. Therefore, environmental quality must be constant on a balanced path. Besides, a constant environmental quality together with the fact that $\partial E/\partial p < 0$ implies that polluting emissions must also be constant on a balanced path.

Denote by g the constant rate of growth of technological knowledge on a balanced path. Since the ratio output/physical capital must be constant and the output production function is linearly homogeneous with respect to physical capital and effective emissions, technological knowledge and physical capital must grow at the same rate on a balanced path. Moreover, dividing equation (10) by k we obtain that c, k and h grow at the same rate.

On the other hand, dividing equation (11) by h it is shown that H grows at the same rate as h and k on a balanced path. So, for a balanced path to be a feasible solution to the problem (8)–(14), function H is required to be linearly homogeneous.

The following proposition lays down the previous properties and new ones which can be directly derived from the preceding explanation.

Proposition 1. *If $(N^*(t), k^*(t), h^*(t), c^*(t), u^*(t), p^*(t))$ is a socially optimal balanced path for this economy, then:*

- *i) Environmental quality and polluting emissions are constant.*
- *ii) Physical capital, technological knowledge, consumption and final output grow at a common constant rate, g.*
- *iii) The shadow price of technological knowledge, q_h, is constant whereas the shadow price of environmental quality, q_N, grows at the same constant rate as the economy does, g.*
- *iv) Marginal productivity of polluting emissions $(\partial Y/\partial p)$ and environmental quality $(\partial Y/\partial N)$ grow at the same rate as the economy, g.*
- *v) Marginal productivities of physical capital $(\partial Y/\partial k_Y, \partial H/\partial k_H)$, efficient emissions $(\partial Y/\partial p_Y)$ and technological knowledge $(\partial H/\partial h)$ are constant on the optimal balanced path.*

Since $\dot{q}_h = 0$ and (16) must be satisfied on an optimal balanced path, we have that

$$u^* = \lambda_{k_Y} \frac{\lambda_{k_H}(g+\theta) + r - g - \eta}{\lambda_{k_H}(g+\theta) + \lambda_{k_Y}(r - g - \eta)}, \tag{26}$$

whereλ_{k_Y} and λ_{k_H} are physical capital production elasticities in the final output sector and knowledge sector respectively, and $r = \partial Y/\partial k_Y$ is physical capital return in the final output sector.

Moreover, since $\dot{k}/k = \dot{h}/h = g$ on a balanced path, we have that $\frac{Y}{k} = g + \eta + \frac{c}{k}$. Besides, $r = \frac{\partial Y}{\partial k_y} = \frac{\lambda_{k_Y}}{u}\frac{Y}{k}$. Therefore,

$$\frac{c^*}{k^*} = \frac{r + (\lambda_{k_H} - \lambda_{k_Y})g + \lambda_{k_H}\theta - \lambda_{k_Y}\eta}{\lambda_{k_H}(g+\theta) + \lambda_{k_Y}(r - g - \eta)}(r - g - \eta). \tag{27}$$

Since $c(t) > 0$ on an optimal solution, $r - \eta > g$ is a necessary condition for a balanced path to be optimal. The contrary together with the fact that $\lambda_{k_Y} < 1$, would imply that $u^* > 1$ which contradicts the feasibility of a balanced path. Therefore, expressions (26) and (27) imply that the feasibility and optimality of a balanced path requires that net physical capital return $r - \eta$ surpasses the economy growth rate g: $r - \eta > g$.

On the other hand, equations (15), (18) and the fact that $\partial Y / \partial k_y$ is constant on a balanced path imply that $\partial U / \partial c$ grows at a constant rate on an optimal balanced path. Moreover, $\frac{\partial U/\partial N}{\partial U/\partial c}\frac{N}{c}$ is constant on an optimal balanced path. Therefore, for the optimality of a balanced path, the utility function must exhibit an elasticity of intertemporal consumption substitution, σ, independent of the level of consumption and on the level of environmental quality. This means that for the existence of an optimal balanced path, the utility function must be of one of the following types:

$$U(c, N) = n(N)\frac{c^{1-1/\sigma}}{1-1/\sigma} \text{ with } n' \lesseqgtr 0 \text{ and } n'' \gtreqless 0 \text{ if } \sigma \lesseqgtr 1$$

$$U(c, N) = \ln c + \ln n(N) \text{with } n' > 0 \text{ and } n'' < 0 if \sigma = 1$$

To establish the existence of an optimal balanced path in this economy we shall verify that there exists a balanced path satisfying the necessary conditions for optimality given in the previous section, and next, after checking its feasibility, we shall confirm that this one really maximizes the discounted utility flow along an infinite horizon using the *catching-up* criterium.

Note that on a balanced path some variables remain constant, N, p, u, and q_h, where others, k, h, c and q_N grow at the same constant rate. Therefore, variables $z = k/h$, $a = c/h$ and q_N/h remain constant on a balanced path. Moreover, taking into account equations (24) and (25), we can establish the following lemma.

Lemma 2. *There exists a balanced path satisfying necessary conditions for optimality if and only if there exists an steady state* $(N^*, z^*, a^*, q_h^*, (q_N/h)^*)$ *for the following system*

$$\dot{N} = E(N, p) = f_1(N, z, q_h, q_N/h) \tag{28}$$

$$\frac{\dot{z}}{z} = \frac{\dot{k}}{k} - \frac{\dot{h}}{h} = f_2(N, z, a, q_h, q_N/h) \tag{29}$$

$$\frac{\dot{a}}{a} = \frac{\dot{c}}{c} - \frac{\dot{h}}{h} = f_3(N, z, q_h, q_N/h) \tag{30}$$

$$\frac{\dot{q}_h}{q_h} = \frac{\dot{\mu}_2}{\mu_2} - \frac{\dot{\mu}_1}{\mu_1} = f_4(N, z, q_h, q_N/h) \tag{31}$$

$$\frac{(q_N\dot{/}h)}{q_N/h} = \frac{\dot{\mu}_3}{\mu_3} - \frac{\dot{\mu}_1}{\mu_1} - \frac{\dot{h}}{h} = f_5(N, z, a, q_h, q_N/h) \tag{32}$$

where control variables u and p have been replaced by the functions obtained in lemma 1, and where we have used the notation f_1, f_2, f_3, f_4 and f_5 to represent the evolution of the variables in a short way.

The following proposition establishes the existence and uniqueness of an optimal balanced path when $\sigma \leq 1$, which is the more realistic case.

Proposition 2. *Consider the dynamic optimization problem (8)–(14) with $\sigma \leq 1$. If the following necessary conditions are satisfied,*

i) Function H is linearly homogeneous
ii) The utility function exhibits a constant elasticity of intertemporal substitution, σ (independent of the level of consumption and environmental quality).
iii) $r - \eta > g$
together with,
iv) $\zeta(p) > \max\left\{\frac{\alpha}{\gamma}, \frac{-\alpha}{\pi\alpha+\gamma\varepsilon}, \frac{\lambda_{k_Y}-1}{\lambda_N+\Phi}\right\}$, where $\Phi = \frac{d}{dN}\left(\frac{U_N}{U_c\ c}\right)\frac{N}{U_N/(U_c\ c)}$.

Then, there exists an interior optimal balanced path.

Condition (iv) requires that the sensitivity of environmental quality to emissions is lower than a critical level given by production technologies and consumers' preferences.

Proof. The first step is to establish the existence of an steady state for the system (28)–(32).

Conditions (3), (5) and (6) guarantee that given N and q_N/h there are unique values $\tilde{z} > 0$ and $\tilde{q}_h > 0$ such that $f_3(N, \tilde{z}, \tilde{q}_h, q_N/h) = 0$, $f_4(N, \tilde{z}, \tilde{q}_h, q_N/h) = 0$. Moreover, taking into account that

$$\det\left[\left(\frac{\partial k_Y}{\partial z}, \frac{\partial k_Y}{\partial q_h}\right), \left(\frac{\partial p}{\partial z}, \frac{\partial p}{\partial q_h}\right)\right] = 0,$$

it can be proved that

$$J(N, \tilde{z}, \tilde{q}_h, q_N/h) = \det\left(\frac{\partial f_i}{\partial j}\right) < 0 \quad \text{for} \quad i = 3, 4 \quad \text{and} \quad j = z, q_h.$$

Particularly,

$$J(N, \tilde{z}, \tilde{q}_h, q_N/h) = \Omega_1 - \Omega_2\left(\frac{p}{\partial Y/\partial k_Y}\frac{\partial Y}{\partial p_Y}\frac{\partial^2 H}{\partial k_H^2} + \frac{\partial^2 H}{\partial k_H \partial h}\right),$$

where Ω_1 and Ω_2 are strictly negative functions evaluated at $N, \tilde{z}, \tilde{q}_h, q_N/h$. However, $f_4(N, \tilde{z}, \tilde{q}_h, q_N/h) = 0$ ensures that (26) is true so that $u(N, \tilde{z}, \tilde{q}_h, q_N/h) > \lambda_{k_Y}$ which implies that

$$\frac{p}{\partial Y/\partial k_Y}\frac{\partial Y}{\partial p_Y}\frac{\partial^2 H}{\partial k_H^2} + \frac{\partial^2 H}{\partial k_H \partial h} < 0.$$

Consequently, $J(N, \tilde{z}, \tilde{q}_h, q_N/h) < 0$, which means that the system

$$\{f_3(N, z, q_h, q_N/h) = 0, f_4(N, z, q_h, q_N/h) = 0\}$$

defines $z = \tilde{z}(N, q_N/h)$ and $q_h = \tilde{q}_h(N, q_N/h)$ as C^1 functions of N and q_N/h.

Let us define the function $g(N, q_N/h) = \overline{N}(p(N, \tilde{z}, \tilde{q}_h, q_N/h)) \in C^1$. It is easy to prove that $\lim_{N\to 0} g(N, q_N/h) > 0$ and $\lim_{N\to N_{\max}} g(N, q_N/h) < N_{\max}$. Then, given q_N/h, we can establish the existence of at least one point $N = \check{N}(q_N/h) \in [0, N_{\max}]$ such that $N = g(N, q_N/h)$, therefore $f_1(\check{N}, \tilde{z}, \tilde{q}_h, q_N/h) = 0$. Moreover,

$$\frac{\partial f_1}{\partial N}(\check{N}, \tilde{z}, \tilde{q}_h, q_N/h) = \frac{\partial E}{\partial N} + \frac{\partial E}{\partial p}\left(\frac{\partial p}{\partial N} + \frac{\partial p}{\partial z}\frac{\partial \tilde{z}}{\partial N} + \frac{\partial p}{\partial q_h}\frac{\partial \tilde{q}_h}{\partial N}\right) < 0,$$

which implies the uniqueness of $N = \check{N}(q_N/h)$. As a consequence, the system

$$\{f_1(N, z, q_h, q_N/h) = 0, f_3(N, z, q_h, q_N/h) = 0, f_4(N, z, q_h, q_N/h) = 0\}$$

defines $z = \check{z}(q_N/h)$, $q_h = \check{q}_h(q_N/h)$ and $N = \check{N}(q_N/h)$ as C^1 functions of q_N/h.

It can be proved that

$$Q(\check{N}, \tilde{z}, \tilde{q}_h, q_N/h) = \det\left(\frac{\partial f_i}{\partial j}\right)_{\substack{i=1,3,4\\ j=N,z,q_h}}$$

$$= \left(\frac{\partial E}{\partial N} + \frac{\partial E}{\partial p}\frac{\partial p}{\partial N}\right) J + \frac{\partial E}{\partial p}\begin{vmatrix} \frac{\partial f_3}{\partial N} & \frac{\partial p}{\partial q_h}\frac{\partial f_3}{\partial z} - \frac{\partial p}{\partial z}\frac{\partial f_3}{\partial q_h} \\ \frac{\partial f_4}{\partial N} & \frac{\partial p}{\partial q_h}\frac{\partial f_4}{\partial z} - \frac{\partial p}{\partial z}\frac{\partial f_4}{\partial q_h} \end{vmatrix} > 0.$$

Taking into account that

$$f_2(N, z, a, q_h, q_N/h) = z^{-1}Y(N, uz, p) - z^{-1}a - H((1-u)z, 1) + \theta - \eta$$

we can establish that the system $\{f_1(N, z, q_h, q_N/h) = 0,\ f_2(N, z, a, q_h, q_N/h) = 0,\ f_3(N, z, q_h, q_N/h) = 0,\ f_4(N, z, q_h, q_N/h) = 0\}$ defines $a = \check{a}(q_N/h) \in C^1$. Moreover, condition (ii) guarantees that $0 < a < Y(N, uz, p)$.

Finally, replacing N, z, a and q_h by the functions $\check{N}$, $\check{z}$, $\check{a}$ and $\check{q}_h$, respectively in the equation $f_5(N, z, a, q_h, q_N/h) = 0$, and deriving with respect to q_N/h we obtain that condition (iv) guarantees that $\frac{df_5}{d(q_N/h)} > 0$.

Particularly,

$$\frac{df_5}{d(q_N/h)} = \Upsilon_1(q_N/h) - \frac{d\check{p}}{d(q_N/h)}\frac{q_N/h}{\check{p}}\{\Upsilon_2(q_N/h)(\gamma\varsigma(p) - \alpha)$$
$$+ \Upsilon_3(q_N/h)((\frac{d}{dN}(\frac{U_N}{U_c\, c})\frac{N}{U_N/(U_c\, c)} + \gamma)\varsigma(p) + (1 - \lambda_{k_Y}))\}$$
$$+ [(1-\sigma)\Upsilon_4(q_N/h) + \Upsilon_5(q_N/h)][(\pi + \frac{\gamma}{\alpha}\varepsilon)\varsigma(p) + 1]$$

where $\Upsilon_1(q_N/h)$, $\Upsilon_2(q_N/h)$, $\Upsilon_3(q_N/h)$, $\Upsilon_4(q_N/h)$ and $\Upsilon_5(q_N/h)$ are strictly positive functions, and $\check{p}(q_N/h) = p(\check{N}, \check{z}, \check{q}_h, q_N/h)$ verifies that $d\check{p}/d(q_N/h) < 0$.

Furthermore,

$$\lim_{q_N/h\to\infty} f_5(\breve{N},\breve{z},\breve{a},\breve{q}_h,q_N/h) > 0 \text{ and } \lim_{q_N/h\to 0} f_5(\breve{N},\breve{z},\breve{a},\breve{q}_h,q_N/h) = -\infty.$$

Then, There exists a unique point $q_N/h > 0$ satisfying the fifth equation.

Therefore, conditions (i)–(iv) ensure the existence of a unique steady state $(N^*, a^*, z^*, q_h^*, (q_N/h)^*)$ for the system (28)-(32). Consequently, Lemma 2 ensures the existence of a unique balanced path for the optimal control problem (8)–(14) which satisfies necessary conditions for optimality. The fraction of physical capital devoted to final output production corresponding to the balanced path is $u^* = u(N^*, z^*, q_h^*, (q_N/h)^*)$ and the constant flow of emissions $p^* = p(N^*, z^*, q_h^*, (q_N/h)^*)$. The constant growth rate of the economy is obtained by the equation (11), $g^* = H((1-u^*)z^*) - \theta$. Finally, $c^*(t) = a^*h^*(t)$ and $k^*(t) = z^*h^*(t)$, where $h^*(t) = h_0e^{g^*t}$. It is also satisfied that $0 < N^* < N_{\max}$, $k^*(t) > 0$, $h^*(t) > 0$, $0 < u^* < 1$, $0 < c^* < Y(N^*, u^*k^*, h^*p^*)$ and $p^* > 0$ so that the feasibility is also established.

To establish the optimality of $(N^*, k^*, h^*, u^*, c^*, p^*)$ we need also to prove that it really maximizes the discounted flow of utility along an infinite horizon, using the *catching-up* criterium.

Because of the constant elasticity of intertemporal substitution and the linear homogeneity of functions H and Y, equation (23) ensures that, if $(N(t), k(t), h(t), u(t), c(t), p(t))$ satisfies necessary conditions for optimality, $c(t)$ cannot grow at an increasing rate. Therefore, if $(N(t), k(t), h(t), u(t), c(t), p(t))$ is different from the unique feasible balanced path $(N^*, k^*, h^*, u^*, c^*, p^*)$, the strict concavity of the utility function implies that

$$\liminf_{T\to\infty} \int_0^T e^{-\rho t}\left(U(c^*,N^*) - U(c,N)\right)dt$$

$$> \liminf_{T\to\infty} \int_0^T e^{-\rho t}\left(\frac{\partial U}{\partial c}(c^*,N^*)\left(c^*-c\right) + \frac{\partial U}{\partial N}(c^*,N^*)\left(N^*-N\right)\right)dt \geq 0,$$

since $c^*(t)$ grows exponentially and $c(t)$ does not. □

Proposition 2 ensures the feasibility and social optimality of an economic grow that keeps constant environmental quality, if some conditions on preferences and environment are met. However, since environmental quality and technological knowledge have public good characteristics, a market economy with a free access environment, and without government control, will not behave in a socially optimal way. Environment will suffer from what is call *The Tragedy of the Commons* due to the fact that, without government control, individual producers will rise their emissions at least till the level $\hat{p}$, which is higher than the social optimum level. In addition, because of the *non-rival* nature of technological knowledge, firms will not have incentives for investing resources in research. Therefore, for the market solution to coincide with the socially optimal solution obtained in the previous preposition, an authority, the government for instance, should tax polluters and subsidize those firms which invest in research.

5 Conclusions

We have studied an endogenous growth model which takes into account a technological sector which aims to increase the efficiency in the use of natural resources. Our model differs from the Bovenberg and Smulders's one basically in the specification of the knowledge production function. In our model the productivity of physical capital invested in knowledge creation depends directly on the current available knowledge. This approach is more realistic than considering the productivity of physical capital dependent on the efficient emissions, as it is done by Bovenberg and Smulders (1995). In additon, we have also assumed general constant-return-to-scale production technologies, not reducing our study to functions of the Cobb-Douglass family. We have also studied the existence of an economic development pattern that respects the environment. To know which are the social and environmental conditions guaranteeing the existence of such a development is a main issue to achieve the objective of a sustainable development. We have obtained conditions on consumers' preferences and production technologies which guarantee the feasibility and optimality of a sustained economic growth that keeps constant environmental quality.

References

Bovenberg, A. L. and Smulders, S. (1995). Environmental Quality and Pollution-Augmenting Technological Change in a Two-Sector Endogenous Growth Model. *Journal of Public Economics* **57**, 369–391.

Brock, W. A. (1977). A Polluted Golden Age. In *Economics of Natural and Environmental Resources*, V. L. Smith (Ed.) Gordon & Breach: New York, Chap.25.

Dasgupta, P. (1993). *Optimal Development and the Idea of Net National Product.* Paris: A Joint CEPR/OECD Development Centre Conference.

Dasgupta, P. (1996). The Economics of the Environment. *Proceedings of the British Academy.*

Foster, B. A. (1973). Optimal Capital Accumulation in a Polluted Environment. *Economic Record* **49**, 534–545.

Gradus, R. and Smulders, S. (1993). The Trade-Off Between Environmental Care and Long-term Growth: Pollution in Three Proto-Type Growth Models. *Journal of Economics* **58**, 25–51.

Hauff, V. (Ed.) (1987). *Unsere gemeinsame Zukunft.* Der Brundtland-Bericht, Greven, Eggenkamp.

Hung, V. T. Y., Chang, P. and Blackburn, K. (1993). Endogenous Growth, Environment and R. and D.. In C.Carraro (Ed.), *Trade, Innovation, Environment.*

Keeler, E., Spence, M. and Zeckhauser, R. (1971). The Optimal Control of Pollution. *Journal of Economic Theory* **4**, 19–34.

Meadows, D. H. et al. (1972). *The Limits of Growth.* Universe Books: New York.

Smulders, S. (1995). Entropy, Environment and Endogenous Economic Growth. *International Tax and Public Finance* **2**, 319–340

Tahvonen, O. and Kuuluvainen, J. (1993). Economics Growth, Pollution and Renewable Resources. *Journal of Environmental Economics and Management* **24**, 101–118.

Sow Model for Decision Aid at Farm Level

Luis M. Plà[1,2], Josep Conde[1] and J. Pomar[2]

[1] Department of Mathematics, University of Lleida, Victor Siurana 1, 25003 Lleida, SPAIN
[2] Animal Production Area, Information Technologies Group, R+D Center, UdL-IRTA, Rovira Roure 177, 25198 Lleida, SPAIN

Abstract

This paper presents a friendly implementation of a dynamic sow model. The aim of the model is to represent sow production through reproduction and replacement management at farm level. A first proposal is validated and later applied to optimize herd dynamics from real farm data. Optimization provides simple rules that farmers can apply to improve their profits. Realistic dynamic models include a large number of state and decision variables, therefore some simplifications are needed both in order to obtain a useful model and to include it in a decision support system (DSS) running on a PC.

Keywords. Decision aid, dynamic model, sow management

1 Introduction

In general, a farmer is faced with the problem of influencing the behavior of a probabilistic system, like a farm, as it evolves through time. He does this by making decisions or choosing actions. The main question is to determine which sequence of actions causes the system to perform optimally with respect to some predetermined performance criterion. Since the farm is not static, decisions must anticipate the opportunities and costs associated with future system evolution, see Chavas et al. (1985).

Mathematical models representing production behaviour of a herd are a popular tool in livestock research. Several models that simulate various biological, physical and management factors influencing population dynamics have been developed in dairy production, and less in pig production, see Huirne et al. (1993). Within the Information Technologies Group of Animal Production Area of the IRTA (Institut de Recerca Tecnico Agroalimentaries) in collaboration with the Mathematics Department of Lleida University decision sow models are being developed to apply modelling techniques that could be integrated in DSS in order to support farmer decision tasks. In this paper we present a friendly implementation of a dynamic sow model, its aim being to represent sow production through reproduction and replacement management at farm level, see Plà et al. (1996). The model is farm specific, its complexity is designed to be enough to solve real problems in field conditions avoiding unpractical complexities that sometimes some research models contain.

2 Markov Decision Processes

Markov decision processes and Markov chains are narrowly related, so that it is easy to induce a new stochastic model from firsts (see, Puterman (1994)), in particular a Markov chain. We assume that the state space S and the action space A are discrete.

Consider now the space Ω:

$$\Omega = \{\omega \,|\, \omega = (i_1, a_1, i_2, a_2, \ldots), i_n \in S, a_n \in A\} = \{S \times A\}^{\infty}.$$

An element of Ω represents a sequence of states and actions. We refer to ω as a possible path. Consider also random variables X_n and Y_n:

$$X_n : \Omega \longrightarrow S \quad \text{and} \quad Y_n : \Omega \longrightarrow A$$

which take values in S and A respectively, defined by:

$$X_n(\omega) = i_n \quad \text{and} \quad Y_n(\omega) = a_n$$

for $n \in I\!N$. X_n represents the system state and Y_n represents the action made at time n.

Given a policy $R = \{d_n\}_{n \in I\!N}$, where d_n is a decision function, it will be stationary if $d_n = d$ for all $n \in I\!N$; thus, the same decision function is considered at each period. We will indicate it as $R = (d)^{\infty}$. Function d in the deterministic case will be denoted by $d : S \longrightarrow A$.

Now we can define a probability P^R on $(\Omega, \mathcal{B}(\Omega))$ by means of the following equations:

$$P^R\{X_n = i\} = q_1(i) \tag{1}$$

$$P^R\{Y_n = a \,|\, X_n = i\} = 1_{\{a\}}(d(i)) \tag{2}$$

$$P^R\{X_{n+1} = j \,|\, X_n = i, Y_n = a\} = p_n(j \,|\, i, a) \tag{3}$$

where (1) are the initial probabilities and (3) is the transition probability associated to policy R, defined by:

$$p_n : (S \times A) \times \mathcal{B}(S) \longrightarrow [0, 1]$$

such that

1.- $p_n(B \,|\, \cdot)$ is a random variable in S for each $B \in \mathcal{B}(S)$.

2.- $p_n(\cdot \mid i, a)$ is a probability on $(S \times A, \mathcal{B}(S \times A))$ for each $(i, a) \in S \times A$.

Thus, the probability of a path $\omega = (i_1, a_1, i_2, a_2, \ldots)$, is given by:

$$P^R(\omega) = q_1(i_1)1_{\{a_1\}}(d(i_1)) \cdot \prod_{n>1} p_n(i_{n+1} \mid i_n, a_n)1_{\{a_n\}}(d(i_n)).$$

Note that the policy determines P^R explicitly through (2) and implicitly through (3). If R is a markovian policy, then:

$$P^R\{Y_n = a \mid X_1 = i_1, Y_1 = a_1, \ldots, X_n = i_n\} = P^R\{Y_n = a \mid X_n = i_n\}$$

and

$$P^R\{X_{n+1} = j \mid X_1 = i_1, Y_1 = a_1, \ldots, X_n = i_n, Y_n = a_n\} =$$

$$= P^R\{X_{n+1} = j \mid X_n = i_n, Y_n = a_n\}$$

so that the induced stochastic processes $\{X_n; n \in \mathbb{N}\}$ is a discrete-time Markov chain.

Let us now consider a family of reward functions $(r_l)_{l \in \mathbb{N} \times S}$, that is real functions, $r_l : S \times A \longrightarrow \mathbb{R}$, $\mathcal{B}(S) \times \mathcal{B}(A)$-measurable and bounded. The reward function represents the cost or income obtained in a time$\times$state, l, depending on the arrival state and the action made.

Finally, a Markovian decision process is a process containing the following elements:

$$\{\mathbb{N}, S, A, p_n(\cdot \mid s, a), r_{n,i}(\cdot, a)\}.$$

3 Model formulation

We have defined the elements needed in Markov decision process from a mathematical point of view. Now we are going to identify these elements with the those of the real world. We assume the process to be time homogeneous, that is, $p_n(j \mid i, a) = p(j \mid i, a)$ and $r_{n,i}(j, a) = r_i(j, a)$. Each sow and its succesors are represented by a Markov decison process. The structure of the model is homomorphic to the sow's life. The model is formulated to take into account, as accurately as possible, the biological and economic inputs needed in sow production dynamics representation.

3.1 State and Action sets

We are concerned in sow production, thus main traits that may influence the future behaviour of the animal would have to be represented in the model. It is obvious that this does not mean taking into account all of controlled traits to get a good model. However, realistic Markov decision models are used to be very complex, and it is usual to encounter several computational problems derived from the curse of dimensionality, see Huirne et al. (1993).

The sow's lifespan is modeled via a Markov chain, therefore an animal begins when it is purchased as a new replacement gilt coming on heat for the first time and finishes when it is sold to slaughter or it has had an involuntary indisposition. The replacement can be made immediately or a delay may be considered.

Sows in a farm will be found in one of the possible states $S = \{s_i : i = 1, \cdots, N\}$ and states are ordered as much as possible depending on the sows's life. The set $S = B \cup E$, is finite ,where $E = \{e_{ijkl} \,|\, i$: reproductive states, j : productive cycle, k : production level, l : genetic merit$\}$ and B represents the set of some artificial states like involuntary indisposal, delay in replacement or mortality.

The sow model can simulate herd production indirectly by aggregating individual sow performance; therefore, the farm is represented by a state vector $\{\Pi_n\}$ where each component represents the probability of sows remaining in their corresponding state. The state vector is made up of four variables: parity number, production level, number of unsuccessful breedings in the present parity and reproductive state.

The initial vector $\Pi_1 = (\pi_{11}^R, \pi_{12}^R, \cdots, \pi_{1N}^R)$ can be obtained from farm recorded data or set as a unit vector representing the farm's beginning, $\Pi_1 = (1, 0, \ldots, 0)$. Optionally this vector can be modified by hand. In case π_{1i}^R were calculated, the procedure is to accumulate the number of sows at each considered state and its normalization provides the initial distribution of the model, thus

$$\widehat{\pi}_{1i}^R = \frac{n_i}{\sum_{i=1}^N n_i}$$

where n_i is the number of sows staying at i-state during the period chosen for estimation, normally one year, and $\sum_{i=1}^N n_i$ is the total number of sows in the same period.

For each state, a set of actions is given. The action set, $A = \{a_i : i = 1, \cdots, N'\}$ is finite and includes all possible controls that the farmer can carry out on the farm. Actions at the sow level all include replacement as one of the alternatives. For solving replacement problems two actions are normaly considered $A = \{\text{Keep, Replace}\}$; however, it is possible to add more actions. The state vector has its relative action vector whose components represent actions taken for each component of the state vector. Actions are given by decision function, so the action vector in a deterministic case equals the policy R applied.

3.2 Transitions and rewards

The model considers a sow in a process moving from one state to another, not all transitions being considered, only those for which there could be a logical biological justification, see Figure 1. This assumption is determined in fact by field conditions, although some filters are introduced to prevent inconsistencies in farm data.

When the order of the chain happens to be greater than 1, it can be reduced to a first order chain by suitable definition of composite states. This implies that the number of states increases. These transformations are used, for example, to take into account production level, but it also may be useful if we want to consider transitions in a daily or weekly basis in order to have an accurate representation of sow age and to be able to make tactical decisions, but then the model becomes more complex, even when most elements of the transition matrix with not feasible transitions equal to zero, see Huirne et al. (1993) and Nogera et al. (1995).

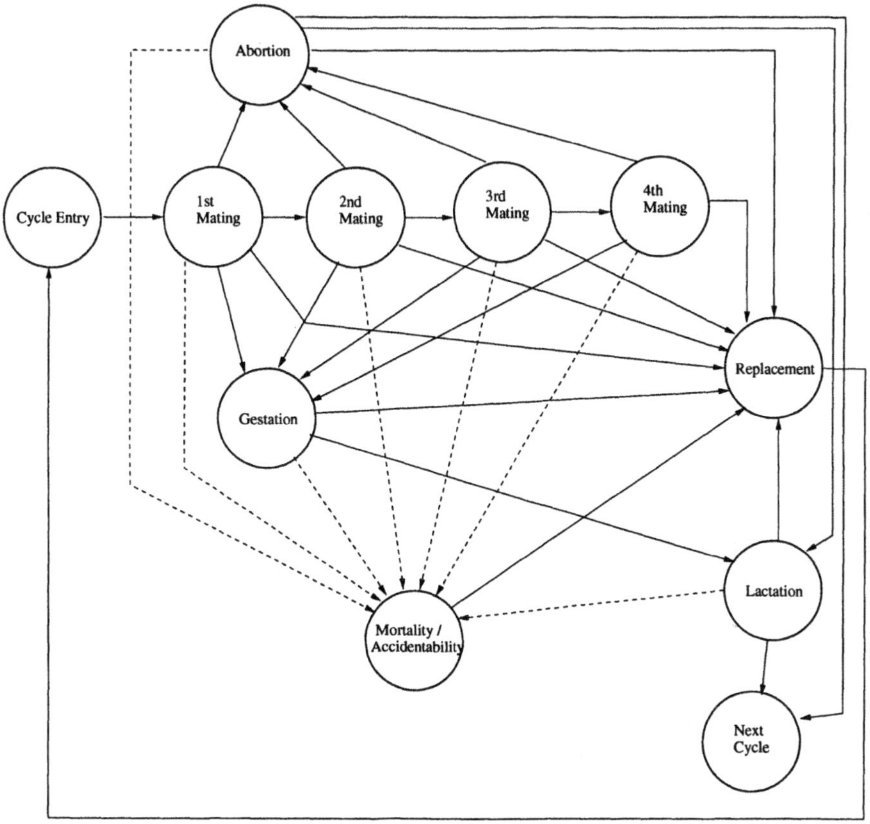

Fig. 1. Graphic representation of a reproductive sow cycle

The probability transitions were estimated from the GTEP-IRTA data-bank or from literature when it was necessary, specially for default values. GTEP-IRTA system is a Pig Management Information System OJO, one of the most importants in Spain. Individual farm data is available and for each farm data recorded for each animal may be classified in reproductive animals inventory and input data: matings, parities and weanings and reproductive animal casualties. Then, maximum likelihood estimates of transition probabilities are computed, see Billingsley (1961):

$$\widehat{p}(j \mid i, a) = \frac{n_{ij}}{n_i}$$

where n_{ij} is the number of sows moving from i state to j state, and $n_i = \sum_{k \in S} n_{ik}$ is the total number of sows passing through state i at the same period of time, usually one year. In case action "Replace"was taken, then $p(j \mid i, a) = 1$ if j is the replacement state, and 0 otherwise. In general, transition probabilities are associated to certain policies. A subset of the data-bank records could be considered to account for these alternative transitions and estimates would be obtained in the same way.

For the moment, the quality of the replacement sow is assumed to be unrelated to that of the particular sow being replaced, all sows having the same expected quality. The model does not take into account improvements in the genetic merit of sows to produce piglets, but it is possible to account for variation in prolificity and its repeatability.

For any stationary policy $R = (d)^\infty$:

$$r^R(i) = \sum_{a \in A} \sum_{j \in S} r_i(j, a) p(j \mid i, a) 1_{\{a\}}(d(i))$$

represents the expected risk at time n and at the state i. The expected value at decision epoch n may be calculated by

$$r(i, a) = \sum_{j \in S} r_i(j, a) p(j \mid i, a).$$

If R is a Markovian policy, we refer to the bivariate stochastic process

$$\{(X_n, r(X_n, Y_n)); n \in I\!N\}$$

as a Markovian rewarded process.

The economic consequences of the decisions made are reflected in the reward function. If at a decision epoch the action a is chosen at state i and the system evolves to j, then an immediate reward $r_i(j, a)$ is obtained with a probability $p(j \mid i, a) = p^a_{i,j}$. In this way the model quantifies the gains or costs obtained in a swine herd.

4 Optimality criteria for infinite-horizon planning

An infinite planning horizon implies that an optimal policy is stationary, see Puterman (1994). We assume from now on that we will have stationary rewards and probability transitions, bounded rewards ($|r(i,a)| \leq M < \infty \quad \forall a \in A, \forall i \in S$) with S and A finite. The discount factor, $0 < \lambda < 1$ expresses the time preference of the decison maker.

The Markov decision problem we are concerned with can be optimized under different objective functions:

- Expected total discounted reward. Let $v_\lambda^R(i)$ represent the expected total reward over the decision making infinite horizon if policy R is used and the system is in state i at the first decision epoch. Then,

$$v_\lambda^R(i) = E_i^R\Big\{\sum_{n=1}^{\infty} \lambda^{n-1} r(X_n, Y_n)\Big\}$$

which can be easily seen to be equal to:

$$v_\lambda^R(i) = \sum_{n=1}^{\infty}\sum_{j\in S} \lambda^{n-1} r(j,a_j) P^R\{X_n = j, Y_n = a_j \,|\, X_1 = i\}$$

when

$$P^R\{X_n = j, Y_n = a_j \,|\, X_1 = i\} = P^R\{Y_n = a_j \,|\, X_n = j\} P^R\{X_n = j \,|\, X_1 = i\}.$$

This criterion maximize the total disounted net revenues per animal. Such a criterion is relevant where a limiting housing capacity is the most limiting herd constraint. For induction purposes we wil use the equivalent formulation:

$$v_\lambda^R(i) = r(i,a_i) + \sum_{j\in S} \lambda p(j \,|\, i, a_i) v_\lambda^R(j) \tag{4}$$

- Average reward.

$$g^R(i) \equiv \lim_{n\to\infty} \frac{1}{n} E_i^R\Big\{\sum_{t=1}^{n} r\{X_t, Y_t\}\Big\}.$$

If all stages are of equal length, and also all states in S are recurrent $g^R = g^R(i) = g^R(j)$, then the function can be rewritten as:

$$g^R = \sum_{i\in S} \Pi_i^R r(i,a_i)$$

where Π_i^R is the limiting state distribution under policy R, and g^R is referred to as a stationary reward. Average reward can be calculated by standard matrix methods, but enumeration does not provide an efficient procedure for computing optimal solutions. For example, for $|S| = k$ and $|A| = 2$ we will have 2^k possible stationary policies. However, induction methods are more suitable. We will use the equivalent formulation:

$$f^R(i) = r(i, a_i) - g^R + \sum_{j \in S} p(j \mid i, a_i) f^R(j) \tag{5}$$

where f^R's are the so-called relative values of policy R and represent for each starting state i, the expected total difference between the reward and the stationary reward, that is

$$f^R(i) = \lim_{n \to \infty} \frac{1}{n} E_i \Big\{ \sum_{t=1}^{n} \Big(r(X_t, Y_t) - g \Big) \Big\}.$$

Practical experience shows that the optimal policies under expected total discounted reward and average reward are almost identical.

- Average reward per unit of output. If a herd restraint is imposed on the physical output we can use this criterion.

$$g^R(i) = \frac{g_r^R}{g_m^R(i)} = \frac{\sum_{i \in S} \Pi_i^R r(i, a_i)}{\sum_{i \in S} \Pi_i^R m(i, a_i)}$$

where $m^R(i)$ is a function defined like r but represents the output produced in the state i when policy R is applied. This function is also relevant when the criterion of maximization is the average reward over time in a model where the stage length varies. To manage such models we must transform it to an equivalent equal stage length model as Howard (1971) and Puterman (1994) discuss. In that case the physical output represents the stage length. For computing reasons we use the equivalent formulation:

$$f^R(i) = r^R(i) - g^R m^R(i) + \sum_{j \in S} p(j \mid i, a_i) f^R(j) \tag{6}$$

When an average criterion is used, the set of simultaneous equations (5) or (6) determines the relative value of each state and the average reward per unit of time under a certain policy.

5 Model implementation

The model has been constructed to be used on a personal computer. It runs with default values according to model formulation if no farm data are available. It allows the user to update these values automatically with estimations made from his own farm records or by hand; further, it is always possible to introduce single modifications. Therefore, the model can be farm specific. There are also a set of filters that can be applied to obtain more elaborate parameters, some for keeping out errors and some for testing different management alternatives.

The sow model prototype was developed with EXTEND^{TM}, an advanced simulation tool for decision support available on personal computers under different operative systems. The advantages of such implementation are very significant and are related to object oriented programming. The process has been split into objects that can be easily identified graphically with the real subprocess represented, see Figure 2. These objects are in fact a partition of the transition function and can be considered as submodels. This implementation helps us structure the model better, modify it and develope it more extensively.

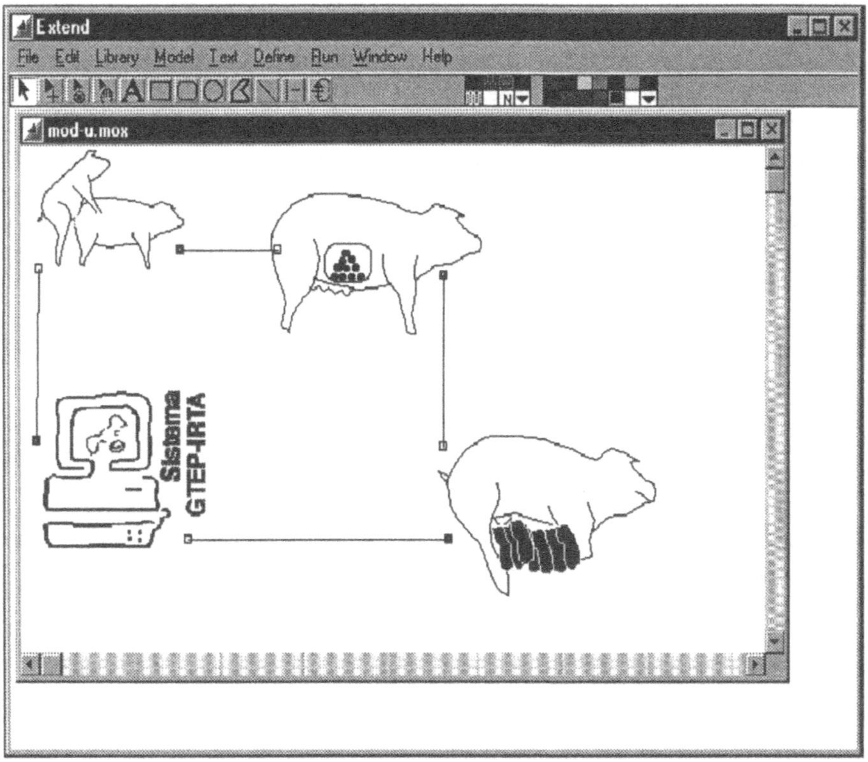

Fig. 2. Model interface

On the other hand, there are also many customizable graphic interfaces and other utility libraries to show off relationships between components in the model. Consequently, the model is an easy-to-use tool that can be used to simulate sow production dynamics in different ways, the most interesting being that of reproducing its behaviour under some management alternatives. This implementation becomes more comprehensive for the user unlike some models published up to now.

6 An application of the model

In order to discuss the suitability of the prototype, a test was carried out with a basic model. The first step was a static analysis derived from the limit distribution at equilibrium, comparing model outputs with the real ones. Several farms were chosen randomly among medium size farms from the GTEP data bank. After that, we were able to carry out a systematic search for optimal management policies and the evaluation of the impact of alternative management policies at operational level that may be used to optimize the replacement policy in a farm. The main purpose is to create operational replacement guidelines under various conditions concerning reproductive performance and delay in replacement.

A limitation to some model variables were established. Hence, maximun lifespan allowed is 15 parities, maximum litter size is 20 piglets, and as soon as an animal is replaced a new gilt is introduced. Availability is not a constraint.

Also some economic parameters were fixed, see Table 1. Inputs in the model are the value of the piglets born alive and weaned (5,500 ptas. each), and the slaughter value of culled sows (25,000 ptas. each). The variable costs are the cost of replacement gilts (25,000 ptas. each) and feed costs. Feed costs are calculated depending on daily intake, reproduction state and feed type. The discount factor in the model is based in a real annual interest rate of 6%.

Feed (Kg.)	Cost (Ptas.)	Consumption (day)	Concept	Ptas.
Open sows	21	2.0	Fix costs	98000 pspy
1st repetition	21	2.0	Variable costs	5000 pspy
2nd repetition	21	2.0	Replacement	25000 ps
3rd repetition	21	2.0	Slaughter	25000 ps
Gestation	21	2.5	Piglet	5500
Lactation	22	4.0		
Abortion	21	2.0		
Piglets	40	0.2		

Table 1. Economic inputs used by the model

For technical results we need to establish the probability of litter size and litter weaned. Average litters of a sow can be used directly, but it is also possible to determine their expected values taking into account the parity number and production level. The length of states is fixed in the basic model, although it can be taken randomly in a more general formulation, see Table 2.

Cycle	LS[a]	LW[b]	IT1M[c]	G[d]	L[e]	A[f]	Oe[g]	Age[h]
1	10.67	9.69	0.05	114.4	31	64.1	26.8	238.7
2	10.52	9.66	6.56	114.4	31	64.1	26.8	
3	11.60	10.58	6.01	114.4	31	64.1	26.8	
4	11.28	10.07	5.46	114.4	31	64.1	26.8	
5	11.97	10.78	4.88	114.4	31	64.1	26.8	
6	11.68	10.66	4.98	114.4	31	64.1	26.8	
7	11.44	10.68	6.47	114.4	31	64.1	26.8	
8	11.32	10.57	4.92	114.4	31	64.1	26.8	
9	10.49	9.51	6.05	114.4	31	64.1	26.8	
10	10.00	9.50	5.21	114.4	31	64.1	26.8	
11	10.75	10.00	4.75	114.4	31	64.1	26.8	

[a] Litter size, [b] Litter weaned, [c] Intervat to 1st mating, [d] Gestation, [e] Lactation. [f] Abortion [g] Oestrus, [h] Age of gilt at the beginning.

Table 2. Litters and length of states by cycle from **Farm 1** during 1996

The marginal probabilities of conception are dependent on the number of unsuccesful breedings and the parity number, see Table 3.

Cycle	CR(1)[a]	CR(2)[b]	CR(3)[c]	CR(4)[d]	AR[e]	CR[f]
1	90.8	100.0	0.0	0.0	0.61	11.24
2	94.0	88.9	100.0	0.0	0.66	9.43
3	91.0	100.0	0.0	0.0	1.39	10.07
4	95.3	100.0	0.0	0.0	1.57	11.54
5	96.7	100.0	0.0	0.0	0.0	13.01
6	92.9	71.4	50.0	100.0	1.01	11.88
7	97.5	100.0	0.0	0.0	0.00	19.05
8	98.1	100.0	0.0	0.0	0.00	26.79
9	97.3	100.0	0.0	0.0	5.41	53.85
10	100.0	0.0	0.0	0.0	14.29	43.75
11	100.0	0.0	0.0	0.0	0.00	50.00

[a,b,c,d] Conception rate for 1st, 2nd, 3rd and 4th mating. [e] Abortion Rate [f] Causalty Rate

Table 3. Main rates obtained by cycle from **Farm 1** during 1996

The stochastic formulation makes it possible, among other things, to account for other involuntary reasons of culling. The casualty rate is calculated for each farm and is divided between mortality/accidentability and involuntary disposal.The marginal probabilities of involuntary disposal are based on the parity number and reproductive state.

6.1 Validation

Model verification was performed by checking for both mathematical and logical consistency. The probability distribution over states at equilibrium is determined and compared with real distribution for validation, but we have also calculated two kinds of indexes: performance indexes and technical indexes. Performance indexes are based on the limit distribution of the herd and they are designed specially to study model dynamics. One of the tests performed with the limit distribution was to compare it with the real distribution through a χ-square test. Some results for herd distribution in 1996 are given in Table 4.

Farm	# sows	χ^2_n	n
1	140	48.88	77
2	184	158.30	105
3	266	82.15	70

Table 4. χ-square test for limit distribution

Technical indexes are equivalents to those of the GTEP-IRTA system because they are used more often and better understood by extension advisers.Sets of input values can be filtered and evaluated by comparing the results of the corresponding herd distribution at equilibrium. The output of the model can be applied in economic analysis, as well as for comparing management alternatives. Some results can be derived directly from the simulated distribution of sows over states; others need more calculations.

From a technical point of view the real technical indexes are very close to indexes calculated by the model at equilibrium, see Table 5. For productivity and mortality the results are not so close. In fact, these results are in accordance with the model formulation and its assumptions. This is because there are some farms that, although technical indexes are good for them, present more differences among sow distribution by cycle and through different states.

6.2 Optimization

The problem can also be optimized by finding the policy $R^* = (d)^\infty$ that prescribes an action for each system state and maximize the average expected profit, that is, when it is most profitable, in the mean, to replace a sow. All parameters in the model are estimated from the GTEP-IRTA data bank, see Noguera et al. (1995), or from the literature, but in fact it is designed to be farm specific.

TECHNICAL INDEXES	Theorical	Real
Average of Sows	140	140
Average of Sires	6	6
♯ Productive Sows	116	116
PRODUCTIVITY		
Piglets/Present Sow/Year	23.6	26.3
Piglets/Sow/Year	25.8	25.9
♯ Piglets weaned	3690	3695
♯ Litters weaned	335	336
% Abortions	2.08	2.24
♯ PIGLETS/LITTER		
Litter size	11.29	12.29
Alive	11.29	11.48
Dead	0	0.81
Weaned	10.24	10.59
% Mortality	9.28	7.74
REPRODUCTIVE RATES		
♯ farrowing/Sow/Year	2.45	2.45
♯ farrowing/Present Sow/Year	2.30	2.49
Index of farrowing	89.0	88.4
% Repetitions	11.2	11.6
Interval weaning-oestrus (d)	5.53	5
Interval weaning-fertile mating	6.72	6
Lactation (d)	28	28
Interval between farrows (d)	149	149
AGE OF SOW		
1st Farrow (d)	340	341
Farrowing Sows (month)	30	30
Replacement ♯:	51	51
Age of replaced Sow (month)	38	37
♯ Litters/Sow replaced	7.0	6.1
% Sows replaced	37.7	36.3

Table 5. Output of technical indexes

Under infinite plannig horizon the policy iteration method may be applied. Unlike the value iteration method, it always provides an optimal policy.

Algorithm:

1) Choose an stationary policy R.
2) Policy evaluation. For current rule R, compute the unique solution $\{g^R, f^R\}$ depending on optimality criteria. The problem is to solve a $|S| \times |S|$ system of linear equations.
   - Total discount revenues. For all $i \in S$ we must solve (4).

- Average rewards per time. For all $i \in S$ we must solve (5) considering the additional equation: $f(k) = 0$ where k is an arbitrary chosen state.
- Average rewards per unit of physical output. For all $i \in S$ we must solve (6) considering the additional equation: $f(k) = 0$ where k is an arbitrary chosen state.

3) Policy improvement. For each state i find the action $d = a \in A$ that maximizes the objective function, $v(i)$, and set $d(i) = a$.

$$\max_{a \in A} \left\{ r(i,a) - g^R + \sum_{j \in S} p(j \mid i, a) f^R(j) \right\}$$

so that we can build a new policy R'. If $R' = R$ stop, an optimal policy is found; otherwise, go back to 2.

The policy iteration algorithm converges after a finite number of iterations, the proof (see Puterman (1994) or Howard (1971)) is based on the finiteness of state and action set and the improvement of succesive policy iterations. It is a robust algorithm that converges very fast in specific problems.The number of iterations is practically independent of the number of states and normally vary between 3 and 15.

The algorithm was tested with Farm 1, the parameters for the model being those calculated before. The output is showed in Table 6. We usually implement the evaluation step of the policy iteration by using Gaussian elimination to solve the linear system. In this case it was enough because there were a maximum of 180 states, but this formulation is equivalent to another with 2100 states on a weekly time base. In case we have a large state space this method may be computationally prohibitive.

Cycle	Mating 1	Mating 2	Mating 3	Mating 4
1	K	R	R	R
2	K	K	R	R
3	K	K	K	K
4	K	K	K	K
5	K	K	K	K
6	K	K	K	R
7	K	K	K	R
8	K	K	K	R
9	R	R	R	R
10	R	R	R	R
11	R	R	R	R

K:*Keep* action, R:*Replace* action

Table 6. Optimal mating policy for **Farm 1**

A modified policy iteration algorithm cited by Puterman (1994) is also available. This algorithm tries to get the best of the two most used algorithms in solving DP problems: policy iteration and value iteration. The key is to avoid the policy evaluation for each policy improvement step, therefore, a partial policy evaluation is carried out by using value iteration methods, which are less expensive in computational time. This algorithm seems to solve in a similar way problems that Kristensen (1993) formulate as hierarchic Markov process applied in farm management.

7 Conclusions

The model formulated may become very large, but we want to use a small version in order to get an idea of its benefits in solving real cases. Results obtained on the model are promising because the implementation is easy to use and there is no need to formulate very complex models for solving common problems. Very often farmers want to have simple rules to apply on their farms, and researchers are not always able to provide them with simple answers. Such models provide more insight into the technical and economic consequences of changes in performances, prices and management policies.

Acknowledgements

The authors would like to thank José L. Noguera and Cándido Pomar for valuable discussions and comments on this paper.

References

Ben-Ari, Y. and Gal, S. (1986). Optimal replacement policy for multi-component systems: An application to dairy herd. *Eur. Jour. of Op. Res.*, **23**, 213–221.

Billingsley, P. (1961). *Statistical Inference in Markov Chains*. University of Chicago Press: Chicago.

Chavas, J. P., Kliebenstein, J. and Crenshaw, Th. D. (1985). Modeling dynamic agricultural production response: The case of swine production. *American Journal of Agricultural Economics* **67**, **3**, 636–646.

Huirne, R. B., Van Beek, P., Hendriks, Th. H. B. and Dijkhuizen, A. A. (1993). Stochastic dynamic programming to support sow replacement decisions. *Eur. Jou. of Op. Res.* **67**, 161.

Kristensen, A. R. (1993). *Markov Decision Programming Techniques Applied to the Animal Replacement Problem*. D. Sc. Diss. University of Copenhaguen.

Howard, R. A. (1971). *Dynamic Probabilistic Systems. Vol.II: Semi-Markov and Decision Processes*. Wiley: New York.

Noguera, J. L., Pomar, J., Plà, L. M., Alfonso, L., Babot, D., Galofré, D. and Estany, J. (1995). *Un modelo operativo para la gestión de las empresas de porcino y sus organizaciones consultivas: el sistema GTEP-IRTA*. IV Seminario Latinoamericano de Agroinformática. San José, Costa Rica.

Plà, L. M., Conde, J. and Pomar, J. (1996). Stochastic dynamic programming. The sow replacement problem. *III Catalan days of Applied Mathematics*, Lleida. 175–18.

Puterman, M. L. (1994). *Markov Decision Processes*. Wiley: New York.

Intelligent Decision Support for Reservoir Operations

D. Ríos Insua[1], C. Bielza[2], J. Martín[2] and K. A. Salewicz[3]

[1] School of Engineering, University Rey Juan Carlos, 28931 Móstoles, SPAIN
[2] Decision Analysis Group, Madrid Technical University, 28660 Madrid, SPAIN
[3] IBM-Austria, 1020 Vienna, AUSTRIA

Abstract

Factors like multiple uncertainty sources, multiple objectives, time-effects over preferences and the hierarchical nature of the planning process increase the complexity of reservoir management problems. We describe developments in a methodology for reservoir operations and its implementation in an intelligent decision support system.

Keywords. Reservoir operations, intelligent decision support, multiattribute utility, dynamic models, dynamic programming, reference trajectory

1 Introduction

Water resources management remains as a very challenging problem, due to complicating features like the hierarchical structure of various planning processes (yearly, seasonal, monthly, weekly, daily, even hourly for some purposes); the sequential nature of the problem; the emergence of complex uncertainty models; the appearance of multiple objectives, stemming from various uses of water; effects of time on preferences, with priorities and targets changing from one period to another; possibly, several groups of users, ... Golden and Wasil (1994) provide a review on water resources management methods.

We shall concentrate here on reservoir operation problems. Specifically, we are interested in determining how much water should we release from a reservoir for various purposes (energy production, irrigation, spill,...) at each time period of interest. In Ríos Insua and Salewicz (1995) and Ríos Insua et al (1997a), we have introduced a methodology to deal with multiobjective stochastic problems for reservoir system management, for monthly planning. In this paper, we extend the methodology to support the hierarchic structure of reservoir operations linking various time-frames of interest. Our method differs from traditional methodologies, which adopt a stationary view of the world. To that end, we shall emphasise how our methodology incorporates a *management by exception principle*, see West and Harrison (1997, WH from now on) discussing how a system built on this methodology may evolve changing its responses when external conditions differ, a feature typically associated with intelligent decision support systems, see Dantzig and Infanger (1997).

We describe our planning methodology in Section 2; after introducing the general problem, we distinguish between short and long term planning, and discuss how various planning processes relate to each other. A key ingredient in our methodology is the provision of inflow forecasting models, again distinguishing between short and long term forecasting, as we describe in Section 3. Section 4 is devoted to a discussion on how intelligence, in an Artificial Intelligence (AI) sense, is built into our system. We conclude with some discussions.

2 Planning Methodology

Reservoir operation problems may be stated as follows: given a planning horizon k, and current time t, we want to determine the controls u_j or volumes of water to be released at times $j = t+1, ..., t+k$. Note that there will usually be several kinds of releases, e.g. for hydro-power generation, irrigation, flood control, spill,... so that $u_j = (u_j^1, u_j^2, ..., u_j^r)$, with u_j^h designating the volume of water released for purpose h at time j.

Assume we have a forecasting model for inflows i to the reservoir, described by a predictive density $h(i_{t+1}, ..., i_{t+k}|D_t)$, where D_t is the inflow history until time t. We have also a model for the relevant consequences $c(u, i)$ associated with control u and inflow i, e.g. storage s_j at time j, energy produced, volume spilled,..., and a preference model for consequences, defined by a utility function F, and an evaluation of the final state given through a function G. Then, at time t, the reservoir management planning problem would consist of finding controls $(u_{t+1}, ..., u_{t+k})$ maximising the expected utility

$$\int \left(\sum_{j=1}^{k} F(c(u_{t+j}, i_{t+j})) + G(s_{t+k+1}) \right) h(i_{t+1}, ..., i_{t+k}|D_t) di_{t+1} ... di_{t+k} \qquad (1)$$

taking into account the dynamics of the reservoir system, and constraints over controls and reservoirs storage. Typical constraints would include bounds on various types of releases, say

$$0 \leq u^i \leq m^i,$$

bounds on the maximum and minimum allowed reservoir storages, say,

$$0 \leq s \leq M,$$

and continuity conditions relating storages from consecutive time periods, given inflows, releases and, possibly, evaporation, for example

$$s_{j+1} = s_j - e_j + i_j - \sum_l u_j^l,$$

where e_j is the evaporated volume.

The above framework is general enough to accomodate most reservoir operation planning problems, whatever the horizon planning is. For example, for some large reservoirs, we could consider monthly planning with a 36 month horizon; for smaller reservoirs, we would consider only a 12 month horizon; we could consider weekly planning with a four week horizon; we could consider daily planning with a 7 day horizon; or, planning for eight three hour periods. The planning hierarchy will vary from one reservoir to another; we shall only assume that time-frames of the planning hierarchy are nested, an example being that above.

Problem (1) is a multi-stage stochastic decision problem. For short-horizon problems, i.e. those with a small number of planning periods, stochastic programming provides appropriate computational and/or approximation schemes, see Birge (1997) for a review and Carlin et al (1997) for alternative approaches based on forward simulation. However, the problem may become unmanageable for some planning horizons, specially if we consider that the evaluation of each control may require the solution of a high dimensional integral, and uncertainty about the inflow process rapidly propagates through time.

For these cases, we adopt a strategy based on 'reference trajectories', which assumes having found a 'reference' storage level for each period. Then, at each period t we would maximise the expected value of a utility function F taking into account the consequences of interest and the deviation from that reference state, i.e.,

$$\int (F(c(u_{t+1}, i_{t+1}) + \delta(s_{t+1}, s^*_{t+1}))h(i_{t+1}|D_t)di_{t+1}, \tag{2}$$

where $\delta(s_{t+1}, s^*_{t+1})$ represents deviation of the final storage s_{t+1} from the reference storage s^*_{t+1}. Intuitively, if reference storages are defined in such a way so as to account for the dynamic aspects of the problem, we would not loose too much with this modified 'myopic' approach.

To compute a reference trajectory, we use a deterministic version of problem (1), where inflows are considered known and fixed at their predictive expected values $\bar{i}_{t+j}$. We use the same dynamics and constraints on storages and controls, and the same planning period of length k as in problem (1), and adopt an initial volume s_0. The objective function includes a term relating to deviation from the initial state s_0 and terms relating to the main objective in the stochastic problem, e.g. energy production. Then, we want to maximise

$$\sum_{j=1}^{k} F(c(u_{t+j}, \bar{i}_{t+j})) - \rho\,(s_{t+k+1} - s_0)^2. \tag{3}$$

The optimal solution of (3) provides a 'reference trajectory'. Problem (3) is a deterministic dynamic programming problem, that we may solve by discrete dynamic programming.

Another issue is how do we link plans for various time-frames. We describe how we could proceed from monthly to weekly planning. Suppose we have a planning model for the next twelve months. We start by computing the reference trajectory and, then, the optimal control for next month, as described above. Suppose we currently have storage s_t, the suggested optimal release is $u_t = (u_t^1, ..., u_t^r)$, the expected predicted inflow is $\bar{i}_t$, and we estimate e_t as the predicted evaporated volume. Then, we would predict as final storage

$$s_{t+1} = s_t - e_t + \bar{i}_t - \sum_j u_t^j.$$

Suppose now that the t-th month is divided in four weeks. Then, we would use s_{t+1} as a reference state for the final state of the planning for the next four weeks. Specifically, if storages for the four weeks are $s_t^1, s_t^2, s_t^3, s_t^4$, we would do in problem (1)

$$G(s_t^4) = -\rho(s_t^4 - s_{t+1})^2.$$

Should we need to solve the four week planning problem by means of our reference trajectory methodology, we could use the term above, in the formulation of the deterministic version of our problem. Though our discussion refers to linking monthly and weekly plans, a similar approach may be used to link weekly and daily plans, and so on.

3 Forecasting methodology

An essential step in our approach is the provision of a forecasting methodology. Again, we may provide a unified approach to various forecasting problems, based on dynamic linear models (DLMs). Numerous recent modeling and computational enhancements have made DLMs readily available for applications, see WH. Berger and Ríos Insua (1997) describe many of their advantages for hydrological modeling.

Our problem is to forecast the next k values of a variable y_t, (say, the inflow or a transformation of it) from instant $t+1$ to instant $t+k$, given the available information D_t. For that we use DLMs which, in their simplest formulation have the following structure, for every instant of time t, $t = 1, 2, 3, \ldots$:

- *Observation equation:*

  $$y_t = F_t z_t + v_t, \quad v_t \sim N(0, V_t)$$

  where y_t denotes the observed value, which depends linearly on the state variables z_t, perturbed by a normal noise.
- *System evolution equation:*

  $$z_t = G_t z_{t-1} + w_t, \quad w_t \sim N(0, W_t)$$

describing the evolution of the state variables, linearly dependent on the variables in the previous state plus a random perturbation.

- *Initial information:*

$$z_0|D_0 \sim N(m_0, C_0)$$

describing the prior beliefs of the forecaster.

The error sequences v_t and w_t are independent, and mutually independent. Moreover, they are independent of $(z_0|D_0)$.

Updating procedures and the use of this model for forecasting are described in WH. Essentially, inferences and forecasts, one or more steps ahead, are based on a normal model, with corresponding parameters computed recursively.

A basic advantage of DLMs is that they allow us to model most features usual in hydrological time series like seasonal patterns and trends, and permit the incorporation of covariates, such as rainfall for inflows, based on the *superposition principle* (WH), which states that linear combinations of independent DLMs provide a DLM. As a consequence, we use a model building strategy based on blocks, representing trends, seasonal patterns, dynamic regression, if covariates are available, and an autorregressive term, to improve short term forecasting.

Depending on the forecasting horizon, we shall use different blocks. For example, long-term planning will require monthly forecasts for, say, the next twelve months, and we typically use:

- A term referring to a constant or a piecewise linear trend.
- A seasonal effects term, where specific components of the harmonic decomposition may be chosen.
- A regression term, based on covariates.
- An autorregresive term, to improve short term forecasting.

For short-term forecasting, we shall usually obviate the seasonal effects term, with only a trend term, an autorregressive term and, possibly, a regression term.

4 Intelligent Decision Support

The above ideas have been implemented in BayRes, an initial version of which we described in Ríos Insua et al (1997b). BayRes may be described as a decision support system for reservoir operations, supporting all phases of the decision process. It includes a module to build a forecasting model, a module to build a preference model, including the definition of a consequence model and the computation of reference trajectories, a module for optimisation and several sensitivity analysis tools, embedded in a user-friendly interface.

In this section, we describe how 'intelligence' is built in BayRes, so that we may describe it as an intelligent decision system. This is done in two ways: first, some phases of the process are fairly sophisticated, hence a number of aids are introduced to facilitate model choice and prior and utility building; second, in a more traditional AI sense, the system will change its recommendations during its operation. As we shall discuss, though these learning aspects are fundamental in good Bayesian modeling, we shall show how this feature is enhanced in our implementation.

4.1 Modelling aids

BayRes includes a number of aids to facilitate model ellaboration, prior assessment, model choice and utility construction. We concentrate here on prior assessment and utility construction, with brief comments on other issues.

A typical criticism to the Bayesian approach is the difficulty in assessing priors, see Berger (1994). To circumvent this difficulty, BayRes provides several facilities. First, it provides the possibility of using non-infomative priors, whose theory is well-developed for DLMs, see West and Harrison (1997). Second, it provides several aids to model informative priors. One is by direct questioning to the expert. Consider, e.g., the case in which we want to provide the prior for a term describing the level of the series. Assuming a normal model, the expert would provide a typical level l and a range r, perhaps through a maximum or a minimum expected level, and we would associate it to a normal distribution with mean l and standard deviation $\sigma = r/4$. Alternatively, BayRes may build a data dependent prior for the level. To do so, it computes the mean value $\bar{l}$ and the maximum M and minimum m of the inflow series; then, it assumes that the level follows a normal distribution with mean $\bar{l}$ and standard deviation $\sigma = \max(\frac{\bar{l}-m}{2}, \frac{M-\bar{l}}{2})$.

A similar approach may be taken if we decide to include a seasonal term. Suppose, e.g., that we are doing monthly planning, and, as a consequence, we are doing monthly forecasting. We would include a level term and a seasonal term, to account for monthly variation. Starting with a representation based on a level term plus a term for each month, we may apply the above method to build a normal prior $N(t_i, r_i)$ for the seasonal term corresponding to each month i. Suppose, first, that l_i is the mean level for each month; then, we just need to do $t_i = l_i - l$. Note that, as a consequence, we have $\sum t_i = 0$, so we have a seasonal effects model. To obtain r_i, assuming independence of level and seasonal term, we write $s_i^2 = \sigma^2 + r_i^2$, and obtain s_i and r as above. From that, we obtain r_i. In cases so far treated r_i was a real number; however, we include a safeguard defining $r_i = \sqrt{s_i^2 - \sigma^2}$ if it is real, and $\sigma/2$, otherwise. From this decomposition, we may obtain the corresponding Fourier decomposition from well-known formulae, see WH, and assess the importance of various harmonics, based on F and χ^2 statistics, retaining only those which are relevant. Similar issues arise for other decompositions. Note, in any case, that sensitivity analysis tools are included to aid in checking the importance of the prior. All cases we have studied suggest that this approach for automated prior choice is reasonable in our context of reservoir operations.

Utility elicitation is also involved in its full generality. We use a restricted, but wide enough for our purposes, class of utility functions. We concentrate on additive decompositions, see French (1986), with a piecewise exponential fit for each component. If $(c_1, ..., c_n)$ are the consequences of interest,

$$F(c_1, ..., c_n) = \lambda_1 F_1(c_1) + ... + \lambda_n F_n(c_n),$$

with $F_i(c_i) = a_1^i + b_1^i \exp(d_1^i c_i)$, if $c_i \leq c_i^0$, and $F_i(c_i) = a_2^i + b_2^i \exp(d_2^i c_i)$, otherwise. This class of models is wide enough in our context of reservoir operations, with components being able of modeling various forms of risk aversion. Once this functional form is fixed, the assessment is relatively simple with a careful implementation of the probability equivalent (PE) method, see Farquhar (1984). BayRes includes an interface designed to obtain interactively the PE of consequences of interest. After the reservoir operator has suggested his preferences over lotteries, the only remaining issue will be the choice of inflection points c_i^0, if any, in the components. Again, a non sophisticated user may have problems when choosing this, which may affect the stability of the least squares algorithm used to fit the component parameters, but this may be identified as follows. Let $(c_i^1, F_i(c_i^1)), ..., (c_i^n, F_i(c_i^n))$ be the values of consequence for which we have assessed the component utility, with $c_i^1 < c_i^2 < ... < c_i^n$ in an appropriate range. Use $G(c_i^{j+1}) = (F_i(c_i^{j+1}) - F_i(c_i^j))/(c_i^{j+1} - c_i^j)$ as an approximation to the derivative. Identify the c_i^j where the maximum of G is attained and suggest it as the inflection point; if it is one of the extreme points of the interval, we identify the minimum of G and suggest it as the inflection point; if this minimum is other extreme point of the interval, we use just one piece. Multimodal cases need some care. BayRes includes, as well, tolerances for cases in which there are several changes in the signs of the approximations of the derivative. Finally, for the complete specification of the utility, recall that we need to specify G in (1) and δ in (2). We use a term $-\rho(s_{t+1} - s_{t+1}^*)^2$ and set ρ automatically, so that the main contribution of that term is 10%. Since we scale utility in [0, 1], this means that the term $\rho(...)^2$ must be at most 0.1, from which an appropriate value of ρ may be deduced.

In any case, we include several sensitivity analysis tools which allow us to check the impact of key parameters.

4.2 Implementing the Management by Exception Principle

We describe how intelligence, in an AI sense, is built into BayRes, if we view it as a system which changes its suggestions as external inputs arrive. In a sense, this is a feature of good Bayesian modeling, but we shall stress how this is enhanced in BayRes.

A first issue to mention is that our forecasting models allow us to move away from stationarity assumptions, since process parameters are time varying, and adapt as information arrives. Moreover, BayRes forecasting module allows for intervention, illustrating in one way the incorporation of a principle of *management by exception*: a set of models is routinely used for processing information, making inferences and predictions, and making decisions, unless exceptional circumstances arise. Examples would include a sudden rainfall, a big release from a reservoir upstream or the detection of a wet period. In those cases, the system is open to external intervention, typically by inclusion of additional subjective information. As described in WH, those interventions may be embedded formally within the DLM framework, so we shall not dwell on them. Also several cases of model deterioration have been well identified, with corresponding remedial actions, so that many of these ideas may be automated. Similarly, there is a well-developed theory for model monitoring of DLMs which may be incorporated in the system, a typical case being that of checking the importance of various harmonics within a seasonal term.

Let us describe interventions in the preference model, a topic in which the literature is not so abundant. We describe interventions on the reference trajectory and the penalty parameter ρ.

Recall that the reference trajectory defines a set of reference storages for the behavior of the reservoir. As such, the concept is close to that of rule curves, used in traditional reservoir operation methods, based on long-term behavior of the reservoir. The computation of a reference trajectory is done via deterministic dynamic program, a computationally intensive procedure. Relatively small changes in the predictive expected inflows produce small changes in the trajectory, suggesting stability of the trajectory. However, the trajectory has a clear impact on performance, specially if we consider unusually wet or dry periods. Hence, the idea would be to use the same reference trajectory, unless an exceptionally wet or dry period arises, another illustration of the management by exception principle.

The detection of wet or dry periods is relatively easy. We use a 95% predictive probability region for inflows in next period; when actual inflows do not fall in that region, an alarm is set and reference trajectories are recomputed, once changes in the predicted inflows have taken place. That would be an example of backward intervention, which may be fully automated. Alternatively, we may have forward interventions, e.g. if we find out about unusual releases upstream. Again, we would modify expected inflows and recompute trajectories. Note though, that this intervention may not be fully automated, requiring the operator to interact with the system to introduce the additional information, external to the system.

Simulations with our methodology have shown us that while performance is appropriate when the reservoir has not very high storage, in some cases reservoirs tend to remain with very high storage for extensive periods, which may be dangerous, see Figure 4.1, with $\rho = 10^{-10}$. This suggests that the deviation term may have little effect, under such circumstances, suggesting, in turn, using different ρ values for different storages as we do in our implementation. Figure 4.2 corresponds to $\rho = 10^{-7}$, showing not so many periods with high storage.

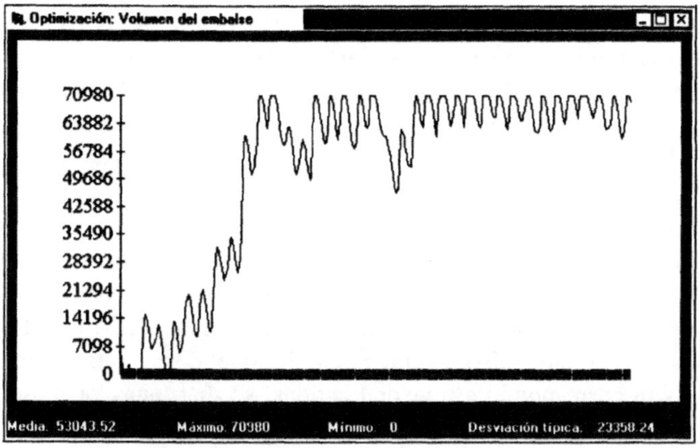

Fig. 4.1. Reservoir storage with $\rho = 10^{-10}$

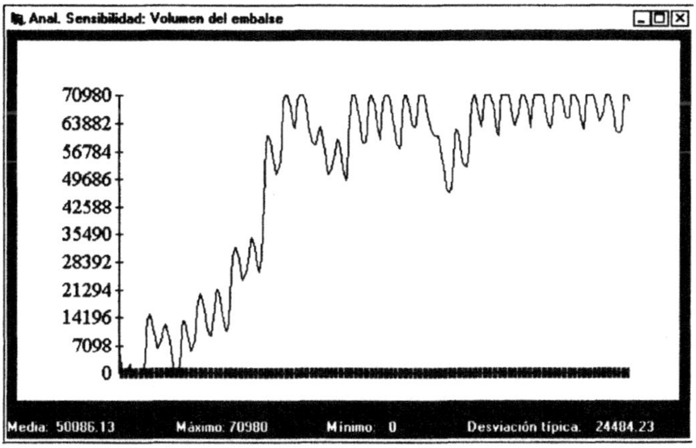

Fig. 4.2. Reservoir storage with $\rho = 10^{-7}$

5 Conclusions

We have described a successful and coherent methodology for reservoir management, which may take into account the hierarchical structure of the planning process. The methodology has been implemented in a system which allows intelligent management of the reservoir, many tasks being completely automated, and others requiring relatively little input from the operator.

A key idea in the implementation is the management by exception principle. When exceptional circumstances arise, the basic models are conveniently modified. Some modifications are fully automated, as when a dry or wet period is detected; others require the intervention of the operator, which may intervene to input additional information. In the end, interaction between reservoir operators and the system will be necessary to cater adequately for events and changes that go beyond the existing model form.

Acknowledgements

This project is supported by grants from IBERDROLA, CICYT and NATO. We are grateful to discussions and the computational work of J. Fuertes, M. Farache and E. Pérez.

References

Berger, J. (1985). *Statistical Decision Theory and Bayesian Analysis*. Springer: New York.

Berger, J. (1994). An overview of robust Bayesian analysis (with discussion), *Test* **3**, 5–26.

Berger, J., Ríos Insua, D. (1997). Recent developments in Bayesian Inference, with applications in Hidrology, *UNESCO*.

Birge, J. (1997). Stochastic programming computation and applications, *INFORMS Jour. Computing* **9**, 111–133.

Carlin, B., Kadane, J. and Gelfand, A. (1997). Approaches for optimal sequential Decision Analysis in clinical trials, Tech. Rep., Univ. of Minnesota.

Dantzig, G. and Infanger, G. (1997). Intelligent control and optimization under uncertainty with applications to hydro-power, *Eur. Jour. Oper. Res.* **97**, 396–407.

Farquhar, P. H. (1984). Utility assessm-ent methods, *Management Science* **30,** 1283–1300.

French, S. (1986). *Decision Theory*. Ellis Horwood: London.

Golden, B. and Wasil, E. (1994). Managing fish, forests, wildlife and water, in Pollock (Ed.) *Handbook in OR*, vol. **6**. North Holland.

Ríos Insua, D. and Salewicz, A. (1995). The operation of Lake Kariba. *J. of Multicriteria Decision Analysis* **4**, 203–222.

Ríos Insua, D., Salewicz, K., D., Müller, P., and Bielza, C. (1997a). Bayesian methods in reservoir operations: the Zambezi river case, in S. French and J. Q. Smith (eds.). *The Practice of Bayesian Analysis*, 107–130. Arnold: London.

Ríos Insua, D., Bielza, C., Martín, J. and Salewicz, K. (1997b). BayRes: a system for stochastic multiobjective reservoir operations, *Proceedings of the Second International Conference in Multi-objective Programming and Goal Programming*, Springer, (in Press).

West, M. and Harrison, J. (1997). *Bayesian Forecasting and Dynamic Linear Models*. Springer: New York.

Analysis of Livestock Production Systems via Compromise Programming

Ana Teruel Doñate[1] and Ana Allueva Pinilla[2]

[1] Department of Animal Production and Food Science. University of Zaragoza, SPAIN
[2] Department of Applied Mathematics. University of Zaragoza, SPAIN

Abstract

Several production systems for ruminants via their modelling by clasical linear programming and compromise programming, are analysed in the framewok of the individual farm and of the whole region of Jacetania (Pyrenees).

Keywords. Compromise programming, livestock, multicriteria, Pyrenees

1 Introduction

Research into agrarian systems has nowadays surpassed the classical paradigm of the single criterion for economic optimisation. The farm can be defined as a system and this approach introduces profound methodological implications. It requires the acceptance of the fact that farms are not only subject to physical conditioning but also to conditions and choices derived from the intentional behaviour of the decision making elements of the system, see Dillon (1992). That is to say, economic problems are more complex than merely technological ones, since they incorporate an element of decision or choice in the strict sense, see Romero (1993).

To the economic-productive function traditionally recognised for farming activity, nowadays we can add, especially in mountain areas, the assignement of the function of protecting the environment and the social function of maintaining a population base in rural areas.

The mountain area of Jacetania in the Huesca Pyrenees (Spain) embraces different ruminant production systems. The traditional extensive systems are characterised by having played a role for centuries which is now revalued.

2 Objectives

The objective of this present research has been to analyse different ruminant production systems, understood as a technical subsystem of the farms and the livestock activity of an area, depending on their suitability to the resources of an area and their contribution to the attainment of a series of objectives.

The analysis has initially been carried out regarding their economic potentials, with a classical approach, carrying out a parallel tracking of the environmental and social effect which they bring about, and then later regarding the various aspects considered as objectives simultaneously via compromise programming.

The study is thought of as a step towards the development of multicriteria models which can be applied to decision making.

3 Methodology

Modelling using mathematical programming is widely used in agrarian research thanks to the possibility of translating problems of the allocation of resources of economic-productive activities into problems of mathematical programming via algebraic algorithms such as the Simplex. Multicriteria methods are ideal for the analysis of agrarian activities, Hazell and Norton (1986), since multiple objectives can be considered simultaneously, which corresponds to the complex reality of the systems.

There are relatively few studies via multicriteria programming which focus on livestock farming activities in relation to the natural pastures and agricultural resources of their area. Amongst these we can mention the work of Bartlett and Clawson (1978), Maino et al.(1987, 1993), Berbel and Vitalina (1993) and Koeijer et al. (1995).

A central tool in the present analysis has been mathematical programming, specifically classical linear and compromise (see, Zeleny (1973)) programming. The latter is considered the most promising multicriteria approach for analytical purposes, see Romero (1994).

Compromise programming:

$$\min L_r = \min \left[\sum_{k=1}^{p} W_k \left| \frac{f_k^* - f_k(x)}{f_k^* - f_k^\bullet} \right|^r \right]^{1/r}$$

$x \in F$.
f_k^* ideal value of k objective.
$f_k^\bullet$ anti-ideal value of k objective.
W_k weighting of k objective.

The analysis is established on two different levels. Initially we study the production systems independently, in the framework of the farm. Next the livestock activity on a regional scale is modelled, via an aggregate model in which the different system participate.

The analysis has been carried out for the agricultural year 1993/4.

3.1 Model structure

In the modelling of the production systems on the farm level the following types of variables, constraints and objectives are involved:

- Variables
  - Variables referring to livestock production systems
  - Variables referring to pasture and cultivated areas
  - Variables referring to externally bought resources
  - "Range" variables to make the nutritional constraints flexible
  - Other variables to facilitate calculations
- Constraints
  - Constraints limiting the number of production units.
  - Balance between nutritional requirements and contributions (UFL, PD).
  - Balance between forage and concentrated foods.
  - Constraints related to ingestion capacity (UL)
  - Related to different surface types in the farm
  - Relation of straw produced, reused and bought (for feeding and bedding)
  - Relation of manure produced by the livestock and use for crops
  - Agronomical balance (between several annual utilizations of the same cultivated area, proporcionalsurface between several crops)
  - Constraints which reflect institutional situations (set-aside percentage, milk production quota)
  - Constraints related to costs and economic results (subsidies, etc.), to labour, petrol, etc. to follow their development
- Objectives included in the compromise approaches
  - Objective related to economic results On the individual farm level we have chosen to maximise the value of the results without subtracting costs for labour nor capital. In the approaches with classical linear programming this is the sole objective.
  - Objectives related to labour In the modelling of individual farms we consider as an objective the minimisation of labour requirements and the seasonal deviations from the average requirements.
  - Objective related to the activity's environmental effect

A global indicator of the environmental effect calculated qualitatively for each activity is maximised. This considers a series of factors which cause an environmental effect, also including fuel consumption, quantitatively valued.

There is a similar structure for the modelling of production systems in the aggregate approaches.

- The variables and restraints which are used in the model are mostly the same as those used in each one of the individual models, in this case all together with particularities such as the following:
  - The limiting constraints for the different types of land are established for each one of the areas distinguished in the region.

- The milk quota for the region is included as a limiting constraint of milk production systems.
- Objectives included in the compromise approaches.
  - Objective related to economic results

We have opted to maximise the value of the results, having previously subtracted labour and capital costs. However, we do not take into account the costs of renting communal meadows which revert to the region, nor the opportunity cost of cultivated land. In the classical linear programming approaches this is the sole objective.

- Objective related to labour.

We fix the regional objective of maximising employment, bearing in mind that at the same time labour is a cost taken into account as the economic results are being maximised.

- Objective related to the environmental effect of the activity.

The global value is maximised.

3.2 Variables

3.2.1 Variables related to the presence of livestock in the different production systems

We analyse various ruminant production systems. For their definition different features are determined:

- Species and race, herd size and the different lots if applicable.
- Reproductive and productive cycle and technical indices.
- Seasonal location (6 periods are differentiated in the year) and the accessibility of pasture resources, cultivated and bought.

We have included cattle systems with births in spring and in autumn, in the latter case with and without milking. Systems are differentiated depending on the area in which they are located and on the corresponding resources that are available, distinguishing two zones, northern "V" and southern "D". In this case we analyse the option of fattening of calves, the specialised production of milk, and cattle in the pre-pyrenean mountains (with scrub).

- "BV.mr-ap" y "BD.mr-ap". 30 cows; births in March-April; calve production; location from June to Sept. in summer ranges, spring and autumn int he valley (V) or depression (D) with access to meadows or pastures, winter in stables.
- "BV.l.nv-dc", "BD.l.nv-dc", "BV.c.nv-dc", "BD.c.nv-dc" and "BD.cc.nv-dc". 30 cows; births in Nov.-Dec.; production of calves and milk(l), only calves(c) or calves older than 10 months(cc); location in summer (June to Sept. in (c, cc) or July to Sep. in (l)) in summer ranges, spring and autumn in the valley (V) or depression (D) with access to meadows and pastures; in stables from December to March.

- "BM.c.mr-ap". 50 cows; births in March-April; calve production; location from June to Sept. in summer ranges, and the rest of the year in hills with scrub without cultivated areas.
- "BD.l.frisón". 30 cows; births troughout the year; production of milk and new born calves; located in the depression; in stables from Dec. to March and with access to meadows the rest of the year; no access to summer ranges.

We analyse sheep systems with a single birthing period per year, which may be in winter, in autumn or in spring. We also include systems with main birthing in the autumn and a secondary period in the spring and systems with three births in two years. Each one of the systems mentioned is considered both for the valleys area and for the pre-pyrenean depression.

- "OV.dc-ja" and "OD.dc-ja". 400 sheep; births in Dec.-Jan.; production of lambs; location Jun. to Sept. in summer ranges, spring and autumn in the valley (V) or depression (D) with access to pastures and meadows, stubble and set-aside land (in D); in stables from Dec. to March.
- "OV.3b/2y" and "OD.3b/2y". 400 sheep in 2 groups; 3 periods of births per year (each group achieves 3 births in 2 years); production of lambs; summer ranges (only one group), spring and autumn in the valley (V) or depression (D) with access to pastures and meadows, stubble and set-aside land (in D); in stables from Dec. to March.
- "OV.sp-oc;mr-ap" y "OD.sp-oc;mr-ap". 400 sheep; main birth period in Sept.-Oct. and secondary in March-April. Production of lambs; located in summer in high ranges, spring and autumn in the valley (V) or depression (D) with access to pastures and meadows, stubble and set-aside land (in D); in stables from Dec. to March.

Furthermore, two transhumant systems are included in some farm models, with a long ("OT8.oc-nv;ap-my") or short ("OT4.dc-ja") period spent in the lowlands and one or two birthing periods.

Once the characteristics have been determined we calculate, for each production system, the seasonal nutritional requirements of each type of animal, seasonal and total labour requirements, environmental indicator, costs and production figures.

3.2.2 Variables related to meadow land and cultivated land

To determine the following aspects are considered:

- location (in one of the two differentiated regional sub-zones, zone "V" Pyrenean valleys, Axial Pyrenees and interior ranges or zone "D" pre-pyrenean depression and exterior ranges) and seasonability.
- technical itinerary

For zone "V" the following land types are included:

- High mountain ranges used from June to September
- Other pasture areas used in June and September
- Scrub used in spring (Apr.-May) and autumn (Oct.-Nov.)

- Natural and artificial non-irrigated and irrigated meadows

For zone "D" the following land types are included:

- High mountain ranges used from June to September
- Other pasture areas and scrub used in spring, autumn and winter
- Natural non-irrigated meadows
- Artificial non-irrigated and irrigated meadows (with several posibilities for usage)
- Non-irrigated and irrigated alfalfa
- Sainfoin (non-irrigated)
- Vetch for pasturing, for hay or grain and straw (non-irrigated)
- Barley and straw (non-irrigated)
- Stubble and set-aside land associated with barley

Once the characteristics have been determined we calculate for each meadow area and cultivated area the productivity and seasonal nutritional value, seasonal and total labour requirements, environmental indicator and production costs. The area of each type of meadow or group of crops in each regional area are quantified, to include as a constraint in the regional model.

3.2.3 Variables related to bought resources

Various resources present in the market which can be used for ruminant farming have been included:

- alfalfa hay, dehydrated alfalfa, barley, maize, soya, bran, straw
- feed stuffs for beef cattle and lactating dairy cattle, for calves, fattering feed for calves, feed for sheep, for lambs and fattering feed for lambs .

For each of these their nutritional value, a value for environmental effect and the market price are determined.

3.3 Generation and processing of the matrices

We have prepared spreadsheets for each variable which plays a part in the model and from these we have obtained the technical-economic variables which make up the matrix. This has meant that the modification of any of the basic data, be they economic factors (prices, subsidies) or technical factors (herd size, reproductive indices, productivity of the meadows or cultivated land, input doses, etc.), automatically leads to the generation of a new matrix.

In the processing of the matrixes both for the individual farm models and the regional aggregate models we have used the Operational Research module (SAS/OR) of the SAS 6.11 package. Its LP procedure uses the Simplex method revised in two phases of Bartels-Golub.

We used SAS and the spreadsheet simultaneously in a multi-task environment via a Dynamic Data Exchange (DDE) subroutine.

4 Results and discussion

4.1 Production systems in the farm context

Among the multiple possibilities for the analysis of individual farms via simulation we have included in this paper the research into the economic results obtained, the requirements and seasonability of labour and the environmental effect of the activity, the quantification of the variation of the results depending on the objectives planned for the farm and the comparison of some production systems with others.

Having predetermined the number of animals and not having introduced constraints in the cultivated area (owned), nor in the access to summer ranges (communal) beyond those imposed by the livestock production system itself, by maximising the economic results (NVA) the systems located in the southern area "D" (with more productive cultivated land suitable for cereals and forage) can achieve better economic results than their homologous systems in the northern zone "V" (with abundant and cheap meadows but whose cultivated land is only suitable for forage and is less productive). The reform of the CAP regarding herbaceous crops contributes to this advantage.

The systems with greatest economic possibilities are those of sheep production with various birthing periods per year in the zone "D" ("OD.sp-oc;mr-ap", "OD.3b/2y") followed by their homologous systems in the zone "V" ("OV.sp-oc;mr-ap", "OV.3b/2y"). The mixed cattle and dairy cattle systems have intermediate possibilities and the beef cattle in the zone "V" together with the transhumant sheep have least possibilities.

If , in the economic results, we take into account the opportunity cost of labour and of capital invested the systems "OT8.oc-nv;mr-ap" and "BM.c.mr-ap" gain importance especially. These have a minimal quantity of capital invested and low labour requirements. The dairy production systems ("B.l.nvdc", "BD.l.frisón") and that with a large cultivated area ("Od.3b/2y") ("OD.sp-oc;mr-ap", "OD.3b/2y") become less interesting.

Labour profitability is relatively greater in the systems with low labour requirements (beef) and the profitability of capital is greater when this is low (transhumant sheep systems and mountain cattle).

The systems with require most labour are cattle systems with milking and the sheep systems with three births in two years. Between homologous systems the labour requirements are greater in the northern area.

The seasonal distribution of labour is always heterogeneous, the positive seasonal variations from the average of labour requirements in percentage terms of hours are between a little less than 10% and a little more than 30%.

In the approaches corresponding to a maximising of economic results the environmental indicator takes widely fluctuating values. The highest value corresponds to the extensive mountain cattle system, mainly thanks to the extensive use of natural meadows, and also the transhumant sheep systems, all of them with no fuel consumption. The environmental indicator is minimal in the specialised dairy system, due to the absence of usage of natural meadows and the estrangement from innate behaviour. It should also be pointed out that homogenous systems usually have a higher environmental indicator in the zone "V", which is economically disfavoured.

Analysing the production systems via compromise programming with the objectives being the maximising of economic results and of the environmental indicator , the minimising of labour requirements and positive seasonal deviations, the pay-off matrixes allow us to see the generalised contradiction between the objectives of minimising labour and maximising economic results, or between minimising labour and maximising the environmental indicator. However, the economic and environmental objectives are not normally opposed.

The compromise solutions with metrics $r = 1$ and with a balanced weighting of objectives lead to efficient solutions in which, regarding the solution of reference to economic maximising, an improvement in the other aspects (labour and environmental effect) is brought about at the expense of a decrease in the economic results which on average is between 10 and 20% (Figure 1).

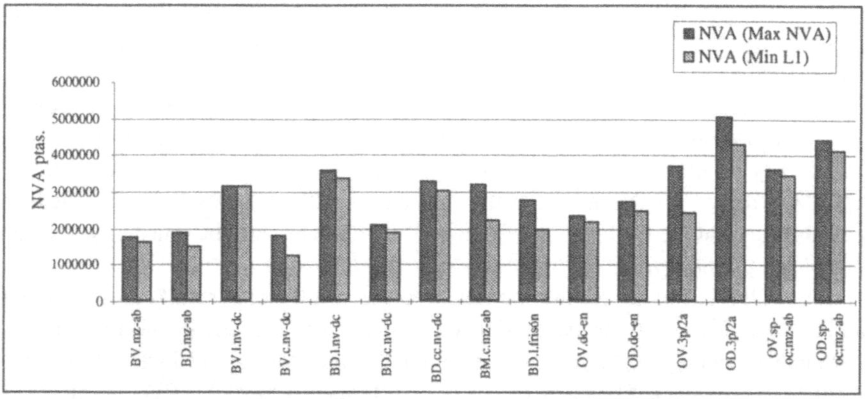

Fig. 1. Comparison of economic results (NVA): max NVA – min L_1

Labour requirements can be reduced in almost all cases, although never more than 25% (Figure 2).

The deviations in labour requirements are also reduced in the majority of the approaches, and a large number of them to a large extent, more than 50%.

The environmental effect indicator, opposed to the objective of reduction in labour requirements suffers very variable changes. For systems in which the reference solution (maximum economic results) shows a margin without using natural meadows the use of this resource generally increases, increasing the environmental indicator and preventing the reduction of labour required (Figure 3).

The greatest global interest (taking into account the four criteria) is in the system "BM.c.mr-ap", cattle in the low level mountain during intermediate periods and in the winter and in summer ranges in the summer. This is justified above all for its positive environmental effect (connected with pasturing) and also because of its low labour requirements and acceptable economic results. Another globally interesting

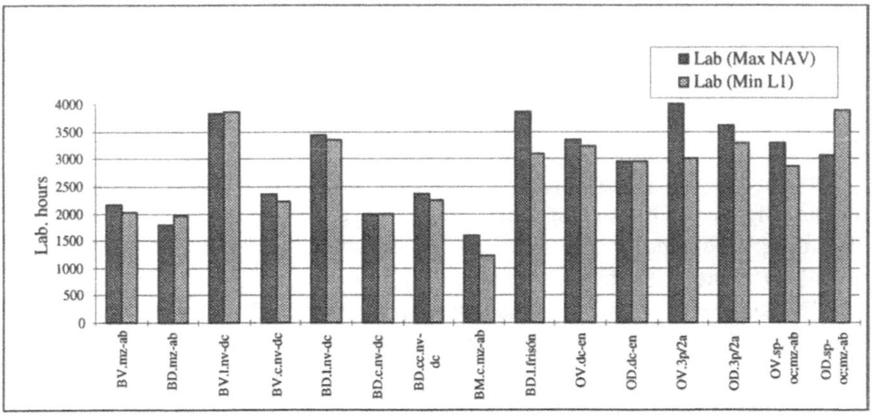

Fig. 2. Comparison of labour requirements: max NVA – min L_1

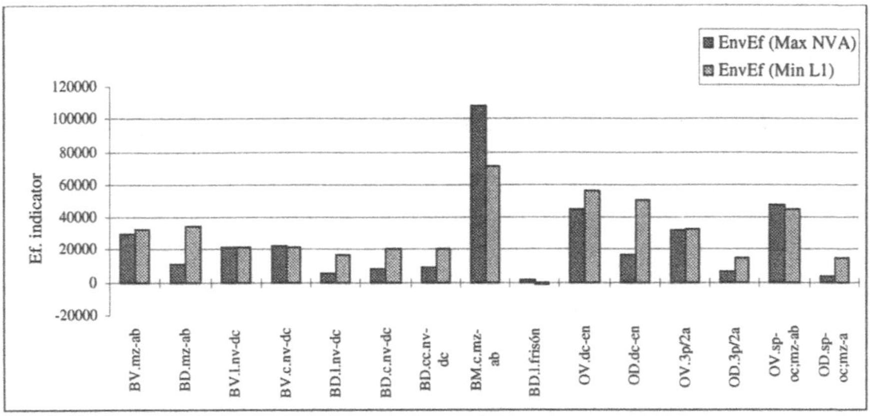

Fig. 3. Comparison of the environmental effect indicator: max NVA – min L_1

system is "OV.sp-oc;mr-ap" of sheep in the southern area with main birthing in September-October and secondary in March-April. Its economic results are quite high, and so is its environmental indicator. On the other hand it requires a lot of labour, although this is quite uniformly distributed.

4.2 Production systems in the regional context

Among the multiple results that can be obtained from the modelling ofproduction systems on a regional scale, we shall mention the participation of production systems in competition for meadow and cultivated areas, assuming an efficient assignation of resources, the economic results obtained, the match between the availability and requirements of labour and the environmental effect of the activity; all this with classical and compromise programming.

Maximising economic results for the region, in this case considering opportunity costs for labour and capital but not the costs of renting communal meadows nor the opportunity cost of cultivated land, the optimum is reached with the systems "BD.l.nv-dc" (15 productive units), "OV.sp-oc;mr-ap" (610 units) and "OD.3b/2y" (264 units).

Adding to the economic objective those of maximising labour occupation and maximising the environmental effect indicator the following systems come into play: "BV.mr-ap" (86 units) and "BD.cc.nv-dc" (189 units). "OV.sp-oc;mr-ap" is reduced to 550 units and "OD.3b/2y" to 99 units.

The value which reflects the maximised economic results in the classical method is 1510 million pesetas. In the multicriteria method the economic results are 1220 million pesetas, that is to say there is a reduction of nearly 20cases it is the subsidies that give rise to these results, even covering some of the losses.

Labour involved turns out to be 1560 AWU when economic results are maximised, and the figure increases to 1660 AWU with the compromise method.

These figures for AWU are greater than the number of workers at the moment, 1014 are involved in the agrarian sector in Jacetania, according to the census of working population in 1991. This is a coherent result bearing in mind the potential for growth in livestock farming found.

The environmental effect indicator, which is positive, is 50% greater in the compromise method.

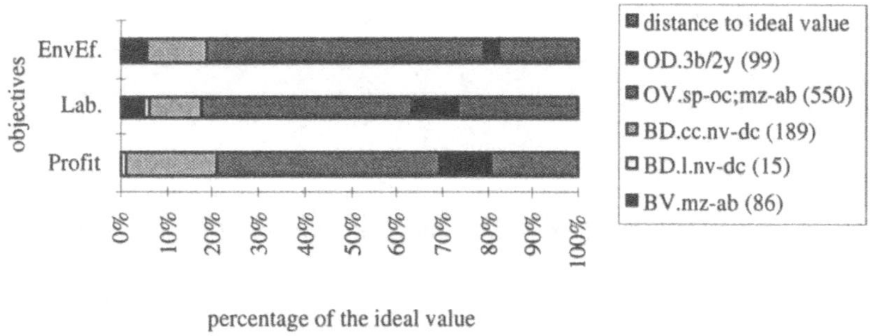

Fig. 4. Profit, labour and environmental effect in compromise solution: contribution of the production systems and distance to the values at the ideal point

Figure 4 shows the relative contribution of each production system in the compromise method to approach the ideal point in the three dimensions considered.

The major production system "OV.sp-oc;mr-ap", mainly contributes to approaching the environmental ideal, its contribution to the economic objective being relatively less, and even less to the labour occupation objective. The system "OD.3b/2y" contributes to a greater extent to the labour objective and also helps to increase the economic results, though it has relatively less impact on the environmental effect indicator. The system "BD.l.nv-dc" contributes to a relatively large extent to the occupation of labour and relatively little to the environmental indicator. "BD.cc.nv-dc" is interesting for the three parameters considered, but to a larger extent for the economic results, followed by its environmental effect, and to a lesser extent by its occupation of labour. The system "BV.mr-ap", of no economic interest contributes significantly to the environmental indicator.

References

Bartlett, E. T. and Clawson, W. J. (1978). Profit, Meat Production or Efficient Use of Energy in Ranching. *Journal of Animal Science* **46**, 812–818.

Dillon, J. L. (1992). The Farm as a Purposeful System. *Miscellaneous Publication,* **10**. The University of New England. Department of Agricultural Economics and Business Management.

Hazell, P. and Norton, R. (1986). *Mathematical Programming for Economic Analysis in Agriculture*. McMillan Publishing Company: New York.

Koeijer, T. J., Renkema, J. A. and Mensvoort, J. J. M. (1995). Environmental-Economic Analysis of Mixed Crop-Livestock Farming. *Agricultural Systems* 515–530.

Maino, M., Alonso, R. and Iruretagoyena, T. (1987). Planificación de fincas ganaderas bovinas mediante modelos de programación multiobjetivo. *Investigación Agraria. Serie Economía* **2** (**1**), 9–30.

Maino, M., Berdegue, J. and Rivas, T. (1993). Multiple Objective Programming. An Application for Analysis and Evaluation of Peasant-Economy of the 8th Region of Chile. *Agricultural Systems* **41**, 387–397.

Romero, C. (1993). *Teoría de la Decisión Multicriterio: Conceptos, Técnicas y Aplicaciones*. Alianza Editorial: Madrid.

Romero, C. (1994). Una aproximación de la aplicación de los enfoques multicriterio en la economía ambiental. In *Economía de los recursos ambientales y naturales* 149–171.

SAS/OR User's Guide.

Zeleny, M. (1973). Compromise programming. In *Multiple Criteria Decision Making*. University of South Carolina Press, Columbia.

Using Mathematical Models in the Management of Forest Industries

Andrés Weintraub[1]

[1] Department of Industrial Engineering, University of Chile, P.O. Box 2777, Santiago, CHILE

Abstract

Mathematical models play an important role in forest planning at different levels. We present four different systems that have been developed for large Chilean forestry firms. The systems deal with dialy truck scheduling, programming of short term harvesting, the location of machine harvesting and medium range planning of forest harvesting and road building. For each case the solution approach is shown as well as the implementation and use by the firms. Solution approaches include: simulation, linear programming with column generation, mixed integer programming solved via strengthening of the formulation and Lagrangean relaxation, and heuristics.

Keywords. Computational implementation, forest management, mathematical model

Introduction

Computational systems, based on mathematical models have been developed for the main Chilean forest firms. These systems have been implemented and are being used for different levels of decision making. A first system is for daily truck scheduling, based on a simulation model with heuristic rules, which is run daily to program all trips of trucks, from origins in the forest to destinations such as sawmills, pulp plant, port. A second system deals with decisions on short term harvesting, which include how much timber to harvest and how to cut up or buck the trees so as to obtain the products needed, defined by length and diameter. The system is based on an LP model with a column generation scheme to generate bucking patterns. A third system is used to locate harvesting machinery and the needed access roads.

The system links with a GIS system and has a graph interactive interphase. The solutions are generated with a heuristic approach. Finally, a tactical model supports decisions on areas to be harvested and roads to be built on a 2 to 5 year horizon. A mixed integer LP model is developed here. To solve more difficult cases, strengthening the LP solution, lifting and Lagrangean relaxation lead to significant improvements in the solutions. We describe the implementation of each system and the results obtained.

1 A Truck Scheduling System

1.1 Description of the Problem

An important problem in forest operations is the daily transport of timber from different stands (origins or sources) being harvested, with known supplies, to destinations, such as pulp mills, sawmills, sorting yards, and ports, with their daily demands. The different timber products transported are characterized basically by the length and diameter of each log. Trucks transport loads of logs from origins to destinations. Although the firms typically subcontract trucks, they usually organize their schedules. The basic decisions a log transport manager has to deal with each day are:

- The origins from which each product demand should be satisfied,
- The trucks and cranes needed at origins and destinations to satisfy all demands, and
- The work schedule for each truck and crane.

The basic objective is to satisfy the demand for different products at each destination, while minimizing transportation costs within technical, policy, and labor constraints. A typical forest firm will operate with about 10 to 90 origins and five to 30 destinations and use between 50 to 300 trucks. Depending on the distance involved, each truck can make between one and four trips per day.

Transportation costs account for about 40% of operating costs, so it is important to define and control efficient truck schedules.

Daily harvesting operations at the origins produce different products defined by the length and diameter of the logs. Each day's supply comes from the logs left over from the previous day plus the present day's production.

The firms typically subcontract trucks and pay them according to agreed-upon formulas based on the number of cubic meters per kilometer, handled by each type of truck (empty trips do not receive pay).

There are different types of trucks according to frame characteristics (e.g. long trucks to handle long logs) and engine power.

For each destination, a daily demand for each product is known, in some cases with higher priority, e.g. to fill an export shipment. For some destinations it is important to deliver products at regular basis, to coordinate with downstream operations.

1.2 The Traditional Management System

A manual, simple scheduling system was used, were each truck was assigned a specific origin-destination pair and truck drivers determine the schedules. This led to poor coordination, long queues and low efficiency.

1.3 The New System

The new system was based on two notions.

a) A centralized administrative system which schedules and control all trips,
b) A simulation model for scheduling decisions.

The model simulates events and decisions as they occur along the day. e.g. a truck being loaded a 9:30 A.M. with export logs, arriving to port at 11:07 unloading and leaving at 11:27 for a new trip. The model assigns decisions on new trips, looking at a one hour horizon, that is, looking jointly at all trucks that will become free in the next hour to avoid near-sighted decisions and assigning those fixed for the first 15 minutes. In this form decisions are made each 15 minutes on a moving horizon scheme. Trip assignments are made based on securing supplying timber to satisfy requirements adequately, at minimum transportation costs.

Because of the unloading capacity at destinations and downstream operations, arrivals at destinations must be regular. This is not trivial as a complete cycle (trip to origin, load, trip to destination, unload) can very significantly (1.5 to five hours) depending on the locations of origins and destinations. The system generates data to determine when a destination will be in critical need of suply in order to maintain regularity.

To evaluate the desirability of each feasible trip, we define an index for each possible trip by all trucks in review that considers the total real cost plus a congestion penalty. Total real costs include operational costs (fuel, tires, maintenance) and fixed costs (capital depreciation, insurance, salaries) prorated by the number of hours the truck is used. The penalty for congestion at origins is a heuristic estimate that depends on (1) the trucks that may load at the same time at a given origin, (2) the alternative trips available for those trucks, and (3) the probability of selecting a conflicting trip. The simulation process estimates the congestion effect as it analyzes possible future trips to origins to be made in addition to those already scheduled. The congestion penalty is not a real cost; it is just a device to reflect the loss efficiency some trip assignments cause to other trucks, and it is not included in the reports. (3) The selection of the next trip to be assigned is based on the desirability index just described but in the context of trip priorities.

Priorities are based on the urgency perceived by the model in scheduling trips. Thus, the first priority is for trips to destinations with urgent requirements. For example, if a destination requires four truckloads per hour, and the simulation has assigned only two between 14:00 and 15:00 with few options available to provide the remaining two truckloads, those trips become first priority.

To minimize transportation costs, schedules program efficient trips and queuing at origins and destinations is minimized.

The system, which is run daily, takes the following as main inputs: supply of timber products at origins or sources, demands at destinations, truck fleet and crane equipment characteristics, costs and times for the different trips, loading and unloading, plus an additional set of relevant constraints. As outputs, the system yields requirements for trucks and cranes, a schedule for each, and basic statistics to evaluate performance.

1.4 Implementation

The system is being used in 8 firms in Chile and one in South Africa. For a typical large firm, with 200 trucks a run takes about 2 minutes on a PC Pentium. Runs are made daily, in the afternoon and truck schedules are given to drivers. Modifications on the schedules during the day induced, for example by the failure of a machine, are handled manually and instructions are given via radio. In the future, it is expected that Global Positioning Systems and satelite communications will be used for on line scheduling. Very important improvements have been obtained in terms of reduction of the number of trucks, global costs and hours spent on the job. For example in one firm daily average queuing was reduced from 41/2 to 1/2 hours. Table 1 shows reduction in the number of trucks used in 4 firms. Global transportation costs were reduced between 15% to 35% (Weintraub et al. 1996).

	Before ASICAM	After ASICAM
Bosques Arauco	156	120
Forestal Millalemu	80	50
Forestal Bío Bío	118	76
Forestal Río Vergara	120	80

Table 1. Number of trucks in four forest firms required for hauling similar volumes of timber before and after the implementation of ASICAM

A mathematical modeling representation of this problem was developed. It corresponds to 2 models, one to define trips and another to assign trucks to trips. Both models are linked through a Lagrangean decomposition scheme (Gallo et al. 1997).

2 A System for Short Term Harvesting

2.1 Description of the Problem

Forest companies use standing timber in their forests to satisfy demand at pulp plants, sawmills and also exports as logs. In our case, the firms handle pine plantations which mature in a cycle of 22-28 years. Forests are divided into reasonably homogeneous stands, were the similarity is given mainly by tree age, site quality and management state. When trees are harvested, they are cut into several products or pieces. This operation is called bucking. The pieces obtained must satisfy demand, which has requirements in terms of volume (m3) of pieces defined by their length and diameter, and often also average diameter of a whole lot. The bucking process can be carried out on the ground and individual pieces transported to their separate destinations from there, or the whole log can be transported to a sorting center, where the bucking is carried out.

Decisions for short term harvesting involve:

1. Which stands to harvest among those which have mature trees ready for harvesting and are already accessible by existing roads.
2. What type of machinery should be used. Areas with steep slopes are harvested using yarders or cable logging while flat areas are harvested with skidders.
3. Volume to be cut each week. The volume harvested is in direct relation to demand. Stocks can be made for future use.
4. Bucking patterns follow simple instructions in terms of lengths and diameters for cutting up each log.
5. Delivery of products, defined by length and diameter to satisfy demand. Typical demands are, in decreasing commercial value, export logs (long pieces of high diameter), sawtimber (short logs of high diameter) and pulp timber (any diameter).

Instructions given to loggers are to obtain as many pieces as possible of each defined piece, in the given order. Thus, in the example of Figure 1, the logger first tries to get a piece which at 12.10 m. has a diameter of at least 26 cm.. If at that length the diameter is below 26 cm., he tries to obtain a piece of length 4.10 m. and diameter at least 24 cm. If he obtains that, he tries again for another piece of length 4.10 and diameter 24 cm. and so on.

2.2 The traditional planning approach

The typical planning approach is carried out by an experienced planner. The planner analyses:

a) The demands for different products in the near future, one to three months ahead.
b) The standing timber available in that period.
c) The capacity for harvesting. This depends mainly on the availability of harvesting equipment (yarders, skidders) and trucks for transportation.

With this information the planner schedules a stand sequence to be harvested and machinery to be allocated. Bucking patterns are defined such as to yield the products needed to satisfy demand each week, including stocks. Feedback by the planner allows to correct production schedules. This system usually leads to losses due to difficulties in matching supply (standing trees) and demand, where timber of higher diameter must be used for lower value purposes (pulp). To avoid this, a mathematical model was developed.

2.3 The Mathematical Model

We show a simplified form of the model.
Variables:

Y_{ijk} = Volume of product k (m^3) transported from stand i, in period t to meet the demand.

K_{ijk} = Volume of timber (m^3) produced in stand i using bucking pattern j in period t.

Constraints:

1. $\sum_{j,t} K_{ijt} \leq \text{Vol}_i \quad \forall i.$
   In each stand i, the total timber harvested is bounded by existing volume (Vol_i).
2. $\sum_j REN_{ijk} \cdot K_{ijt} = Y_{ijk} \quad \forall i, j, t.$
   The amount of product k produced in stand i considering all bucking patterns used is transported. REN_{ijk} is the volume obtained of product k when pattern j is used in stand i.
3. $\sum_i Y_{ikt} = DD_{k,t} \quad \forall k, t.$
   Demand, $DD_{k,t}$, for each product k in each period t must be satisfied.

Additional constraints relate to harvesting limitations due to machine capacity, having different destinations, and satisfying diameter constraints for groups of products involved in export orders.

The yields parameters REN_{ijk} are obtained from a timber simulation model, which based on sample plots determines volumes available in different lengths and diameters for each bucking pattern.

Since the number of bucking patterns is exponential, a column generating scheme was developed for generating new improving patterns. The subproblem is based on a specially designed Branch and Bound scheme, (Chevalier 1995) where branches at each node represent different cutting options. The scheme is described in Epstein et.al. (1997).

Figure 1 shows a schematic version of the branch and bound tree. Each arc represents a decision for a next piece cut. Thus, at node 1 the arc (12) represents getting a first piece of length 12.10 m. and a minimum diameter of 24 m. Special rules were derived for branching in an efficient way and for bounding, which allows to eliminate a large fraction of nodes in the tree.

2.4 Implementation

The system has been implemented in four firms. The model is typically run about every two weeks, in a rolling horizon of 3 months. The LP model runs on a commercial code on a PC with improvements of about 5% to 10% in relation to the traditional system, the main advantage being in the better use of timber of satisfy demand by reducing the amount of degradation of timber.

3 A Machinery Location System

3.1 Description of the problem

Suppose you have already defined an area of 400 Hectares which you plan to harvest in the next 3-6 months. One question to answer is how to allocate harvesting machinery in a most efficient way to carry out the harvesting operations. Cable logging or towers are used for steep areas and skidders for flat areas. So, first we wish to define which areas will be harvested with towers and with skidders. We also need to know at which points to assign towers, and what type of tower (range, typically, from 300

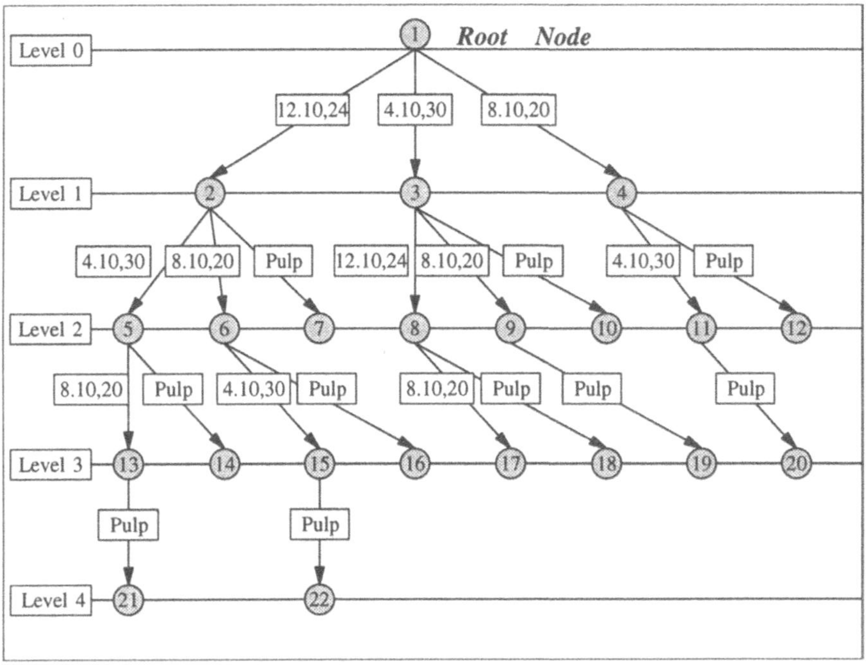

Fig. 1. Nodes in a branch and bound tree for the generation of bucking patterns

meters, to 1000 meters, and direction of pull, upwards or downwards). Finally we need to define the roads needed both to access tower landings, where a small flat area is needed to store logs and load then into trucks and so that skidders work close enough to roads. It is considered economical for skidders to work at distances no longer than 300 meters or so from roads.

The main decisions involved in the planning are:

i) Areas to be harvested by skidders.
ii) Areas to be harvested by towers
iii) Location of landings for towers, and the area to be harvested by each tower.
iv) New roads to be built
v) Old roads to be repaired
vi) Volume of timber harvested and transported

The system must satisfy a set of technical constraints:

i) Locate the landing for towers in adequate locations, according to topographical conditions.
ii) Comply with the range of reach of each tower. This will depend on the type of tower, operating conditions and the characteristics of the terrain (the reach of the cable for logging will be interrupted for example by a river).

iii) Satisfy technical and economical constraints for harvesting with skidders. Elements to consider here are the slope of the terrain, the length of the cable, the loading capacity.
iv) Characteristics of roads. In the design of the road network we must consider acceptable slope, minimum radious of turn for trucks, how to link new roads to existing roads.
v) Availability of equipment.

The objective is to harvest all of the volume that is profitable to harvest, while minimizing costs, which include machine installation and operation, road building and transportation.

3.2 The Traditional Approach

Solutions were obtained manually, as an experiented planner looked at maps of each area, which include altitude level curves and information on existing timber volumes, roads and topographical accidents. The planner would then locate the machinery and design accessing roads by trial and error. Typically, it was a time consuming process and very few options could be analyzed.

3.3 The New System

PLANEX, the system designed system interacts with a Geographic Information System (GIS) which provides information on topography, volumes of standing timber, and roads. The system requires a large amount of information provided by a GIS. A raster format is used to divide the area in question into squares or poligons for analysis. The size of the squares are a parameter, defined usually as 10×10 meters. Information that comes from the GIS in vector format is transformed into raster format.

The GIS provides basic information on the area to be harvested, while the user provides additional information both manually and through a visual interactive interphase.

The system has an internal heuristic algorithm which determines a solution based on the following steps.

i) The user defines the area under study and a set of points where towers could be located. This is done graphically with a mouse. Users are familiar with the problem and can define possible locations of towers by examining the topographical altitude level curves and additional information at their disposal.
ii) With this information, the algorithm finds a solution, which is based on
    a) According to slopes assign areas to be harvested with skidders and towers.
    b) Find sequentially the most attractive locations for installing machinery, based on a criteria of minimum cost por m3 obtained, where costs include harvesting, road building and transportation.
    c) Once all locations are defined redefine heuristic calls a road network of minimum cost.

A graphic interphase allows to analyze possible modifications to solutions. Using the mouse on the screen the user can for example choose towers that should be selected, or design a road that should be build. The system then optimizes the remaining part of the problem and presents a new global solution. This option allows the user to analyze different scenarios in a simple and visual way.

3.4 Implementation

The System is presently used in four firms. It runs on PC Pentium and a typical run takes about 10 minutes. The system is tied to a GIS system and the graphic visual interphase allows the user to test alternatives solutions (Epstein et. al. 1995).

A Mathematical model has been developed to solve this problem. It can be described as a problem with two main components: a plant location part (to define the machinery location were the timber cells act as potential customers) plus a roading and transportation part. This is difficult combinatorial problem. A Lagrangean relaxation solution approach to solve it is shown in Vera, et. al. (1997).

4 A Tactical Forest Planning Model

4.1 Description of the problem

We consider a planning horizon of 2–5 years. Plantation lands are divided into areas, which are continuous lands owned by a firm. Within each area there are different stands, considered homogeneous as defined by the age of trees, quality of land, volume available per hectare and number of hectares. Pine trees mature at age 22 to 28, so stands that can be harvested during the planning horizon are known. These stands are located in geographically different areas. Growth simulator models estimate timber yields in future periods. Timber production goes to export as logs, to sawmills and to pulp plants. While in reality there are many different products, defined mainly by length and diameter of the logs, at this level of planning we define only a few basic aggregate products, such as export, sawmill quality 1, sawmill quality 2, pulp. Usually the higher level quality can be used for lower level purposes, at a loss in sale price. For example, the pulp mill takes any type of timber, while only export quality can be exported. One of the objectives of planning is to minimize the degradation of timber products.

Most timber areas are near paved public roads, but inside the areas private roads are needed. At any moment there is a combination of roads already built and roads that are projected to be built. Private roads are built of gravel or dirt. The more expensive gravel roads can be used year round, while dirt roads are only useful in summer. Road building should be carried out in proper sequence so as to be consistent and timed with stand harvests, and to avoid excessive road building. There are a few cases of sand roads, than can only be used in winter, when rains compact the sand and allow their use. Road building can only be carried out in summer. Harvested timber can be stocked from winter to summer in stocking yards, this allows timber harvested in summer to be hauled through dirt roads to stocking yards near final destinations, and then sent to final destinations in winter using gravel roads.

Aggregate demand is projected to future periods, often as lower and upper bounds as well as expected prices. Harvesting is carried out by cable logging (or towers) for steep areas, while skidders harvest flat areas. Timber hauling is carried out by trucks to destinations such as ports, pulp plant, sawmills or stocking yards. The harvesting machinery and crews are usually subcontracted, with yearly contracts. Since there is a fixed cost associated with installing a harvesting operation, one typically wants to harvest a minimum number of hectares to justify this fixed cost. A typical policy is in case of larger stands to harvest at least 15 hectares. For smaller stands the policy is to harvest the whole stand if at all.

4.2 The Traditional Planning Method

Planning was carried out manually, based on experience. The basic decisions to be considered are:

- Stands to be harvested in each period.
- Timber production, by aggregate product to be harvested in each period to satisfy demand.
- Roads to be built each period, in gravel or dirt.
- Timber transported to destinations.
- Timber stocked from winter to summer.
- Use of harvesting machinery and trucks.

These decisions were developed using maps, on a trial and error approach. The main drawbacks of this approach were in terms of finding a proper sequencing of stands to harvest to match expected demand and roads to build.

4.3 The New System

A mixed integer programming LP model was developed to solve this problem. A simplified form is presented here. A detailed version is presented in Andalaft et al. (1997).

Variables:

X_{st} : Number of hectares of stand s harvested in period t.

Y_{it}^{k} : Volume of timber of type k harvested in origin i, period t (m^3). We note that an origin may be defined for several stands.

$F_{ij,r}^{k,t}$: Flow of timber type k transported on arc (ij) built at standard r, in period t (can exist if the standard is compatible with the season represented by the period).

$$W_{ij,r}^{t} = \begin{cases} 1 & \text{if road } (ij) \text{ is built at standard } r \text{ in period } t. \\ 0 & \text{otherwise} \end{cases}$$

Constraints:

1. Production by origin.

$\sum_{s e(i)} a_{st}^k \cdot X_{st}^k = Y_{it}^k$ for all origins i, products k, periods t, where a_{st}^k is the timber volume of type k produced in stand s if harvested in period t.

2. Harvesting by area
   $\sum_t X_{st} \leq A_s$ for all stands s. The total area of a stand s harvested in all periods is bounded by the total area of the stand, A_s.
3. Flow conservation at origin nodes
   In each production node, for each product, timber production plus incoming timber equals outgoing timber.
   $Y_{it}^k + \sum_r \sum_s F_{si,r}^{k,t} - \sum_r \sum_s F_{ip,r}^{k,t} = 0$ for all production nodes i, products k, periods t.
4. Flow conservation at intersection nodes.
5. Flow conservation at destination to satisfy demand nodes. Note that in this case, export and saw timber can also be used at the pulp plant and export timber can be used at sawmills, by allowing timber degradation.
6. Flow conservation at stocking yards, where timber can be stocked in Summer for use in Winter.
7. Road Building
   $\sum_k Fij, r^{k,t} \leq U_{ij,r}^t \cdot \sum_{\theta \leq t} W_{ij,r}^{\theta} \quad \forall ij, t, r.$
   If (ij) is a potential road, there can be a flow on it up to the capacity $U_{ij,r}^t$ in period t only if it has been previously built.
8. A dirt road can be upgraded to gravel, so it can be used year round.
9. Existing roads can be used year round if in gravel, only in Summer if in dirt.
10. If a stand is harvested, it is harvested completely, if it is smaller than 15 Hectares. If it is larger than 15 Hectares, at least that area is harvested.

Objective function:

Maximize net present value, were revenues originate from timber sales and costs originate through harvesting, road building or upgrading and transportation.

4.4 Implementation

The model has been used by one firm for about 2 years. It is used in the regular planning process, run about twice a year, and also in evaluating possible purchases of forest land. In this case the model is run with and without the new area to be evaluated. The difference in objective value indicates the value of the area to the firm.

The software runs on a PC using a commercial LP code.

The 0-1 variables involved are due to decisions in road building and defining minimum areas that can be harvested. To obtain integer solutions based on LP continuous runs, a set of heuristic rules was developed, which leads to approximate solutions in reasonable CPU time. This type of heuristics were shown to lead to acceptable solutionis in Weintraub et. al. (1994).

Further algorithmic development were carried out in order to obtain more exact solutions for problems difficult to solve using a commercial 0-1 LP code in a straightforward form. Several improved solutions techniques were developed:

Strengthening of the model:

a) Several logical, redundant constraints, were added to the model to strengthen the LP formulation, such as adding constraints that allow harvesting in a stand only if an accessing road is built (such constraints are redundant, given constraints, (3) and (6)).
b) Reducing capacities of roads in the formulation, to an estimated maximum flow that could go through them, which reduces the gap between the continuous and integer solutions.
c) Lifting, which adds superfluous but legitimate terms to the LHS of the constraints

Lagrangean relaxation: The plantations are composed of 15 separate areas. So, by relaxing the demand constraints, the problem separates areas into 15 individual, smaller problems, which are easier to solve. A subgradient approach was used to obtain a bound and a Lagrangean heuristic to obtain feasible solutions.

For the more difficult problems, using all these techniques provided a very significant improvement as shown in Table 2, where Gap measures the difference in % between the best feasible solution and bound obtained.

Problem		Original Formulation	Using Strengthening and Lagrangean relaxation	
	Gap %	CPU Time (s)	Gap %	CPU Time (s)
1	0,51	148	0,35	14
2	1,46	176	0,52	402
3	7,84	3600	0,95	102
4	5,80	3600	0,47	673
5	15,44	3600	1,17	3626

Table 2. Results for 5 problems of increasing difficulty to solve

References

Andalaft, N., Andalaft, P., Guignard, M., Magendzo, A., Wainer A. and Weintraub. A. (1997). A Problem of Forest Harvesting and Road Building. To be submitted for Publication.

Chevalier, P. (1995). *Boabab, Instructions Manual.* Dept. of Industrial Engineering. University of Chile.

Equi, L., Gallo, G., Marziale, S., Weintraub, A. (1996). A Combined Transportation and Scheduling Problem. *European Journal of Operations Research.* (accepted).

Epstein, R., Weintraub, A., Sapunar, P., Nieto, E., Sesions, J. and Sessions, B. (1995). PLANEX: A System for Optimal Assignment of Harvesting Machinery. *Annals of the LIRO Harvest Planning Conference.* Nelson, New Zealand.

Vera, J., Weintraub, A., Koenig, M., Bravo, G., Guignard, M. and Barahona, F. (1997). A Lagrangean Relaxation Approach for a Machinery Location Problem in Forest Harvesting. *Working Paper.* Dep. of Industrial Engineering, University of Chile.

Weintraub, A., Epstein, R., Morales, R., Serón, J., and Traverso, P. (1996). A Truck Scheduling System Improves efficiency in the Forest Industries. *Interfaces* **26**, 4, 1–12.

Weintraub, A., Jones, G., Magendzo,, A., Meacham, M.L. and Kirby, M.W. (1994) A Heuristic System to Solve Mixed-Integer Forest Planning Models. *Operations Research* **42**, 1010–1024.

Part II

Medical Decision Making

Automatic Diagnostic of Breast Cancer: A Case Study

F. Javier Girón[1], M. Lina Martínez[1] and Elías Moreno[2]

[1] Dept. de Estadística, Universidad de Málaga, Campus de Teatinos s/n, Málaga, SPAIN
[2] Dept. de Estadística, Universidad de Granada, Campus de Fuente Nueva s/n Granada, SPAIN

Abstract

The examination of mammograms along with some (historical) information on the patients lead physicians, in some informal way, to declare a patient as having or not breast cancer. This diagnostic is usually based on historical variables, such as age, familiar antecedents, etc. and other semiologic variables derived from the analysis of the mammogram. Most of these variables are usually of an ordinal nature.

We have developed an automated decision diagnostic system based on a logistic model which may help physicians improve the task of diagnosing patients.

Keywords. Gibbs sampling, importance sampling, Laplace approximation, logistic model, mammography, outliers, semiologic variables

1 Introduction

Radiologists get useful information about the possibility of a patient having breast cancer by considering some historiacal factors and by looking at the mammograms of the patients.

How this information is turned into a uselful diagnostic, either by declaring the patient as not having cancer or by performing a biopsy to the patient, depends on the experience and expertise of the radiologist.

With the purpose of helping radiologists improve their diagnosis, we developed a simple decision model, which can be described as follows.

First, as explained in section 2, the variables —obtained from the patient's records, as shown in Fig. 1— are mapped into an interval scale with the help of the medical experts. These transformed variables are then used, in section 3, in modelling a binary logistic model, which is estimated using Bayesian techniques such as Gibbs and importance sampling, and the Tierney-Kadane Laplace approximation.

NAME:
HISTORY Nº:
RADIOLOGIC RECORD Nº:
AGE: < 35 years / 35–50 years / 50–65 years / > 65 years

1. CLINIC HISTORY:
   - FAMILIAR ANTECEDENTS (BREAST CANCER): YES / NO
   - PREGNANCY: NO
     YES: < 35 years / > 35 years
   - PERSONAL HISTORY OF CANCER: NO
     YES: BREAST
     OTHER LOCATIONS

2. CLINIC BREAST EXPLORATION:
   - NEGATIVE
   - POSITIVE: SUSPICIOUS
     UNSUSPICIOUS

3. MAMMOGRAM / DIAGNOSTIC IMPRESSION:
   - POSITIVE
   - DOUBTFUL
   - NEGATIVE

3.A. NODULES:
   - NUMBER: SINGLE / MULTIPLE
   - SIZE: < 2 cm. / 2–5 cm. / > 5 cm.
   - MARGINS: CRISP / ILL DEFINED
   - DISTRIBUTION: SCATTERED / GENERALIZED
   - FORM: ROUNDED / LOBULATED / SPICULATED

3.B. ARCHITECTURAL CHANGES:
   - NO
   - YES: ASSOCIATED TO MASS
     NOT ASSOCIATED TO MASS

3.C. MICROCALCIFICATIONS: NO /YES
   - SIZE: < 1 mm. / > 1 mm.
   - CHARACTER: SCATTERED / MULTIPLE
   - DISTRIBUTION: GROUPED / UNGROUPED
   - FORM: IRREGULAR / REGULAR
   - LOCALIZATION: DUCTAL / NO DUCTAL
   - ASSOCIATED TO MASS: YES / NO

4. BIOPSY:
   - NEGATIVE
   - POSITIVE: (specify histopathological class)

Fig. 1.1. Patient's Record

In order to simplify the computation of the true predictive distribution, the appropriateness of the normal approximation to the posterior distribution of the parameters in the model, from which the predictive distribution is obtained, was checked up using Gibbs and importance sampling techniques as shown in section 3.

Outlier detection was carried out, as shown in section 4 using a simple scheme, and the sensitivity and specificity of the test based on this model was compared with the corresponding values of the informal test based on the examination of the mammogram, showing the advantage of the automated decision model.

The emphasis of the proposed model was in predicting the probability for a new patient of having or not cancer. The whole predictive distribution of this random quantity, along with some useful features of it (such as the reliability of the diagnostic), and the losses associated to the decision problem (elicited with the help of the medical experts), were used as inputs for building the automated decision model that has been implemented recently in the University Hospital of Granada to help physicians classify new patients. This is described in section 5.

2 Coding of variables

The result of the biopsy actually reveals whether a patient has or has not cancer, which is represented by a binary variable y.

$$y = \begin{cases} 1 & \text{if patient has cancer;} \\ 0 & \text{if patient has not cancer.} \end{cases}$$

It is supposed that this variable depends on the following historical variables, x_1, x_2, x'_3, x''_3, x_4, obtained from the patient record; and the semiological variables x_5, x_6, x_7, x_8,, e.i., obtained from the examination of the mammogram, respectively. These variables, which we describe below, were mapped into an interval scale, after an elicitation procedure based on the opinion of a group of expert radiologists, as follows. The higher values in every scale of any variable presume greater risk of having cancer. This was confirmed later, after the model was estimated, by the fact that all coefficients of these variables in the model were of the same sign (positive in our model). Following the suggestion of the radiologists, variables x'_3 and x''_3 were considered alongsise, and the pairs were coded as the new variable x_3.

2.1 Historical variables

$$x_1 : \textbf{Age Group} \begin{cases} \text{age} < 35 & \longrightarrow 0 \\ 35 < \text{age} < 50 & \longrightarrow 1 \\ 50 < \text{age} & \longrightarrow 2 \end{cases}$$

$$x_2 : \textbf{Familiar Antecedents} \begin{cases} \text{No antecedents of breast cancer} & 0 \\ \text{Antecedents of breast cancer} & 1 \end{cases}$$

$$x'_3 : \textbf{Maternity} \begin{cases} \text{No pregnancy} & 0 \\ \text{Pregnancy before 30} & 1 \\ \text{Pregnancy after 30} & 2 \end{cases}$$

$$x_3'' : \textbf{The breast gave milk?} \begin{cases} \text{No} & 0 \\ \text{Yes} & 1 \end{cases}$$

The joint pairs of (x_3', x_3'') are equated to the new variable x_3 which is coded as follows:

$$x_3 = (x_3', x_3'') = \begin{cases} (0,1) & \text{does not hold} \\ (1,1) & \longrightarrow 0 \\ (1,0) & \longrightarrow 1 \\ (2,1) & \longrightarrow 2 \\ (2,0) & \longrightarrow 3 \\ (0,0) & \longrightarrow 4 \end{cases}$$

$$x_4 : \textbf{Any sort of cancer before?} \begin{cases} \text{No} & 0 \\ \text{Yes} & 1 \end{cases}$$

2.2 Semiologic variables

$$x_5 : \textbf{Nodules} \begin{cases} \text{No nodules} & 0 \\ \text{Rounded nodules} & .5 \\ \text{Spiculated nodules} & 3 \\ \text{Ill defined nodules} & 2 \end{cases}$$

$$x_6 : \textbf{Microcalcifications} \begin{cases} \text{No microcalcifications} & 0 \\ \text{Ductal scattered microcalcifications} & .5 \\ \text{Ductal grouped microcalcifications} & 3 \\ \text{No ductal microcalcifications} & 2.2 \end{cases}$$

$$x_7 : \textbf{Architectural changes} \begin{cases} \text{No architectural changes} & 0 \\ \text{Changes associated to mass} & 2 \\ \text{Changes not associated to mass} & .7 \end{cases}$$

$$x_8 : \textbf{Is there assymetry?} \begin{cases} \text{No} & 0 \\ \text{Yes} & 1 \end{cases}$$

2.3 Description of the data set

The database D used to build up the model were obtained from 338 medical records of patients —consisting in the values of the original and encoded variables, plus the information provided by the result of the biopsy— 328 of which were complete, and 10 had some missing variables. These data were gathered from the Radiology Department of the *Clinic Hospital* in Granada. Once the model was operative, the database is updated periodically, when the results of new biopsies are available, and the new data is used to update the model and/or to crossvalidate the existing model.

3 The model

In this section we describe the Bayesian model used mainly with the purpose of making predictions about the possibility of future patients of having breast cancer, based on historical and semiological data obtained from mammography.

The data $\boldsymbol{D} = \{(y_1, \boldsymbol{x}_1), \ldots, (y_n, \boldsymbol{x}_n)\}$ is modelled by

$$\begin{aligned} y_i \,|\, p_i &\sim Ber(p_i), \\ p_i &= F(\boldsymbol{x}_i'\boldsymbol{\beta}), \\ &\pi(\boldsymbol{\beta}); \end{aligned} \tag{1}$$

where $F(.)$ is the link function, $\boldsymbol{\beta} = (\beta_0, \beta_1, \ldots, \beta_k)'$ is a $k+1$-dimensional vector of regressor coefficients, and $\pi(\boldsymbol{\beta})$ is the prior distribution.

For this particular application we used the logistic link

$$F(z) = \frac{1}{1+e^{-z}} \tag{2}$$

and a flat prior on $\boldsymbol{\beta}$, i.e., $\pi(\boldsymbol{\beta}) \propto$ constant.

Thus, the posterior distribution of $\boldsymbol{\beta} \,|\, \boldsymbol{D}$ is

$$\begin{aligned} \pi(\boldsymbol{\beta} \,|\, \boldsymbol{D}) &\propto \pi(\boldsymbol{\beta}) \prod_{i=1}^{n} F(\boldsymbol{x}_i'\boldsymbol{\beta})^{y_i}(1 - F(\boldsymbol{x}_i'\boldsymbol{\beta}))^{1-y_i} \\ &\propto \exp\left\{ \sum_{i=1}^{n} \left[y_i\boldsymbol{x}_i'\boldsymbol{\beta} - \log(1 + \exp(\boldsymbol{x}_i'\boldsymbol{\beta})) \right] \right\}. \end{aligned} \tag{3}$$

3.1 Sampling from the posterior

Sampling from this posterior is described in Dellaportas & Smith (1993) (based on Gibbs sampling, adaptive rejection algorithms and log-concavity of the likelihood function) and Albert & Chib (1993) (data augmentation and Gibbs sampling).

Instead, we obtained a simulated sample $\boldsymbol{S} = \{\boldsymbol{\beta}^{(g)}\}$, of size $G = 10000$, from the true posterior distribution of $\boldsymbol{\beta}$ based on the *Sampling Importance Resampling* SIR technique of Rubin (1987) and the well known rejection algorithm, see, e.g. Bernardo and Smith (1994).

As mentioned above, the emphasis was in computing, from $\boldsymbol{S}$, the whole predictive distribution of the probability of having cancer, for a new patient with regressors $\boldsymbol{x}_{n+1}$, i.e., the predictive distribution of the random quantity

$$p_{n+1} = P\{y_{n+1} = 1 \,|\, \boldsymbol{\beta}, \boldsymbol{x}_{n+1}\} = \frac{1}{1 + \exp\{-\boldsymbol{x}_{n+1}'\boldsymbol{\beta}\}}. \tag{4}$$

The SIR sample $\boldsymbol{S}$ of $\boldsymbol{\beta}$ induces a sample of p_{n+1}. From this sample, say $\{p_{n+1}^{(g)}\}$ several useful summary values of the predictive distribution, including the histogram and the mean, needed for probabilistic diagnosis, can easily be obtained. If other loss functions are considered for diagnostic purposes, the computation of the predictive risks associated to the possible diagnosis are straightforward (see section 5).

3.2 Normal approximations

Using the fact that, for large n, $\beta \mid \boldsymbol{D} \approx N_k(\beta \mid \tilde{\beta}_n, \tilde{\Sigma}_n)$, where $\tilde{\beta}_n$ is the maximum likelihood estimator of β and and $\tilde{\Sigma}_n$ its asymptotic variance, then the approximate posterior distribution of $z = \boldsymbol{x}'_{n+1}\beta$ given $\boldsymbol{D}$ is

$$z = \boldsymbol{x}'_{n+1}\beta \approx N(z \mid \boldsymbol{x}'_{n+1}\tilde{\beta}_n, \boldsymbol{x}'_{n+1}\tilde{\Sigma}_n\boldsymbol{x}_{n+1}), \tag{5}$$

and that of p_{n+1} follows, approximately, a univariate logistic-normal distribution (see, e.g., Aitchison and Shen (1980).) Therefore, denoting the logistic-normal distribution with parameters μ, σ^2 by $LN(\cdot \mid \mu, \sigma^2)$, we have

$$p_{n+1} \mid \boldsymbol{D} \approx LN(p_{n+1} \mid \boldsymbol{x}'_{n+1}\tilde{\beta}_n, \boldsymbol{x}'_{n+1}\tilde{\Sigma}_n\boldsymbol{x}_{n+1}). \tag{6}$$

Instead of considering the asymptotic normality based on maximum likelihood estimates, we contemplated, alternatively, the normal approximation based on the SIR estimates of the mean vector and covariance matrix, $\tilde{\beta}_n^{\mathrm{SIR}}$ and $\tilde{\Sigma}_n^{\mathrm{SIR}}$, respectively. From this, we obtain the following approximation

$$p_{n+1} \mid \boldsymbol{D} \approx LN(p_{n+1} \mid \boldsymbol{x}'_{n+1}\tilde{\beta}_n^{\mathrm{SIR}}, \boldsymbol{x}'_{n+1}\tilde{\Sigma}_n^{\mathrm{SIR}}\boldsymbol{x}_{n+1}). \tag{7}$$

The comparison of the two estimates of β shows that even for a sample size of $n = 328$ there are some differences.

$$\tilde{\beta}_n = (-3.594, 0.751, 0.366, 0.145, 2.000, 1.212, 0.734, 2.531, 1.578);$$
$$\tilde{\beta}_n^{\mathrm{SIR}} = (-3.746, 0.789, 0.378, 0.151, 2.235, 1.258, 0.767, 2.738, 1.625).$$

Note that all coefficients of the variables, excluding that of the constant term, are positive and those of the SIR estimate are uniformly larger that those of the maximum likelihood one. This means, in general, that SIR based estimates of the posterior probability of patients having cancer are greater than the corresponding ones based on maximum likelihood *for patients having large values of the regressors.* This implies that the specificity of the test based on the SIR estimates is higher than that of the same test based on maximum likelihood estimates, without impairing the sensitivity of the test. However, the sensitivity of both tests is roughly the same.

3.2.1 How good are the normal approximations?

As our emphasis is on prediction, not in estimating the model, a natural question arises: how close is the SIR histogram of $\{p_{n+1}^{(g)}\}$ to the corresponding logistic-normal approximations (6) and (7) for a new patient?

For purposes of both probabilistic and decision-based diagnosis both approximations performed rouhgly equally well, very close to the exact results obtained from SIR sampling, as described in section 5; though, obviously, approximation (7) performed better than (6) for patients having very low or high probabilities of having cancer. For patients with probabilities of having cancer close to .5, both approximations were practically indistinguishable. However, when trying to determine the sensitivity and specificity, the test based on the posterior mode of the jackknifed distribution outperformed other tests (see subsection 4.2).

3.3 The Laplace approximation

A simple way of computing $E(p_{n+1} \mid \boldsymbol{D})$ approximately is based in the Laplace approximation. Thus, using the results of Tierney and Kadane (1986) and Kass, Tierney, and Kadane (1988), we obtain

$$E(p_{n+1} \mid \boldsymbol{D}) \approx \frac{|\tilde{\Sigma}_{n+1}|^{1/2}}{|\tilde{\Sigma}_n|^{1/2}} \exp\{\ell(\tilde{\boldsymbol{\beta}}_{n+1}; \boldsymbol{D}_{n+1}) - \ell(\tilde{\boldsymbol{\beta}}_n; \boldsymbol{D})\}; \tag{8}$$

where $\boldsymbol{D}_{n+1} = \boldsymbol{D} \cup (1, \boldsymbol{x}_{n+1})$, ℓ denotes the likelihood function and $\tilde{\boldsymbol{\beta}}_{n+1}$, $\tilde{\Sigma}_{n+1}$ denote the maximum likelihood estimator of $\boldsymbol{\beta}$ and its asymptotic variance for the augmented data $\boldsymbol{D}_{n+1}$, respectively. The computation of this estimators can be, in turn, simplified using the following approximate recursive formulae, also based on the asymptotic normality of the posterior distribution (see, Girón, Martínez and Moreno (1997)).

3.3.1 Approximate Recursive Estimation

$$\begin{aligned} \tilde{\boldsymbol{\beta}}_{n+1} &= \tilde{\boldsymbol{\beta}}_n + (y_{n+1} - \tilde{p}_{n+1})\boldsymbol{g}_{n+1}, \\ \tilde{\Sigma}_{n+1} &= \tilde{\Sigma}_n - \tilde{p}_{n+1}(1 - \tilde{p}_{n+1})\boldsymbol{g}_{n+1}\boldsymbol{x}'_{n+1}\tilde{\Sigma}_n; \end{aligned} \tag{9a}$$

where

$$\begin{aligned} \tilde{p}_{n+1} &= \frac{1}{1 + \exp\{-\boldsymbol{x}'_{n+1}\tilde{\boldsymbol{\beta}}_n\}}; \\ \boldsymbol{g}_{n+1} &= \frac{\tilde{\Sigma}_n \boldsymbol{x}_{n+1}}{1 + \tilde{p}_{n+1}(1 - \tilde{p}_{n+1})\boldsymbol{x}'_{n+1}\tilde{\Sigma}_n \boldsymbol{x}_{n+1}}. \end{aligned} \tag{9b}$$

This approximation also holds good for the SIR estimates.

4 Validation of the model

4.1 Outliers in the model

The analysis of outliers and influence measures in binary regression from a Bayesian perspective is a relatively new field. Albert and Chib (1993, 1995) propose the computation of the posterior distribution of the ordinary residuals given $\boldsymbol{D}$,

$$r_i = y_i - p_i = y_i - F(\boldsymbol{\beta}'\boldsymbol{x}_i), \tag{10}$$

from the simulated sample (The SIR $\boldsymbol{S}$ sample, in our case) and plotting it against the fitted probabilities $E(p_i \mid \boldsymbol{D})$.

The problem with this approach is that we are conditioning the i-th residual r_i on the whole data $\boldsymbol{D}$ not on the jackknifed data $\boldsymbol{D}_{(i)} = \boldsymbol{D} \setminus (y_i, \boldsymbol{x}_i)$. This problem is unimportant if the sample size is large, but for small data sets there can be substantial differences, specially if observation i is influential or an outlier.

Based on the asymptotic normality of $\boldsymbol{\beta} \,|\, \boldsymbol{D}$, the "false posterior"distribution of the residuals can be approximated by

$$\begin{aligned} r_i \,|\, \boldsymbol{D} &\approx LN(.\,|\, -\tilde{m}_i, \tilde{v}_i) \quad \text{if} \quad y_i = 1, \\ -r_i \,|\, \boldsymbol{D} &\approx LN(.\,|\, \tilde{m}_i, \tilde{v}_i) \quad \text{if} \quad y_i = 0; \end{aligned} \tag{11}$$

where

$$\begin{aligned} \tilde{m}_i &= \boldsymbol{x}_i' \tilde{\boldsymbol{\beta}}_n, \\ \tilde{v}_i &= \boldsymbol{x}_i' \tilde{\Sigma}_n \boldsymbol{x}_i; \end{aligned} \qquad \text{or} \qquad \begin{aligned} \tilde{m}_i &= \boldsymbol{x}_i' \tilde{\boldsymbol{\beta}}_n^{\text{SIR}}, \\ \tilde{v}_i &= \boldsymbol{x}_i' \tilde{\Sigma}_n^{\text{SIR}} \boldsymbol{x}_i; \end{aligned} \tag{12}$$

depending on whether the normal approximation is based either on the maximum likelihood estimates or the importance sample ones, respectively.

We, instead, used the simpler approach of Girón, Martínez y Morcillo (1992), based on the computation of a highest posterior set of probabilistic content $1-\alpha$, $C_i(1-\alpha)$, of the jackknifed predictive distribution of the dicotomous variable y_i given $\boldsymbol{D}_{(i)} = \boldsymbol{D} \setminus (y_i, \boldsymbol{x}_i)$.

As H.P.D.'s can only be of the form $\{0\}$, $\{1\}$ or $\{0,1\}$, the rule for deciding if an observation is one outlier is the following:

If $C_i(1-\alpha) = \{1-y_i\}$, observation i is an outlier at the specified probabilistic level $1-\alpha$, which is equivalent to the following simple rule:

Observation i is an outlier if

$$y_i = 0 \quad \text{and} \quad E(p_i \,|\, \boldsymbol{D}_{(i)}) > 1 - \alpha,$$

or (13)

$$y_i = 1 \quad \text{and} \quad E(p_i \,|\, \boldsymbol{D}_{(i)}) < \alpha.$$

This approach implies the computation of the expectation of the predictive of p_i given $\boldsymbol{D}_{(i)}$, $E(p_i \,|\, \boldsymbol{D}_{(i)})$, which can be carried out by either using a sample $\boldsymbol{S}_{(i)}$ of the posterior of $\boldsymbol{\beta} \,|\, \boldsymbol{D}_{(i)}$ —this sample can be easily and efficiently generated from the sample $\boldsymbol{S}$ by adaptive rejection algorithms— or by using the normal approximation and the recursive estimation procedure discussed above. It can be shown that

$$p_i \,|\, \boldsymbol{D}_{(i)} \approx LN(p_i \,|\, \tilde{\mu}_{(i)}, \tilde{\sigma}^2_{(i)}), \tag{14}$$

where if

$$\tilde{\pi}_i = \frac{1}{1 + e^{-\tilde{m}_i}}, \tag{15a}$$

then,

$$\begin{aligned} \tilde{\mu}_{(i)} &= \tilde{m}_i - (y_i - \tilde{\pi}_i)\tilde{v}_i; \\ \tilde{\sigma}^2_{(i)} &= \frac{\tilde{v}_i}{1 - \tilde{\pi}_i(1 - \tilde{\pi}_i)\tilde{v}_i}. \end{aligned} \tag{15b}$$

Using this approach, and setting $1-\alpha = .95$ we detected two extreme outliers; namely, patient 145 which had no cancer, yet $E(p_{145} \,|\, \boldsymbol{D}_{(145)}) \approx .995$ and patient 75 which had no cancer, yet $E(p_{75} \,|\, \boldsymbol{D}_{(75)}) \approx .975$.

The above approach to outliers can be extended easily to the detection of multiple outliers and will be described somewhere, Girón, Martínez and Moreno (1997).

4.2 Sensitivity and specificity of the test

As a measure of the performance of the logistic model we used the quantity $E(p_i \mid D_{(i)})$ for probabilistic classification of the i-th patient in the database D, which can be easily computed as described in subsection 4.1.

This allows for the estimation of the *sensitivity* $s(p)$ and *specificity* $\sigma(p)$ of the test based on a *cut off* value of p—generally set to $p = .5$ for probabilistic classification, and some other value based on a decision criteria that takes into account utilities or losses associated to wrong decisions.

The Bayesian estimates (using a non-informative prior) of the sensitivity and specificity of the test for $p = .5$ were $s(.5) = .743$ and $\sigma(.5) = .741$, respectively.

The radiologists suggested increasing the sensitivity by setting p to a higher value $p = K/(K+1)$ for values of $1 \leq K \leq 3$, where K represents or measures the relative importance of the sensitivity versus specificity. But this dramaticaly decreases the specificity. Thus, for example, with $K = 3$ the values of the sensitivity and specificity for $p = .75$ are .949 and .321, respectively. To circumvent this problem, we suggested to introduce a new category in the diagnosis of new patients, apart from the diagnosis of *having cancer* and *not having cancer*; namely, that of being classified as *doubtful*, based on the formulation of a loss function associated to the new problem. This is discussed, with some detail, in section 5.

4.3 Sensitivity analysis on the coding

The coding of all the variables in the model, but the dicotomous ones, was assesed subjectively by the team of radiologists, based on their previous experience on the influence of the variables upon the desease. Nevertheless, we raised the following question: Is there any recoding of the variables that might improve sensitivity and/or specificity?

To answer this question we performed several single and joint monotonic transformations on the variables so as to study the sensitivity of the test to these transformations. The results, though not conclusive, were that the diagnostic ability of the test was not too sensitive to reasonable departures from the actual coding.

5 Model Implementation

Probabilistic classification has its drawbacks as it ignores other characteristics of the predictive distribution but the mean. It also ignores other possible diagnostics on the patient (the possibility of a close follow up) and the losses associated to this diagnostics.

The automated procedure for diagnosis that we have developed, and has been recently implemented in the *Clinic Hospital* in Granada, provides —among other facilities discussed below— a plot of the approximate predictive density of having cancer for any future patient, along with some useful summaries that may help radiologists improve their diagnosis.

The appropiateness of the logistic-normal approximation to the predictive distribution can be gathered from the plots in Figures 5.1 and 5.2, —which also show the histograms of the *true* predictive distribution obtained from the SIR sample— and from the values of the quantities of interest for probabilistic diagnosis shown in Tables 5.1 and 5.2.

For illustrative purposes we show the way the procedure works for two potential patients having the same values of the regressors as patients 2 and 32 in the database. Note that there is not a great difference among the different estimates —exact and based on the normal approximation— and, as expected, the Laplace approximation is practically equal to the predictive mean.

- Maximum likelihood estimation: 0.824
- SIR mean estimation: 0.829
- Probabilistic diagnosis: Cancer
- Probability that the diagnosis be correct: 1.000

Normal approximation

- Mean: 0.820
- Laplace approximation: 0.820
- Mode: 0.833

Table 5.1. Summary of the true and approximate predictive distribution of the probability for patient 2 of having cancer

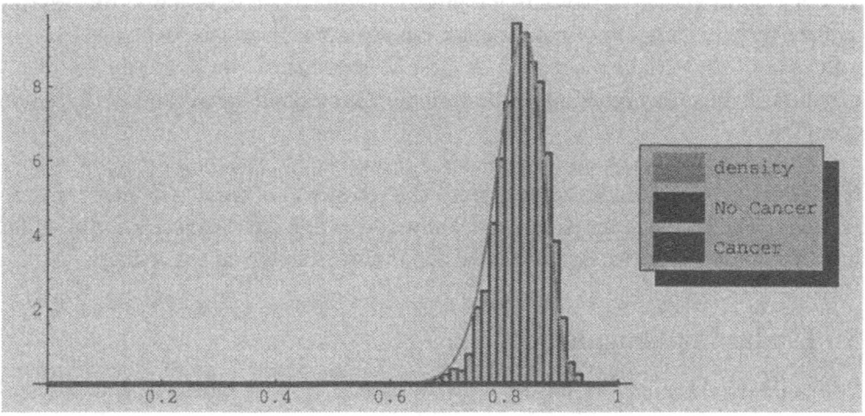

Fig. 5.1. Predictive distribution of the probability for patient 2 of having cancer

As expected from looking up at Table 5.1 and Figure 5.1, the probabilistic diagnostic of patient 2 is *patient 2 has cancer*, and in fact patient 2 had cancer. However, even though the the probabilistic diagnostic of patient 32 is *patient 32 has cancer*, the confidence in that the diagnostic should be correct is only 0.836, a high value but not a conclusive evidence. In fact, patient 32 had no cancer.

In order to minimize the number of missclassified patients (false positives + false negatives) —80 from a total of 328, using probabilistic diagnosis with a cut off

- Maximum likelihood estimation: 0.595
- SIR mean estimation: 0.593
- Probabilistic diagnosis: Cancer
- Probability that the diagnosis be correct: 0.836

Normal approximation

- Mean: 0.592
- Laplace approximation: 0.591
- Mode: 0.602

Table 5.2. Summary of the true and approximate predictive distribution of the probability for patient 32 of having cancer

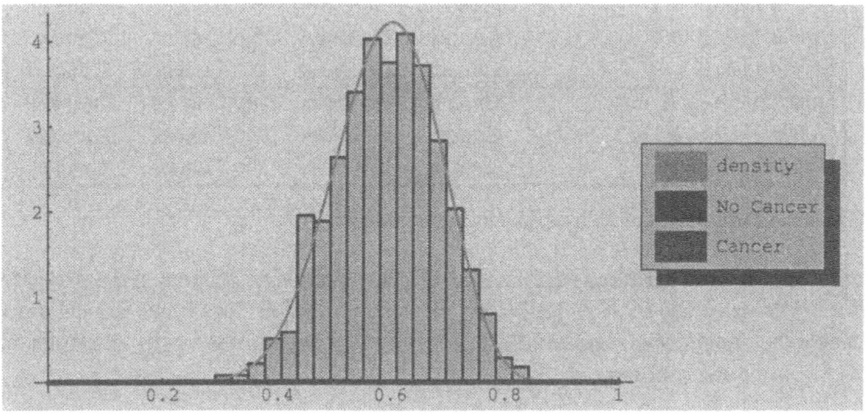

Fig. 5.2. Predictive distribution of the probability for patient 32 of having cancer

value of $p = .5$— we added, apart from declaring a patient as having or not cancer, a new diagnostic possibility; namely, that of a patient being declared as *doubtful*, by treating the diagnosis as a decision problem with losses involved. In the case a patient is declared *doubtful* he is subjected to a closer follow up than patients being diagnosed as not having cancer. Patients diagnosed as having cancert are directly sent for biopsy. The computer program provides the predictive risks of the three possible actions (diagnosis) and chooses the diagnosis that minimize the risk. In the case the patient is declared doubtful, how close the follow up of the patient should be depends on these values.

With this possibility in mind, and from a decision viewpoint, we introduced the following *piecewise linear* L^1 and *piecewise quadratic* L^2 loss functions with action space $\mathcal{A} = \{c, nc, d\}$, where c, nc and d stands for cancer, no cancer and doubtful, respectively, and parametric space $p \in (0, 1) = \Omega$, the unknown probability of having cancer. Note that the loss functions depend on the constant K which is chosen by the radiologist as described in subsection 4.2.

$$L_c^1(p) = 1 - p \qquad L_c^2(p) = (1-p)^2$$
$$L_{nc}^1(p) = Kp \qquad L_{nc}^2(p) = Kp^2$$
$$L_d^1(p) = \begin{cases} 2(1/2 - p) & \text{if } p \leq 1/2 \\ 2K(p - 1/2) & \text{if } p \geq 1/2 \end{cases} \qquad L_d^2(p) = \begin{cases} 4(1/2 - p)^2 & \text{if } p \leq 1/2 \\ 4K(p - 1/2)^2 & \text{if } p \geq 1/2 \end{cases}$$

Table 5.3 shows the results obtained from applying this procedure to patients 2, 3, 23 and 32 of the database, for several values of the constant K.

Patient	2	3	23	32
True status	Cancer	Cancer	No Cancer	No Cancer
Probabilistic Classification	Cancer	No Cancer	No Cancer	Cancer
Linear loss $K = 1$	Cancer	Doubtful	No Cancer	Doubtful
Linear loss $K = 2$	Cancer	Doubtful	No Cancer	Cancer
Linear loss $K = 3$	Cancer	Doubtful	No Cancer	Cancer
Quadratic loss $K = 1$	Cancer	Doubtful	No Cancer	Doubtful
Quadratic loss $K = 2$	Cancer	Doubtful	No Cancer	Doubtful
Quadratic loss $K = 3$	Cancer	Doubtful	No Cancer	Cancer

Table 5.3 Comparison of various diagnostic procedures

After testing both loss functions to the classification of patients in the database, for different values of $K \in [2, 3]$, the *piecewise linear* L^1 loss function performed worse that the *piecewise quadratic* L^2 loss function, which was finally implemented in the computer program.

6 Discussion

The implementation of a computer program based on the model discussed above serves the purpose of aiding physicians, usually radiologists, to make decision on the possibility for new patients of having developed breast cancer. The program is not intended as a substitute to medical skills, independent of the doctors (see, e.g. the final comments in the paper by de Dombal, Clamp and Chan (1997)), but as a decision support system which aims at improving breast cancer diagnostic.

The computer program also serves as a mean to construct a permanent database of patients in the hospital, which is updated upon arrival of new patients, so that the model can be validated or changed dynamically.

Acknowledgments

This paper has been partially supported by the *Dirección General de Investigación Científica y Técnica* (DGICYT) as part of the project PB93-1154 and by *La Consejería de Educación de la Junta de Andalucía* as part of one *Marroquí-Andaluz* project.

References

Aitchison, J. and Shen, S. M. (1980). Logistic-normal distributions: some properties and uses. *Biometrika* **67**, 261–272.

Albert, J. and Chib, S. (1993). Bayesian analysis of binary and polychotomous response data. *J. Amer. Statist. Assoc.* **88**, 669–679.

Albert, J. and Chib, S. (1995). Bayesian residual analysis for binary response regression models. *Biometrika* **82**, 747–759.

Bernardo, J. M. and Smith, A. F. M. (1994). *Bayesian Theory*. John Wiley and Sons: Chichester.

Dellaportas, P. and Smith, A. F. M. (1993). Bayesian inference for generalized linear and proportional hazards models via Gibbs sampling. *Appl. Statist.* **42**, 443–459.

de Dombal, F. T., Clamp, S. E. and Chan, M. (1997). Bayes' theorem and decision support in 'Front Line'clinical medicine. In *The Practice of Bayesian Analysis*. (S. Frech and J. Q. Smith, eds.), 55–70. Arnold: London.

Gir6n, F. J., Martínez, M. L. and Morcillo, C. (1992). A Bayesian justification to the analysis of residuals and influence measures. In *Bayesian Statistics* **4**. (J. M. Bernardo, A. P. Dawid, D. V. Lindley and A. F. M. Smith, eds.), 651–660. Oxford University Press: Oxford.

Gir6n, F. J., Martínez, M. L. and Moreno, E. (1997). Approximate recursive estimation in binary regression models with applications to the detection of outliers. *Unpublished Tech. Rep.*. U. de Málaga.

Kass, R. E., Tierney, L. and Kadane, J. B. (1988). Asymptotics in Bayesian computation. In *Bayesian Statistics* **3**. (J. M. Bernardo, M. H. DeGroot, D. V. Lindley and A. F. M. Smith, eds.), 261–278. Oxford University Press: Oxford.

Rubin, D. B. (1987). The SIR algorithm. A discussion of Tanner and Wong's: The calculation of posterior distributions by data augmentation. *J. Amer. Statist. Assoc.* **82**, 543–546.

Tierney, L. and Kadane, J. B. (1986). Accurate approximations for posterior moments and marginal densities. *J. Amer. Statist. Assoc.* **81**, 82–86.

Decision Analysis for a Data Monitoring Committee of a Clinical Trial

Joseph B. Kadane[1], Pantelis Vlachos[1] and Samuel Wieand[2]

[1] Department of Statistics, Carnegie-Mellon University, Pittsburgh, Pennsylvania 15213-3890, USA
[2] National Surgical Adjuvant Breast and Bowel Program, University of Pittsburgh, USA

Abstract

A data monitoring committee holds a position of great trust within the structure of a US clinical trial, as it alone receives the accumulating data and decides whether to continue the trial. The committee generally meets at regularly scheduled intervals, e.g. six months. Recent advances in computation allow us to find optimal group-sequential strategies for each member of such a committee. This paper reviews how we plan to use the newly available computational ability to advise members of a data monitoring committee.

Keywords. backwards induction; elicitation; forward algorithm; group-sequential methods; hybrid algorithm

> "In theory there is no difference between theory and practice; in practice, there is."
>
> Chuck Reid
> `www.starling.tech.com/quotes`

1 Introduction

Work on applied problems is important to decision analysis for several reasons. First, applications are an opportunity to make a contribution to society by improving the quality of the decisions made. Second, working on applied problems, one can learn a lot about parts of the theoretical structure that require more thought. For these benefits to be realized, it is critical to work with people who have real decisions to make, and who care about the quality of those decisions.

This paper explores a decision analysis application about to be launched, studying the decisions of a Data Monitoring Committee (DMC) in a clinical trial. The context is adjuvant therapy (i.e. chemotherapy and radiation) in addition to surgery for breast (and bowel) cancer. Section 2 gives the background of the decision problem; Section 3 shows how we plan to conduct the necessary elicitations. In Section 4 we review recent progress in computing optimal group-sequential strategies, and Section 5 gives our conclusions.

2 Background

For most adjuvant trials, the decisions regarding early stopping of clinical trial derive from two factors; in most studies the experimental regimen(s) has the potential for more toxic side-effects than the standard regimen, but also is believed to have some potential for extending survival and possibly curing a new subset of patients. However, in many instances, the new regimen ultimately offers no therapeutic advantage.

There are three instances when stopping a trial may be beneficial.

- The experimental regimen has so much toxicity that it is deemed unethical to continue, e.g. several patients die from the therapy or have debilitating strokes.
- There is sufficient evidence that the experimental regimen is not offering a benefit to warrant release of the results.
- There is such strong evidence of benefit for a new regimen that it seems unethical to continue assigning patients to the standard regimen (on or off-study).

Determining whether to stop a trial in the first instance may be the most straightforward case, particularly in the adjuvant setting. Since a large subset of patients on adjuvant trials will survive for many years when receiving the standard regimen, an experimental regimen which is causing death in several patients will almost always be discontinued.

The situation is more complicated in the second and third instance. One factor influencing a decision is whether patients on the trial are still receiving therapy. Another is that once a trial is terminated, it is very difficult to start a new trial addressing the same question. Investigators who have a strong opinion regarding the efficacy of a regimen may not be willing to change therapies if they feel a trial was stopped too soon to provide definitive data. In addition, if a trial is stopped "too early", a few events among patients still on the study may be sufficient to make the results more equivocal than it appeared at the time the trial was stopped.

The DMC meets on a regularly scheduled basis, and decides by majority vote at each meeting whether to continue or to stop each trial. The physicians seeing patients are blinded to the accumulating data, and rely on the judgment of the DMC. We are working with the DMC of the National Surgical Adjuvant Breast and Bowel Program (NSABP), which monitors 20-30% of all breast cancer trial patients in the US. The DMC, which meets every six months, has agreed to let us do elicitation of their probabilities and utilities, and to observe their meetings.

3 Elicitation

There are standard steps to take in elicitation:

- identify the available decisions
- identify the sources of uncertainty
- as a function of both decision and sources of uncertainty, identify a loss (or utility) function
- conduct probability elicitation, for both the prior distribution and the likelihood

The identification of the available decisions is simple: at every meeting except the last, the DMC may stop and recommend treatment 1, stop and recommend treatment 2, or continue. At the last meeting, to continue is not an option.

The sources of uncertainty must include something about how toxic the treatments are, and something about how effective they are. To the extent feasible, we would look for standard ways to express these, such as five-year survival rates, and standard scales of toxicity.

Utility elicitation asks the question: as a function of recommending each treatment, given the toxicities and effectivenesses of both the treatments, how pleased or sorry would you be? The expected utility of continuing is derived from the other utilities and the posterior probabilities at each stage. There is no obviously correct way to tradeoff between toxicity and effectiveness, and members of the DMC may reasonably differ in their views about this. Our plan is to use the Keeney and Raiffa (1976,1983) methods of multi-attribute utility elicitation as a starting point.

Probability elicitation needs to be used to discover both a likelihood and a prior distribution for the resulting parameters for each member of the DMC. We would want to use predictive methods to avoid heavy reliance on DMC members' understanding of the parameterization of the model. It may well be necessary to restrict the class of priors considered, but the class needs to be wide enough to encompass a reasonable representation of each member's views. The recent *RSS* meeting on elicitation (Kadane and Wolfson (1998), O'Hagan (1998), Craig, et al. (1998)) gives a good overview of current methods.

4 Computational Methods

The computation of optimal group-sequential strategies has gone through several phases; recent progress makes us confident of our ability to do the needed computations for this project.

As an illustration consider the following clinical trial setting. Suppose the DMC is interested in estimating the effect θ of a new treatment. Each DMC member, prior to the conduct of the trial, summarizes the available information on θ in a form of a prior distribution $\pi(\theta)$. Such information may rely on clinical experience, basic biology or other clinical trials. K prespecified meeting dates are set to discuss the trial's progress and make decisions regarding the future of the trial. At each of the prespecified meetings, k, the cost of observing a new group of patient responses is C_k. The new treatment is considered superior to the standard (or placebo) when

$\theta < c_2$, while it is considered inferior when $\theta > c_1$, for $c_1 \geq 0$ and $c_2 < 0$. When $c_2 < \theta < c_1$ both of the treatments are acceptable. Hence the decisions available to the DMC, at any monitoring stage, are:

d_1 : stop and decide in favor of the new therapy

or

d_2 : stop and decide in favor of the standard therapy

or

d_3 : continue and decide after y_{k+1} is available for observation

At the final monitoring stage (K) the DMC has to choose between d_1 and d_2. Following Carlin et al. (1996), at any stage, the decision space might suggest the use of loss functions of the following form for true values of the treatment effect θ:

$$l_1^{(K)}(d_1, \theta) = s_1^{(K)}(\theta - c_1) \quad \text{and} \quad l_2^{(K)}(d_2, \theta) = s_2^{(K)}(c_2 - \theta) \tag{1.1}$$

for $s_1^{(K)}, s_2^{(K)} > 0$. After the final group of patient responses have been observed, the DMC can either choose decision d_1, which yields a posterior expected loss (PEL)

$$L_1^{(K)} \equiv E[l_1^{(K)}(d_1, \theta)]$$

or choose d_2 with PEL

$$L_2^{(K)} \equiv E[l_2^{(K)}(d_2, \theta)].$$

Going backwards, at stage $K-1$, the DMC can either choose d_1 with PEL $L_1^{(K-1)}$, choose d_2 with $L_2^{(K-1)}$ or choose d_3(continue the trial) with PEL

$$L_3^{(K)} = E_{y_K|y_{K-1}} \min\{L_1^{(K)}, L_2^{(K)}\} + C_K.$$

The traditional method of doing such computations relies on backwards induction (see DeGroot (1970).) Here the idea is to study first the last decision to be made, after all the data that might be collected have been collected. For each data set (or, in special cases for each value of the sufficient statistics), there is an optimal final decision to make (which treatment to recommend), and a resulting expected utility. Here the expectation is with respect to the decision-maker's posterior distribution on the parameters.

The next-to-last decision is analyzed next. For each data set that might be available at this point (or, again, each value of sufficient statistics) there are three decisions that might be taken: to stop and decide on treatment 1, to stop and decide on treatment 2, or to continue. The expected utility of continuing can be assessed (one must include the cost of sampling until the last decision point). Similarly, the expected utility of each terminal decision can be assessed, and hence the optimal decision and its expected utility can be found. In principle, this process can be continued, backwards in time, to the first decision to be made. This method is implemented Vlachos and Gelfand (1996) in a categorical data setting who find that beyond 3 decision points, it becomes computationally infeasible due to the bookkeeping required by backwards induction.

A second method of computation, called a forward algorithm, works as follows: Approximate the expected utility of a sequential strategy by sampling from the prior, sampling from the likelihood a "complete" data set that includes all the data that would be available if the trial is allowed to proceed to completion, applying the sequential strategy to the data set, and recording the consequent obtained utility. By repeatedly sampling, and averaging the sampled values, an arbitrarily good approximation to expected utility can be achieved. By varying the sequential strategy, an optimum, or very good strategy can be found (the same sample of parameters and data can be reused). Carlin et al. (1996) use this method to compute optimal group-sequential strategies. They find that they can handle more than three decision times, but the expected utility surface is quite flat as a function of early decisions, making optimization problematic. Using the notation introduced previously in this section and for group sequential settings where the optimal sequential rule is of the form

- choose d_1 if $E(\theta|y_1, \ldots, y_k) \leq \gamma_{k,L}$,
- choose d_2 if $E(\theta|y_1, \ldots, y_k) > \gamma_{k,U}$,
- choose d_3 if $\gamma_{k,L} < E(\theta|y_1, \ldots, y_k) \leq \gamma_{k,U}$,

the decision rules can be represented in a $2K + 1$ dimensional vector

$$\gamma = (\gamma_{0,L}, \gamma_{0,U}, \gamma_{1,L}, , \gamma_{1,U}, \cdots, \gamma_{K-1,L}, \gamma_{K-1,U}, \gamma_K)'.$$

For the simple case of $K = 2$ we end up with the 5-dimensional vector

$$\gamma = (\gamma_{0,L}, \gamma_{0,U}, \gamma_{1,L}, \gamma_{1,U}, \gamma_2)'.$$

Drawing, via the compositional method, an independent sample $\theta_j^*, y_{1,j}^*, y_{2,j}^*$, $j = 1, \ldots, G$ from the joint density of θ, y_1 and y_2 the loss incurred under the current rule $\gamma^{(i)}$ will be $\bar{L} = G^{-1} \sum_{j=1}^{G} L_j$ where the L_j are obtained as follows:

$$\begin{array}{rl}
\text{If } E(\theta) \leq \gamma_{0,L}^{(i)}, & L_j = s_1^{(0)}(\theta_j^* - c_1) \\
\text{else if } E(\theta) > \gamma_{0,U}^{(i)}, & L_j = s_2^{(0)}(c_2 - \theta_j^*) \\
\text{else if } E(\theta|y_{1,j}^*) \leq \gamma_{1,L}^{(i)}, & L_j = s_1^{(1)}(\theta_j^* - c_1) + C_1 \\
\text{else if } E(\theta|y_{1,j}^*) > \gamma_{1,U}^{(i)}, & L_j = s_2^{(1)}(c_2 - \theta_j^*) + C_1 \\
\text{else if } E(\theta|y_{1,j}^*, y_{2,j}^*) \leq \gamma_{2,L}^{(i)}, & L_j = s_1^{(2)}(\theta_j^* - c_1) + C_1 + C_2 \\
\text{else,} & L_j = s_2^{(2)}(c_2 - \theta_j^*) + C_1 + C_2
\end{array}$$

If $\gamma^{(i)}$ does not yield the minimum value for $\bar{L}$ then it is adjusted to $\gamma^{(i+1)}$ and the process is repeated until convergence.

More recently a third, hybrid, method has been explored. The hybrid algorithm works backwards as far as is feasible, deriving the expected utility of the optimal continuation as a callable function. It then proceeds as a forward algorithm from the start of the trial to where the backwards algorithm takes over. Consider a $K = 3$ stage scenario where the optimal rules are indexed by the 7-dimensional vector

$$\gamma = (\gamma_{0,L}, \gamma_{0,U}, \gamma_{1,L}, \gamma_{1,U}, \gamma_{2,L}, \gamma_{2,U}, \gamma_3)'.$$

At any iteration i, for fixed values of $\gamma_{0,L}^{(i)}, \gamma_{0,U}^{(i)}$ the 2 stage backward induction can be used to calculate estimates of $\gamma_{1,L}, \gamma_{1,U}, \gamma_{2,L}, \gamma_{2,U}$ and γ_3 as well as the expected loss $\hat{L}_{(0)}$ of the procedure. The loss incurred under $\gamma^{(i)}$ can be computed as follows:

$$\begin{aligned} \text{If } E(\theta) \leq \gamma_{0,L}^{(i)} \quad & L_j = s_1^{(0)}(\theta_j^* - c_1) \\ \text{else if } E(\theta) > \gamma_{0,U}^{(i)}, \quad & L_j = s_2^{(0)}(c_2 - \theta_j^*) \\ \text{else} \quad & L_j = \hat{L}_{(0)} \end{aligned}$$

Then $\bar{L} = G^{-1} \sum_{j=1}^{G} L_j$ will be a Monte Carlo estimate of the posterior expected loss under $\gamma^{(i)}$. If the current estimate is not the minimum value then it is adjusted to $\gamma^{(i+1)}$ and the process is repeated until convergence. Note here that the forward part of the algorithm no longer requires a minimization over a $2K + 1 = 7$ dimensional space but over a 2-dimensional one. Thus the algorithm reduces the space, and hence the difficulty, of the optimization confronted by the forwards algorithm, but retains its ability to compute group sequential strategies of length greater than three. Kadane and Vlachos (1997) explore this algorithm, and find that it retains the strengths, and compensates for the weaknesses, of the other two.

5 Critique, Further Work and Conclusions

One source of uncertainty about these ideas is the extent to which the elicitations will prove feasible. Only performing them will answer that question. A second source of uncertainty is about whether the computations of optimal group-sequential strategies will go well. The examples used in Vlachos and Gelfand (1996), Carlin et al. (1996) and Kadane and Vlachos (1997) all rely on sufficient statistics to reduce the space of sequential strategies that must be considered. Outside the exponential family, however, the computations will be more difficult. Nonetheless, very good strategies (nearly, but not exactly optimal) can be found using the forwards algorithm on a reduced, but reasonable, set of possible sequential strategies.

The largest gap we see in our reasoning is that optimal group-sequential strategies do not necessarily determine optimal votes, since the former assumes (contrary to fact) that the DMC member whose strategy is being calculated controls when to stop. It will require further algorithmic design to calculate optimal votes, as opposed to optimal sequential strategies. Nonetheless, it is reasonable to hope and expect that the optimal sequential strategies will, in general, indicate optimal votes.

In any study plan, there are many gaps that can only be filled by doing the project. We are eager to do so.

References

Carlin, B. P., Kadane, J. B. and Gelfand, A. E. (1996). Approaches for optimal sequential decision analysis in clinical trials. *Tech. Rep.*. Department of Biostatistics, University of Minnesota.

Craig, P. S., Goldstein, M., Seheult, A. H. and Smith, J. A. (1998). Constructing partial prior specifications for models of complex systems. *The Statistician*. To appear with discussion.

DeGroot, M. H. (1970). *Optimal Statistical Decisions*. MacGraw Hill: New York.

Kadane, J. B. and Vlachos, P. (1997). Hybrid methods for calculating optimal sequential strategies: data monitoring for a clinical trial.

Kadane, J. B. and Wolfson, L. (1998). Experiences in elicitation. *The Statistician*. To appear with discussion.

Keeney, R. L. and Raiffa, H. (1976, 1983). *Decisions with Multiple Objectives: Preferences and Value Tradeoffs*. Cambridge University Press: Cambridge. 1976 printing by J.Wiley & Sons, NY.

O'Hagan, A. (1998). Eliciting expert beliefs in substantial practical applications. *The Statistician*. To appear with discussion.

Vlachos, P. K. and Gelfand, A. E. (1996). Bayesian decision theoretic design for group sequential clinical trials having multivariate patient response. *Tech. Rep.*. Department of Statistics, University of Connecticut.

Optimal Design in Longitudinal Data Models

Peter Müller[1] and J. Lynn Palmer[2]

[1] Institute of Statistics and Decision Sciences, Duke University, Durham NC 27708-0251, USA
[2] Department of Biomathematics, The University of Texas M.D. Anderson Cancer Center, Houston, TX 77030, USA

Abstract

We discuss expected utility optimization in the context of population models. This class of models covers a variety of important models, including pharmacokinetic/pharmacodynamic models, growth curve models, and repeated measurement models. The discussion will be focused on a specific application. We consider optimal design of apheresis schedules to collect blood stem cells from cancer patients. Blood stem cells are collected prior to the patient undergoing high-dose chemoradiotherapy and are returned after this treatment to enable reconstitution of the white blood cell components. Maximizing the number of cells collected in as few aphereses as possible is desirable.

We use a longitudinal data model with random effects (population model) to describe profiles of individual patients. A hierarchical prior model introduces common mean profiles for patients undergoing different treatments. The optimal apheresis schedule for a new patient is found by minimizing an expected loss over the posterior predictive distribution of the patient's predicted CD34 profile. Estimation of the model and solution of the optimal design problem are implemented by a simulation approach, which allows us to accommodate arbitrary shapes for the profiles and realistic loss functions which include relative penalties for the number of scheduled stem cell collections and for collecting fewer than a specified target quantity of total collected stem cells.

Keywords. apheresis schedules, Bayesian optimal design, longitudinal data, population models

1 Introduction

Over the last ten years a barrage of literature has appeared concerned with the implementation of posterior inference by methods collectively known as Markov chain Monte Carlo (MCMC) simulation. See, for example, Tierney (1994) and Gilks et al. (1993) for a summary. It is now possible to consider inference in essentially any well specified probability model. Most work related to MCMC simulation was focused on posterior estimation, including posterior predictive estimates and model comparison. However, the same impetus which has so dramatically changed the narrower field of statistical estimation has yet to permeate the wider context of decision making. In this paper we argue for the use MCMC simulations to address steps of the decision making process beyond the basic inference problem. We demonstrate how with minor computational effort the same MCMC output which is used for parameter estimation can be used to solve an optimal design problem. We will make the argument in the context of a specific probability model. But the ideas are more general, and do not depend on the specific example. The discussion is based on methodological developments in Bielza, Müller and Rios Insua (1996) and Palmer and Müller (1998). Ideas similar to the approach discussed in Section 4 have been used in Wakefield (1994) with the specific aim of determining an optimal dose in a pharmacokinetic study.

In Section 2 we state the optimal design problem, using a problem specific utility function related to treatment success and sampling cost. In Section 3 we introduce the probability model in which we will address the optimal design question. Using the same MCMC simulation output which is generated to estimate posterior means, we propose in Section 4 a numerical solution to the optimal design problem. Section 5 discusses an alternative approach based on MCMC simulation in a different, augmented probability model. Section 6 concludes with a discussion.

2 The decision problem

In Palmer and Müller (1998) we consider optimal apheresis (stem cell collection process) designs for cancer patients undergoing high-dose chemotherapy. Between a pre-treatment and start of the chemotherapy stem cells are collected to allow later reconstitution of white blood cell components. Depending on the pre-treatment the first stem cell collection process is scheduled on the fifth or seventh day after pre-treatment. The design problem is to decide for which of the remaining days further aphereses should be scheduled. Clearly the optimal solution should propose stem cell collections on days with high predicted stem cell concentrations. The prediction is based on observations of stem cell levels (represented by CD34 antigen levels) from past patients.

Let y_{ij}, $i = 1, \ldots, I$ and $j = 1, \ldots, n_i$ denote the observed CD34 count for patient i on day t_{ij}. Let $y_i = (y_{i1}, \ldots, y_{i,n_i})$ and $y = (y_1, \ldots, y_I)$ denote the i–th patient's data and the combined data vector, respectively. For a new patient $h = I + 1$ denote with $y_h = (y_{h1}, \ldots, y_{h,n_h})$ the (unknown) stem cell counts on days $t_{h1}, \ldots, t_{h,n_h}$. Denote with $a = (d_1, \ldots, d_{n_h})$ a vector of indicators with $d_j = 1$ if a stem cell collection is to be scheduled for day t_{hj} and $d_j = 0$ otherwise. For a first day t_{h0} we already have a count y_{h0}. Let $n_a = 1 + \sum d_j$ denote the number of scheduled aphereses, where the additional 1 appears because of the already realized apheresis at day t_{h0}. Let A be the event of failing to collect a specified target number y^* of stem cells: $A = \{\sum_j d_j y_{hj} L_h < y^*\}$, where L_h is the volume of blood processed at each stem cell collection for the new patient. Assuming a sampling cost p_1 and a penalty p_2 for under-achievement of the target, we formalize the aim of the optimal design as maximizing a utility function

$$u(a, y_h) = -p_1\, n_a - p_2\, I(A),$$

where $I(A)$ is the indicator function of event A. Since at the time of decision the data y_h is unknown, the optimal design a^* is determined by maximizing $u(a, y_h)$ in expectation:

$$a^* = arg \max_a \underbrace{E_{y_h}[u(a, y_h)]}_{\mathcal{U}(a)} \tag{1.1}$$

The relevant distribution on y_h with respect to which the expectation is defined depends on the underlying probability model, details of which will be discussed in Section 3. We will then in (1.4) rewrite the optimal design problem with the expectation explicitly stated as integral with respect to the relevant distributions.

3 A longitudinal data model

To complete the formal specification of the optimal design problem (1.1) we still need to define a probability model $p(\omega, y) = \pi(\omega)l(y|\omega)$, consisting of the prior $\pi(\omega)$ on the unknown parameter vector, and a sampling model $l(y|\omega)$ on the data given the parameters. In a general design problem this probability model could depend on the decision. For example, if the decision was to chose the covariates in a non-linear regression, we would then write $p_d(\omega, y) = \pi(\omega)l_d(y|\omega)$. All of the following discussion would remain valid, except for p_d and l_d replacing p and l.

Figure 1 shows data y_i for some typical patients in the study. Although different patients vary significantly in their specific profile, some characteristic features are common to all patients. Profiles start at some baseline count, rise to a mode, and then decrease again to the same baseline count. The day of maximum CD34 count depends on the type of pre-treatment. Patients under pre-treatment 2 show an earlier peak than patients under pre-treatment 1. Data with these features are common in many applications, for example pharmacokinetic and pharmacodynamic models (Wakefield, 1996), white blood cell counts of chemotherapy patients (Müller and Rosner, 1997), or income of individuals on the labor market (Hirano 1998). Depending on the focus of the application such data are referred to as longitudinal data models, repeated measurement models, population models, growth curve models, etc. See, for example, Davidian and Giltinan (1995) for a review. Wakefield, Smith, Racine-Poon and Gelfand (1994) discuss common modelling issues for such data, using hierarchical models of the form

$$l(y_i|\theta_i), \quad p(\theta_i|\eta), \quad p(\eta).$$

In words, observations $y_i = (y_{i1}, \ldots, y_{i,n_i})$ are generated from some sampling model $l(y_i|\theta_i)$. Often this sampling model includes a dependence on occasion-varying

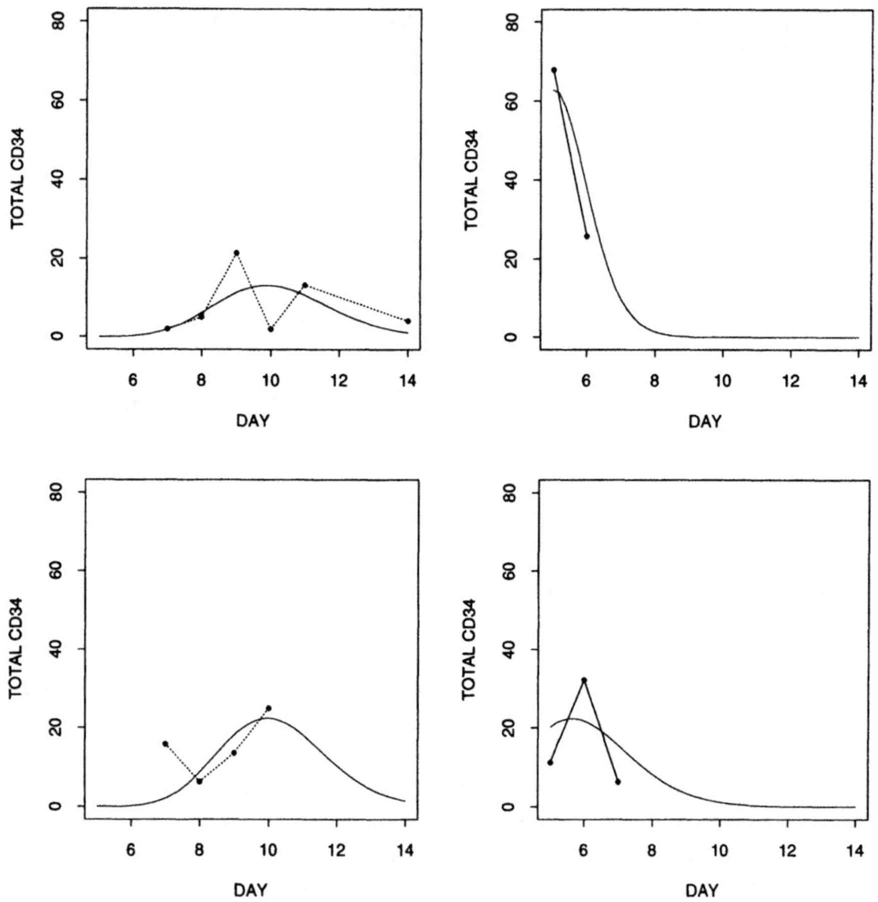

Fig. 1. Stem cell counts (CD34) over days for four typical patients. The patients in the left two panels were treated with pre-treatement 1. The right two panels show patients under pre-treatment 2

covariates t_{ij}, i.e. $l(y_i|t_i, \theta_i)$. For example, this could be a non-linear regression $y_{ij} = f(t_{ij}, \theta_i) + \epsilon_{ij}$ of y_{ij} on day t_{ij}. Patients are different, i.e., each patient has a separate parameter vector θ_i, but all patients come from the same underlying population. This is formalized by assuming that all θ_i are generated from the same prior model $p(\theta_i|\eta)$, also referred to as the "population distribution". Here η is some hyperparameter in the prior distribution. Often, the prior model depends on patient specific covariates x_i, such as age, body mass, etc., replacing $p(\theta_i|\eta)$ by a regression $p(\theta_i|x_i, \eta)$.

Based on exploratory data analysis and substantive knowledge of the problem we decided to use a non-linear regression $y_{ij} = f(t_{ij}, \theta_i) + \epsilon_{ij}$ with a unimodal, smooth regression curve $f(t_{ij}, \theta_i)$. Also, the relatively sparse data does not allow estimation of high dimensional parameter vectors θ_i. Thus we decided for a non-linear regression using rescaled gamma curves for the mean profiles for each patient. Patients undergo one of two possible pre-treatments. A covariate $x_i = 1$ or 2 records each patient's pre-treatment and is used as a regressor in the population distribution. Specifically, we use the following model.

$$\begin{aligned}
y_{ij} &= z_i\, g(t_{ij}; e_i, s_i) + \epsilon_{ij}, i = 1, \ldots, I,\ j = 1, \ldots, n_i \\
\epsilon_{ij} &\sim N(0, \sigma^2), \\
\theta_i &\sim \begin{cases} N(\eta_1, V), & \text{if } x_i = 1, \\ N(\eta_2, V), & \text{if } x_i = 2, \end{cases} \qquad (1.2) \\
\theta_i &= (e_i, s_i, z_i), \\
\eta_k &\sim N(\mu, \Sigma),\ k = 1, 2 \\
V^{-1} &\sim W[q, (qQ)^{-1}], \\
\sigma^{-2} &\sim Gamma(a_0/2, b_0/2). \qquad (1.3)
\end{aligned}$$

Here $g(t; e, s) = 1/c\Gamma(t; a, b)$ is a Gamma function with parameters $b = e/s^2$ and $a = e \cdot b$ chosen to have mean and variance matching e and s^2, and rescaled by $c = [(a-1)/b]^{a-1} \exp[-(a-1)]$ such that $\sup(g) = 1.0$. Figure 1 shows observed counts y_{ij} and fitted values $\hat{y}_{ij} = E\left[z_i\, g(t_{ij}; e_i, s_i) \middle| y\right]$ for some typical patients. Let $\omega = (\eta_1, \eta_2, V, \sigma^2, \theta_1, \ldots, \theta_I)$ denote the full parameter vector. Using MCMC posterior simulation it is possible to generate by computer simulation a Monte Carlo sample $M = \{\omega^1, \ldots, \omega^T\}$ with $\omega^t \sim p(\omega|y)$. Here ω^t is the imputed parameter vector after t iterations of the Monte Carlo simulation. For details of the setup of the Monte Carlo simulation see Palmer and Müller (1998). The fitted curves in Figure 1 are posterior means of fitted values $f(t_{ij}, \theta_i)$ estimated by averages over the Monte Carlo sample M.

4 Solving the optimal design problem using the MCMC output

A formal solution of (1.1) requires to find the design a^* which maximizes $u(a, y_h)$ in expectation, i.e., which maximizes the expected utility $\mathcal{U}(a)$. For the sake of a clear presentation we start the discussion without considering the first observation y_{h0}. A simple modification introduced later will allow us to include conditioning on y_{h0}.

$$\begin{aligned}
\mathcal{U}(a) &= \int u(a, y_h) p(y_h|y) dy_h, \\
&= \int u(a, y_h) p(y_h|\theta_h) p(\theta_h|\omega) p(\omega|y) dy_h\, d\theta_h\, d\omega,
\end{aligned} \qquad (1.4)$$

where y_h denotes the stem cell counts for the new patient $h = I + 1$, and θ_h parametrizes the mean profile for the new patient. Since y_h is unknown at the time of decision making, $\mathcal{U}(a)$ includes an expectation over y_h. The relevant distribution with respect to which this expectation is evaluated is the posterior predictive distribution given the already available data $p(y_h|y) = \int p(y_h|\theta_h)p(\theta_h|y)d\theta_h$, which we can further rewrite as a posterior expectation

$$p(y_h|y, y_{h0}) = \int p(y_h|\theta_h)p(\theta_h|\omega)p(\omega|y)d\omega,$$

leading to the expression in (1.4).

This allows us to approximately evaluate expected utilities as ergodic averages over the generated posterior Monte Carlo sample M. We augment the Monte Carlo sample $\omega^t \sim p(\omega|y)$ to a Monte Carlo sample

$$(\omega^t, \theta_h^t, y_h^t) \sim p(y_h^t|\theta_h^t)p(\theta_h^t|\omega^t)p(\omega^t|y)$$

by generating for each simulated ω^t a value for θ_h and for the future data y_h from the given distributions. Then

$$\hat{U}(a) = \frac{1}{M}\sum_{t=1}^{T} u(a, y_h^t). \tag{1.5}$$

We derived (1.5) without conditioning on the already observed y_{h0}. To account for y_{h0}, note that $p(\theta_h, \omega|y, y_{h0}) \propto p(y_{h0}|\theta_h)p(\theta_h, \omega|y)$. In other words, expression (1.4) needs to be modified only by an additional factor $p(y_{h0}|\theta_h)$ in the integrating measure. Thus (1.5) remains valid if the average over $u(a, y_h^t)$ is replaced by a weighted average, weighting with $p(y_{h0}|\theta_h^t)$. Alternatively, θ_h and the additional observation y_{h0} could be included when implementing the MCMC for posterior simulation.

Evaluation of (1.5) for all possible designs a reveals the optimal design a^*. Each evaluation (1.5) is a simple sum over all T posterior simulations in the posterior Monte Carlo sample M. Table 1.1 shows the optimal design and the two next best suboptimal solutions for a future patient $h = I + 1$ under each of the two pre-treatments. For a patient undergoing treatment $x_h = 1$, with a first observation $y_0 = 20.0$ on day $t_{h,0} = 5$, the optimal apheresis schedule for the remaining six days was found to be given by $d_1 = 1, d_j = 0, j = 2, \ldots, 6$ with an expected utility $T(a^*) = 2.03$.

$\hat{U}(a)$	d_0	d_1	d_2	d_3	d_4	d_5	d_6
			Treatment $x_{I+1} = 1$				
2.03	1	1	0	0	0	0	0
3.00	1	1	1	0	0	0	0
4.00	1	1	1	1	0	0	0
			Treatment $x_{I+1} = 2$				
5.14	1	0	1	1	0	0	0
5.18	1	0	1	1	1	0	0
5.47	1	1	0	1	1	0	0

Table 1.1. Optimal (and 2nd and 3rd best) design for two future patients

5 Optimal design by MCMC in an augmented probability model

In Bielza, Müller and Rios Insua (1996) we explored another numerical solution strategy for optimal design problems such as (1.1). The approach is very different from the scheme described in the previous section. The scheme proposed in Section 4 was based on evaluating for each possible design a the expected utility integral by an ergodic average $\hat{\mathcal{U}}(a)$ over a posterior Monte Carlo sample M. Generating the posterior Monte Carlo sample involved a MCMC simulation from the posterior distribution.

In contrast, in Bielza et al. (1996) we propose to consider the expression

$$h(a, \theta_h, y_h) \propto u(a, y_h) p(\theta_h | y) p(y_h | \theta_h)$$

and interpret it as a probability density function on (a, θ_h, y_h). Of course, this requires some technical constraints on $u(a, y_h)$, such as non-negativity and integrability of the product $h(a, \theta_h, y_h)$. In the current application this is achieved by adding a constant shift u_0 to $u(a, \theta_h, y_h)$. Note that adding a constant to the utility function does not change the solution of the optimal design problem (1.1). By construction, under $h(\cdot)$ the marginal distribution $h(a)$ on a is proportional to the expected utility $\mathcal{U}(a)$.

$$h(a) \propto \int u(a, y_h) p(\theta_h | y) p(y_h | \theta_h) d\theta_h \, dy_h = \mathcal{U}(a).$$

If we could simulate a large Monte Carlo sample from $h(a, \theta_h, y_h)$, we could solve the original optimal design problem by inspection of the marginal distribution of the simulated a values. The mode a^* of $h(a)$ is the optimal design. Thus we can change the optimal design problem into a simulation problem similar to the well studied posterior simulation problem. In Bielza et al. (1996) we propose several schemes to simulate from $h(\cdot)$, all of them based on similar simulation schemes used for posterior simulations.

We used this approach to find the solution in the optimal apheresis design problem introduced earlier. A simple observation simplified the implementation. The unimodality of fitted profiles suggests that any optimal apheresis scheme should be of the type "start on day d_1 and continue to schedule stem cell collections until day d_2 or until the target amount is collected, whatever occurs first". Thus we can index actions by the two parameters $a = (d_1, d_2)$. Figure 2 shows a histogram of simulated values for (d_1, d_2). The optimal design can readily be read off.

6 Discussion

Using a case study concerned with optimal apheresis designs we have shown how MCMC simulation can be used to solve optimal design problems. This takes the use of MCMC beyond the narrower statistical problem of estimating a given probability model. Parameter estimation, including prediction and model comparison, is but one step in decision making. We see our discussion as a contribution towards applying MCMC methods originally developed with the posterior estimation problem in mind to a wider context of the decision problem.

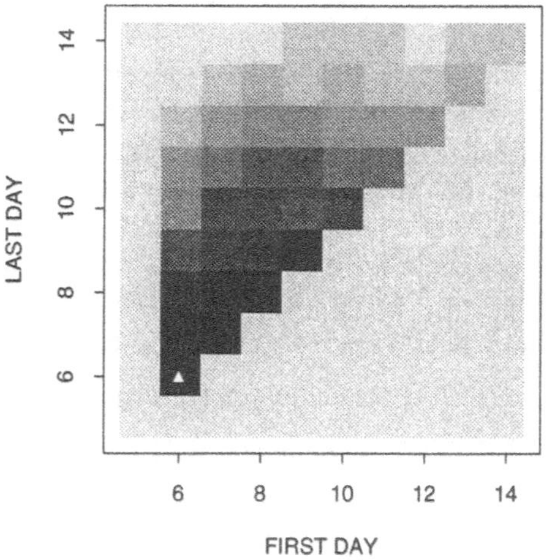

Fig. 2. Histograms of simulated values $a = (d_1, d_2)$ from $h(a) \propto \mathcal{U}(a)$. Here d_1 and d_2 are the first and last day of stem cell collection, respectively, for a patient under pre-treatment 1. The optimal design can be readily read off as $a = (6, 6)$

References

Bielza, C., Müller, P. and Ríos-Insua, D. (1996). Monte Carlo Methods for Decision Analysis with Applications to Influence Diagram. *Discusssion paper 96-07*, ISDS, Duke University.

Davidian, M. and Giltinan, D. M. (1995). *Nonlinear Models for Repeated Measurement Data*. Chapman and Hall: London.

Gilks, W. R., Clayton, D. G., Spiegelhalter, D. J., Best, N. G., McNeil, A. J., Sharples, L. D. and Kirby, A. J. (1993). Modelling complexity: applications of Gibbs sampling in medicine. *Journal of the Royal Statistical Society Ser. B* **55**, 39–52.

Hirano, K. (1998), Semiparametric Bayesian Models for Longitudinal Earnings Data. In *Practical Nonparametric and Semiparametric Bayesian Statistics* (Dey, D., Müller, P. and Sinha, D., eds.), Springer Lecture Notes, Springer-Verlag: New York, to appear.

Müller, P. and Rosner, G. (1997). A semiparametric bayesian population model with hierarchical mixture priors. *Journal of the American Statistical Association*, to appear.

Palmer, J. and Müller, P. (1998). Bayesian optimal design in population models of hematologic data. *Statistics in Medicine*. To appear.

Tierney, L. (1994). Markov chains for exploring posterior distributions. *Annals of Statistics* **22**, 1701–1728.

Wakefield, J. C. (1994). An expected loss approach to the design of dosage regimens via sapling-based methods. *The Statistician* **43**, 13–29.

Wakefield, J. C. (1996). The Bayesian analysis of population pharmacokinetic models. *Journal of the American Statistical Association* **91**, 62–75.

Wakefield, J. C., Smith, A. F. M., Racine-Poon, A. and Gelfand, A. (1994). Bayesian analysis of linear and nonlinear population models using the Gibbs sample. *Applied Statistics* **43**, 201–221.

An Intelligent Decision System for Jaundice Management in Newborn Babies

S. Ríos-Insua[1], C. Bielza[1], M. Gómez[1], J.A. Fdez. del Pozo[1], M. Sánchez Luna[2] and S. Caballero[2]

[1] Dept. of Artificial Intelligence, Madrid Technical University, SPAIN.
[2] Neonatology Service, Gregorio Marañón General Hospital, Madrid, SPAIN

Abstract

Jaundice management in newborn babies is a complex problem faced almost everyday by neonatology services. This suggests the development of a decision support system integrating the beliefs and preferences of members of a neonatology service. In this paper, we introduce one such system called IctNeo. We describe first the basic representation of the problem by means of influence diagrams, including admission and treatment decisions. The corresponding uncertainty model is built with the aid of both historical data and subjective judgements. We then describe the multiattribute preference structure. Finally, we provide some ideas on the system implementation and use.

Keywords. Decision analysis, influence diagrams, neonatal jaundice

1 Introduction

The diagnosis and medical treatment of full-term newborn jaundice is aimed at reducing the toxic effects of bilirubin in the central nervous system. Bilirubin is derived from the body's heme-containing proteins, Syskes and Epstein (1990) and Gartner (1995). Relationships between bilirubin and brain damage were found by Mollison and Cutbush (1951). At that time blood exchange was the only way of treatment, and it was applied when the infant had a bilirubin level higher than 20 mg/dl, since such value was considered a risk factor for neurologic abnormalities. However, later studies proved that lower values of bilirubin were able to promote less showy neurological alterations, bilirubin encephalopathy being the most dangerous one. The introduction of phototherapy in jaundice management, led to the treatment of lower bilirubin cases and produced a drastic reduction of blood exchanges.

Current jaundice protocols are based on the control of bilirubin with variable periodicity, depending on the newborn weight and age, suggesting several medical tests when bilirubin goes over certain levels. The type of treatment, observe, phototherapy or exchange, at each moment, depends on the bilirubin levels and is independent of the cause of jaundice. These recommendations are based, on one hand, on the appraisal of some laboratory tests sometimes unnecessary and with nonnegligible costs whose results have not been proved always useful and, on the other, on avoiding the risk due to the indirect hyperbilirubinemia.

Recently, Newman and Maisels (1992) have proposed a less aggressive approach based on the fact that the neurological risk associated with high concentrations of bilirubin in healthy full-term newborns is small with respect to the risk due to treatments whose benefits are very limited or no longer existent. Thus, the morbid-mortality derived from exchanges is more relevant than the benefits obtained from avoiding an each more infrequent pathology as nuclear jaundice is. The use of phototherapy has shown an important decrease in the number of exchanges and it does not seem to have any effect over the neurological evolution and development of the baby, but it requires keeping away the baby from the mother, hence disrupting lactation.

The new recommendation implies reducing the number of laboratory tests, postponing the beginning of phototherapy treatment in cases of a jaundiced newborn without hemolysis until bilirubin levels are higher than the classic ones (23–29 mg/dl), and having a greater control of newborns with hemolysis in an attempt to keep bilirubin levels at lower values (19–23 mg/dl).

The present study aims at developing a knowledge-based system to aid in neonatal jaundice management decisions, that permits with these new recommendations the analysis of multiple variables which take part in the pathogeny. It will yield a decrease in the costs of diagnostic and therapeutic phases, will define better the limits to change the treatment, and will take into account the preferences of parents and doctors.

We use Decision Analysis (DA) to integrate several uncertain factors and decisions to control neonatal jaundice, and thus, determine the expected utilities of different medical treatments. To deal with multiple uncertainties, we construct an influence diagram (ID) whose qualitative structure models current knowledge about jaundice management. IDs, Shachter (1986), are a very appealing DA tool because of their expressiveness, probabilistic coherency, and computational power, and can be viewed as a useful instrument for representing and solving decision-making problems, the medical ones included, see, e.g., Owens et al. (1997) and Nease and Owens (1997).

The paper includes four more sections. In Section 2, we provide the qualitative structure of the ID with the description of the decisions and uncertain variables, as well as conditional dependencies and independencies among variables. In Section 3, we specify conditional probability distributions which model the relationship among a node and its parents, and describe the assessment of such distributions. Section 4 describes the evaluation of possible outcome scenarios based on a multiattribute utility function. Section 5 illustrates the implemented system and provides some conclusions.

2 Structuring the problem

After several interviews with doctors we modelled the structure of the problem, identifying decisions to be made, the sequence in which they would arise and uncertain events, as well as the information available at each moment. As decisions are concerned, the doctor would decide first whether to admit or not the newborn to hospital and confine it, eventually, to the ICU. Therefore, we call it *admission.* If the infant is not admitted, the problem is over. Otherwise, the baby receives a *treatment* in several consecutive stages, between 0 and 10 phases of 6 hours, until either doctors discharge the newborn or s/he receives a treatment that is outside our specific problem, e.g., for hepatitis, Gilbert's syndrome, ...

Hence, we have a repetitive structure in which the alternatives are:

1. Observe the baby.
2. Perform a phototherapy for 6, 12 or 18 hours.
3. Perform a blood exchange.
4. Discharge the neonate.
5. Give an outside treatment.

We could have up to 13 decision nodes, by applying several phases of phototherapy of 6 hours, since the treatment may last up to 4 days, typical duration being between 2 and 2.5 days. Note, however, that the structure is not symmetric, since there are several combinations of treatment that are not allowed. Table 2.1 lists these constraints. For example, constraint 4 is due to the danger (1% of mortality) that is involved with blood exchange. The handling of asymmetric IDs is still a not very developed topic, though some initial ideas may be seen in Smith et al. (1993).

1	Start treatment with observation or phototherapy
2	End treatment with discharge or outside treatment
3	Not to observe during two consecutive phases, if tests are performed
4	Not to perform more than two exchanges per treatment
5	Exchange followed and preceded by phototherapy
6	Observe with analyses before discharge or outside treatment
7	Whole treatment lasts at most 10 phases of 6 hours

Table 2.1. Constraints on sequences of treatments

Concerning uncertain events, there are a lot of them, see Figure 2.1, which shows the whole ID without value nodes and with a general i-th treatment phase, for convenience. All variables with arcs into the admission node represent information available at the time of making this decision. At that moment, the doctor knows the value of some factors related to the mother like her age, Rh factor, race, blood group, delivery with or without instruments or whether this is her first delivery. The social level of the mother is reflected in several social variables: *mother discharge* (at 48 hours or at 72 hours), which depends on the *social level*and on the *place of residence*, since mothers with lower social level and who live not very close to the hospital remain in it longer if the baby may be likely admitted. The doctor also knows important data from the baby like *birth weight*, depending obviously on the *gestational age*; *age* in hours; *blood group* and *Rh factor*; and *jaundice*. Two clinical findings demand special attention for each decision: serum concentration of bilirubin and of hemoglobin, whose dependencies will be explained in the next section.

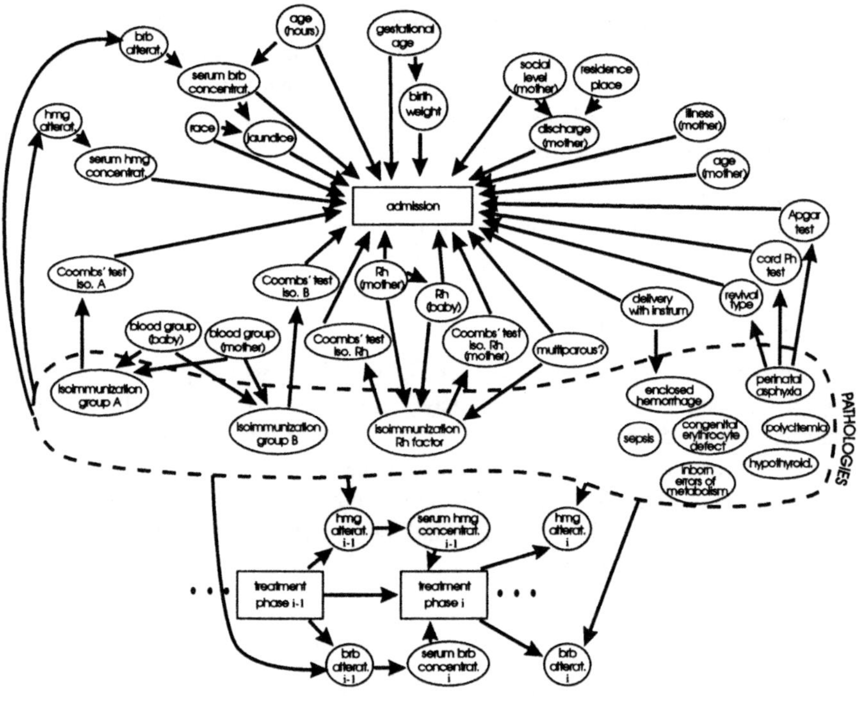

Fig. 2.1 Decision and chance nodes of the influence diagram for the jaundice problem

A number of pathologies may have influence on hyperbilirubinemia: *sepsis, congenital erythrocyte defect, inborn erors of metabolism, enclosed hemorrhage, hypothyroidism, polycitemia, perinatal asphyxia*, and *isoimmunization*. We decompose the last one into three nodes related to blood group A, group B and Rh factor. Isoimmunization reveals incompatibility between mother and baby bloods. Finally, the results of some tests are included like *Coombs' test*, related with isoimmunization; *Apgar test*, and others, to study potential baby asphyxia.

The value node will be additively decomposed, Tatman and Shachter (1990), for each decision stage, leading us to define some new variables, as will be shown later.

3 Assessing uncertainty

Following the decision analysis cycle to construct a *requisite* decision model, Phillips (1984), we model now the uncertainty inherent in the problem by means of probabilities, i.e., we fill the tables contained in the chance nodes. To accomplish it, we use both historical data and subjective judgements. Historical data are taken from the Neonatology Service of the hospital and date from 1994. This historical data correspond to babies admitted to hospital. One issue is whether this sample is actually representative, since non-admitted babies take part in our study as well, hence, raising the question of whether the probabilities would be the same should we consider non-admitted babies. Experts detected that it is more frequent for a high social level baby to return home without being admitted than for a low social level baby. As a consequence, we decided to work with a wider sample taken from the whole hospital to assign probabilities of two variables: social level and place of residence. Examples of such quantified probabilities are shown in Tables 3.1 and 3.2.

For example, for the distribution of mother blood group, 2381 historical cases were studied, whereas for birth weight given gestational age, we used 356 cases. This last variable is continuous but doctors felt more comfortable working with four intervals as a discrete approximation. In general, doctors suggested the discretization of continuous variables like those related to age (*gestational age, baby age, mother age*). For example, *gestational age* had three levels: preterm (< 37 weeks), full-term (37–41 weeks) and posterm (≥ 42 weeks) as indicated in Table 3.2; while *mother age* was discretized according to young (15–18 years old), middle (19–34) and advanced (≥ 35). For *baby age*, doctors distinguished between 12 hours intervals, leading to 6 intervals, since in our context babies were younger than 72 hours.

Blood group	A	B	AB	O
Probability	.4271	.0979	.0331	.4419

Table 3.1. Probability of mother blood group

	Birthweight (g.)			
Gestational age	499–999	1000–1499	1500–2499	≥ 2500
Preterm	.204	.243	.361	.192
Full-term	.013	.218	.324	.445
Posterm	.001	.152	.303	.544

Table 3.2. Probability of birthweight given gestational age

Probability encoding based on historical data was only possible for 21 chance nodes, out of 37, providing 48 probability values, the remaining 29 probability values being inferred by their complement to one. The biggest probability table had 12 entries, like Table 3.2.

Empirical data were insufficient to quantify the remaining 16 random variables. Hence, judgemental probabilities were required. We followed the SRI encoding process and its extensions, see Merkhofer (1987) and Shephard and Kirkwood (1991), as a formal protocol for probability elicitation. We were the interviewers and three doctors served as the experts. The process tried to overcome biases, mainly the expert bias, see Morgan and Henrion (1990), in our case, to motivate doctors and structure uncertain quantities, exploring the way doctors think about them. Many interviews were needed. Most variables were clearly defined at this stage together with their possible outcomes and appropriate measurement scales. Then, the process guided the doctors to quantify the uncertainty by means of basic encoding procedures (probability, value, or probability/value methods), presented in an indirect response mode employing a probability wheel. *Cord PH test, serum bilirubin concentration,* and *hemoglobin concentration* were the unique continuous random variables but, as before, they were discretized. Bilirubin concentration was classified in two levels: high (> 5 mg/dl) and normal, whereas low (< 14 g), medium (14–23 g) and high (> 23 g) was the resolution for hemoglobin concentration.

Initial structurations of the ID did not include *bilirubin alteration* and *hemoglobin alteration* nodes having instead a huge probability table to be elicited for *bilirubin* and *hemoglobin concentration* nodes, since each of them had many predecessors, i.e., all pathologies. This posed problems related to the obtainment from experts, the tables with so many entries, storage of so much information and the decrease of the computational burden. By adding the alteration nodes with arcs into the corresponding concentrations (see Figure 2.1), the model we get for alterations is of causal nature so that we may use a noisy OR-gate, Pearl (1988).

As a consequence, we assume that each pathology i may act to produce *bilirubin alteration* (BA) but there exist inhibitors I_i representing exceptions or abnormalities that interfere with the normal relationship between BA and pathologies, taken implicitly into account. We checked that the required assumptions hold, i.e., causes and inhibitors act as independent variables, and BA is absent only if either the pathologies are absent or for each present pathology the associated inhibitor has acted. Let q_i denote the probability that I_i is active. Then,

$$P(BA = \text{present} \mid Path_i = \text{present}, Path_j = \text{absent}, j \neq i) = c_i = 1 - q_i$$

is the probability that the isolated i-th pathology can cause BA to be present. Only from the assignment of the values c_i, we may derive the probability distribution of BA given any configuration $\boldsymbol{x}$ of its parents by

$$P(BA = \text{absent}|\boldsymbol{x}) = \prod_{i \in \{i : Path_i = \text{present}\}} q_i.$$

Table 3.3 shows the values c_i for BA only for the admission stage. Note that *hemoglobin alteration* may be modelled in a similar fashion by means of another OR-gate.

	Status	Rest	$P(AB)$ =pres.		Status	Rest	$P(AB)$ =pres
A-iso.	pres.	abs.	.75	Hypothyr.	pres.	abs.	.50
B-iso.	pres.	abs.	.70	MBD	pres.	abs.	.80
Rh-iso.	pres.	abs.	.97	Asphyx.	pres.	abs.	.50
Sepsis	pres.	abs.	.95	Hemorr.	pres.	abs.	.70
CBD	pres.	abs.	.97	Polycit.	pres.	abs.	.80

Table 3.3. OR-gate assigments for BA given the set of pathologies

Note that without an OR-gate model, we would have needed to assign 2^{10} = 1024 values, against just 10. An additional strength of the OR-gate will be the provision of simple linguistic explanations. All judgements obtained were checked for consistency. We assigned individual judgements from the three doctors and retained them for sensitivity analysis. Group probabilities were obtained through behavioral aggregation, sharing knowledge by interaction among the doctors. In our case, there were not significant differences among individuals after their exchange of information.

4 Multiattribute evaluation

In this section we develop a framework to assess and quantify preferences and systematically include them in the decision making process.

4.1 Generation of objectives and attributes

The question we wished to answer in determining objectives and attributes was, what are the intangible and direct effects of concern in our particular problem and how do we measure them.

With the aid of the doctors, we constructed an objectives hierarchy, Keeney and Raiffa (1976), with the well being of the newborn baby as the major objective. We went down considering *direct effects* and *intangible effects*. Several subobjectives for direct effects, like costs at the minimal care unit and at ICU, number of days in both places,... could be considered, but we noted that all these might be included and condensed in only one named "minimize cost of stay in hospital", avoiding redundancies. We took care to ensure that all facets of the higher objective were accounted for in one of the subobjectives. Furthermore, tests of importance were repeatedly considered before any objective was included in the hierarchy, and doctors were asked whether they felt the best course of action could be altered if that objective were excluded. For intangible effects we included as subobjectives "baby-mother gap", "minimize the risk of being admitted to hospital" and "injuries". Finally, the baby-mother gap was broken into "minimize social cost", and "minimize emotional cost", and injuries was broken into two lower-level objectives, named "minimize injuries due to the treatment" and "minimize injuries due to the hyperbilirubinemia".

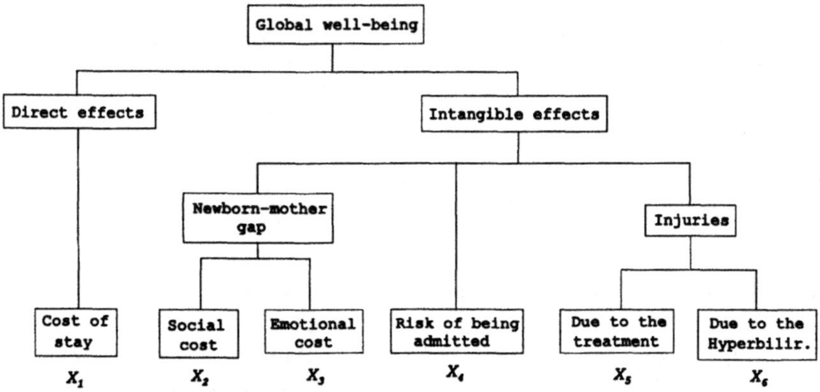

Fig. 4.1. An objectives hierarchy for the jaundice management problem

Figure 4.1 shows the objectives hierarchy for jaundice management in newborns. As a summary, the objective of our problem was to minimize the patient risk, the parents worries and the cost of the treatment. Next, we identified an attribute for each one of the six lowest-level objectives. We considered for the objective "minimize cost of stay in hospital" the obvious attribute thousands of pesetas. However, for the remaining objectives it was much harder to determine an attribute and we had to construct an ad hoc scale for each objective. Table 4.1 shows the attributes X_i, $i = 1, ..., 6$, with their measurement units and ranges with worst and best levels. For all attributes, less was preferred to more.

Attribute	Measure (units)	Level Worst	Level Best
X_1 : cost of stay	thousands of ptas.	1260	0
X_2 : social cost	constructed scale	2	0
X_3 : emotional cost	constructed scale	2	0
X_4 : risk of being admitted	constructed scale	3	0
X_5 : injuries due to treatment	constructed scale	4	0
X_6 : injuries due to hyperbilir.	constructed scale	5	0

Table 4.1. Attributes for evaluating strategies

As an example, we describe the scale constructed for attribute X_4 in Table 4.2.

4.2 Multiattribute assessment

We have specified an objectives hierarchy, and appropriate attributes X_i, $i = 1, ..., 6$, have been identified for our problem. If x_i designates a specific level of X_i, then our task is to assess a utility function $u(x_1, x_2, x_3, x_4, x_5, x_6)$. It is clear that a direct assessment of u presents major practical shortcomings, so we investigated various sets

Value	Level of impact
0	Newborn not admitted to hospital. Under observation.
1	Newborn admitted + receives some test.
2	Newborn admitted + receives medium care.
3	Newborn admitted + receives intensive care.

Table 4.2. Constructed scale for risk of being admitted to hospital

of independence assumptions, Keeney (1980), about the basic preferences attitudes of the DM, so as to derive a functional form of the multiattribute utility function consistent with these assumptions. The first important step in selecting the form of the utility function involves investigating how reasonable are preferential and utility independence conditions. To facilitate checking independence conditions and due to the homogeneity, on one hand, of attributes X_2 and X_3, and on the other, X_5 and X_6, we assume that such attributes might be structured temporarily substituting X_2 and X_3 by only one attribute Y_2, which represents "newborn-mother gap", and X_5 and X_6 by Y_4 meaning "injuries", both Y_2, Y_4 with their particular scales. For a moment, we shall consider four attributes denoted $Y_1 = X_1$, $Y_2 = (X_2, X_3)$, $Y_3 = X_4$ and $Y_4 = (X_5, X_6)$. Then, we intend to determine a utility function of the form

$$u(y_1, y_2, y_3, y_4) = f\left[u_1(y_1), u_2(y_2), u_3(y_3), u_4(y_4)\right]$$

where f is a scalar-valued function, and u_i a utility function over y_i.

We found that Y_4 was utility independent of (Y_1, Y_2, Y_3) and that $\{Y_4, Y_i\}$ was preferential independent of their complement, for $i = 1, 2, 3$. Thus, we concluded that the utility function u is multiplicative of the form

$$u(y_1, y_2, y_3, y_4) = \sum_{i=1}^{4} k_i u_i(y_i) + k \sum_{\substack{i=1 \\ j>i}}^{4} k_i k_j u_i(y_i) u_j(y_j) + \\ k^2 \sum_{\substack{i=1 \\ j>i \\ l>i}}^{4} k_i k_j k_l u_i(y_i) u_j(y_j) u_l(y_l) + k^3 k_1 k_2 k_3 k_4 u_1(y_1) u_2(y_2) u_3(y_3) u_4(y_4) \tag{1}$$

where k, k_i, $i = 1, 2, 3, 4$, are scaling constants, Keeney and Raiffa (1976). The logical next step in assessing u is to try to identify functions f_2 and f_3 such that

$$u_2(y_2) = f_2\left[u_2^x(x_2), u_3^x(x_3)\right] \quad \text{and} \quad u_4(y_4) = f_3\left[u_5^x(x_5), u_6^x(x_6)\right]$$

where the u_i^x's are utility functions over their respective domains. In both cases, we undercovered an additive independence assumption. Hence, we obtained additive utility functions, given by

$$u_2(y_2) = k_2^x u_2^x(x_2) + k_3^x u_3^x(x_3) \quad \text{and} \quad u_4(y_4) = k_5^x u_5^x(x_5) + k_6^x u_6^x(x_6). \qquad (2)$$

Once with the structure, we assessed the component utility functions with the aid of Logical Decision (1991). This program fits exponential functions, $a+be^{-cx}$, using the midvalue splitting technique, see, e.g., Farquhar (1984). To set the midvalue point, we asked the doctors to provide the mid-preference level for a sub-range. We ran many consistency checks to find out possible inconsistencies and obtain a coherent set of compatible responses. Table 4.3 shows the fitted utility functions for the attributes.

Attribute	u_i	Range
X_1	$u_1(x_1) = 1.386 - .386\exp(.001015x_1)$	$[0, 1260]$
X_2	$u_2^x(x_2) = -.09575 + 1.096\exp(-1.219x_2)$	$[0, 2]$
X_3	$u_3^x(x_3) = 1 - .5x_3$	$[0, 2]$
X_4	$u_4(x_4) = 1.277 - .2766\exp(.5098x_4)$	$[0, 3]$
X_5	$u_5^x(x_5) = 1.096 - .09574\exp(.6094x_5)$	$[0, 4]$
X_6	$u_6^x(x_6) = 1.063 - .06309\exp(.5649x_6)$	$[0, 5]$

Table 4.3. Single-attribute utility function

Utility functions were assessed by doctors, except for the attributes "emotional and social cost" which were assessed with the aid of a doctor and several mothers.

Once the measures had been made comparable by defining a utility function for each attribute, the next step was to combine the individual utility functions into the overall function (1). To establish the relative importance of each attribute, we assessed the weights or scaling constants based on tradeoffs obtained with Logical Decision. We made several consistency checks based on the sensitivity analysis facility included in Logical Decision to revise existing tradeoffs. Table 4.4 shows the scaling constants for multiplicative utility function (1) and additive utility functions (2) which were also assessed with the aid of tradeoffs.

k_i	Value	k_i^x	Value
k	13.9656	k_2^x	.5644
k_1	.6247	k_3^x	.4356
k_2	.0184	k_5^x	.6488
k_3	.0125	k_6^x	.3512
k_4	.0030		

Table 4.4. Scaling constants

Since $k = 13.9656 > 0$ and $\sum_{i=1}^{4} k_i = .6586 < 1$, a destructive interaction is implied: a low utility on any one attribute leads to a low overall utility. All this structuration led to add some variables to the ID to determine the value node assessment. Its additive decomposition is defined by two types of value nodes: v_0 related to admission stage; and v_i related to i-th treatment phase. v_o depends on the new chance nodes *social cost, emotional cost, cost of stay* and *risk of being admitted*, being the last two deterministic nodes. v_i is a function of the random variable *risk due to the treatment*, which has the treatment decision node as its predecessor; and of *risk due to hyperbilirubinemia*, which is a deterministic function of birthweight, serum bilirubin concentration (i), lifetime, and pathologies seriousness.

5 Description of the system and conclusions

IctNeo is developed in C++ under Windows, with three basic modules: a compiler, a solving engine and a user interface. The compiler has its own grammar to define the ID: nodes, relationships and the relevant information, being easily modifiable. Some rules are checked (no cycles, coherent probability distributions,...) before the diagram is composed and compiled. Then, the solving engine applies Shachter's algorithm, Shachter (1986), to obtain optimal strategies once that those that do not verify the constraints are ruled out. The user typically enters a whole case of a patient with the treatments already performed, and IctNeo looks for the optimal strategy corresponding to that case for comparison purposes. The system tries also to explain the results, e.g., it looks for irrelevant variables, those which lead to the same decisions regardless the values they take. Currently, IctNeo is being tested. It will become an important aid for doctors, who will have deeper insight and understanding of the jaundice problem. Some features will be incorporated to IctNeo: sensitivity analysis options to check the robustness to the structure, the probabilities and the utilities; pathology diagnosis by looking at the final updated probabilities of the diagram; incomplete cases inclusion; and a constructor of utility functions to be used in different hospitals.

Acknowledgments

This paper has been supported by FIS project 97/0003-02 and CICYT project TIC 95-0028. D. Ríos Insua provided the initial influence diagram and many discussions. We are also grateful to S. Ríos, P. García Barreno and J. Díez Vegas for useful comments and suggestions, and to F. Almarza for his valuable cooperation in the implementation of the system.

References

Farquhar, P. H. (1984). Utility Assessment Methods, *Management Science* **30**, 1283–1300.

Gartner, L. M. (1995). Neonatal Jaundice, *Ped. in Review* **16**, 22–31.

Keeney, R . L. and Raiffa, H. (1976). *Decisions with Multiple Objectives. Preferences and Value Tradeoffs*. Wiley: New York.

Keeney, R. L. (1980). *Siting Energy Facilities*. Academic Press.

Logical Decision (1991). Multi-Measure DA Software V. 2.04.

Merkhofer, M. W. (1987). Quantifying Judgmental Uncertainty: Methodology, Experiences and Insights. *IEEE Trans. on Sys., Man. and Cyber.* **17**, 741–752.

Mollison, P. L. and Cutbush, M. (1951). A Method of Measuring the Severity of a Series of Cases of Hemolytic Disease of the Newborn, *Blood* **6**, 777–788.

Morgan, M. G. and Henrion, M. (1990). *Uncertainty: A Guide to Dealing with Uncertainty in Quantitative Risk and Policy Analysis*. Cambridge U. P.

Nease, R. F. and Owens, D. K. (1997). Use of Influence Diagrams to Structure Medical Decisions. *Medical Decision Making* **17**, 263–275.

Newmann, T. B. and Maisels, M. J. (1992). Evaluation and Treatment of Jaundice in the Term Infant: A Kinder, Gentler Approach, *Pediatrics* **89**, 809–830 (with discussion).

Owens, D. K., Shachter, R .D. and Nease, R. F. (1997). Representation and Analysis of Medical Decision Problems with IDs, *Medical Decision Making* **17**, 241–262.

Pearl, J. (1988). *Probabilistic Reasoning in Intelligent Systems: Networks of Plausible Inference*. Morgan Kaufmann: San Mateo, CA.

Phillips, L. D. (1984). Requisite Decision Modelling, *J. O. R. S.* **33**, 303–312.

Shachter, R. D. (1986). Evaluating Influence Diagrams, *Operations Research* **34**, 871–882.

Shephard, G. G., and Kirkwood, C. W. (1991). The Process of Eliciting a Judgmental Probability Distribution. *Tech. Rep. DIS 91/92-1*, Arizona State University.

Smith, J. E., Holtzman, S. and Matheson, J. E. (1993). Structuring Conditional Relationships in Influence Diagrams. *Operations Research* **41**, 280–297.

Sykes, E. and Epstein, E. (1990). Laboratory Measurement of Bilirubin. *Clin. in Perinatology* **17**, 397–416.

Tatman, J. and Shachter, R. (1990). Dynamic Programming and Influence Diagrams, *IEEE Trans. on Sys., Man. and Cyber.* **20**, 365–379.

Part III

Economics and Finance

A Theory of Possibility Approach to The Solution of a Fuzzy Linear Programming

M. Mar Arenas[1], Amelia Bilbao[1], M. Victoria Rodríguez Uría[1] and Mariano Jiménez[2]

[1] Dpto. Matemáticas. Univ. Oviedo, SPAIN
[2] Dpto. Econ. Aplicada I. Univ. País Vasco, SPAIN

Abstract

In conventional decision making problems, the estimation of the parameters of the model is often a problematic task. Normally they are either given by the decision maker (DM) who has imprecise information and/or expresses his/her considerations subjectively, or by statistical inference from past data and, consequently, their stability is doubtful. Therefore, it is reasonable to construct a model reflecting imprecise data or ambiguity in terms of fuzzy sets. This is the reason why a lot of fuzzy approaches to linear programming have been developed.

Our purpose in this paper is to present the solution of fuzzy linear programming problems in terms of a fuzzy number considered as a possibility distribution, i.e., the possibility distribution of the optimal value of the objective function. The method relies on α-cuts of the fuzzy solution to generate its possibility distribution. Finally, a bank balance sheet problem is solved for illustrating our approach.

Keywords. Decision making, fuzzy number, fuzzy programming, linear programming, possibility distribution

1 Introduction

A lot of real world decision problems are described by linear programming models and sometimes it is necessary to formulate them including elements of imprecision or uncertainty. It is possible to handle imprecision with the help of some results obtained from the theory of fuzzy sets, which gives a conceptual and theoretical framework for handling ambiguity or vagueness. A lot of fuzzy methods have been developed to solve this kind of problems, see Lai (1992). In particular Buckley (1988,1989) has used possibility theory to solve fuzzy linear programming problems. In this paper we have chosen to work out the method that considered the parameters of the problem as being represented by fuzzy numbers and to find the solution by applying the extension principle and the joint possibility distribution of the parameters of the problem.

Our purpose in this paper is to present the solution of fuzzy linear programming problems in terms of a fuzzy number considered as a possibility distribution, i.e., the possibility distribution of the optimal value of the objective function. The method relies on α-cuts of the fuzzy solution to generate its possibility distribution.

We shall consider the following possibilistic linear programming problem (FLP):

$$\left.\begin{array}{r} \max \tilde{z} = \tilde{c}x \\ \text{subject to} \\ \tilde{A}x \leq \tilde{b} \\ x \geq 0 \end{array}\right\} (FLP)$$

where $x = [x_j]$ is a crisp decision vector $n \times 1$ and symbols with a 'tilde' on top, like $\tilde{c} = [\tilde{c}_j]$, $\tilde{A} = [\tilde{a}_{ij}]$ and $\tilde{b} = [\tilde{b}_i]$ denote fuzzy parameters. We shall suppose that they are given by fuzzy numbers, i.e., they are fuzzy matrices.

A fuzzy number is defined differently by different authors. The most frequently used definition is that a fuzzy number is a fuzzy set in the real line which is a normal and bounded convex set.

From the definition of a fuzzy number $\tilde{N}$, it is important to note that the set of level α, N_α, can be represented by the closed interval which depends on the value of $\alpha : N_\alpha = [n_\alpha^L, n_\alpha^R]$.

The fuzzy numbers will represent the continuous possibility distributions for fuzzy parameters and hence place a restriction on the possible values the variable may assume. We will assume that all fuzzy numbers $\tilde{c}_j$, $\tilde{a}_{ij}$ and $\tilde{b}_i$ are weakly noninteractive, see Zadeh (1975). Weakly noninteractive means that there exists a t-norm T, such that we can find the joint possibility distribution of all the fuzzy variables by calculating the T-intersection of their possibility distributions. Following Buckley (1989) and Luhamdjula (1987) we used the minimum operator to intersect all the fuzzy parameters. The joint possibility distribution $\Pi(A, b, c)$ is just the minimum of $\mu_{\tilde{c}_{kj}}(c_j)$, $\mu_{\tilde{a}_{ij}}(a_{ij})$ and $\mu_{\tilde{b}_i}(b_i)$ over all $\tilde{c}_j$, $\tilde{a}_{ij}$ and $\tilde{b}_i$.

2 Possibility distribution of the solution of a fuzzy linear programming problem

The solution of the FLP is also fuzzy and we will describe it through the possibility distribution of the optimum value of the objective function.

Let us consider the crisp LP(A, b, c) problem:

$$\left.\begin{array}{r} \max \tilde{z} = \tilde{c}x \\ \text{subject to} \\ \tilde{A}x \leq \tilde{b} \\ x \geq 0 \end{array}\right\} (LP(A, b, c))$$

Following the classical scheme for fuzzy decision-making defined by Bellman and Zadeh, the possibility distribution of the optimum value of the objective function is given by the extension principle and the joint possibility distribution of all parameters. We define $\Pi[\tilde{z}^* = z^*]$, the possibility distribution of optimum value of the objective function $\tilde{z}$:

$$\Pi(\tilde{z}^* = z^*) = \sup_{A,b,c} \{\Pi(A, b, c) : z^* \text{ is the optimum of the LP}(A, b, c)\}$$

We will construct the possibility distribution of $\tilde{z}^*$ in terms of its α-cuts, $z^*_\alpha = [z^{*L}_\alpha, z^{*R}_\alpha]$ with $\alpha \in [0, 1]$. For this we need some definitions and results.

Definition 1.

$$\Omega(\alpha) = \{z^* : z^* \textit{ is the optimum of the } LP(A, b, c) \textit{ with } A \in A_\alpha, b \in b_\alpha, c \in c_\alpha\}$$

where A_α, b_α, c_α *are the* α*-cuts of* $\tilde{A}, \tilde{b}, \tilde{c}$.

This allows us to describe the α-cut of the fuzzy solution, z^*_α, as we shall proof (theorem 3) it is equal to $\Omega(\alpha)$.

Definition 2. *Let the function* f *be such that*

$$f(A, b, c) = z^*$$

where z^* *is the optimum finite —provided it exists— of the LP*(A, b, c)*. Then*

$$\Omega(\alpha) = \{f(A, b, c) : A \in A_\alpha, b \in b_\alpha, c \in c_\alpha\}.$$

Theorem 1. *The function* f *is continuous in its domain,* $\mathcal{D}$*, i.e., in all points* (A, b, c) *where the problem LP*(A, b, c) *is feasible and has a finite optimum.*

Proof. Let (A_0, b_0, c_0) be any point in $\mathcal{D}$ and $z^*_0 = f(A_0, b_0, c_0)$. We are going to prove that

$$\forall \epsilon > 0\ \exists \delta > 0 : z^* = f(A, b, c) \in B(z^*_0, \epsilon) \text{ and } \forall (A, b, c) \in B((A_0, b_0, c_0), \delta). \quad (1)$$

If $z^*_0 = f(A_0, b_0, c_0)$ then there exists $x_0 \geq 0$ such that $A_0 x_0 \leq b_0$, $A_{0_B} x_{0_B} = b_0$ and $z^*_0 = c_0 x_0$, and if $z^* = f(A, b, c)$ then there exists $x \geq 0$ such that $Ax \leq b$, $A_B x_B = b$ and $z^* = cx$.

Let

$$\| z^* - z^*_0 \| = \| cx - c_0 x + c_0 x - c_0 x_0 \| \leq \| c - c_0 \| \, \| x \| + \| c_0 \| \, \| x - x_0 \| \quad (2)$$

Because $x_B = A_B^{-1} b$ and $A_{0_B} x_{0_B} = b_0$, then

$$\begin{aligned} x_B &= A_B^{-1} b = A_B^{-1}(b_0 + b - b_0) = A_B^{-1} b_0 + A_B^{-1}(b - b_0) \\ &= A_B^{-1}(A_{0_B} x_{0_B}) + A_B^{-1}(b - b_0) = A_B^{-1}(A_B + A_{0_B} - A_B) x_{0_B} \cdot \\ &\quad + A_B^{-1}(b - b_0) = x_{0_B} + A_B^{-1}(A_{0_B} - A_B) x_0 + A_B^{-1}(b - b_0) \end{aligned}$$

From above it follows

$$x_B - x_{0_B} = A_B^{-1}(A_{0_B} - A_B)x_{0_B} + A_B^{-1}(b - b_0).$$

If $A \in B(A_0, \delta')$, i.e., $\| A - A_0 \| < \delta'$, using the norm that provides convergence element to element then $\| A_{0_B} - A_B \| < \delta'$, if $b \in B(b_0, \delta'')$, i.e., $\| b - b_0 \| < \delta''$, and $c \in B(c_0, \delta''')$, i.e., $\| c - c_0 \| < \delta'''$.

Taking

$$\delta' < \frac{\epsilon}{4\|A_B^{-1}\| \, \|x_0\| \, \|c_0\|}, \quad \delta'' < \frac{\epsilon}{4\|A_B^{-1}\| \, \|c_0\|}, \quad \delta''' < \frac{\epsilon}{2\|x\|}$$

and $\delta = \min(\delta', \delta'', \delta''')$, it follows that

$$\|z^* - z_0^*\| < \frac{\epsilon}{2} + \|c_0\| \left[\frac{\epsilon}{4\|c_0\|} + \frac{\epsilon}{4\|c_0\|} \right] = \epsilon.$$

□

Theorem 2. *Consider the problems LP(A, b, c) and LP(A′, b′, c′). If* $z^* = f(A, b, c)$ *and* $z'^* = f(A', b', c')$*, where* $c < c'$*,* $b < b'$ *and* $A' < A$*, then:*

$$z^* = f(A, b, c) < z'^* = f(A', b', c').$$

Proof. Let $\mathcal{X}_{(A,b)}$ and $\mathcal{X}_{(A',b')}$ be the feasible sets of the problems LP(A, b, c) and LP(A', b', c'), we are going to prove that $\mathcal{X}_{(A,b)} \subset \mathcal{X}_{(A',b')}$.

If $x \in \mathcal{X}_{(A,b)}$, then $Ax \leq b$, $x \geq 0$ and so

$$A'x < Ax \leq b < b'$$

we concluded that $x \in \mathcal{X}_{(A',b')}$.

Let $x \in \mathcal{X}_{(A,b)}$ be such that $z^* = cx$ and $x' \in \mathcal{X}_{(A',b')}$ such that $z'^* = c'x'$. As $x \in \mathcal{X}_{(A',b')}$ and $c < c'$ then

$$z^* = cx < c'x \leq c'x' = z'^*.$$

□

From the previous theorems we may affirm that

Theorem 3. *If*

(i) the problem $LP(A_0^R, b_0^L, c_0^L)$ *is feasible and*
(ii) the problem $LP(A_0^L, b_0^R, c_0^R)$ *has finite optimum,*

then $\Omega(\alpha)$ *is a closed interval.*

This result holds because $\Omega(\alpha)$ is the image of a connected set, $A_\alpha \times b_\alpha \times c_\alpha$, through a continuous function, f. Condition (i) assures that all problems with parameters varying in the joint α-cut are feasible because the previous theorem states that $LP(A_0^R, b_0^L, c_0^L)$ is the problem with the smaller feasible set. Also condition (ii) allows us to assure that all problems with parameters varying in the joint α-cut have finite optima because theorem 2 states that $LP(A_0^L, b_0^R, c_0^R)$ is the problem with the larger optimum. We conclude that $LP(A, b, c)$ is feasible and has finite optimum for all $A \in A_\alpha, b \in b_\alpha$, $c \in c_\alpha$ and, then, the function f is definite in the whole set $A_\alpha \times b_\alpha \times c_\alpha$.

Theorem 4.

$$\Omega(\alpha) = z^*_\alpha$$

Proof.

(i) $\Omega(\alpha) \subset z^*_\alpha$ is evident.
(ii) Let $z^* \in z^*_\alpha$, then $\Pi(\tilde{z^*} = z^*) \geq \alpha$ and it follows that:

$$\sup_{A,b,c} \{\Pi(A, b, c)/z^* = f(A, b, c)\} = \alpha^* \geq \alpha.$$

If $\Upsilon_{z^*} = \{\Pi(A, b, c)/z^* = f(A, b, c)\}$, from (3) there exists a sequence $(\alpha_n) \subset \Upsilon_{z^*}$ converging to α^*.

Given $\alpha_n \in \Upsilon_{z^*}$, there are A_n, b_n, c_n such that

$$z^* = f(A_n, b_n, c_n) \quad \text{and} \quad \Pi(A_n, b_n, c_n) = \alpha_n,$$

then $A_n \in A_{\alpha_n}$, $b_n \in b_{\alpha_n}$, $c_n \in c_{\alpha_n}$, $z^* \in \Omega(\alpha_n)$ and $(A_n)_{n\in\mathcal{N}} \subset A_{\alpha=0}$, $(b_n)_{n\in\mathcal{N}} \subset b_{\alpha=0}$, $(c_n)_{n\in\mathcal{N}} \subset c_{\alpha=0}$, $A_{\alpha=0}, b_{\alpha=0}, c_{\alpha=0}$ are compact sets, hence there are convergent subsequences:

$$(A_{n_k}) \longrightarrow A^*, (b_{n_k}) \longrightarrow b^*, (c_{n_k}) \longrightarrow c^*,$$

and because $\lim_{n\to\infty} \alpha_n = \alpha^*$, then $A^* \in A_{\alpha^*}, b^* \in b_{\alpha^*}, c^* \in c_{\alpha^*}$ and f is continuous, it follows that

$$\forall \epsilon > 0 \quad \exists k \geq k_0 : f(A_{n_k}, b_{n_k}, c_{n_k}) \in \mathcal{B}(f(A^*, b^*, c^*), \epsilon) \quad \forall k \geq k_0;$$

also $z^* = f(A_{n_k}, b_{n_k}, c_{n_k})$, then $z^* = f(A^*, b^*, c^*) \in \Omega(\alpha^*)$ since $\alpha \leq \alpha^*$, hence $\Omega(\alpha^*) \subset \Omega(\alpha)$ and we conclude that $z = f(A^*, b^*, c^*) \in \Omega(\alpha)$. □

From the previous theorems we may affirm that

Proposition 1.

$$z^{*^L}_\alpha = f(A^R_\alpha, b^L_\alpha, c^L_\alpha) \qquad z^{*^R}_\alpha = f(A^L_\alpha, b^R_\alpha, c^R_\alpha)$$

where $z^{*^L}_\alpha$, $z^{*^R}_\alpha$ *denote the lower and upper extremes of the closed interval* z^*_α*, respectively.*

From theorem 2 and the α-cuts properties, we have that

Proposition 2. *If* $\alpha_1 < \alpha_2$ *, then:*

$$(i) \quad z^{*^L}_{\alpha_1} < z^{*^L}_{\alpha_2}$$
$$(ii) \quad z^{*^R}_{\alpha_2} < z^{*^R}_{\alpha_1}$$

This proposition means that the α-cuts of the possibility distribution of z^* are closed and nested intervals and, finally, we can conclude that

Theorem 5. *If conditions (i) and (ii) of theorem 3 are satisfied, then*

$$\tilde{z}^* \text{ is a fuzzy number.}$$

If conditions (i) and (ii) of theorem 3 are not satisfied, then we should point out to the DM that estimates of the parameters in the model leads to unfeasible or unbounded problems. DM must to consider a posible modification of his/her estimates.

3 An application: A bank balance sheet

The interest rate problem in bank balance sheet management has been formulated and studied by numerous authors. In practice, the unit costs, the unit profits and the interest rates are usually imprecise. This imprecise nature has long been studied with the help of probability theory. However, probability theory might not provide the correct interpretation to solve some practical decision-making problems. Stochastic programming is built on the assumption that some of the parameters used in describing the problem are random variables, which are difficult to determine exactly. Stochastic programming models are often very complex in structure and therefore rarely used in practice. In addition, applying probability theory to some optimization problems has a negative effect on the computational efficiency. To solve this kind of problems, the possibility theory might be more appropriate.

Let us consider an interest rate problem in bank balance sheet management and assume that the interest rate is imprecise and has a possibilistic distribution, instead of a probabilistic distribution. The interest rate cannot be described through precise and reliable data needed to set up the random variables. Then, possibility theory may be helpful in describing this kind of imprecision and allows us to construct flexible models and obtain the possibilistic distribution of the solution that permits the decision-maker to choose the one that best fits his/her goal.

The basic bank hedging decision problem we consider is based on Lai and Hwang's model (1992). The fuzziness of interest rates and the price of futures is modelled by triangular possibilistic distributions. The objective of the problem is to maximize the expected final balance sheet value of stockholders' equity or to maximize expected profit. Stockholders' equity at the end of period E equals: beginning equity ($E*$); plus the net revenues associated with non-maturing

$$r*_{STS}(1-b_{STS})STS*+r*_{LTS}(1-b_{LTS})LTS*+r*_{L}(1-b_{L})L*$$

and newly acquired securities and loans

$$r_{STS}P_{STS}+r_{LTS}P_{LTS}+r_{L}P_{L}$$

minus the net revenues corresponding to securities sold

$$r*_{STS}S_{STS}+r*_{LTS}S_{LTS}$$

plus (or minus) capital gains or losses (book value minus anticipated ending price)

$$K_{STS}S_{STS} + K_{LTS}S_{LTS}$$

where the capital gains (losses) of the short-term security sales (K_{STS}) and the capital gains (losses) of the long-term security sales (K_{LTS}) are

$$K_{STS} = 1 - \left\{ r*STS \left[\sum_{t=1}^{(0.5/b_{STS})} (1+\tilde{r}_{STS})^{-t} \right] + (1+\tilde{r}_{STS})^{-(0.5/b_{STS})+0.5} \right\},$$

$$K_{LTS} = 1 - \left\{ r*LTS \left[\sum_{t=1}^{(0.5/b_{LTS})} (1+\tilde{r}_{LTS})^{-t} \right] + (1+\tilde{r}_{LTS})^{-(0.5/b_{LTS})+0.5} \right\}$$

plus (or minus) the gain (or loss) on the hedging transaction

$$[1 - (\tilde{p}_{PF}/p_{SF})]S_F$$

minus the cost of deposits

$$\tilde{r}_D D.$$

It should be noted that futures and spot prices are not mechanically related and allow the bank to be subject to basic risk; thus, the per dollar profit of selling futures is $1 - (\tilde{p}_{PF}/p_{SF})$.

The first constraint requires that at the period's end the bank's cash and reserve holdings are at least a certain portion of deposits plus a margin requirement associated with the sale of future contracts

$$aD + mS_F - R \leq 0$$

The second constraint indicates that the bank can sell short-term, non-maturing securities but cannot sell securities purchased

$$S_{STS} \leq (1 - b_{STS})STS*$$

Similarly, we have

$$S_{LTS} \leq (1 - b_{LTS})LTS*$$

As only the interest rate risk associated with long-term securities is hedged and the magnitude of this hedge is determined by the maximum dollar volume of long-term securities that could be sold, we have

$$S_F \leq (1 - b_{LTS})LTS*$$

The bank cannot make loans in excess of that supplied: $P_L \leq ld$, and it cannot obtain more deposits than are supplied: $D \leq d$. The managerially determined relationship between loans and deposits is indicated in the following constraint

$$L = (1 - b_L)L* + P_L \leq cD$$

Variable Parameter	Historical value	Current value	Future value
R Reserves	\$200		
STS Short-term securities	\$100		
LTS Long-term securities	\$300		
L Loans	\$400		
D Deposits	\$900		
E Equity	\$100		
r_{STS} STS interest rate (annual)	0.07	0.08	about 0.08
r_{LTS} LTS interest rate (annual)	0.08	0.09	about 0.09
r_L L Interest rate (annual)	0.11	0.14	
r_D D Interest rate (annual)			about 0.04
p_{SF} Price of futures contract sold		\$92	
p_{PF} Price of futures contract purchased			about \$92
m Margin per dolar of S_F		0.025	
ld Maximum new loan demand		\$424	
d Maximum new deposite supply			\$986
a Portion of D associated with R		0.2	
b_{STS} Portion of STS maturing		0.5	
b_{LTS} Portion of LTS maturing		0.125	
b_L Portion of L maturing		0.125	
c Maximum desired L to D ratio		0.83	
P_{STS} Purchase STS			
P_{LTS} Purchase LTS			
P_L Purchase L			
S_{STS} Sell STS			
S_{LTS} Sell LTS			
S_F Sell futures			
R Reserves			

Table 1. Variable and parameter definitions and numerical quarterly data

Finally, the last constraint indicates that the total assets cannot exceed the deposits plus equity

$$R + STS + LTS + L \leq D + E$$

where

$$STS = (1 - b_{STS})STS{*}{+}P_{STS} - S_{STS}, \quad LTS = (1 - b_{LTS})LTS{*}{+}P_{LTS} - S_{LTS}.$$

With the data appearing in Table 1, the fuzzy bank model can be modelled as a maximization problem

$$\begin{aligned}
\max E = {} & 115.75 + 0.02P_{STS} + 0.0225P_{LTS} + 0.035P_L \\
& + (-0.024217, -0.0223775, -0.0205436)S_{STS} \\
& + (-0.0320299, -0.0214892, -0.016166)S_{LTS} \\
& + (-0.0227391, 0, 0.0108696)S_F \\
& + (-0.0125, -0.01, -0.00875)D
\end{aligned}$$

subject to

$$\begin{aligned}
& 0.2D + 0.025S_F - R \leq 0 \\
& P_L \leq 424, \;\; D \leq 986 \\
& S_{STS} \leq 50, \;\; S_{LTS} \leq 262.5, \;\; S_F \leq 262.5 \\
& P_L - 0.83D \leq -350 \\
& 0.98P_{STS} + 0.9775P_{LTS} + 0.965P_L + \\
& \quad + (-0.9794564, -0.9776245, -0.975783)S_{STS} + \\
& \quad + (-0.983834, -0.9785108, -0.9679701)S_{LTS} + \\
& \quad + (-0.0108696, 0, 0.0217391)S_F + \\
& \quad + (-0.99125, -0.99, -0.9875)D + R \leq -546.75
\end{aligned}$$

The lowest optimum at a level of possibility α, $E{*}_{\alpha}^{L}$, can be determined by solving the worst linear program at the possibility level α and the highest optimum, $E{*}_{\alpha}^{R}$, can be obtained solving the best linear program. We also solve the problems at possibility levels 0, 0.2, 0.4, 0.6, 0.8 and 1.

α	0	0.2	0.4	0.6	0.8	1
E	112.6611	113.5516	114.3685	115.1819	115.9918	116.9342
P_{STS}	0	0	0	0	0	0
P_{LTS}	0	0	0	0	0	131.7343
P_L	424	424	424	424	424	424
S_{STS}	50	50	50	50	50	50
S_{LTS}	134.9689	134.1489	133.3315	132.518	131.7082	262.5
S_F	0	0	0	0	0	0
D	986	986	986	986	986	986
R	197.2	197.2	197.2	197.2	197.2	197.2
α	0.8	0.6	0.4	0.2	0	
E	117.9238	119.0644	120.2051	121.3457	122.4863	
P_{STS}	0	0	0	0	0	
P_{LTS}	126.1614	127.302	128.4426	129.5232	130.7238	
P_L	424	424	424	424	424	
S_{STS}	50	50	50	50	50	
S_{LTS}	262.5	262.5	262.5	262.5	262.5	
S_F	262.5	262.5	262.5	262.5	262.5	
D	986	986	986	986	986	
R	203.7625	203.7625	203.7625	203.7625	203.7625	

Table 2. The optimal balance sheet and decisions

Table 2 presents the solution of the balance sheet and the corresponding decisions. From this table, the bank should obtain the funds through the maturing of its existing short-term securities, long-term securities and loan balance, and accept all the deposits supplied to it. Reserve balances should be reduced to 197.2 . All of the non-maturing short-term securities should be sold. The amount of sales and purchases of long-term securities is very sensitive to the possibility degree.

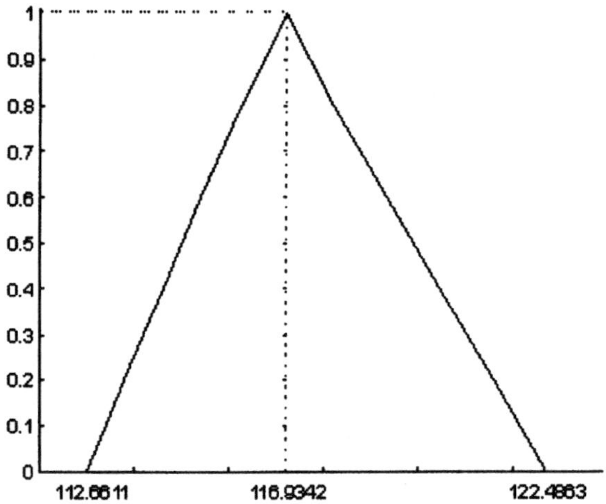

Fig. 1. The posibility distribution of the objective function

The possibility distribution of the optimal equity is presented in Figure 1, it is a non linear bell-shaped distribution.

4 Summary and conclusions

In this paper we have considered a linear programming problem where all the parameters are imprecise data. This imprecise nature has long been studied with the help of probability theory. However, probability theory might not give us the correct answer to solve some practical decision-making problems and applying probability theory to some optimization problems has a negative effect on the computational efficiency. In these cases, possibility theory might be helpful.

We have shown a fuzzy solution of the FLP whose α-cuts are connected and nested and whose bounds have been obtained solving the "worst" LP($A^R_\alpha, b^L_\alpha, c^L_\alpha$), and the "best" LP($A^L_\alpha, b^R_\alpha, c^R_\alpha$) problems defined for each $\alpha \in [0, 1]$. That solution is a fuzzy number (theorem 5) and it allows us to specify the possibility distribution for the objective function.

An advantage of the proposed approach is that the DM can also participate fruitfully in the process because, the concept of fuzzy sets is very well suited to practical situations, where the process has been operating for some time and the DM has a fairly good idea about the process.

To illustrate our approach we have solved a linear programming with a maximization objective of a investment discounted value where the interest rate is imprecise and has a triangular possibility distribution. Solving the numerical bank hedging decision problem, has shown that the distribution of the objective function has a non-linear bell shape, even though the interest rates and the price of futures contracts purchased have simple triangular possibility distributions.

References

Arenas, M. M., Rodríguez, M. V. (1994). A formulation of a fuzzy linear goal programming problem with fuzzy constraints and fuzzy target values. Proceeding of MOPGP94. Springer-Verlag: New York.

Arenas, M. (1997). *Programación Multiobjetivo en Ambiente Difuso*. Tesis Doctoral. Dpto. Matemáticas. Universidad de Oviedo.

Bellman, R. E. and Zadeh, L. A. (1970). Decision-making in a fuzzy environment. *Management Science* **17**, 141–164.

Buckley, J. J. (1989). Solving possibilistic linear programming problems. *Fuzzy Sets and Systems* **31**, 329–341.

Dubois, D. and Prade, H. (1980). *Fuzzy Sets and Systems: Theory and Applications*. New York, London, Toronto.

Lai, Y-J. and Hwang Ch-L. (1992). *Fuzzy Mathematical Programming*. Springer-Verlag: Berlin.

Lai, Y-J.;Hwang Ch-L. (1993). Possibilistic linear programming for managing interest rate risk. *Fuzzy Sets and Systems*, **54**, 135–146.

Julien, B. (1994). An extension to possibilistic linear programming. *Fuzzy sets ans Systems* **64**, 195–206.

Luhandjula, M. K. (1987). Multiple objective programming problems with possibilistic coefficients. *Fuzzy Sets and Systems* **21**, 135–145.

Tanaka, H. and Asai, K. (1984). Fuzzy linear programming problems with fuzzy numbers. *Fuzzy Sets and Systems* **13**, 1–10.

Yang, Y. (1991). An new approach to uncertain parameter linear programming. *European Journal Of Operational Research* **54**, 95–114.

Zadeh, L. A. (1965): Fuzzy sets. *Information and Control* **8**, 338–353.

Measuring the Arbitrage Opportunities in an Intertemporal Dynamic Asset Pricing Model

A. Balbás[1], P. Jiménez Guerra[2] and M.J Muñoz Bouzo[3]

[1] Departamento de Economía de la Empresa. Universidad Carlos III. C/ Madrid 126. 28903 Getafe. Madrid, SPAIN
[2] Departamento de Matemáticas Fundamentales. Facultad de Ciencias. UNED. C/ Senda del Rey s/n. 28040. Madrid, SPAIN
[3] Departamento de Economía. Universidad Carlos III. C/ Madrid 126. 28903 Getafe. Madrid, SPAIN

Abstract

This paper gives a measure of the arbitrage opportunities in an intertemporal dynamic asset pricing model. The measure is introduced by means of a stochastic process, and extends previous results obtained for static models in the literature. Two interesting applications of this theory can be considered. First, the measure of the cross-market arbitrage gives information about the integration between two or more financial markets. Second, dynamic asset pricing models with transaction costs can be analyzed.

The main results have also interesting consequences from a mathematical point of view, since we provide a procedure to solve certain infinite multiobjective optimization problems with (non-differentiable) objective function.

Keywords. Arbitrage portfolio, dynamic asset pricing model, infinite-dimensional optimization program, multiobjective program

1 Introduction

The absence of arbitrage opportunities is a basic assumption common to all the asset pricing models. However, some empirical studies have presented evidence supporting the existence of arbitrage strategies (see Kamara and Miller (1995), Chen and Knez (1995), Protopapadakis and Stoll (1983) or Harris et al. (1995)). As a consequence, some authors have proposed different ways to estimate the size of these arbitrage strategies, and so for instance Chen and Knez (1995) give a measure of the cross-market arbitrage opportunities which helps to asess the integration level among different markets. In Balbás and Muñoz (1996) we provide an alternative measure with some interesting properties, like giving the size of the arbitrage opportunities in monetary terms (relative profits obtained from an arbitrage portfolio). Also, it is not necessary to be working with more than one market. However, both measures are defined for static models. The purpose of this paper is to define a measure in a dynamic setting, following the approach of Balbás and Muñoz (1996) in order to measure in monetary terms. The analysis of dynamic models with transaction costs and the measurement of market integration are two interesting applications of the theory we develop here. So, our results are an alternative to the ones presented in Prisman (1986), Leland (1985), Davis et al. (1993) or Toft (1996).

The paper proceeds as follows. The model is presented in Section 2. In Section 3 we introduce the measure of arbitrage opportunities: the infinite-dimensional linear optimization problem (1_h) leads to the maximum expected profit derived from an arbitrage portfolio with short-sales constraints h. Considering that the portfolio h depends on the investor (for instance if we assume that an agent cannot sell what he/she does not have), Problem (4) leads to the maximum expected relative profit with respect to the price of h. Thus, Theorem 3.6 is one of the most important results of the present paper, since it guarantees that problem (4) is solvable. It allows us to introduce a random variable (or adapted stochastic process in a dynamic setting) to measure the arbitrage opportunities. In Section 4 we show that our measure also analyzes the level of the arbitrage opportunities after absolutely relaxing the short-selling constraints. From a mathematical point of view Theorems 4.4 and 4.5 show that the results in Section 3 provide a procedure to reduce the solution of an optimization program with a non differentiable function (Problem (5)) to succesively solving two linear programs. Furthermore, Problem (5) is also equivalent to the infinite multiobjective optimization programs (6) and (7). As a consequence we show that the measure tests the maximum relative profit in almost every state of nature and not only the expected maximum.

2 Preliminaries

In many papers (e.g., Harrison and Kreps (1979), Chamberlain and Rothschild (1983), Chen and Knez (1995)) Hilbert space methods are used to represent pricing functions and to characterize the absence of arbitrage across a market. Thus, much of their analysis leads them to consider an economy endowed with a probability space on which the space of all square-integrable functions is defined. In order to derive a general framework for analyzing the profits obtained by arbitrage opportunities in a multiperiod model we focus our attention in a arbitrary single period model from the intertemporal arbitrage problem. This leads us to not assume that the price at first time of the period of each security is constant.

Thus, consider an economy endowed with probability spaces (Ω, Σ_1, P) and (Ω, Σ_2, P) (with $\Sigma_1 \subseteq \Sigma_2$) on which the linear spaces $L^2(\Sigma_1)$ and $L^2(\Sigma_2)$ of Σ_1 or Σ_2-measurable square-integrable functions over $\boldsymbol{R}$, are defined. Let the number of assets be finite and indexed by $\{1, \ldots n\}$. The prices of the assets at time 1 are $p = (p_1, p_2, \ldots, p_n) \in (L^2(\Sigma_1))^n$, and the price on the ith asset at time 2 is $\alpha_i \in L^2(\Sigma_2)$. Let us introduce the following assumptions:

A$_1$. For every $i = 1, \ldots, n$, $p_i \in L^2(\Sigma_1)$ and there exists $k_i > 0$ such that $p_i(\omega) > k_i$.

A$_2$. For every $i = 1, \ldots, n$, $\alpha_i \in L^2(\Sigma_2)$ and $\alpha_1(\omega) > 0$.

For a portfolio $x = (x_1, x_2, \ldots, x_n) \in (L^2(\Sigma_1))^n$, the sum $\sum_{i=1}^n x_i\alpha_i$ is its total price at time 2 and $\sum_{i=1}^n x_i p_i$ is its total price at time 1.

Definition 2.1. *The portfolio $x \in (L^2(\Sigma_1))^n$ is said to be an arbitrage opportunity (strong form) if there exists $A \in \Sigma_1$ with $P(A) > 0$ such that $\sum_{i=1}^n x_i\alpha_i \geq 0$ a.e. in A, then $\sum_{i=1}^n x_i p_i < 0$ a.e. in A.*

3 Measurement of the arbitrage opportunities

In order to define a measure indicating the level of arbitrage opportunities, consider for every $h = (h_1, \cdots h_n) \in (L^2_+(\Sigma_1))^n$ the following optimization problem

$$(1_h)\ \max -\sum_{i=1}^n \int_\Omega x_i p_i \, dP \quad \text{s.t.} \quad \begin{cases} \sum_{i=1}^n x_i\alpha_i \geq 0 \\ x_i \geq -h_i \quad i = 1, \ldots, n. \end{cases}$$

The problem (1_h) describes the process of identifying the portfolio (constrained by the bounds in a short position $h_i \geq 0$) which minimizes the initial expected investment needed to purchase a portfolio that generates a a nonnegative payoff in every state of nature. Thus, a solution to the problem (1_h) represents the maximum expected profit obtained by an agent implementing arbitrage in such a way that he/she cannot sell more than h_i units in each asset i.

Denote by F'_h the feasible set in (1_h).

Lemma 3.1. *If $h \in (L^2_+(\Sigma_1))^n$ is such that $\sum_{i=1}^n h_i p_i \in L^2(\Sigma_1)$ then Program (1_h) is solvable.*

Proof. First note that the feasible set F'_h in (1_h) is non void since $x = 0 \in F'_h$. Furthermore, the optimum value in (1_h) is nonnegative.

Take $x \in F'_h$ such that $-\sum_{i=1}^n \int_\Omega x_i p_i \, dP \geq 0$.

For $A = \{\omega \in \Omega \mid -\sum_{i=1}^n x_i(\omega)p_i(\omega) > 0\}$ and $x' = x.chi_A$ where χ_A is the characteristic function of A we get, $x' \in F'_h$ and $-\sum_{i=1}^n \int_\Omega x'_i p_i \, dP \geq -\sum_{i=1}^n \int_\Omega x_i p_i \, dP$. Then, the original problem is equivalent to

$$(2_h)\ \max -\sum_{i=1}^n \int_\Omega x_i p_i \, dP \quad \text{s.t.} \quad \begin{cases} \sum_{i=1}^n x_i\alpha_i \geq 0 \quad \text{and} \quad \sum_{i=1}^n x_i p_i \leq 0 \\ x_i \geq -h_i \quad i = 1, \ldots, n. \end{cases}$$

Taking into account that $-h_i \leq x_i \leq (\sum_{j \neq i} p_j h_j)/p_i$ if x feasible in (2_h), the assumption (A_2) and the fact that $\sum_{i=1}^n h_i p_i \in L^2(\Sigma_1)$ we get that the feasible set in (2_h) is weakly-compact. Then, the weak-continuity of the objective function guarantees that there exists x feasible in (2_h) where the optimum value of (1_h) is achieved. □

Denote by F_h the feasible set of (2_h) and by $\varphi(h)$ the optimal value in (1_h), i.e., $\varphi(h) = \max\{-\sum_{i=1}^n \int_\Omega x_i p_i \, dP \,|\, x \in F_h\}$. It is easily verified that

$$\varphi(h+h') \geq \varphi(h) + \varphi(h') \quad \text{and} \quad \varphi(\delta h) = \delta\varphi(h)$$

for every $h, h' \in (L^2_+(\Sigma_1))^n$ such that $\sum_{i=1}^n h_i p_i$, $\sum_{i=1}^n h'_i p_i \in L^2(\Sigma_1)$ and $\delta > 0$, so φ is a concave function. Also, $\varphi(h) \geq \varphi(h')$ if $h \geq h'$ in the product order generated by the cone $L^2_+(\Sigma_1)$.

Finally, from $-\sum_{i=1}^n \int_\Omega x_i p_i \, dP \leq \sum_{i=1}^n \int_\Omega h_i p_i \, dP$ for every feasible x, we get that

$$\varphi(h) \leq \sum_{i=1}^n \int_\Omega h_i p_i \, dP \tag{3.1.1}$$

Lemma 3.2. *Suppose $x \in (L^2(\Sigma_1))^n$ and $A \in \Sigma_1$ with $P(A) > 0$ are such that $\sum_{i=1}^n x_i \alpha_i \geq 0$ a.e. in A and $\sum_{i=1}^n x_i p_i < 0$ a.e. in A. Then for every $\epsilon > 0$ there exists $B \in \Sigma_1$, $B \subseteq A$ with $P(A - B) < \epsilon$ such that $\hat{x} = x.chi_B \in (L^\infty(\Sigma_1))^n$, $\sum_{i=1}^n \hat{x}_i \alpha_i \geq 0$ and $\sum_{i=1}^n \hat{x}_i p_i < 0$ a.e.*

Proof. Let $A_k = \{\omega \in A \,|\, |x_i(\omega)| \leq k,\ i = 1, \cdots, n\}$. Since $\lim_k P(A_k) = P(A)$, then for every $\epsilon > 0$, there exists $k' \in \mathbb{N}$ such that $P(A - A_k) < \epsilon$ whenever $k \geq k'$. Then $B = A_{k'}$ is the required subset. □

Theorem 3.3. *No arbitrage opportunity exists on the market if and only if $\varphi(h) = 0$ for every $h \in (L^2_+(\Sigma_1))^n$ such that $\sum_{i=1}^n h_i p_i \in L^2(\Sigma_1)$.*

Proof. Suppose there exists an arbitrage porfolio $x \in (L^2(\Sigma_1))^n$ and let $A \in \Sigma_1$ such that $P(A) > 0$, $\sum_{i=1}^n x_i \alpha_i \geq 0$ a.e. in A and $\sum_{i=1}^n x_i p_i < 0$ a.e. in A. From Lemma 3.2, let be B and $\tilde{x} = x.chi_B$ such that $P(B) > 0$ and $\tilde{x} \in (L^\infty(\Sigma_1))^n$. Then $\sum_{i=1}^n |\tilde{x}_i| p_i \in L^2(\Sigma_2)$. Setting $h = (|\tilde{x}_1|, \cdots, |\tilde{x}_n|)$, $\tilde{x} \in F_h$. Consequently, $\varphi(h) \geq -\sum_{i=1}^n \int_\Omega \tilde{x}_i p_i \, dP = -\sum_{i=1}^n \int_B x_i p_i \, dP > 0$.

Assume now that no arbitrage opportunity exists. If $h \in (L^2_+(\Sigma_1))^n$ and $x \in F_h$ then, $P\{\omega \mid \sum_{i=1}^n x_i p_i < 0\} = 0$ holds. Consequently, $\varphi(h) = 0$ for every $h \in (L^2_+(\Sigma_1))^n$ such that $\sum_{i=1}^n h_i p_i \in L^2(\Sigma_1)$. □

Let $x^h \in F_h$ be a solution where the optimum value $\varphi(h)$ is achieved. We first prove that x^h solves a multiobjective optimization program. For this purpose, we adopt the following notations. For every $A \in \Sigma_i$, $i = 1, 2$ set $\Sigma_i^A = \{B \cap A \,|\, B \in \Sigma_i\}$ and the restricted optimization program:

$$(1_h^A) \ \max -\sum_{i=1}^n \int_A x_i p_i \, dP \quad \text{s.t.} \quad \begin{cases} \sum_{i=1}^n x_i \alpha_i \geq 0 & \text{a.e. in } A \\ x_i \geq -h_i & \text{a.e. in } A \quad i = 1, \ldots, n. \end{cases}$$

Lemma 3.4. *Let $h \in (L^2_+(\Sigma_1))^n$ such that $\sum_{i=1}^n h_i p_i \in L^2(\Sigma_1)$ and suppose that x^h solves (1_h). Then, x^h solves (1_h^A) for every $A \in \Sigma_1$.*

Proof. Proceeding by contradiction suppose there exists x feasible in (1_h^A) such that

$$-\sum_{i=1}^{n} \int_A x_i p_i \, dP > . - \sum_{i=1}^{n} \int_A x_i^h p_i \, dP$$

Define

$$x' = \begin{cases} x^h & \text{if } \omega \notin A \\ x & \text{if } \omega \in A. \end{cases}$$

Obviously x' is feasible in (1_h) and $-\sum_{i=1}^n \int_\Omega x_i p_i \, dP > \varphi(h)$. □

Lemma 3.5. *Let $h \in (L^2_+(\Sigma_1))^n$ such that $\sum_{i=1}^n h_i p_i \in L^2(\Sigma_1)$ and suppose that x^h solves (1_h). Then, x^h solves the following multiobjective optimization program:*

$$(3_h) \quad \max - \sum_{i=1}^{n} x_i p_i \quad \text{s.t.} \quad \begin{cases} \sum_{i=1}^n x_i \alpha_i \geq 0 \\ x_i \geq -h_i \quad i = 1, \dots, n. \end{cases}$$

Furthermore, $-\sum_{i=1}^n x_i^h p_i$ is a strong maximum in (3_h), i.e., an upper bound for (3_h), and not only a maximal element.

Proof. It follows immediately from Lemma 3.4. □

We try to define a measure as the maximum expected profit obtained by an investor among all the priced one portfolios h of the bounds in a short position. Then we look for $h = (h_1, \cdots h_n) \in (L^2_+(\Sigma_1))^n$ so as to solve

$$(4) \quad \max \; \varphi(h) \quad \text{s.t.} \quad \begin{cases} \sum_{i=1}^n h_i p_i = 1 \\ h_i \geq 0 \quad i = 1, \dots, n. \end{cases}$$

Denote by H the feasible set in (4), i.e., $H = \left\{h \in (L^2_+(\Sigma_1))^n \mid \sum_{i=1}^n h_i p_i = 1\right\}$. Since $0 \leq h_i \leq 1/p_i$ and $1/p_i$ is in $L^2(\Sigma_1)$ it follows that H is order bounded and hence compact in the weak topology (it is obviously non void and closed).

Theorem 3.6. *Under assumptions A_1 and A_2 Program* (4) *is solvable.*

Proof. From 3.1.1 we obtain $0 \leq \varphi(h) \leq 1$ for every $h \in H$. Therefore, there exists a finite optimal value $\mathfrak{M}$ $(0 \leq \mathfrak{M} \leq 1)$ in (4). We prove in four steps that $\mathfrak{M}$ is achieved in H.

First step: There exist a sequence $(h^k)_{k \in N}$ in H and an associated sequence $(x^k)_{k \in N}$, $x^k \in F_{h^k}$ such that, setting $m^k(\omega) = -\sum_{i=1}^n x_i^k(\omega) p_i(\omega)$, $(m^k)_{k \in N}$ is an increasing sequence in $L^2(\Sigma_1)$ and $\lim_k \int_\Omega m^k \, dP = \mathfrak{M}$.

For this purpose, take a sequence $(\hat{h}^k)_{k \in N}$ in H and an associated sequence $(\hat{x}^k)_{k \in N}$, $\hat{x}^k \in F_{\hat{h}^k}$ such that $\varphi(\hat{h}^k) = -\sum_{i=1}^n \int_\Omega \hat{x}_i^k p_i \, dP$ converges to $\mathfrak{M}$.

Let $h^1 = \hat{h}^1$, $x^1 = \hat{x}^1$ and $A_1 = \{\omega \in \Omega \,|\, -\sum_{i=1}^n x_i^1 p_i \geq -\sum_{i=1}^n \hat{x}_i^2 p_i\}$. Setting

$$x_i^2(\omega) = \begin{cases} x_i^1(\omega) & \text{if } \omega \in A_1 \\ \hat{x}_i^2(\omega) & \text{otherwise,} \end{cases} \quad \text{and} \quad h_i^2(\omega) = \begin{cases} h_i^1(\omega) & \text{if } \omega \in A_1 \\ \hat{h}_i^2(\omega) & \text{otherwise.} \end{cases}$$

then h^2 is feasible in (4) and $x^2 \in F_{h^2}$. Consequently,

$$\mathfrak{M} \geq \varphi(h^2) \geq -\sum_{i=1}^n \int_\Omega x_i^2 p_i \, dP \geq -\sum_{i=1}^n \int_\Omega \hat{x}_i^2 p_i \, dP = \varphi(\hat{h}^2)$$

and $-\sum_{i=1}^n x_i^2 p_i \geq -\sum_{i=1}^n x_i^1 p_i$. Proceed in a similar way with h_2 and $\hat{h}^3$ in order to define h_3 and x_3 such that

$$\mathfrak{M} \geq \varphi(h^3) \geq -\sum_{i=1}^n \int_\Omega x_i^3 p_i \, dP \geq -\sum_{i=1}^n \int_\Omega \hat{x}_i^3 p_i \, dP = \varphi(\hat{h}^3)$$

and $-\sum_{i=1}^n x_i^3 p_i \geq -\sum_{i=1}^n x_i^2 p_i \geq -\sum_{i=1}^n x_i^1 p_i$. Following this procedure we obtain (h^k) and (x^k) verifying the desired requirements.

Second step: There exists an aglomeration point x of the sequence (x^k) in the weak topology of $(L^2(\Sigma_1))^n$.

In fact, since $x^k \in F_{h^k}$ and $h^k \in H$ we get

$$-\frac{1}{k_i} \leq -\frac{1}{p_i} \leq -h_i^k \leq x_i^k \leq \frac{\sum_{j \neq i} p_j h_j^k}{p_i} = \frac{1 - p_i h_i}{p_i} \leq \frac{1}{p_i} \leq \frac{1}{k_i}.$$

Then, the Banach-Alaoglu theorem leads to a weak-aglomeration point x of the sequence (x^k) such that $\sum_{i=1}^n x_i \alpha_i \geq 0$.

Third step: $-\sum_{i=1}^n x_i p_i = m$, where m is defined by $m = \lim_{k \in N} m^k$.

First, note that $(m^k(\omega))$ is an increasing bounded sequence for every $\omega \in \Omega$, thus there exists $m(\omega) = \lim_k m^k(\omega)$. Moreover, $0 \leq m(\omega) \leq 1$ and consequently, from the bounded convergence theorem $m = \lim_{k \in N} m_k$ in $L^2(\Sigma_1)$.

Suppose that $P(A) > 0$, where $A = \{\omega \in \Omega \,|\, -\sum_{i=1}^n x_i(\omega) p_i(\omega) < m(\omega)\}$.

Take $\delta = \int_A \left(m - \left(-\sum_{i=1}^n x_i p_i\right)\right) dP > 0$, and k' such that for every $k \geq k'$ the inequality $\int_A \left|m - \left(-\sum_{i=1}^n x_i^k p_i\right)\right| dP < \delta/2$ holds. Since x is a weak-aglomeration point, there exists $k_0 \geq k'$ such that

$$\left| \int_A \left(-\sum_{i=1}^n x_i p_i - \left(-\sum_{i=1}^n x_i^{k_0} p_i \right) \right) dP \right| < \delta/2.$$

Thus, combining both inequalities we get a contradiction. Hence $P(A) = 0$. In a similar way, we obtain that $P(B) = 0$, where $B = \{\omega \in \Omega \,|\, -\sum_{i=1}^n x_i(\omega) p_i(\omega) > m(\omega)\}$.

Fourth step: $P\{\omega \in \Omega_1 \mid \sum_{i=1}^n x_i^- p_i = 1\} = P(\Omega_1)$ where $\Omega_1 = \{\omega \in \Omega \mid m(\omega) \neq 0\}$ and $x_i^-(\omega) = \max(-x_i(\omega), 0)$.

Define $\epsilon(\omega) = \sum_{i=1}^n x_i^-(\omega)p_i(\omega)$ and note that $\epsilon(\omega) > 0$ whenever $m(\omega) \neq 0$. Furthermore, since $m(\omega) \leq \epsilon(\omega)$ holds, we get $0 < m(\omega)/\epsilon(\omega) \leq 1$ for every $\omega \in \Omega_1$. Hence m/ϵ is an integrable function. Denote by D and E the following sets:

$$D = \{\omega \in \Omega_1 \,|\, 0 < \epsilon(\omega) < 1\} \text{ and } E = \{\omega \in \Omega_1 \,|\, \epsilon(\omega) > 1\}.$$

Suppose first that $P(D) > 0$ and assume without loss of generality that $x^k(\omega) = x(\omega) = 0$ whenever $\omega \notin \Omega_1$. Let $\beta = \int_D \big((m/\epsilon) - m\big)\, dP > 0$. Choose $C \in \Sigma_1$ and $a > 0$ such that $P(C) > 0$, $P(D - C) \leq \beta/2$ and $0 < a < \epsilon(\omega) < 1$ in C, and take $h^k \in H$ and x^k such that $\int_\Omega \big(m - (-\sum_{i=1}^n x_i^k p_i)\big)\, dP < \beta/2$. Setting,

$$y_i(\omega) = \begin{cases} x_i(\omega)/\epsilon(\omega) & \text{if } \omega \in C \\ x_i^k(\omega) & \text{otherwise,} \end{cases} \quad \text{and } h_i'(\omega) = \begin{cases} \max(-y_i(\omega), 0) & \text{if } \omega \in C \\ h_i^k(\omega) & \text{otherwise.} \end{cases}$$

it follows that $h' \in H$ and consequently $\varphi(h') \leq \int_\Omega m\, dP$.

Besides, since $y \in F_{h'}$ we get $-\int_\Omega \sum_{i=1}^n p_i y_i\, dP \leq \varphi(h')$. Combining both inequalities we get $-\int_\Omega \sum_{i=1}^n p_i y_i\, dP \leq \int_\Omega m\, dP$. Nevertheless, from the choice of y we have that

$$\begin{aligned} -\int_\Omega \sum_{i=1}^n p_i y_i\, dP &= \int_C m/\epsilon\, dP - \int_{\Omega - C} \sum_{i=1}^n x_i^k p_i\, dP \\ &> \int_D m/\epsilon\, dP - \int_{D-C} m/\epsilon\, dP + \int_{\Omega - C} m\, dP - \beta/2 \\ &> \beta + \int_D m\, dP - \beta/2 + \int_{\Omega - C} m\, dP - \beta/2 \\ &> \int_\Omega m\, dP. \end{aligned}$$

Thus, $P(D) = 0$.

Finally, suppose that $P(E) > 0$ and take $\gamma = \int_E \epsilon\, dP > P(E)$ and

$$g_i(\omega) = \begin{cases} p_i(\omega) & \text{if } \omega \in E \text{ and } x_i(\omega) < 0 \\ 0 & \text{otherwise.} \end{cases}$$

Then, there exists $k \in \mathbb{N}$ such that $\int_E \big(\epsilon - (-\sum_{i=1}^n x_i^k g_i)\big)\, dP < \gamma - P(E)$ and consequently, $-\int_E \sum_{i=1}^n x_i^k g_i\, dP > P(E)$. Then, there exists $G \in \Sigma_1$ such that $P(G) > 0$ and $-\sum_{i=1}^n x_i^k g_i > 1$ in G which contradicts the fact that $x^k \in F_{h^k}$, since $-\sum_{i=1}^n x_i^k g_i \leq \sum_{i=1}^n h_i^k g_i \leq \sum_{i=1}^n h_i^k p_i = 1$.

We are now in the situation to conclude the proof of the theorem. Choose an arbitrary $h' \in H$ and define h as follows:

$$h_i(\omega) = \begin{cases} \max(-x_i(\omega), 0) & \text{if } \omega \in \Omega_1 \\ h_i'(\omega) & \text{otherwise.} \end{cases}$$

Then, $h \in H$, $x \in F_h$ and consequently $\varphi(h) = \mathfrak{M}$. □

This leads to the following definition.

Definition 3.7. *For a market satisfying A_1 and A_2 we define a measure of the level of arbitrage opportunities by*

$$m(\omega) = -\sum_{i=1}^{n} x_i^*(\omega)p_i(\omega)$$

where $x^* \in F_{h^*}$, $h^* \in H$ are such that $\mathfrak{M} = \varphi(h^*) = -\sum_{i=1}^{n} \int_\Omega x_i^* p_i \, dP$.

Observe that $0 \leq m(\omega) = -\sum_{i=1}^{n} x_i^*(\omega)p_i(\omega) \leq \sum_{i=1}^{n} h_i^*(\omega)p_i(\omega) = 1$ and hence $m \in L^2(\Sigma_1)$.

The following proposition states the consistency of the definition of m.

Proposition 3.8. *Assume that the market satisfies A_1 and A_2. Let $h^*, \tilde{h}$ be feasible in (4) such that $\mathfrak{M} = \varphi(h^*) = \varphi(\tilde{h})$ and $x^* \in F_{h^*}$, $\tilde{x} \in F_{\tilde{h}}$ such that $\mathfrak{M} = -\sum_{i=1}^{n} \int_\Omega x_i^* p_i \, dP = -\sum_{i=1}^{n} \int_\Omega \tilde{x}_i p_i \, dP$. Then,*

$$\sum_{i=1}^{n} x_i^* p_i = \sum_{i=1}^{n} \tilde{x}_i p_i$$

Proof. Proceeding by contradiction suppose that $-\sum_{i=1}^{n} x_i^* p_i \neq -\sum_{i=1}^{n} \tilde{x}_i p_i$. Then $P(A) > 0$ or $P(B) > 0$ (or both), where $A = \{\omega | -\sum_{i=1}^{n} x_i^* p_i > -\sum_{i=1}^{n} \tilde{x}_i p_i\}$ and $B = \{\omega | -\sum_{i=1}^{n} x_i^* p_i < -\sum_{i=1}^{n} \tilde{x}_i p_i\}$. If $P(A) > 0$, take

$$x_i(\omega) = \begin{cases} x_i^*(\omega) & \text{if } \omega \in A \\ \tilde{x}_i(\omega) & \text{otherwise,} \end{cases} \text{quad and} \quad h_i(\omega) = \begin{cases} h_i^*(\omega) & \text{if } \omega \in A \\ \tilde{h}_i(\omega) & \text{otherwise.} \end{cases}$$

Then h is feasible in (4) and $x \in F_h$ and consequently,

$$\varphi(h) \geq -\sum_{i=1}^{n} \int_\Omega x_i p_i \, dP \geq -\sum_{i=1}^{n} \int_\Omega x_i^* p_i \, dP = \varphi(h^*)$$

Hence, $\sum_{i=1}^{n} \int_\Omega x_i^* p_i \, dP = -\sum_{i=1}^{n} \int_\Omega x_i p_i \, dP$ and therefore,

$$\int_A \left(\sum_{i=1}^{n} x_i^* p_i - \sum_{i=1}^{n} \tilde{x}_i p_i \right) dP = 0$$

Thus, $P(A) = 0$. In a similar way we get $P(B) = 0$. □

One can check that, with this definition, m verifies the first requirement to be a measure of the level of arbitrage opportunities, that is,

Theorem 3.9. *Under assumptions A_1 and A_2 the following conditions are equivalent.*

i) No arbitrage opportunity exists on the market.
ii) $\mathfrak{M} = 0$.
iii) $m = 0$.

The no existence of arbitrage opportunities is thus made testable by estimating m directly. The closer the value of $\mathfrak{M}$ to zero, the lower the maximum expected quotient between the profit and the total price of short-selling restrictions

Such a test is also valid for a measurement of market integration: for two or more not integrated markets, treated as parts of one combined market, $\mathfrak{M}$ also indicates the level of arbitrage opportunities across the markets.

4 Other interpretations of the measure m

Of special interest is the relation between the maximum expected profit with short-selling restrictions with total current price one and the maximum expected profit obtained from a portfolio relative to the price of the sold assets. First we prove that $\int_A m\,dP$ solves the same optimization programs restricted to $A \in \Sigma_1$. Second, we establish a relation between this maximum expected profit and the maximum expected profit obtained from a portfolio relative to the price of all exchanged (sold and purchased) assets. This relation could be useful to study arbitrage opportunities in economies with frictions.

For every set $A \in \Sigma_1$ consider the programs (1_h^A) and

$$(4_A) \quad \max\ \varphi_A(h) \quad \text{s.t.} \quad \begin{cases} \sum_{i=1}^n h_i p_i = 1 \text{in} A \\ h \in (L_+^2(\Sigma_1^A))^n, \end{cases}$$

where $\varphi_A(h)$ is the optimal value attained in (1_h^A). Finally, we denote by $\mathfrak{M}_A$ the optimal value attained in (4_A).

Proposition 4.1. *Assume that the market satisfies A_1 and A_2. Let $h^* \in H$ and $x^* \in F_{h^*}$ such that $\mathfrak{M} = \varphi(h^*) = -\sum_{i=1}^n \int_\Omega x_i^* p_i\,dP$. Then,*

$$\mathfrak{M}_A = \varphi_A(h^*) = -\sum_{i=1}^n \int_A x_i^* p_i\,dP.$$

Consequently, $\mathfrak{M}_A = \int_A m\,dP$

Proof. Proceeding by contradiction, suppose that (4_A) does not achieve the optimum in h^*. Then there exist $\hat{h}$ feasible in (4_A) and $\hat{x}$ feasible in $(1_{\hat{h}}^A)$ such that $\varphi_A(\hat{h}) = -\sum_{i=1}^n \int_A \hat{x}_i p_i\,dP > \varphi_A(h^*) \geq -\sum_{i=1}^n \int_A x_i^* p_i\,dP$. Let

$$x_i(\omega) = \begin{cases} \hat{x}_i(\omega) & \text{if } \omega \in A \\ x_i^*(\omega) & \text{otherwise,} \end{cases} \quad \text{and} \quad h_i(\omega) = \begin{cases} \hat{h}_i(\omega) & \text{if } \omega \in A \\ h_i^*(\omega) & \text{otherwise.} \end{cases}$$

Then h is feasible in (4) and $x \in F_h$ and consequently,

$$\begin{aligned} \varphi(h) &\geq -\sum_{i=1}^n \int_\Omega x_i p_i\,dP = -\sum_{i=1}^n \int_A x_i p_i\,dP - \sum_{i=1}^n \int_{\Omega - A} x_i p_i\,dP \\ &> -\sum_{i=1}^n \int_\Omega x_i^* p_i\,dP = \varphi(h^*). \end{aligned}$$

□

Corollary 4.2. *Assume that the market satisfies A_1 and A_2. Let be $h^* \in F$ and $x^* \in F_{h^*}$ such that $\mathfrak{M} = \varphi(h^*) = -\sum_{i=1}^n \int_\Omega x_i^* p_i\,dP$. Then for every $x \in F_{h^*}$ the inequality $-\sum_{i=1}^n x_i p_i \leq m$ holds a.e.*

From now on, denote by $\Omega_1 = \{\omega \in \Omega \mid m(\omega) \neq 0\}$. Then for every $A \subseteq \Omega_1$, $\mathfrak{M}_A = 0$ if and only if $P(A) = 0$.

Lemma 4.3. *Assume that the market satisfies* A_1 *and* A_2 *and let* $h^* \in F$ *and* $x^* \in F_{h^*}$ *such that* $\mathfrak{M} = \varphi(h^*) = -\sum_{i=1}^{n}\int_\Omega x_i^* p_i\, dP$. *Then,*

$$P(\{\omega \in \Omega_1 \,|\, x_i^*(\omega) > -h_i^*(\omega) \neq 0\}) = 0$$

for every $i = 1, \ldots, n$

Proof. In order to simplify the notation and without loss of generality, we will prove for $i = n$. Proceeding by contradiction, suppose that $P(\{\omega \in \Omega_1 \,|\, x_n^*(\omega) > -h_n^*(\omega) \neq 0\}) > 0$. Then, setting $A = \{\omega \in \Omega_1 \,|\, h_n^*(\omega) \neq 0\}$, $B = \{\omega \in A \,|\, x_n^*(\omega) \geq 0\}$ and $C = \{\omega \in A \,|\, 0 > x_n^*(\omega) > -h_n^*(\omega)\}$, one has $P(B) > 0$ or $P(C) > 0$ and $B, C \subseteq \Omega_1$. First assume that $P(B) > 0$, and let $h_0 = (h_1^*, \cdots, h_{n-1}^*, 0)$ and $\gamma = \sum_{i=1}^{n-1} p_i h_i^*$. $\varphi_B(h_0) \leq \varphi_B(h^*)$, since the feasible sets $F_{h_0}^B$ and $F_{h^*}^B$ are such that $F_{h_0}^B \subseteq F_{h^*}^B$. From $x^* \in F_{h_0}^B$ we get $\varphi_B(h^*) = \varphi_B(h_0)$.

Besides, $P(E) = 0$ holds, where $E = \{\omega \in B \mid p_n^*(\omega)h_n^*(\omega) = 1\}$ since $\varphi_E(h_0) = \varphi_E(h^*) = \mathfrak{M}_E = 0$. Then, $\gamma > 0$ in B. Taking into account that $h_n^* > 0$ and $p_n^* > 0$ in B , we get $\gamma < 1$ in B. Then, there exists $D \subseteq B$, $D \in \Sigma_1$ such that $P(D) > 0$ and $0 < b < \gamma(\omega) < a < 1$ in D and consequently $1/\gamma \in L^\infty(\Sigma_1^D)$ and hence $h_0/\gamma \in (L_+^2(\Sigma_1^D))^n$. Finally, from the fact that $h_0/\gamma \in H^D$ we have that $\varphi_D(h^*) = \varphi_D(h_0) = a\varphi_D(h_0/a) < \varphi_D(h_0/a) \leq \varphi_D(h_0/\gamma) \leq \varphi_D(h^*)$, getting a contradiction. Thus, $P(B) = 0$.

Proceeding in a similar way for $h^0 = (h_1^*, \cdots, h_{n-1}^*, |x_n^*|)$ and $\delta = \sum_{i=1}^{n-1} p_i h_i^* + p_n|x_n^*|$. we get $0 < \delta < 1$ and $G \subseteq C$, $G \in \Sigma_1$ such that $P(G) > 0$ and $0 < b < \delta(\omega) < a < 1$ in G and consequently $1/\delta \in L^\infty(\Sigma_1^G)$ and hence $h_0/\delta \in (L_+^2(\Sigma_1^G))^n$. Thus, we derive that $\varphi_G(h^*) = \varphi_G(h^0) = a\varphi_G(h^0/a) < \varphi_G(h^0/a) \leq \varphi_G(h^0/\delta) \leq \varphi_G(h^*)$ and we get again a contradiction. Thus, $P(C) = 0$. □

Lemma 4.3 says basically that the portfolio where the maximum expected profit is achieved either sells all the stock or purchases in each asset.

For a portfolio $x \in (L^2(\Sigma_1))^n$, denote by $S_{x,\omega}$ the set of indices of the sold assets, that is, $S_{x,\omega} = \{i = 1, \cdots, n \,|\, x_i(\omega) < 0\}$. Let $\Omega_x = \{\omega \in \Omega \,|\, \sum_{i \in S_{x,\omega}} x_i(\omega)p_i(\omega) \neq 0\}$ and $\Omega_x' = \{\omega \in \Omega \,|\, \sum_{i=1}^n x_i(\omega)\alpha_i(\omega) \geq 0\}$ and consider for every $\omega \in \Omega_x$ the function

$$f(x,\omega) = \left(\sum_{i=1}^{n} x_i(\omega)p_i(\omega) \Big/ \sum_{i \in S_{x,\omega}} x_i(\omega)p_i(\omega) \right)$$

Theorem 4.4. *Under assumptions* A_1 *and* A_2 *and given* $x \in (L^2(\Sigma_1))^n$ *one has,*

i) $P\left(\{\omega \in A \,|\, f(x,\omega) \leq m(\omega)\}\right) = P(A)$ *for every* $A \in \Sigma_1$, $A \subseteq \Omega_x \cap \Omega_x'$. *In particular,* $\int_A f(x,\omega)\, dP \leq \int_A m(\omega)\, dP$.

ii) If $x = x^*$ *then* $P\left(\{\omega \in B \,|\, f(x^*,\omega) = m(\omega)\}\right) = P(B)$ *for every* $B \subseteq \Omega_{x^*}$ *such that* $B \in \Sigma_1$. *In particular,* $\int_B f(x^*,\omega)\, dP = \int_B m(\omega)\, dP$.

Proof. i) First note that $f(x,\omega) \leq 1$ whenever $\omega \in A$. Proceeding by contradiction suppose that $P(D) > 0$, where $D = \{\omega \in A | f(x,\omega) > m(\omega)\}$. Set

$\epsilon(\omega) = -\sum_{i \in S_{x,\omega}} x_i(\omega)p_i(\omega)$. Then, $\epsilon > 0$ in D since $f(x,\omega) \geq 0$ in D and $\epsilon \in L^1(\Sigma_1^D)$. Thus, there exist $C \subseteq D$, $C \in \Sigma_1$ and a, b such that $P(C) > 0$ and $0 < a < \epsilon(\omega) < b$ in C. Consequently, the functions $y_i = x_i/\epsilon \in L^2(\Sigma_1^C)$. Define $h' = (h'_1, \cdots, h'_n)$ by $h'_i = \max(-y_i, 0)$ for every $i = 1, \cdots, n$.

Since $h' \in H^C$ we get $\varphi_C(h') \leq \mathfrak{M}_C = \int_C m\,dP$. Besides, from y feasible in $(1_{h'}^C)$ we get $\int_C f(x,\omega)\,dP(\omega) = -\int_C \sum_{i=1}^n p_i y_i\,dP \leq \varphi_C(h')$.

Thus, combining both inequalities, we obtain a contradiction and i) is proved.

ii) Assume $x = x^*$. Since $m(\omega) = -\sum_{i=1}^n x_i^*(\omega)p_i(\omega)$ and from the fact that $x_i^*(\omega) = -h_i(\omega)$ whenever $i \in S_{x^*,\omega}$ and $h_i^*(\omega) = 0$ otherwise B a.e., we get $-\sum_{i \in S_{x^*,\omega}} x_i^*(\omega)p_i(\omega) = \sum_{i \in S_{x^*,\omega}} h_i^*(\omega)p_i(\omega) = \sum_{i=1}^n h_i^*(\omega)p_i(\omega) = 1$ and the proof of ii) is concluded. □

Consider now for every $x \in (L^2(\Sigma_1))^n$ the function,

$$g(x,\omega) = \left(-\sum_{i=1}^{n} x_i(\omega)p_i(\omega) \Big/ \sum_{i=1}^{n} |x_i(\omega)|\, p_i(\omega) \right)$$

for every $\omega \in \{\omega' \in \Omega \,|\, x(\omega') \neq 0\}$. The function g is the quotient between the profit generated by x and the price of all interchanged assets. Manipulating g, it is easy to prove that $g(x,\omega) = \big(f(x,\omega) / 2 - f(x,\omega)\ \big)$ for every $x \in (L^2(\Sigma_1))^n$ and $\omega \in \Omega_x$. These observations and the fact that $t/(2-t)$ is a increasing continuous function in $[0, 1]$ $(0 \leq m(\omega) \leq 1)$ lead to the following theorem.

Theorem 4.5. *Assume that the market satisfies A_1, A_2. Let $x^* \in (L^2(\Sigma_1))^n$ be such that $m(\omega) = -\sum_{i=1}^n x_i^*(\omega)p_i(\omega)$. Then for every $A \in \Sigma_1$ x^* solves the following optimization problem*

$$(5)\quad \max \int_A g(x,\omega)\,dP \quad \text{s.t.} \quad \begin{cases} \sum_{i=1}^n x_i\alpha_i \geq 0 \text{ in } A \\ x \neq 0 \text{ in } A. \end{cases}$$

Proof. Let be x feasible in (5) and $A_1 = \{\omega \in A \,|\, \sum_{i=1}^n x_i p_i < 0\}$. If $P(A_1) = 0$, then we get $\int_A g(x,\omega)\,dP \leq 0 \leq \int_A \big(m(\omega)/2 - m(\omega)\big)\,dP$.

If $P(A_1) > 0$, note that from Theorem 4.4 it follows that $f(x,\omega) \leq f(x^*,\omega)$ a.e. in A_1 and consequently,

$$\begin{aligned}\int_A g(x,\omega)\,dP &= \int_{A-A_1} g(x,\omega)\,dP + \int_{A_1} g(x,\omega)\,dP \\ &= \int_{A_1} g(x,\omega)\,dP \leq \int_{A_1} (f(x^*,\omega)/2 - f(x^*,\omega))\,dP \square \\ &= \int_{A_1} g(x^*,\omega)\,dP \leq \int_A g(x^*,\omega)\,dP.\end{aligned}$$

Remarks.

1. Extending $f(x,\omega)$ by 0 whenever $\omega \notin \Omega_x$, we conclude from Theorem 4.4 that

$$f(x,\omega) = \left(\sum_{i=1}^{n} x_i(\omega)p_i(\omega) \Big/ \sum_{i \in S_{x,\omega}} x_i(\omega)p_i(\omega) \right) \leq m(\omega)$$

for every $x \in (L^2(\Sigma_1))^n$ such that $\sum_{i=1}^n x_i\alpha_i \geq 0$.
In other terms x^* solves the following nonlinear multiobjective program

$$(6) \quad \max \; f(x,\omega) \text{s.t.} \; \sum_{i=1}^{n} x_i\alpha_i \geq 0$$

given a strong maximum.

2. Setting $l(\omega) = \frac{m(\omega)}{2-m(\omega)}$, we conclude from Theorem 4.5 that

$$g(x,\omega) = (-\sum_{i=1}^{n} x_i(\omega)p_i(\omega) \Big/ \sum_{i=1}^{n} |x_i(\omega)|\, p_i(\omega)\ ) \leq l(\omega)$$

for every $x \in (L^2(\Sigma_1))^n$ such that $\sum_{i=1}^n x_i\alpha_i \geq 0$ where $g(x,\omega)$ is extended by 0 whenever $x(\omega) = 0$. In other terms x^* solves the following non linear multiobjective optimization problem

$$(7) \quad \max \; g(x,\omega) \text{s.t.} \; \sum_{i=1}^{n} x_i\alpha_i \geq 0$$

Once again x^* gives a strong maximum of (7).

3. Extension to a multiperiod economy.

Assume that we are in front of an intertemporal model. Let $\Sigma_1, \Sigma_2, \ldots$ be a series of σ-algebras of subsets of Ω representing of all past events through times $1, 2, \ldots$ ($\Sigma_1 \subseteq \Sigma_2 \subseteq \cdots$). Take $\Sigma_0 = \{\emptyset, \Omega\}$ and let $p^t \in (L^2(\Sigma_t))^n$ be the vector price for the n assets at time t, $t = 0, 1 \ldots$. Then for every $t \in \boldsymbol{N}$ such that $\mathbf{H}_1$:

i) for every $i = 1, \ldots, n$, $p_i^t \in L^2(\Sigma_t)$ and $p_i^t(\omega) > k_i^t > 0$.
ii) for every $i = 1, \ldots, n$, $p_i^{t+1} \in L^2(\Sigma_{t+1})$ and $p_1^{t+1}(\omega) > 0$, we can procede as below and define $\mathfrak{M}_t$ and $m_t \in L^2(\Sigma_t)$. The family $\{m_t\}$ is then adapted to $\{\Sigma_t\}$ and $\{m_t\}$ is a filtered stochastic process. In the absence of all arbitrage opportunities, $m_t = 0$ and inversely.

4. On the transaction costs.

By means of the measure l it could be tested if the market frictions affect to the absence arbitrage. In fact, since l computes the maximum profit relative to the total price of the exchanged assets and assuming that the transaction costs are a.e determined by the price $V(\omega)$ of the exchanged assets, the maximum profit an investor can obtain for V is then lV. Discounting then the transaction costs we can verify if there is no arbitrage opportunity.

5 Extension of the model

Suppose now we do not assume in A_1 that $p_i > k_i > 0$ but $p_i > 0$. For every $k \in N$ denote by $A^k = \{\omega \in \Omega \,|\, p_i(\omega) > 1/k,\ i = 1, \cdots n\}$. Obviously, $\lim_k P(A^k) = 1$. Set $p_i^k = p_i.chi_{A^k}$ and consider the programs (1_h^k), (2_h^k) and (4^k) where each p_i is replaced by p_i^k. Choose corresponding zero valued in $\Omega - A^k$ functions h_{ik}^*, l_{ik}^*, x_{ik}^* and m^k. It follows from Proposition 3.8 that $m^j.chi_{A^k} = m^k$ for every $j \geq k$. Hence $(m^k)_{k \in N}$ is an a.e. pointwise convergent sequence such that $0 \leq m^k \leq 1$, then $m = \lim_{k \in N} m^k \in L^2(\Sigma_1)$. Notice that $\int_\Omega m\,dP$ is the optimum value in Program (4), but this optimum is not necessarily attained in H. Nevertheless, for every $\epsilon > 0$ there exist $A \in \Sigma_1$ such that $P(A) \geq 1 - \epsilon$, $h_\epsilon \in H$ such that Program (4^A) achieves its optimum $\int_A m\,dP$ in h_ϵ and $x_\epsilon \in F_{h_\epsilon}$ such that Program (1_{h_ϵ}) achieves its optimum in x_ϵ.

6 Conclusions

The present paper introduces a measure of the level of arbitrage opportunities in a discrete dynamic time asset pricing model. Among other possibilities, our measure is useful to analyze markets with frictions and to test the level of integration of different financial markets. Our measure does not depend on the assumed short-selling restrictions.

The results are also interesting from a mathematical point of view since they show how a multiobjective optimization problem with a (non-differentiable) objective function may be transformed into an equivalent pair of scalar linear problems, a procedure which may be useful in more general situations.

Acknowledgements

This research has been supported by grant D.G.I.C.Y.T. Ref. PB95-0729-C02.

References

Balbás, A., and Muñoz, M. J. (1996). Measuring the degree of fulfillment of the Law of One Price. Applications to Financial Markets Integration. Working Paper **75**. Economics Series 31. Universidad Carlos III de Madrid.

Chamberlain, G., and Rothschild, M. (1983). Arbitrage, Factor Structure, and Mean-Variance Analysis on Large Assets. *Econometrica* **51**, 1281–1304.

Chen, Z., and Knez, P. J. (1995). Measurement of Market Integration and Arbitrage. *The Review of Financial Studies* **Vol. 8, 2**, 545–560.

Davis, M. H. A., Panas, V. G. and Zariphopoulou, T. (1993). European Option Pricing with Transaction Costs. *Siam Journal of Control and Optimization* **31**, 470–493.

Harris, F. H., McInish, T. H., Shoesmith, G. L. and Wood, R. A. (1995). Cointegration, Error Correction, and Price Discovery on Informationally Linked Security Markets. *Journal of Financial and Quantitative Analysis* **30, 4**, 563–579.

Harrison, J., and Kreps, D. (1979). Martingales and Arbitrage in Multiperiod Securities Markets. *Journal of Economic Theory* **20**, 381–408.

Kamara, A., and Miller, T. W. Jr. (1995). Daily and Intradaily Tests of European Put-Call Parity. *Journal of Financial and Quantitative Analysis* **30, 4**, 519–541.

Leland, H., (1985). Option Pricing and Replication with Transaction Costs. *The Journal of Finance* **40**, 1283–1301.

Prisman, E. Z, (1986). Valuation of Risky Assets in Arbitrage Free Economies with Frictions. *The Journal of Finance* **41, 3**, 545–56.

Protopapadakis A., and Stoll, H. (1983). Spot and Future Prices and Law of One Price. *The Journal of Finance* **5**, 1431–1455.

Toft, K. B. (1996). On the Mean-Variance Tradeoff in Option Replication with Transaction Costs. *Journal of Financial and Quantitative Analysis* **31, 2**, 233–263.

Work-leisure Trade-off in a Workers' Enterprise: A Decision Analysis Approach

Enrique Ballestero[1] and Carlos Romero[1]

[1] Technical University of Madrid, Ciudad Universitaria s/n, 28040 Madrid, SPAIN

Abstract

An explanatory model of workers' enterprise is proposed in this paper. The model is based upon a utility function with two arguments (leisure and income) which is optimised over the corresponding production possibility frontier. The model proposed provides approximations to the working-leisure mix, output supply and income as the output price increases. In this way typical "perverse behaviours" usually reported in the literature are avoided. The theoretical presentation is illustrated with the help of some numerical examples.

Keywords. compromise programming, multiple criteria decision making, workers' enterprise

1 Introduction

Since the pioneer paper by Ward (1958) an extensive literature on labour-managed firms has aroused. Thus, journals like Managerial and Decision Economics (1993) and the Journal of Comparative Economics (1986) have devoted entire issues to this topic. Specific books [e.g. Vanek (1970), Ireland and Law (1982), Bonnin and Putterman (1987), etc.] as well as an impressive range of journal articles have also come out.

Labour-managed firms seem to be of sufficient interest for economists. Indeed, they are neither a historical curiosity of the former centrally planned economies nor firms related to the co-operative sector but appearing under several forms in developed countries. In a market economy we find a great variety of activities where labour-managed firms play a primary role in one way or in another.

Lawyers, financial consultants, taxi-drivers, grocers and other retailers, artisans, writers and artists, insurance agents, small restaurant owners, and many other white or blue collar workers can often be considered as self-employment firms in intensive labour units or intensive human capital ones. Sometimes, these firms get certain advantages as outsiders within an underground economy (e.g. tax evasion) but this is not a rule among them.

A behavioural analysis for labour-managed firms leads to the maximisation of profit per worker instead of the maximisation of profits of traditional firms. This behavioural hypothesis suggests a certain kind of "perverse behaviour" since the maximisation of profit per worker seems to involve some contraction in both output and employment when the firm faces increasing prices of the output [see e.g., Chiarella (1993)].

A rehabilitation of labour-managed firms theory has been introduced by Sertel (1982) within which he calls a workers' enterprise as a firm whose workers coincide with their partners. The income of the partnership (i.e. the workers) coincides with the value added by labour (i.e. sales revenue minus all non-labour costs). In order to avoid "perverse behaviour" Sertel suggests as behavioural hypothesis the maximisation of the value added per-worker as a function of any variable other than labour (Sertel, 1993).

Another possible way to address the explanation of the workers' enterprise behaviour consists in assuming, that the partnership (i.e. workers) instead of maximising profit or value added per worker maximises a utility function with two arguments, worker's income (value added) and his leisure. Something of this approach has been suggested by Chiarella (1992) by accepting that the partnership faces a work-leisure preference choice. However, the standard optimisation of a work-leisure utility function is not undertaken in the cited literature.

We think that introducing a decision analysis approach for addressing this problem is to move a step closer to reality. Regardless of the analysis on "perverse behaviour", a model based on work-leisure utility seems to be a key tool in achieving a good understanding and explanation of workers' enterprises. In this paper this task is undertaken by resorting to a methodology different that the one used by Chiarella. Thus, it will be shown how some recent results in decision theory allow for a boundness of the work-leisure equilibrium mix on the opportunity set with the standard utility function of an average decision-maker, even in a context of incomplete information (Ballestero and Romero, 1991, 1994).

2 Workers' enterprise: An optimum utility solution

Let us assume a workers' enterprise where all workers are identical producing an output which is sold in a competitive market. The following variables are defined.

P = net market price; i.e. output market price minus non-labour cost (per unit of output) attached to the production process.

Y = income of partnership.

S = net sales revenue, that is, $S = PQ$.

C_0 = fixed costs.

L = level of self-employment (hours per year or per other unit of time).

L_0 = vital maximum time for working (hours per unit of time).

E = level of leisure.

Q = amount of output produced and sold by the firm.

$Q(L)$ = production function (describing the output produced and sold).

$U(E, Y)$ = utility function measuring the preferences of the partnership for leisure and income.

The partnership's income is given by:

$$Y = S - C_0 = PQ(L) - C_0 \tag{1}$$

since non-labour variable costs (per unit) have already been subtracted from the output price. From (1), taking into account that $E = L_0 - L$, the following leisure-income trade-off is obtained:

$$Y = PQ(L_0 - E) - C_0. \tag{2}$$

As an approximation to Q we assume the diminishing marginal output expression:

$$Q(L) = qL^h \text{ where } q > 0 \text{ and } 0 < h < 1. \tag{3}$$

From (3) the trade-off frontier (2) turns into:

$$Y = Pq(L_0 - E)^h - C_0. \tag{4}$$

By maximising the utility function $U(E, Y)$ subject to the trade-off (4) we obtain the following Lagrangean:

$$\max \phi = U(E, Y) + \lambda[Y - Pq(L_0 - E)^h + C_0]. \tag{5}$$

From (5) we get the following first-order conditions:

$$\begin{aligned} \phi_E &= U_E + \lambda qPh(L_0 - E)^h - 1 = 0, \\ \phi_Y &= U_Y + \lambda = 0; \end{aligned} \tag{6}$$

where ϕ_E and ϕ_Y as well as U_E and U_Y represent partial derivatives. From (6) the following equilibrium condition is straightforwardly derived:

$$U_E / U_Y = qPh(L0 - E)^{h-1}. \tag{7}$$

According to a well-known property of the equilibrium, condition (7) can be read as follows: the marginal rate of substitution between leisure and income must be proportional to income diminution caused by a marginal increase in leisure.

For different utility functions $U(E, Y)$ different mixes (E, Y) are obtained. Thus, for a linear utility function such as: $U = Y + \theta E$ the following optimum mix is obtained:

$$E = L_0 - \left(\frac{\theta}{qhP}\right)^{\frac{1}{h-1}} \tag{8}$$

$$Y = qP\left(\frac{\theta}{qhP}\right)^{\frac{h}{h-1}} - C_0 \tag{9}$$

The corresponding supply function is given by:

$$Q = q\left(\frac{\theta}{qhP}\right)^{\frac{h}{h-1}} \tag{10}$$

The above equations are well-behaved since we have $dQ/dP > 0$, $dE/dP < 0$ and $dY/dP > 0$, that is both income and the output supply grow as the net market price P increases. Moreover, notice the following results:

a) The lower q (that is, preference for leisure) the higher are both income and output at the equilibrium point, and the lower is leisure.
b) The higher q and h (technological parameters related to productivity) the higher are both income and output, and the lower is leisure.
c) From the structure of dQ/dP we obtain that high values of technological parameters q and h as well as low values of preferences θ for leisure involve a quicker growing of the output as the net market price increases.

The utility approach seems theoretically sound leading to no-perverse results, since $dQ/dP > 0$. However, its main drawback lies in the serious difficulties associated to the estimation of a reliable utility function $U(E, Y)$. In the next section it will be presented a surrogate which keeps the main advantages of the utility approach, avoiding the conceptual and operational problems derived from the precise estimation of a bi-criteria utility function.

3 Workers' enterprise: A best-compromise solution

As a first step to obtain a best-compromise (E, Y) the following ideal (E^*, Y^*) and anti-ideal points (E_*, Y_*) are derived by elemental calculations:

$$E^* = L_0 - (C_0/qP)^{1/h} \qquad E^* = 0$$
$$Y^* = qPL_0^h - C_0 \qquad Y^* = 0$$

In what follows the equilibrium point of the workers' enterprise will be approximated by the point of the frontier given by (2) or (4) nearest with respect to the ideal point (E^*, Y^*)—Zeleny's axiom of choice (see Zeleny 1974). Accepting this behavioural axiom and with different metrics several solutions can be obtained by solving the following optimisation problem:

$$\min L_\pi = [W_1^\pi(E^* - E)^\pi + W_2^\pi(Y^* - Y)^\pi]^{1/\pi} \tag{11}$$

subject to $Y = qP(L_0 - E)^h - C_0$.

By solving (11) for metrics $\pi = 1$ and $p\pi = \infty$ a compromise set as a portion of the frontier with respect to the ideal is obtained (Yu 1973, 1985 and Zeleny 1974).

To implement model (11) weights W_1 and W_2 have to be determined. A sensible and commonly used normalising system consists in setting the weights inversely proportional to the ranges of both criteria (i.e. ideal minus anti-ideal values). Among the different reasons in favour of this normalising system it can be pointed out that this systems is the best normalising procedure from a shadow prices perspective. In other words weights inversely proportional to the corresponding ranges represent the best shadow prices within an economic scenario (Ballestero and Romero, 1993). Therefore, in our case we have:

$$\begin{aligned} W_1 &= \frac{1}{E^* - E_*} = \frac{1}{L_0 - (C_0/qP)^{1/h}} \\ W_2 &= \frac{1}{Y^* - Y_*} = \frac{1}{qPL_0^h - C_0} \end{aligned} \tag{12}$$

Bound L_1 (i.e. $\pi = 1$) of the compromise set is the point where the path $W_2T_1 - W_1T_2 = 0$ intercepts the frontier, being T_1 and T_2 the partial derivatives of the corresponding frontier curve (Ballestero and Romero, 1991). Making the corresponding calculations and taking into account weights given by (12) the following L_1 bound is obtained:

$$E = L_0 - \left[\frac{PqL_0^h - C_0}{L_0 - (C_0/qP)^{1/h}} \cdot \frac{1}{Pqh}\right]^{\frac{1}{h-1}}. \tag{13}$$

$$Y = qP\left[\frac{PqL_0^h - C_0}{L_0 - (C_0/qP)^{1/h}} \cdot \frac{1}{Pqh}\right]^{\frac{h}{h-1}} - C_0. \tag{14}$$

Since $L = L_0 - E$, from (13) is straightforward to obtain the level of self-employment L. By substituting this value of L in the production function (3) the following supply function associated to the L_1 bound is obtained:

$$Q = q\left[\frac{PqL_0^h - C_0}{L_0 - (C_0/qP)^{1/h}} \cdot \frac{1}{Pqh}\right]^{\frac{h}{h-1}}. \tag{15}$$

Bound L_∞ (i.e. $\pi = \infty$) of the compromise set is the point where the path $W_1(E^* - E) = W_2(Y^* - Y)$ intercepts the frontier. Making the corresponding calculations and considering again weights given (12) the L_∞ bound will be obtained by solving the following system of equations:

$$\begin{aligned} Y &= \frac{qPL_0^h - C_0}{L_0 - (C_0/qP)^{1/h}} E; \\ Y &= qP(L_0 - E)^h - C_0. \end{aligned} \tag{16}$$

First equation of (16) represents the L_∞ path $W_1(E^* - E) = W_2(Y^* - Y)$ and the second equation represents the frontier.

L_∞ path represents balanced allocations among leisure and income. It is also interesting to notice that to the L_∞ bound corresponds the maximisation of a maximin or Rawlsian utility function, where the maximum deviation is minimised.

It is now tempting to interpret the compromise set as the portion of the feasible frontier where the maximum of $U(E,Y)$ will likely occur. That is, the compromise set can be interpreted as something like a landing area for the iso-utility curves. This fuzzy and not rigorous statement will be theoretically justified in what follows with the help of a theorem proved elsewhere (Ballestero and Romero, 1991) which suitably adapted to our context reads as follows:

Theorem. *With any utility function $U(E,Y)$ involving a non-satiation scenario, the necessary and sufficient condition under which the maximum of U always belongs to the compromise set on every given transformation curve or frontier is:*

Marginal rate of substitution = $MRS(E,Y) = U_E/U_Y = W_1/W_2$ *on the path* $W_1(E^* - E) = W_2(Y^* - Y)$.

For weights given by (12) the theorem says:

$$MRS(E,Y) = U_e/U_Y = \frac{Y^* - Y_*}{E^* - E_*} = \frac{qPL_0^h - C_0}{L_= - (C_0/qP)^{1/h}}$$

on the path $E/[L_0 - (C_0/qP)^{1/h}] = Y/(qPN_0^h - C_0)$.

The condition underlying the Theorem seems sensible since it simply implies a behaviour coherent with the diminishing marginal rate of substitution (MRS) law. In fact, the Theorem underlies the following behaviour: If the leisure is large workers can wish to give up a significant amount of leisure for a marginal increase in income without loosing utility (and viceversa). On the contrary when the mix leisure-income is already balanced (i.e. belongs to the L_∞ path or to a neighbourhood of it) workers likely do not want to sacrifice a large amount of leisure in favour of a small increase in income; that is, $MRS \cong 1$ when leisure-income allocation is balanced (i.e. belongs to the path L_∞). In short, it can be stated that a "normal" behaviour of marginal rates of substitution in the utility function $U(E,Y)$ will guarantee that the optimum mix (E,Y) lies on the compromise set. For more details about the economic meaning of the Theorem see (Ballestero and Romero, 1994). In Morón et. al. (1997) is proved the existence of large families of utility functions holding the condition which underpins the above Theorem what reinforces the compromise sets as good surrogates of the utility optima.

4 Numerical illustrations

Let us assume the case of a small workshop which owns to two workers (partners). In this workshop an homogeneous output is made according to the following technology:

$$Q = 2L^{0.7}. \tag{17}$$

The net market price of the output is \$ 170. No casual labour is hired. The fixed costs of the workshop are estimated in \$ 20000. The maximum amount of work that the two workers (partners) can provide is 8000 hours/year. From these data and according to (4) the following attainable frontier in the (E, Y) space is obtained:

$$Y - 340(8000 - E)^{0.7} + 20000 = 0 \tag{18}$$

The ideal and anti-ideal values are:

$E^* = 7664$ hours	$E_* = 0$
$Y^* = 163502$ dollars	$Y_* = 0$

Making the corresponding substitutions and calculations in (13), (14) and (16) the following best-compromise solution is obtained:

$$L_1 \longrightarrow L = 3100 \text{ hours}, Y = 74530 \text{ dollars}$$
$$L_\infty \longrightarrow L = 4075 \text{ hours}, Y = 94635 \text{ dollars}$$

Hence the surrogate optimum will be to work between 3100 and 4071 hours, obtaining an income (value added by labour) between 74530 and 94635 dollars, respectively. This solution represents a volume of production between 556 and 673 units. The actual optimum will belong to the intervals defined by the above figures when:

$$MRS(E, Y) = U_E/U_Y = \frac{Y^* - Y_*}{E^* - E_*} = 24.02 \text{ along the path: } Y = 24.02E$$

Taking into account (15) and leaving the net market price P as a parameter the following supply function associated to the L_1 bound is obtained:

$$Q = 2\left[\frac{771 - 14200P^{-1}}{8000 - 517940P^{-1.43}}\right]^{-2.33} \tag{19}$$

it can be checked the well-behaved character (i.e. $dQ/dP > 0$) of (19).

Acknowledgements

The work of Carlos Romero was supported by CICYT project AGF95-0014. Technical help by Dr. Luis Díaz-Balteiro is appreciated. English language was checked by Ms. Christine Mendez.

References

Ballestero, E. and Romero, C. (1991). A theorem connecting utility function optimization and compromise progamming. *Operations Research Letters* **10**, 421–427.

Ballestero, E. and Romero, C. (1993). Weighting in compromise progamming a theorem on shadow prices. *Operations Research Letters* **13**, 325–330.

Ballestero, E. and Romero, C. (1994). Utility optimization when the utility function is virtually unknown. *Theory and Decision* **37**, 233–243.

Bonnin, J. P. and Putterman, L. (1987). *Economics of Cooperation and the Labor-Managed Economy*. London and New York: Harwood Academic Publishers.

Chiarella, C. (1992). Dynamic interaction of profit maximising an workers' enterprises in a doupolistic industry. *Workshop on Workers' Enterprises, EIASM Brussels*, April 1992.

Chiarella, C. (1993). The dynamic operation of the market for partnership deeds in a doupolistic industry of a profit-maximizing firm and workers' enterprise. *Managerial and Decision Economics* **14**, 541–458.

Ireland, N. Y. and Law,P. Y. (1982). *The Economics of Labour-Managed Enterprises*. London: Croom Helm.

Morón, M. A., Romero, C. and Ruiz del Portal, F. R. (1996). Generating well-behaved utility functions for compromise programming. *Journal of Optimization Theory and Applications* **91**, 643–649.

Sertel, M. R. (1982). *Workers and Incentives*. Amsterdam: North-Holland.

Sertel, M. R. (1993). Workers' enterprise in price competition. *Managerial and Decision Economics* **14**, 445–449.

Vanek, J. (1970). *The General Theory of Labor-Managed Market Economies*. Ithaca, New York: Cornell University Press.

Ward, B. (1958). The firm in Illyria: market syndicalism. *American Economic Review* **48**, 566–589.

Yu, P. (1973). A class of solutions for group decision problems. *Management Science* **19**, 936–946.

Yu, P. (1985). *Multiple-Criteria Decision Making: Concepts, Techniques, and Extensions*. New York: Plenum Press.

Zeleny, M. (1974). A Concept of compromise solutions and the method of displaced ideal. *Computers and Operations Research* **1**, 479–496.

Implementing Financial Equilibrium of Incomplete Markets : Bounded Portfolios and the Limiting Case

Monique Florenzano[1], Pascal Gourdel[2] and Valeri Marakulin[3]

[1] CNRS-CEPREMAP, 140 rue du Chevaleret, 75013 Paris, FRANCE
[2] CERMSEM, Université de Paris 1, 90 rue de Tolbiac, 75013 Paris, FRANCE
[3] Institute of Mathematics, Russian Academy of Sciences, Novosibirsk, 630090, RUSSIA

Abstract

A financial equilibrium existence theorem is proved under very mild assumptions on a two-period exchange model with bounded portfolios. We also characterize the asset trading that supports allocations, prices and financial transfers at the limit, when bounds are relaxed to infinity.

Keywords. Financial equilibrium, incomplete markets, pseudo-equilibrium, Radner-limits

1 Introduction

In the classical two-period exchange model with incomplete markets, it is well-known that equilibrium exists under reasonable assumptions, if asset returns are denominated in units of account or in units of a commodity bundle chosen as numeraire. With real assets, a long time ago, Radner (1972) was the first to remark that equilibrium exists if a priori bounds are put on forward transactions, that is on short selling of assets. Whithout limitation on short sales, equilibrium is only shown to exist for generic asset structures and endowments of agents. The key tool for proving this result is the concept of pseudo-equilibrium, a weaker equilibrium concept which "always" exists.

In this paper, based on results of Marakulin (1994), we give a partial answer to a problem mentioned by Geanakoplos (1990) in its Introduction to the JME Special Issue on Incomplete Markets : how to characterize the set of allocations and prices that can be obtained as limits of "Radner" equilibria as the a priori bounds are relaxed to infinity? More precisely, on what kind of asset trading are based the financial transfers which support these limit allocations and prices?

We first prove the existence of an equilibrium with bounded portfolios. Such an equilibrium obviously depends on the chosen lower bounds for portfolios. We also prove that a limit exists, using a limiting process involving no other mathematical tool than standard analysis and linear algebra. Both results are obtained under very mild assumptions, even weaker than the ones used in Keiding (1992), on the asset structure and agents' characteristics.

The kind of weak equilibrium concept obtained at the limit appears to be a possible alternative to the conventional pseudo-equilibrium concept, which may "coincide" with it. Moreover, the limiting process used to prove its existence can be thought of as a way for a government of proceeding by trial and error on (Radner) equilibria under decreasing institutional lower bounds on portfolios before allowing a limit equilibrium to exist when these bounds are relaxed to infinity.

2 The model

Let us consider an exchange model with two periods $t = 0, 1$, I consumers $i = 1, \cdots, I$ and L commodities $\ell = 1, \cdots, L$, available either today (with certainty) or tomorrow (contingent on each of a finite number S of possible states of nature). For convenience, we denote by $s = 0$ the state of nature today. At each state $s = 0, 1, \cdots, S$, there is a spot market for each of the L commodities ; at time 0, there exists also a financial market for J assets which deliver a random return across the states at $t = 1$. Let $\Pi = \{(p, q) \in \boldsymbol{R}^{L(1+S)} \times \boldsymbol{R}^J \mid \forall s \ \|p(s)\| \leq 1, \|q\| \leq 1\}$ denote the set of admissible prices for commodities and assets. Each consumer i is characterized by a consumption set $X^i \subset \boldsymbol{R}^{L(1+S)}$, a portfolio set $Z^i \subset \boldsymbol{R}^J$, a preference correspondence $P^i : X \to X^i$ where $X = \prod_{i=1}^I X^i$ and by a vector-function $\alpha^i = (\alpha^i_s)$, $\alpha^i_s : \boldsymbol{R}^{L(1+S)} \times X \to \boldsymbol{R}$ giving for each state s the wealth of consumer i, given prices p and actions of the other agents. $\omega \in \boldsymbol{R}^{L(1+S)}$ denotes the endowment of the whole economy.

As usually, consumption sets express sociological and physiological restrictions on consumption bundles, independently of any limitation of resources of the agents. Portfolio sets describe (possibly individual) institutional restrictions on asset trading, independently of current prices. For $x \in X$, $P^i(x)$ is interpreted as the set of consumption plans in X^i which are strictly preferred to x^i by the consumer i, given the consumption plans $(x^j)_{j \neq i}$ of the other agents. It should be emphasized that $P^i(x)$ expresses, as much as a comparison between different goods, the time preference of consumer i and his/her attitude toward risk. Such a framework obviously encompasses the case where each consumer i is assumed to have a complete preorder on his/her consumption set X^i ; a fortiori, it encompasses the case where the preferences of consumer i are represented by a von Neumann - Morgenstern expected utility function $u^i(x) = \sum_{s=1}^S \rho^i_s u^i(x^i(0), x^i(s))$, where $\rho^i_s \geq 0$ and $\sum_{s=1}^S \rho^i_s = 1$. Finally, if consumer i is given with an individual endowment vector $\omega^i = \big(\omega^i(s)\big) \in \boldsymbol{R}^{L(1+S)}$, then $\alpha^i_s(p, x) = p(s) \cdot \omega^i(s)$.

A general asset structure is given by a map V defined on $\boldsymbol{R}^{L(1+S)} \times X$; the image $V(p,x)$ is a $(S \times J)$-matrix of which the jth column vector denotes, given p and x, the financial return of asset j across states of nature at period 1, denominated in units of account. The previous framework encompasses three basic types of assets which are of practical significance and generally considered in the literature. With real assets: $a^1, a^2, \cdots, a^J \in \boldsymbol{R}^{LS}$,

$$V(p,x) = (p(s) \cdot a^j(s))_{\substack{s=1,\ldots,S \\ j=1,\ldots,J}}.$$

If a consumption bundle $e \in \boldsymbol{R}^L$ is chosen as a unit of "numeraire", numeraire assets are given by $a^j(s) = r^j(s)e,\ r^j(s) \in \boldsymbol{R}$ and

$$V(p,x) = \left((p(s) \cdot e)r^j(s)\right)_{\substack{s=1,\ldots,S \\ j=1,\ldots,J}}.$$

With purely financial securities, V does not depend on p.
In all cases, the full matrix of returns (i.e. period 0 and period 1), given p, q, and x, is

$$W(p,q,x) = \begin{pmatrix} -q \\ V(p,x) \end{pmatrix}.$$

Taking as given the actions of the other agents and a market system of commodity and asset prices, the budget set of consumer i is

$$B^i(p,q,x) = \{x'^i \in X^i \mid \exists z^i \in Z^i, p \,\square\, x'^i \leq \alpha^i(p,x) + W(p,q,x)z^i\}$$

where the standard notation $p \,\square\, x'^i$ denotes the vector $(p(s) \cdot x'^i(s))_{s=0}^S$.

Let us resume by $Z = \prod_{i=1}^I Z^i$ the list of data concerning the portfolio restrictions.

Definition 2.1. *A financial Z-equilibrium is a pair of actions and admissible prices* $\left((\bar{x}^i, \bar{z}^i)_{i=1}^I, (\bar{p}, \bar{q})\right)$ *such that*

(i) for each i, $\bar{x}^i \in X^i$, $\bar{z}^i \in Z^i$, $\bar{p} \,\square\, \bar{x}^i = \alpha^i(\bar{p}, \bar{x}) + W(\bar{p}, \bar{q}, \bar{x})\bar{z}^i$ and

$$P^i(\bar{x}) \bigcap B^i(\bar{p}, \bar{q}, \bar{x}) = \emptyset$$

(ii) $\sum_{i=1}^I \bar{x}^i = \omega$ and $\sum_{i=1}^I \bar{z}^i = 0$.

Classically, (i) means that each $(\bar{x}^i, \bar{z}^i)$ is an optimal budget feasible plan for agent i, given $(\bar{p}, \bar{q}, \bar{x})$. (ii) is a couple of market clearing conditions under the assumption that no production or intertemporal storage is possible and assets are in zero net supply. In (ii), if $\sum_{i=1}^I \alpha^i(\bar{p}, \bar{x}) = \bar{p} \,\square\, \omega$, the condition $\sum_{i=1}^I \bar{z}^i = 0$ is obviously redundant when the rank of $W(\bar{p}, \bar{q}, \bar{x})$ is equal to J.

If for each i, the set Z^i is equal to the whole space $\boldsymbol{R}^J$, that is if there is no restriction on short selling of assets, then the following definition is a particular case of the previous one.

Definition 2.2. *A financial equilibrium is a pair of actions and admissible prices* $((\bar{x}^i, \bar{z}^i)_{i=1}^I, (\bar{p}, \bar{q}))$ *such that*

(i) for each i,

$$\bar{x}^i \in X^i, \bar{z}^i \in \mathbf{R}^J, \bar{p} \,\Box\, \bar{x}^i = \alpha^i(\bar{p}, \bar{x}) + W(\bar{p}, \bar{q}, \bar{x})\bar{z}^i \text{ and } P^i(\bar{x}) \bigcap B^i(\bar{p}, \bar{q}, \bar{x}) = \emptyset$$

with $B^i(\bar{p}, \bar{q}, \bar{x})$ *defined by*

$$B^i(\bar{p}, \bar{q}, \bar{x}) = \{x'^i \in X^i \mid \exists z^i \in \mathbf{R}^J, \bar{p} \,\Box\, x'^i \leq \alpha^i(\bar{p}, \bar{x}) + W(\bar{p}, \bar{q}, \bar{x})z^i\}$$

(ii) $\sum_{i=1}^I \bar{x}^i = \omega$ *and* $\sum_{i=1}^I \bar{z}^i = 0$.

Note that in Definition 2.2, if $\sum_{i=1}^I \alpha^i(\bar{p}, \bar{x}) = \bar{p} \,\Box\, \omega$, even if the matrix $W(\bar{p}, \bar{q}, \bar{x})$ has a rank strictly less than J, the condition $\sum_{i=1}^I \bar{z}^i = 0$ is redundant in the following sense: by changing the portfolio of any one agent, it is easy to associate a financial equilibrium with any $((\bar{x}^i, \bar{z}^i)_{i=1}^I, \bar{p}, \bar{q})$ satisfying all the other conditions of Definition 2.1 but not necessarily $\sum_{i=1}^I \bar{z}^i = 0$.

3 Equilibrium with bounded portfolios

We will use in this paper the following assumptions on the economy:

A.1 For every i, X^i is closed, convex and bounded below

A.2 The correspondences P^i are lower semicontinuous on X and have open values in X^i.

A.3 For each $x \in X$, for every i, $x^i \notin \text{co}\, P^i(x)$ ($\text{co}\, P^i(x)$ denotes the convex hull of $P^i(x)$)

A.4 The functions α^i and the map W are continuous on $\Pi \times X$. Moreover, the functions α^i_s are homogeneous of degree one with respect to $p(s)$, for all $s = 0, \ldots, S$.

A.5 $\forall p \in \mathbf{R}^{L(1+S)}$, $\forall x \in X$, $\forall s$, $\sum_{i=1}^I \alpha^i_s(p, x) = p(s) \cdot \omega(s)$

A.6 (Survival assumption) For every i, $\forall p \in \mathbf{R}^{L(1+S)}$, $\forall x \in X$,

$$p(s) \neq 0 \Rightarrow \inf_{x'^i \in X^i} p(s) \cdot x'^i(s) < \alpha^i_s(p, x).$$

Let $\hat{X} = \{x \in X \mid \sum_{i=1}^I x^i = \omega\}$ denote the set of attainable consumption allocations.

A.7 (nonsatiation at every date-event pair and at every component of an attainable consumption allocation) For every $x \in \hat{X}$, for every i, for every s, there exists an $x'^i \in X^i$, differing from x^i only at s, such that $x'^i \in P^i(x)$.

The assumptions A.1–A.4 are standard in a nontransitive framework. Assumption A.2 will be reinforced later with

A$'$.2 The correspondences P^i have an open graph in $X \times X^i$.

The survival requirement in A.6 and the specific form of nonsatiation in A.7 characterize incomplete market economies.

The first stated result uses the ideas of Radner (1972). More precisely, we prove an existence result for a model with a simpler stochastic structure, a more general asset structure and weaker assumptions on the characteristics of the agents.

Theorem 3.1. *Under Assumptions A.1–A.7, if for each* i, Z^i *is a closed, convex and bounded below subset of* $\mathbf{R}^J$, *then there exists a financial* Z*-equilibrium. Moreover, the equilibrium prices satisfy* $\bar{p}(s) \neq 0\ \forall s = 0, 1, \cdots, S$.

Proof. As Gale and Mas-Colell (1975-1979), replacing original preferences by "augmented preferences"

$$\hat{P}^i(x) = \{x'^i \in X^i \mid x'^i = x^i + \lambda(x''^i - x^i), 0 < \lambda \leq 1, x''^i \in P^i(x)\}$$

we can assume that preference correspondences satisfy the following additional convexity property :

A.8 $x'^i \in P^i(x)$ and $0 < \lambda \leq 1 \Rightarrow x^i + \lambda(x'^i - x^i) \in P^i(x)$.

Noticing that the set of attainable plans $\{(x, z) \in X \times Z \mid \sum_{i=1}^I x^i = \omega, \sum_{i=1}^I z^i = 0\}$ is bounded, we can also replace the original economy by an "equivalent" one. Let us denote by $\tilde{X}^i$ and $\tilde{Z}^i$ the bounded consumption and portfolio sets of i in this economy and set $\tilde{X} = \prod_{i=1}^I \tilde{X}^i$, $\tilde{Z} = \prod_{i=1}^I \tilde{Z}^i$. Given $(p, q) \in \Pi$, $(x, z) \in \tilde{X} \times \tilde{Z}$, following ideas originating from Bergstrom (1976), we define the "modified" budget sets of i

$$B'^i(p, q, x) = \{(x'^i, z'^i) \in \tilde{X}^i \times \tilde{Z}^i \mid p \,\square\, x'^i \leq \alpha^i(p, x) + W(p, q, x)z'^i + \gamma(p, q)\}$$

$$B''^i(p, q, x) = \{(x'^i, z'^i) \in \tilde{X}^i \times \tilde{Z}^i \mid p \,\square\, x'^i \ll \alpha^i(p, x) + W(p, q, x)z'^i + \gamma(p, q)\}$$

where $\gamma(p, q) \in \mathbf{R}^{1+S}$ is defined by

$$\gamma_0(p, q) = 1 - \min\{1, \|p(0)\| + \|q\|\}$$

$$\gamma_s(p, q) = 1 - \|p(s)\|, \ s = 1, \ldots, S.$$

Note that, in view of Assumption A.6, with well-chosen truncated consumption sets $\tilde{X}^i$ (for technical details, we refer to Gale and Mas-Colell (1979)), the resulting budget sets $B''^i(p, q, x)$ (and consequently $B'^i(p, q, x)$) are always non empty.
As in Gale and Mas-Colell (1975-1979), we set the following reaction correspondences

$$\psi^i(p, q, x, z) = \begin{cases} B'^i(p, q, x) & \text{if } (x^i, z^i) \notin B'^i(p, q, x) \\ B''^i(p, q, x) \cap (P^i(x) \times \tilde{Z}^i) & \text{if } (x^i, z^i) \in B'^i(p, q, x) \end{cases}$$

$$\psi^0(p, q, x, z) = \{(p', q') \in \Pi \mid (p' - p) \cdot (\sum_{i=1}^I x^i - \omega) + (q' - q) \cdot \sum_{i=1}^I z^i > 0\}.$$

The correspondences ψ^i can easily be shown to satisfy the assumptions of Gale and Mas-Colell's theorem (as stated in the Corollary 1 of Proposition 12 in Florenzano (1981)) and the relations $(p, q) \notin \psi^0(p, q, x, z)$ and $(x^i, z^i) \notin \text{co}\, \psi^i(p, q, x, z)$. Therefore, there exists $(\bar{p}, \bar{q}, \bar{x}, \bar{z})$ such that $\psi^i(\bar{p}, \bar{q}, \bar{x}, \bar{z}) = \emptyset$, $i = 0, 1, \ldots, I$, i.e.

$$(\bar{x}^i, \bar{z}^i) \in B'^i(\bar{p}, \bar{q}, \bar{x}) \text{ and } B''^i(\bar{p}, \bar{q}, \bar{x}) \cap (P^i(\bar{x}) \times \tilde{Z}^i) = \emptyset, \ i = 1, \ldots, I$$

$$p \cdot (\sum_{i=1}^{I} \bar{x}^i - \omega) + q \cdot \sum_{i=1}^{I} \bar{z}^i \leq \bar{p} \cdot (\sum_{i=1}^{I} \bar{x}^i - \omega) + \bar{q} \cdot \sum_{i=1}^{I} \bar{z}^i, \ \forall (p, q) \in \Pi.$$

To complete the proof, we must now show that $\big((\bar{x}, \bar{z}), (\bar{p}, \bar{q})\big)$ is a financial $\tilde{Z}$-equilibrium of the bounded economy, therefore a financial Z-equilibrium of the original economy. First, we prove that the allocation $(\bar{x}, \bar{z})$ is attainable.

We cannot have $\sum_{i=1}^{I} \bar{z}^i \neq 0$, for if so, then $\|\bar{q}\| = 1$, $\gamma_0(\bar{p}, \bar{q}) = 0$, $\bar{q} \cdot \sum_{i=1}^{I} \bar{z}^i > 0$ and $\bar{p}(0) \cdot \big(\sum_{i=1}^{I} \bar{x}^i(0) - \omega(0)\big) + \bar{q} \cdot \sum_{i=1}^{I} \bar{z}^i > 0$. Summing on i the budget constraints at $s = 0$, we get

$$0 < \bar{p}(0) \cdot \big(\sum_{i=1}^{I} \bar{x}^i(0) - \omega(0)\big) + \bar{q} \cdot \sum_{i=1}^{I} \bar{z}^i \leq \sum_{i=1}^{I} \alpha_0^i(\bar{p}, \bar{x}) - \bar{p}(0) \cdot \omega(0)$$

which contradicts A.5.

We cannot have $\sum_{i=1}^{I} \bar{x}^i - \omega \neq 0$, for if so, then for some $s = 0, 1, \cdots, S$, $\|\bar{p}(s)\| = 1$, $\gamma_s(\bar{p}, \bar{q}) = 0$ and $\bar{p}(s) \cdot \big(\sum_{i=1}^{I} \bar{x}^i(s) - \omega(s)\big) > 0$. As previously, summing on i the budget constraints at s, we get $0 < \sum_{i=1}^{I} \alpha_s^i(\bar{p}, \bar{x}) - \bar{p}(s) \cdot \omega(s)$, which contradicts A.5.

Finally, it follows from A.2 that each $(\bar{x}^i, \bar{z}^i)$ is optimal in $B'^i(\bar{p}, \bar{q}, \bar{x})$. It now follows from A.7 and A.8 that $\gamma(\bar{p}, \bar{q}) = 0$. Therefore, $\|\bar{p}(0)\| + \|\bar{q}\| = 1$ and $\forall s$, $\|\bar{p}(s)\| = 1$, hence for each i, $\bar{p} \,\square\, \bar{x}^i = \alpha^i(\bar{p}, \bar{q}, \bar{x}) + W(\bar{p}, \bar{q}, \bar{x})\bar{z}^i$ and $P^i(\bar{x}) \bigcap B^i(\bar{p}, \bar{x}) = \emptyset$. Moreover, it follows from A.7 that $\bar{p}(0) \neq 0$. In view of Assumption A.4, it is possible to modify $\bar{q}$ in order to get a price $\bar{p}$ normalized by 1, even at date 0. This is this equilibrium that we will consider in the following limit argument presented below. □

Note that the existence of a pure spot market equilibrium (i.e. an equilibrium without financial transfers) under the assumptions A.1–A.7 is an obvious corollary of the previous proposition.

4 Limits of equilibria with bounded portfolios

Since, as pointed in Hart (1975), the financial equilibrium existence may fail even with stronger assumptions than A.1–A.7, a weaker equilibrium concept has been introduced in the literature. The so-called pseudo-equilibrium concept, together with the Grassmanian manifold approach, is used to prove the existence of financial equilibrium for generic asset structures and endowments. We propose here an alternative concept which may "coincide" with the previous one. This definition will take more sense later when looking up at limits of equilibria with bounded portfolios. Let us denote by 1_J the vector of $\boldsymbol{R}^J$ with all coordinates equal to 1.

Definition 4.1. *A generalized-equilibrium is a pair of actions and admissible prices* $\left((\bar{x}^i, \bar{z}^i)_{i=1}^I, (\bar{p}, \bar{q})\right)$, *a* $((1+S)\times J)$*-matrix* B *defining compensating assets, a* $(J\times J)$*-matrix* Δ *of short sale constraints, such that*

(i) *for each* i, $\bar{x}^i \in X^i$, $\bar{z}^i = (\bar{z}_1^i, \bar{z}_2^i) \in \boldsymbol{R}^J \times \boldsymbol{R}^J$,

$$\bar{p}\,\square\,\bar{x}^i = \alpha^i(\bar{p},\bar{x}) + W(\bar{p},\bar{q},\bar{x})\bar{z}_1^i + B\bar{z}_2^i,$$

$\Delta\bar{z}_2^i \geq -1_J$, *and* $P^i(\bar{x}) \bigcap B^i(\bar{p},\bar{q},\bar{x},B,\Delta) = \emptyset$ *where* $B^i(\bar{p},\bar{q},\bar{x},B,\Delta) =$

$$\{x \in X^i \mid \exists z \in \boldsymbol{R}^{2J}, \bar{p}\,\square\, x \leq \alpha^i(\bar{p},\bar{x}) + W(\bar{p},\bar{q},\bar{x})z_1 + Bz_2 \text{ and } \Delta z_2 \geq -1_J\},$$

(ii) $\sum_{i=1}^I \bar{x}^i = \omega$ *and* $\sum_{i=1}^I \bar{z}^i = 0$,

(iii) *the matrix* $\begin{pmatrix} 0 & \Delta \\ W(\bar{p},\bar{q},\bar{x}) & B \end{pmatrix}$ *has rank* J.

The following proposition is an immediate consequence of the previous definition

Proposition 4.1. *If the generalized equilibrium* $\left((\bar{x}^i, \bar{z}^i)_{i=1}^I, (\bar{p}, \bar{q}), B, \Delta\right)$ *satisfies the condition:* rank $W(\bar{p},\bar{q},\bar{x}) = J$, *then* $\left((\bar{x}^i, \bar{z}^i)_{i=1}^I, (\bar{p}, \bar{q})\right)$ *is a financial equilibrium of the economy* $\mathcal{E}$.

Let us now assume that $(\varepsilon_\nu)_{\nu\in N}$ is a sequence of positive real numbers converging to 0. For each agent i, we define $Z_\nu^i = \{z \in \boldsymbol{R}^J \mid z_j \geq -1/\varepsilon_\nu, j = 1, \cdots, J\}$ and set $Z_\nu = \prod_{i=1}^{I} Z_\nu^i$. Looking at the limit properties of a sequence $\left((\bar{x}_\nu, \bar{z}_\nu), \bar{p}_\nu, \bar{q}_\nu\right)_{\nu\in N}$ of Z_ν-equilibria, one obtains the following result.

Theorem 4.1. *Under Assumptions A.1, A'.2, A.3–A.7, there exist* $(\bar{x}^i, \bar{z}^i)_{i=1}^I, (\bar{p}, \bar{q})$, *a* $\left((1+S)\times(J-m)\right)$*-matrix* B *defining* $(J-m)$ *compensating assets, a* $\left(J\times(J-m)\right)$*-matrix* Δ *of short sale constraints on portfolios of compensating assets such that* m *is the rank of* $W(\bar{p},\bar{q},\bar{x})$ *and* $\left((\bar{x}^i, \bar{z}^i)_{i=1}^I, (\bar{p}, \bar{q}), (B,\Delta)\right)$ *is a generalized equilibrium (after completing with columns of* 0 *terms the matrix* B *and* Δ *so as to get the desired format). If* $m = J$, $\left((\bar{x}^i, \bar{z}^i)_{i=1}^I, (\bar{p}, \bar{q})\right)$ *is a financial equilibrium.*

Proof. The limit properties of a sequence $\left((\bar{x}_\nu, \bar{z}_\nu), \bar{p}_\nu, \bar{q}_\nu\right)_{\nu\in N}$ of Z_ν-equilibria will be studied, using the following technical lemma whose proof is left to the reader. [1]

[1] The proof constructs by induction a sequence of subspaces L_{m+k}, $0 \leq k \leq J-m$ such that each L_{m+k} is the linear hull of the first $(m+k)$ column-vectors of matrix G and defines $\tilde{g}^{m+k+1}$ as the normalized normal vector dropped from g^{m+k+1} onto L_{m+k}. One easily checks that, constructed in this way, the matrix $\tilde{G}$ satisfies conditions b) - d) of Lemma 4.1.

Lemma 4.1. *For every J, for every $K \geq J$, for every $m \leq J$, for every real matrix G with J columns and K rows such that the rank of G is J, if we set $G = (g^j)_{1 \leq j \leq J}$, then there exists some matrix $\tilde{G} = (\tilde{g}^j)_{1 \leq j \leq J}$ satisfying :*

a) $\tilde{g}^j = g^j$ *for all* $j = 1, \ldots, m$;
b) $\|\tilde{g}^j\| = 1$ *for all* $j = m+1, \ldots, J$;
c) $\tilde{g}^j \perp \tilde{g}^k$ *for all* $j = m+1, \ldots, J$ *and* $k < j$;
d) the matrix $\tilde{G}$ *and* G *have the same rank* J *and the same range.*

In view of the proof of Theorem 3.1, one can assume that for every ν and for every $s = 0, 1, \ldots, S$, $\|\bar{p}_\nu(s)\| = 1$. Since the set of all attainable consumption plans is bounded, the sequence $(\bar{p}_\nu, \bar{q}_\nu, \bar{x}_\nu)$ has a subsequence, denoted by $(\bar{p}_\nu, \bar{q}_\nu, \bar{x}_\nu)$ for simplicity of notations, converging to $(\bar{p}, \bar{q}, \bar{x})$ with, at the limit, for every s, $\|\bar{p}(s)\| = 1$, $\sum_{i=1}^I \bar{x}^i(s) = \omega$. Since for each i,

$$\bar{p}_\nu \,\Box\, \bar{x}^i_\nu = \alpha^i(\bar{p}_\nu, \bar{x}_\nu) + W(\bar{p}_\nu, \bar{q}_\nu, \bar{x}_\nu)\bar{z}^i_\nu = \alpha^i(\bar{p}_\nu, \bar{x}_\nu) + t^i_\nu$$

we have also at the limit:

$$\bar{p} \,\Box\, \bar{x}^i = \alpha^i(\bar{p}, \bar{x}) + t^i$$

with $t^i = \lim_\nu t^i_\nu = \lim_\nu W(\bar{p}_\nu, \bar{q}_\nu, \bar{x}_\nu)\bar{z}^i_\nu$.

We will now distinguish two cases following the rank m of the limit-matrix $W(\bar{p}, \bar{q}, \bar{x})$.

- If $m = J$, for ν big enough, J is also the rank of $W(\bar{p}_\nu, \bar{q}_\nu, \bar{x}_\nu)$, so that we can deduce from $W(\bar{p}_\nu, \bar{q}_\nu, \bar{x}_\nu)\bar{z}^i_\nu = t^i_\nu$ that $\bar{z}^i_\nu$ converges to $\bar{z}^i$ with at the limit $W(\bar{p}, \bar{q}, \bar{z})\bar{z}^i = t^i$ and $\sum_{i=1}^I \bar{z}^i = 0$.

- If $m < J$, we will assume for simplicity that the m first column-vectors of $W(\bar{p}, \bar{q}, \bar{x})$ are linearly independant. For ν big enough ($\nu \geq \nu_0$), the m first column-vectors of $W(\bar{p}_\nu, \bar{q}_\nu, \bar{x}_\nu)$ are also linearly independant. We now consider the $((J + 1 + S) \times J)$-matrices $G_\nu = \begin{pmatrix} I_\nu \\ W_\nu \end{pmatrix}$ where I_ν is the diagonal matrix $I_\nu = \begin{pmatrix} \varepsilon_\nu & & 0 \\ & \ddots & \\ 0 & & \varepsilon_\nu \end{pmatrix}$ and W_ν stands for $W(\bar{p}_\nu, \bar{q}_\nu, \bar{x}_\nu)$ and observe that for each ν, $-1_J \leq I_\nu \bar{z}^i_\nu \leq (I-1)1_J$ and $W_\nu \bar{z}^i_\nu = t^i_\nu$. For $\nu \geq \nu_0$, let us denote by W^m_ν the $((1 + S) \times m)$-matrix with the m first column-vectors of W_ν as column-vectors and by I^m_ν the matrix with the m first column-vectors of I_ν as column-vectors. Applying Lemma 4.1 to each G_ν ($\nu \geq \nu_0$), we get the existence of a $(J \times (J-m))$-matrix: Δ_ν, a $((1 + S) \times (J - m))$-matrix: B_ν and, for each i, a vector: $\bar{z}^i_\nu = (\bar{z}'^i_\nu, \bar{z}''^i_\nu) \in \boldsymbol{R}^m \times \boldsymbol{R}^{J-m}$ such that $\tilde{G}_\nu = \begin{pmatrix} I^m_\nu & \Delta_\nu \\ W^m_\nu & B_\nu \end{pmatrix}$ and $\tilde{G}_\nu \begin{pmatrix} \bar{z}'^i_\nu \\ \bar{z}''^i_\nu \end{pmatrix} = G_\nu \bar{z}^i_\nu$, i.e.

$$-1_J \leq I^m_\nu \bar{z}'^i_\nu + \Delta_\nu \bar{z}''^i_\nu \leq (I-1)1_J, \tag{1}$$

and

$$W^m_\nu \bar{z}'^i_\nu + B_\nu \bar{z}''^i_\nu = t^i_\nu. \tag{2}$$

By definition of $\tilde{G}_\nu$, one can assume that $\begin{pmatrix} \Delta_\nu \\ B_\nu \end{pmatrix} \to \begin{pmatrix} \Delta \\ B \end{pmatrix}$ where Δ and B are respectively a $(J \times (J-m))$ and a $((1+S) \times (J-m))$-matrix, so that $\tilde{G}_\nu \to \begin{pmatrix} 0 & \Delta \\ W^m & B \end{pmatrix}$. Recalling (1) and (2), one can also assume that $\tilde{G}_\nu \begin{pmatrix} \bar{z}'^i_\nu \\ \bar{z}''^i_\nu \end{pmatrix}$, $\nu \geq \nu_0$, tends to a limit so that, since $\tilde{G}_\nu$ has rank J, the vector $(\bar{z}'^i_\nu, \bar{z}''^i_\nu)_{\nu \geq \nu_0}$ converges to $(\bar{z}'^i, \bar{z}''^i)$ satisfying $\Delta \bar{z}''^i \geq -1_J$ and $W^m \bar{z}'^i + B\bar{z}''^i = t^i = \bar{p} \,\square\, \bar{x}^i - \alpha^i(\bar{p}, \bar{x})$. For $\nu \geq \nu_0$, $\sum_{i=1}^I \tilde{G}_\nu \begin{pmatrix} \bar{z}'^i_\nu \\ \bar{z}''^i_\nu \end{pmatrix} = G_\nu \sum_{i=1}^I \bar{z}^i_\nu = 0$ and since $\operatorname{rank} \tilde{G}_\nu = J$, we have $\sum_{i=1}^I \bar{z}'^i_\nu = 0$, $\sum_{i=1}^I \bar{z}''^i_\nu = 0$ and, by passing to limit, $\sum_{i=1}^I \bar{z}'^i = 0$ and $\sum_{i=1}^I \bar{z}''^i = 0$.

Finally, we prove that for each i, $\left((\bar{x}^i, \bar{z}^i)_{i=1}^I, \bar{p}, \bar{q}\right)$ is optimal in $B^i(\bar{p}, \bar{q}, \bar{x})$ if $m = J$, $\left(\left(\bar{x}^i, (\bar{z}'^i, \bar{z}''^i)\right)_{i=1}^I, \bar{p}, \bar{q}\right)$ is optimal in $B^i\left(\bar{p}, \bar{q}, \bar{x}, \Delta, (W^m, B)\right)$ if $m < J$.

- If $m = J$, assume that $x^i \in P^i(\bar{x})$ and $\bar{p} \,\square\, x^i \leq \alpha^i(\bar{p}, \bar{x}) + W(\bar{p}, \bar{q}, \bar{x}) z^i$. By Assumptions A.6 and A.2, we can assume $\bar{p} \,\square\, x^i \ll \alpha^i(\bar{p}, \bar{x}) + W(\bar{p}, \bar{q}, \bar{x}) z^i$. Since $\begin{pmatrix} I_\nu \\ W(\bar{p}_\nu, \bar{q}_\nu, \bar{x}_\nu) \end{pmatrix} \to \begin{pmatrix} 0 \\ W(\bar{p}, \bar{q}, \bar{x}) \end{pmatrix}$, $\bar{x}^i_\nu \to \bar{x}^i$, using A$'$.2 and A.4 we get for large enough ν, $x^i \in P^i(\bar{x}_\nu)$ and

$$I_\nu z^i \geq -1_J,$$

$$\bar{p}_\nu \,\square\, x^i \ll \alpha^i(\bar{p}_\nu, \bar{x}_\nu) + W(\bar{p}_\nu, \bar{q}_\nu, \bar{x}_\nu) z^i$$

i.e. $x^i \in B^i(\bar{p}_\nu, \bar{q}_\nu, \bar{x}_\nu)$, which contradicts the optimality of $\bar{x}^i_\nu$.

- If $m < J$, assume that $x^i \in P^i(\bar{x})$ and $\bar{p} \,\square\, x^i \leq \alpha^i(\bar{p}, \bar{x}) + W^m z'^i + B z''^i$ with $\Delta z''^i \geq -1_J$. By Assumptions A.6 and A.2, one can assume $\bar{p} \,\square\, x^i \ll \alpha^i(\bar{p}, \bar{x}) + W^m z'^i + B z''^i$ and $\Delta z''^i \gg -1_J$. Since $\tilde{G}_\nu \to \begin{pmatrix} 0 & \Delta \\ W^m & B \end{pmatrix}$, $\bar{x}^i_\nu \to \bar{x}^i$, using A$'$.2, we get for large enough ν, $x^i \in P^i(\bar{x}_\nu)$ and

$$I^m_\nu z'^i + \Delta_\nu z''^i \geq -1_J$$

$$W^m_\nu z'^i + \Delta z''^i \gg \bar{p}_\nu \,\square\, x^i - \alpha^i(\bar{p}_\nu, \bar{x}_\nu).$$

Since G_ν and $\tilde{G}_\nu$ have same range, $x^i \in B^i(\bar{p}_\nu, \bar{q}_\nu, \bar{x}_\nu)$, which contradicts the optimality of $\bar{x}^i_\nu$. □

Let $e \in \mathbb{R}^L$ be a commodity bundle chosen as numeraire. Recalling the form of the return matrix

$$V(p) = \left((p(s) \cdot e) r^j(s)\right)_{\substack{s=1,\ldots,S \\ j=1,\ldots,J}}$$

in case of numeraire assets, Proposition 4.1 has the obvious following corollary where we assume some desirability of numeraire:

Corollary 4.1. *Under Assumptions A.1, A'.2, A.3–A.7, if the matrix*

$$R = \left(r^j(s)\right)_{\substack{s=1,\dots,S \\ j=1,\dots,J}}$$

has rank J and if A.7 is replaced by

A.9 For every $x \in \tilde{X}$, for every i, for every s, defining $e_s \in \boldsymbol{R}^{L(1+S)}$ by $e_s(s) = e$ and $e_s(s') = 0$ if $s' \neq s$, $x^i + e_s \in P^i(x^i)$
then the model with numeraire assets has a financial equilibrium.

Proof. Indeed, it follows from A.9 that $\bar{p}(s) \cdot e > 0\ \forall s = 0, 1, \cdots S$, hence, rank $V(\bar{p}) = J$. A fortiori, rank $W(\bar{p}, \bar{q}) = J$. □

5 Generalized and pseudo-equilibria

We now recall formally the definition of a pseudo-equilibrium.

Definition 5.1. *A pseudo-equilibrium is a pair of actions and admissible prices $\left((\bar{x}^i)_{i=1}^I, (\bar{p}, \bar{q})\right)$, a J-dimensional space of transfers L ($L \subset \boldsymbol{R}^{1+S}$), such that*

(i) for each i, $\bar{x}^i \in X^i$, there exists $\bar{t}^i \in L$ such that $\bar{p} \,\square\, \bar{x}^i = \alpha^i(\bar{p}, \bar{x}) + \bar{t}^i$ and $P^i(\bar{x}) \bigcap B^i(\bar{p}, \bar{q}, \bar{x}, L) = \emptyset$ where $B^i(\bar{p}, \bar{q}, \bar{x}, L) =$

$$\{x \in X^i \mid \exists t \in L, \bar{p} \,\square\, x \leq \alpha^i(\bar{p}, \bar{x}) + t\},$$

(ii) $\sum_{i=1}^I \bar{x}^i = \omega$,
(iii) for all $z \in \boldsymbol{R}^J$, $W(\bar{p}, \bar{q}, \bar{x})z \in L$.

It can easily be checked that this definition, which involves as space of authorized financial transfers a linear subspace L of $\boldsymbol{R}^{1+S}$ (and not $\boldsymbol{R}^S$), coincides with the usual one if the preference correspondences P^i satisfy the two following properties :

- $\forall x \in X$, $(\{x^i\} + \boldsymbol{R}_+^{L(1+S)} \setminus \{0\}) \subset P^i(x)$ (monotonicity of preferences)
- $\forall x \in X$, $(P^i(x) + \boldsymbol{R}_+^{L(1+S)}) \subset P^i(x)$ (free disposal of preferences).

Comparing Definition 4.1 with Definition 5.1, we see that if rank $W(\bar{p}, \bar{q}, \bar{x})$ is less than J, at a pseudo-equilibrium as at a generalized equilibrium, consumers are allowed to use income transfers outside the actual space generated by the initial asset structure. At a pseudoequilibrium, they do that using income transfers belonging to some J-dimensional subspace L of $\boldsymbol{R}^{1+S}$ which is a component of the pseudo-equilibrium. At a generalized equilibrium, they use compensating assets defined by a matrix B which is a component of the generalized equilibrium ; the corresponding portfolios are constrained by the condition $\Delta \bar{z}_2^i \geq -1_J$, where Δ is also a component of the generalized equilibrium. Obviously, a pseudo-equilibrium is a generalized equilibrium. The following proposition gives a partially converse statement.

Proposition 5.1. *Under the convexity assumption A.8, if the generalized equilibrium* $\left((\bar{x}^i, \bar{z}^i)_{i=1}^I, (\bar{p}, \bar{q}), B, \Delta\right)$ *is such that for each consumer* i, $\Delta \bar{z}_2^i \gg -1_J$ *and if the rank of the matrix* $(W(\bar{p}, \bar{q}, \bar{x}) \quad B)$ *is equal to* J, *it is possible to construct a linear space* L *such that* $\left((\bar{x}^i)_{i=1}^I, (\bar{p}, \bar{q}), L\right)$ *is a a pseudo-equilibrium.*

Proof. Indeed, if we define the linear space of transfers L as the range of the matrix $(W(\bar{p}, \bar{q}, \bar{x}) \quad B)$, the condition (iii) of the definition of pseudo-equilibrium is obviously satisfied. Hence, it only remains to prove that for all i, the intersection $P^i(\bar{x}) \bigcap B^i(\bar{p}, \bar{q}, \bar{x}, L) = \emptyset$; this will be done by contradiction. Let $x \in P^i(\bar{x}) \bigcap B^i(\bar{p}, \bar{q}, \bar{x}, L)$ for some i ; it is possible to associate with x the transfer $t \in L$ and the portfolio $z = (z_1, z_2)$ such that $t = W(\bar{p}, \bar{q}, \bar{x}))z_1 + Bz_2$. It follows from Assumption A.8 that for all $\alpha \in]0, 1[$, the consumption plan $\alpha x + (1 - \alpha)\bar{x}^i \in P^i(\bar{x})$. Since $\Delta \bar{z}_2^i \gg -1_J$, for all α small enough the consumption plan $\alpha x + (1-\alpha)\bar{x}^i$ (associated to the portfolio plan $\alpha z + (1-\alpha)\bar{z}^i$) belongs to the budget set $B^i(\bar{p}, \bar{q}, \bar{x}, B, \Delta)$. This contradicts the optimality of $\bar{x}^i$ in $B^i(\bar{p}, \bar{q}, \bar{x}, B, \Delta)$. □

References

Bergstrom, T .C. (1976). How to dicard "free disposability" - at no cost. *Journal of Mathematical Economics* **3**, 131–134.

Florenzano, M. (1981). *L'équilibre économique général transitif et intransitif : problèmes d'existence*. Monographies du séminaire d'économétrie. Editions du C.N.R.S.: Paris.

Gale, D. and Mas-Colell, A. (1975). An equilibrium existence theorem for a general model without ordered preferences. *Journal of Mathematical Economics* **2**, 9–15.

Gale, D. and Mas-Colell, A. (1979). Corrections to an equilibrium existence theorem for a general model without ordered preferences. *Journal of Mathematical Economics* **6**, 297–298.

Geanakoplos, J. (1990). An introduction to General Equilibrium with incomplete asset markets. *Journal of Mathematical Economics* **19**, 1–38.

Hart, O. (1975). On the optimality of equilibrium when the market structure is incomplete. *Journal of Economic Theory* **11**, 418–443.

Keiding, H. (1992). Existence of pseudo-equilibria in economies with incomplete markets. Working paper. Copenhagen.

Marakulin, V. (1994). On the notion of generalized equilibrium in incomplete markets and its existence theorem. Working paper. Novosibirsk.

Radner, (1972). Existence of equilibrium of plans, prices and price expectations in a sequence of markets. *Econometrica* **40, 2**, 289–303.

Part IV

Educational Applications

A Decision Analysis Approach to Multiple-Choice Examinations

José M. Bernardo[1]

[1] Departament d'Estadística i I.O., Facultat de Matemàtiques, Universitat de València, 46100–Burjassot, Valéncia, SPAIN

Abstract

We present a decision analysis approach to the problems faced by people subject to multiple-choice examinations, as often encountered in their education, in looking for a job, or in getting a driving permit.

From the candidate's viewpoint, each question in this form of examination is a *decision problem*, where the decision space depends on the examination rules and the expected utility is some function of the expected score. We analyse this problem for the two basic situations which occur in practice, namely when the candidate wants to maximize his or her expected score, and when he or she wants to maximize the probability of obtaining the minimum grade required to pass, and we derive the corresponding optimal strategies.

We argue that for multiple-choice examinations to be *fair*, candidates should be required to provide a *probability distribution* over the possible answers to each question, rather than merely marking the answers judged to be more likely; we then discuss the appropriate scoring rules and the corresponding optimal strategies. As an interesting byproduct, we deduce some illuminating consequences on the scoring procedures of multiple-choice examinations, as they are currently performed.

Keywords. Bayesian education, decision analysis, multiple-choice questionnaires, probability assessment, scoring rules, utility assessment

1 Introduction

Young citizens are increasingly subject to a number of formal examinations whose results are often very important to their future. Many of these examinations take the form of a multiple-choice questionnaire; important examples include educational examinations, obtaining a driving licence, and interviewing for a job. In this paper, we present a decision analysis approach to the problems faced by people subject to multiple-choice questionnaires.

From the candidate's viewpoint, each question in this form of examination is a *decision problem*, where the decision space depends on the examination rules, and where the expected utility is some function of the expected score. We analyse this problem for the two basic situations which occur in practice, namely when the candidate wants to maximize his or her expected score, and when he or she wants to maximize the probability of obtaining the minimum grade required to pass. We avoid tiresome repetition, 'he or she' will systematically be replaced by a generic 'she' in the rest of the paper.

The literature on non decision-based analysis of conventional multiple-choice tests is huge, specially is psychology-oriented journals. Relevant signposts include see Lierly (1951), Solomon (1955), Chernoff (1962), Nogaki (1984), Thissen and Steinberg (1984), Pollard, (1985), Martín and Luna (1989, 1990), Hsu, Leonard and Tsui (1991), Hutchinson (1991, 1993), Klein (1992), Post (1994), and references therein.

The problem is sociologically important, and a knowledge of the optimal strategy will certainly be of interest to people taking this type of examinations. Moreover, the analysis presented has strong *pedagogical* motivations, for it may successfully be used to introduce the basic elements of decision theory to undergraduate candidates of *any* discipline. Indeed, whether or not it is considered appropriate to include some axiomatic foundations in the course, we argue that it is pedagogically best to begin with a *detailed* example of a decision problem where the basic concepts may be illustrated; ideally, this should be a simple but *realistic* problem, within a context which students understand and care for. We claim that the decision problems posed by multiple-choice examinations are ideally suited for this purpose.

In Section 2 we analyze the conventional decision problem where, for each question, the candidate is required to mark that answer which she judges to be more likely, or to leave that question blank, and we derive the candidate's optimal strategy if she wants to maximize her expected score. In Section 3, we argue that for multiple-choice examinations to be *fair*, candidates should be requested to provide a complete *probability distribution* over the answers proposed, rather than to merely mark that answer which they judge to be more likely; we analyze the corresponding candidate's optimal strategy if she wants to maximize her expected score, and we make use those results to derive some possible improvements on the scoring procedure, if conventional multiple-choice examinations are nevertheless to be performed. In Section 4, we analyze the more complex problem posed when the candidate's preferences are to maximize her probability of obtaining a minimum grade, rather than maximizing her total score. In Section 5 we make a specific proposal for an appropriate implementation of multiple-choice examinations, and suggest areas for additional research.

2 The conventional decision problem

The structure of any finite decision problem may formally be described in terms of the set $A = \{a_1, \ldots, a_k\}$ of possible *alternatives*, the set $\Theta = \{\theta_1, \ldots, \theta_m\}$ of exhaustive, mutually exclusive *relevant uncertain events*, and the set of *consequences*, $c_{ij} = c(a_i, \theta_j)$ which may possibly result; it is well known that sensible set of axiom requirements on coherent decision making (see Bernardo and Smith, 1994, Ch. 2, and references therein, for some options) logically imply (i) that preferences among consequences must be quantified with a real-valued *utility function* $u(c_{ij}) = u(a_i, \theta_j)$, (ii) that the plausibility of the uncertain events must be described with a *probability distribution* $\{p(\theta_1), \ldots, p(\theta_m)\}$ $(p(\theta_j) \geq 0, \sum_j p(\theta_j) = 1)$ over the relevant uncertain events, and (iii) that the optimal alternative a^* is that which *maximizes the expected utility*

$$\overline{u}(a_i) = \sum_{j=1}^{m} u(a_i, \theta_j)\, p(\theta_j); \tag{1}$$

It should be stressed that the word *probability* is to be understood in its common *semantic* use, that is, as a *degree of belief*.

Let $\{\delta_1, \ldots, \delta_k\}$ be the k possible answers to a multiple-choice question, which are assumed to be mutually exclusive and to contain the true answer δ^*. Following conventional practice, we suppose that (i) the candidate is required to either mark the answer which she considers to be correct or to leave the question blank, and that (ii) the scoring rule is such that one point is awarded if the correct answer is marked, zero points if left blank, and $c \geq 0$ points are subtracted if an incorrect answer is marked.

We will first consider the simplest situation, where the candidate wants to maximize her expected total grade. In that case, since her total grade is just the sum of the scores obtained in each question, she clearly has to maximize her expected score in each individual question.

For each question, the set of alternatives is $\{a_0, a_1, \ldots, a_k\}$, where a_0 denotes the option of leaving the question blank, a_i denotes the option of marking δ_i as the correct answer, and the score function may be written as

$$u(a_0, \delta_j) = 0, \qquad u(a_j, \delta_j) = 1, \quad u(a_j, \delta_l) = -c, \text{ if } l \neq j. \tag{2}$$

Thus, if $p_j = \Pr[\delta^* = \delta_j]$ denotes the probability which the candidate actually associates to the event that δ_j is the true answer, then it follows from (1) that her expected utility for each possible alternative is given by

$$\overline{u}(a_0) = 0, \qquad \overline{u}(a_j) = (1 + c)p_j - c, \quad j = 1, \ldots, k, \tag{3}$$

and, therefore,

$$\begin{aligned} \overline{u}(a_j) > \overline{u}(a_l) &\iff p_j > p_l \\ \overline{u}(a_j) > \overline{u}(a_0) &\iff p_j > c/(1 + c). \end{aligned} \tag{4}$$

Thus, to maximize her expected score in one particular question, the candidate must determine her most likely answer (or anyone of them if there are several equally likely), that is one *mode* of her belief distribution $\{p_1, \ldots, p_k\}$, and to mark such a mode in the examination paper if, and only if, its associated probability $p^* = \max_j p_j$ is larger or equal than $c/(1+c)$. It follows from (4) that the expected score in one question for a candidate which acts optimally is

$$\overline{u}(a^*) = \max_{j=0,\ldots,k} \overline{u}(a_j) = \max\{(1+c)p^* - c,\, 0\}. \tag{5}$$

In particular, the score that a candidate may *expect* in one question if she is *convinced* that a particular answer is true is one, while the score she may expect if she has no idea of what the true answer might be, so that her belief distribution ($p_j = 1/k$) is uniform over the k possible answers, is given by $\max\{(1+c)/k - c,\, 0\}$.

From the instructor's point of view, it may seem natural to set the penalty *cost* c of marking a wrong answer such that the expected score associated to random guessing would be zero, and this is achieved if, and only if, $(1+c)/k - c = 0$, that is if, and only if, $c = 1/(k-1)$, in which case the optimal strategy of the candidate is to mark a mode if its associated probability p^* is such that $p^* \geq c/(1+c) = 1/k$. Since this condition is satisfied by the mode of *any* belief distribution over the k possible answers, the optimal strategy of the candidate would then *always* be to mark what she believes to be the more likely answer, no matter how small her associated probability might be, a less than satisfactory solution for an instructor who is interested in learning about the candidate's level of knowledge!

Example 1. In Spain, candidates to postgraduate medical schools are selected in the order established by the total score they achieve in a multiple-choice questionnaire (the *MIR* examination) which consists of $n = 250$ questions, each of which has $k = 5$ possible answers, of which one, and only one, is correct. Candidates are requested to mark one answer from each question or to leave it blank. A point is awarded for each correct answer, zero points are awarded for blank answers and $c = 1/3$ points are subtracted for each incorrect answer. If more than one possibility is marked, the answer is considered to be incorrect. Since, in this case, $c/(1+c) = 1/4$, the argument above shows that the candidate's optimal strategy is *to mark all questions such that,* $p^* \geq 1/4$, that is to mark all questions for which the probability of the more likely answer is, at least, $1/4$. In particular, this is automatically achieved if the candidate may rule out at least one of the answers. It also follows that random guessing with no knowledge (so that $p^* = 1/5$) diminishes the candidate's expected score. $\triangleleft$

3 The relevant decision problem

The conventional practice in multiple-choice examinations described above, where for each question candidates are supposed to mark as correct one of the possible alternative answers, is clearly inappropriate: the candidate is often encouraged to always mark an answer, no matter what her level of knowledge is, and the instructor has no way of discriminating between a correct answer from a knowledgeable candidate, and a correct answer obtained from random guessing. The axiomatic arguments mentioned in Section 1 prescribe that *all* uncertainties *must* be described by probabilities; hence, candidates should be required to specify a complete *probability distribution* over the possible answers, and not merely to quote a mode. Thus, for instance, an answer of the form $(0, 1, 0, \ldots, 0)$ would indicate that the candidate is *absolutely convinced* that the true answer is δ_2, while $(1/2, 1/2, 0, \ldots, 0)$ would indicate that she does not know whether the true answer is δ_1 or δ_2 but has ruled out all other possibilities, and $(1/k, 1/k, \ldots, 1/k)$ would indicate she has no relevant information about what is the true answer to the question posed.

Naturally, an appropriate evaluation function, or *scoring rule*, is needed to score each question as a function of the probability distribution written and the correct answer. We now turn to discuss the crucial question of how the scoring rule should be chosen. As before, we will still assume that the candidate wants to maximize her expected total grade, so that she has to maximize her expected score in each individual question.

From the candidate point of view, each question in this form of examination is a decision problem, where the set of alternatives is the class $Q = \{\boldsymbol{q} = (q_1, \ldots, q_m)\}, q_j \geq 0, \sum_j q_j = 1\}$, of probability distributions over the set $(\delta_1, \ldots, \delta_m)$ of possible answers, and the expected utility is the *expected score*

$$\overline{u}(\boldsymbol{q}) = \sum\nolimits_{j=1}^{m} u(\boldsymbol{q}, \delta_j)\, p_j, \tag{6}$$

where $u(\boldsymbol{q}, \delta_j)$ is the score awarded to a candidate who quotes the probability distribution $\boldsymbol{q}$ when the correct answer is δ_j and where, as before, $p_j = \Pr\{\delta^* = \delta_j\}$ is the personal probability which the candidate associates to the event that the correct answer is δ_j. Note that, in principle, there is no reason to expect that the probability distribution $\boldsymbol{q}$ written by the candidate on the examination form will be the same as the distribution $\boldsymbol{p} = (p_1, \ldots, p_m)$ which describes her actual beliefs.

The instructor is naturally interested in encouraging honesty and, therefore, she should choose a scoring function $u(\boldsymbol{q}, \delta_j)$ whose expected value (6) is maximized if, and only if, $\boldsymbol{q} = \boldsymbol{p}$, that is if, and only if, the candidate writes in the examination form her true beliefs. A scoring rule with this property is called a *proper* scoring rule. The quadratic scoring function

$$\begin{aligned} u(\boldsymbol{q}, \delta_j) &= a\Big[1 - \sum\nolimits_{j=1}^{k} (q_j - \mathbf{1}_{\delta_j})^2\Big] + b_j, \quad a > 0, \quad b_j \in \Re, \\ &= a\Big[2q_j - \|\boldsymbol{q}\|\Big] + b_j, \quad \|\boldsymbol{q}\| = \sum\nolimits_{j=1}^{k} q_j^2, \quad a > 0, \quad b_j \in \Re, \end{aligned} \tag{7}$$

where $\mathbf{1}_{\delta_j}$ is the indicator function of δ_j, is perhaps the simplest *bounded* proper scoring rule. This imposes as a penalty some linear transformation of the squared euclidean distance between a perfect response (a degenerate distribution which gives probability one to the true answer) and the stated answer, $(q_1, q_2, \ldots, q_k)$; it also has the interesting additional property of remaining proper, that is encouraging honesty, even if the q_j's are *not* a priori required to be a probability distribution. The quadratic scoring function was introduced by Brier (1950); major developments were due de

Finetti (1962, 1965); further discussion was provided by Savage (1971) and by Lindley (1982).

The arbitrary constants in (7) are fixed with side conditions; thus, if one point is awarded to a perfect reply giving probability one to the right answer, and zero points are awarded to the lack of knowledge described by a uniform distribution, the quadratic scoring rule (7) becomes standardized to

$$u(\boldsymbol{q}, \delta_j) = \frac{k}{k-1}\Big[2q_j - \|\boldsymbol{q}\|\Big] - \frac{1}{k-1}, \quad \|\boldsymbol{q}\| = \sum\nolimits_{j=1}^{k} q_j^2, \tag{8}$$

which, as one would anticipate, yields *negative* values to distributions which associate high probabilities to wrong answers; in particular, a candidate who gives probability one to a wrong answer would get, using (8), the negative score $-(k+1)/(k-1)$, that is, she would be penalized by $c = (k+1)/(k-1)$ points. The condition of zero points awarded to a uniform distribution automatically implies that blank questions may be treated as questions for which a uniform distribution is stated as the answer; thus, without loss of generality, it may be assumed that probability distributions are specified for all questions.

The result described above indicates that, in conventional multiple-choice examinations, a far more serious penalty should be used for wrong answers than the often suggested value $c = 1/(k-1)$. Indeed, if a conventional multiple-choice questionnaire was scored using the penalty value indicated by the quadratic scoring rule, the analysis in Section 2 establishes that, to maximize her expected score, the candidate should only mark the mode of those questions for which the probability p^* associated to that mode verifies the inequality

$$p^* \geq \frac{c}{1+c} = \frac{k+1}{2k} > \frac{1}{2}, \tag{9}$$

so that an 'absolute (probability) majority' is required, and random guessing in *not* encouraged.

Example 1. (continued). In the *MIR* example discussed before, where future medical postgraduates face a multiple-choice questionnaire with $k = 5$ possible answers associated to each question, one has

$$c = \frac{k+1}{k-1} = \frac{3}{2}, \qquad p^* \geq \frac{k+1}{2k} = \frac{3}{5}, \tag{10}$$

so that the quadratic scoring rule suggests a penalty of $3/2$ points for each incorrect answer (rather than the penalty $c = 1/3$ currently used!); if this were implemented, the optimal candidate's strategy would be to mark the mode of a question if, and only if, its associated probability were larger than $3/5$ (a kind of 'absolute majority'). This would immediately lead to a much better discrimination of good candidates against merely lucky candidates, with the corresponding obvious social benefits. ◁

The case $k = 2$ is specially interesting both by its simplicity and by its pedagogic value: it simply requires to propose a statement and to ask the candidate to quote her probability, say p, of this statement being true, with no need for the instructor to provide alternative answers, which are often artificially confusing. If T denotes the event that the statement is true, then the scoring rule (8) simply reduces to

$$u(p, T) = 1 - 4(1-p)^2, \quad u(p, \overline{T}) = 1 - 4p^2, \tag{11}$$

plotted and tabulated in Figure 1.

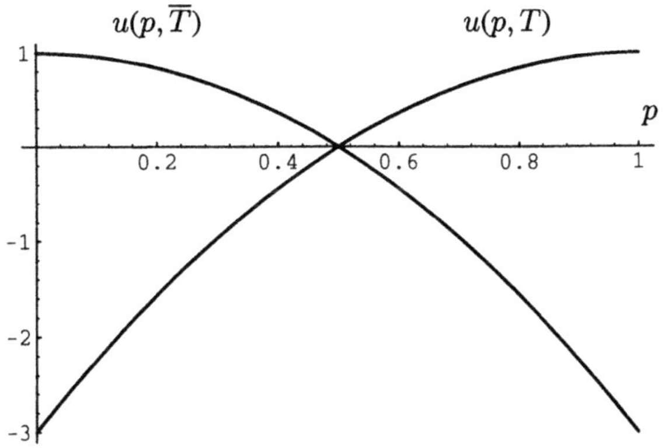

p	$u(p,T)$	$u(p,\overline{T})$
0.00	-3.00	1.00
0.10	-2.24	0.96
0.25	-1.25	0.75
0.50	0.00	0.00
0.75	0.75	-1.25
0.90	0.96	-2.24
1.00	1.00	-3.00

Figure 1. Standardized quadratic scoring rule when $k = 2$, as a function of $p = \Pr(T)$

Proper scoring rules heavily penalize false *presumed* knowledge. Thus, using the quadratic scoring rule described above, a totally ignorant candidate would have a total score of zero, which would *also* be the total score of a candidate with 75% perfectly correct answers ($p^* = 1$) and 25% total blunders ($p^* = 0$), while a candidate with 50% perfect answers and openly ignorant on the rest would get 50% of the maximum score. Thus, a candidate with strong *misconceptions* on 25% of the questions is considered far worst than one which only shows her knowledge on half the questions but *realizes* her ignorance on the rest. We believe this is appropriate: people should be taught that assigning high probability to false statements may be very damaging in real life (if treated by a less than knowledgeable doctor, most of us would rather prefer him to realize his ignorance than to be convinced of a false diagnosis!). Thus, proclaiming false statements with high probability should be seriously penalized.

A similar analysis may be carried out with any other *proper* evaluation function, that is one which encourages honesty by guaranteeing that the maximum expected score is obtained if, and only if, the stated probability distribution $\boldsymbol{q}$ is that describing the candidates actual beliefs, $\boldsymbol{p}$. An alternative candidate to (8) is the *logarithmic* scoring rule

$$u(\boldsymbol{q}, \delta_j) = a \log(q_j) + b_j, \quad a > 0, \quad b_j \in \Re, \tag{12}$$

which reduces to

$$u(\boldsymbol{q}, \delta_j) = 1 - \frac{\log(q_j)}{\log(k^{-1})}, \tag{13}$$

if, as before, it is required that one point is awarded to a perfect reply and zero to a uniform distribution. Introduced by Good (1950), the logarithmic scoring rule is the *only* proper scoring rule which *exclusively* depends on the probability q_j associated to the true answer δ_j (Savage, 1971), and also has a rather nice decision-theoretical interpretation (Bernardo, 1979). However, its use in the context of multiple-choice examinations is problematic because it is *not* bounded; thus, the score associated to a response which gives probability zero to the correct answer is $-\infty$. Although this is mathematically sound (the worst possible mistake is to dogmatically declare false the correct conclusion, and this has the worst possible score, namely $-\infty$), it would be rather rash in practice: it would mean to automatically exclude from the examination any candidate which commits such a mistake. Besides, to be proper, the logarithmic scoring rule requires the stated q_j's to be probability values, ($0 \leq q_j \leq 1$) while the quadratic scoring rule encourages honesty *even* if the candidate is allowed to write any numerical values for the q_j's.

4 Maximizing the probability of a minimum grade

We will now turn to consider the situation where the candidate wants to maximize the probability of getting a minimum grade, such as that needed to simply pass the examination, or that required to qualify for a grant. This is a far more complex decision problem, for it involves a *joint* analysis of the answers given to *all* the questions posed.

Let us consider a multiple-choice questionnaire consisting of n questions with k alternative answers, one of which is assumed to be true, associated to each question. We denote by $\delta_i^* \in \{\delta_{i1}, \ldots, \delta_{ik}\}$ the correct answer to the i-th question, so that $\delta_i^* = \delta_{ij}$ means that δ_{ij} is the correct answer to the i-th question, and we denote by $\boldsymbol{\delta} = \{\delta_1^*, \ldots \delta_n^*\}$ the set of all correct answers. Furthermore, we represent the candidate's true beliefs on the questions posed by the $n \times k$ matrix $\boldsymbol{P}$, with rows

$$\{\boldsymbol{p}_1, \ldots, \boldsymbol{p}_n\}, \quad \boldsymbol{p}_i = \{p_{i1}, \ldots, p_{ik}\}, \quad p_{ij} \geq 0, \quad \sum\nolimits_{j=1}^{k} p_{ij} = 1, \tag{14}$$

where p_{ij} is the probability which the candidate associates to the event that δ_{ij} is the correct answer to the i-th question.

4.1 Conventional Multiple-Choice Questionnaires

Suppose that a conventional multiple-choice examination is performed, so that, for each question, the candidate is required to mark one, and only one of its associated possible answers, or to leave the question blank. We denote by $a_{(i)} \in \{a_{i0}, a_{i1}, \ldots, a_{ik}\}$ the answer provided to the i-th question, so that $a_{(i)} = a_{i0}$ means that the candidate has left the i-th question blank, and $a_{(i)} = a_{ij}$ means that the candidate has marked the j-th answer within the i-th question, and we denote by $\boldsymbol{a} = \{a_{(1)}, \ldots, a_{(n)}\}$ the set of all answers, that is, the complete answer to the examination. As before, we assume that the scoring rule is such that

$$u(a_{i0}, \delta_{ij}) = 0, \qquad u(a_{ij}, \delta_{ij}) = 1, \quad u(a_{ij}, \delta_{il}) = -c, \text{ if } l \neq j. \tag{15}$$

It follows that, if r and s respectively denote the number of correct and incorrect answers contained in $\boldsymbol{a}$, therefore leaving $n - r - s \geq 0$ questions left blank, then the *total score* t associated to the set of answers $\boldsymbol{a}$ is given by

$$t = t(\boldsymbol{a}, \boldsymbol{\delta}) = r(\boldsymbol{a}, \boldsymbol{\delta}) - c\, s(\boldsymbol{a}, \boldsymbol{\delta}), \quad c \geq 0, \tag{16}$$

where, again, c is the penalty associated to one incorrect answer. The preferences of a candidate who wants to maximize her probability of getting an score equal or larger than t_0 are described by the dichotomous utility function

$$\begin{aligned} u(\boldsymbol{a}, \boldsymbol{\delta}) = u(t(\boldsymbol{a}, \boldsymbol{\delta})) &= 1, \quad \text{if } t \geq t_0 \\ &= 0, \quad \text{otherwise.} \end{aligned} \tag{17}$$

It follows that the expected utility $\overline{u}(\boldsymbol{a})$ associated to a particular answer $\boldsymbol{a}$ will therefore be

$$\overline{u}(\boldsymbol{a}) = \Pr[t \geq t_0 \,|\, \boldsymbol{a}, \boldsymbol{P}]. \tag{18}$$

It is easily established that the expected utility $\overline{u}(\boldsymbol{a})$ is maximized by *marking the m more likely modes*, where $t_0 \geq m \geq n$, and where the optimal value of $m = m(t_0, n, \boldsymbol{P}, c)$ depends both on the probability matrix $\boldsymbol{P}$ and on the penalty constant c. Computationally, this is a simple exercise, for it only involves $n - t_0 + 1$ evaluations of $\overline{u}(\boldsymbol{a})$; however this means that, in order to be able to implement her optimal strategy, the candidate would need access to a preprogrammed calculator. As one would expect, $m(t_0, n, \boldsymbol{P}, 0) = n$ so that, if there is no penalty for a wrong answer ($c = 0$), then the candidate's optimal strategy is to mark *all* the modes. Thus, *a null penalty strongly encourages blind guessing.*

Example 2. The theoretical knowledge required to obtain a driving permit is usually controlled with multiple-choice examinations, where a minimum score is required to pass and where there is no penalty for incorrect answers. For instance, in Spain the test consists of $n = 40$ questions, each of which has $k = 3$ possible answers, of which one, and only one, is correct. Candidates are requested to mark one answer from each question or to leave it blank. A point is awarded for each correct answer, zero points are awarded for blank answers and nothing is subtracted for incorrect answers. Candidates pass the exam if they get a minimum of $t_0 = 36$ correct answers. Since, in this case, $c = 0$, the argument above shows that the candidate's optimal strategy is *to mark all questions* using a relevant mode if available, or randomly guessing the correct answer if no knowledge is held. ◁

4.2 Probabilistic Multiple-Choice Questionnaires

Let us now suppose that candidates are requested to specify their probability distributions over the sets of alternative answers to each question. We represent the candidate's statements on the questions posed by $\boldsymbol{a} = \{a_{(1)}, \ldots, a_{(n)}\}$ where $a_{(i)} \in \{q_{i0}, \boldsymbol{q}_i\}$ is the answer provided to the i-th question, so that $a(i) = q_{i0}$ means that the candidate has left the i-th question blank, and $a_{(i)} = \boldsymbol{q}_i = \{q_{i1}, \ldots, q_{ik}\}$

means that the candidate has marked $\{q_{i1}, \ldots, q_{ik}\}$ as the probability distribution which she associates with the answer to the i-th question.

The total score will typically be of the form

$$t(\boldsymbol{a}, \boldsymbol{\delta}) = \sum_{i=1}^{n} f(a_{(i)}, \delta_{ij}), \tag{19}$$

where $f(q_{i0}, \delta_{ij}) = 0$ and $f(\boldsymbol{q}_i, \delta_{ij})$ is an evaluation function possibly, but not necessarily, of the form specified by (8), and where the candidate preferences are again described by the utility function (17). If the evaluation function f is chosen such that the score associated to a uniform distribution is zero, than blank answers may be treated as those which specify a uniform probability distribution and hence, without loss of generality, the set $\boldsymbol{a}$ of all the answers in the examination may be represented as the $n \times k$ matrix $\boldsymbol{Q}$, whose rows are

$$\{\boldsymbol{q}_1, \ldots, \boldsymbol{q}_n\}, \quad \boldsymbol{q}_i = \{q_{i1}, \ldots, q_{ik}\}, \quad q_{ij} \geq 0, \quad \sum\nolimits_{j=1}^{k} q_{ij} = 1, \tag{20}$$

where q_{ij} is the probability which the candidate *states* as her belief on the event that δ_{ij} is the correct answer to the i-th question.

The candidate's optimal strategy would then be described by that matrix $\boldsymbol{Q}$ which maximizes the expected utility

$$\overline{u}(\boldsymbol{Q}) = \Pr[t \geq t_0 \,|\, \boldsymbol{Q}, \boldsymbol{P}]. \tag{21}$$

The solution will depend on the evaluation function f which is used. Note that, in general, the optimal strategy for the candidate will *not* be to be honest, that is to write $\boldsymbol{Q} = \boldsymbol{P}$, therefore revealing her true beliefs, *even* if f is chosen to be a proper scoring rule. Intuitively, if she is convinced that she 'must' get a minimum of t_0 points, then she would tend to pretend to have enough knowledge to have a chance to get those t_0 points, even if this is bound to decrease her *expected* total score.

5 Discussion

In our many years of teaching experience, a detailed analysis of the decision problems associated to multiple-choice examinations has proved to be a very valuable introduction to the main ideas in decision analysis. Moreover, when candidates are required to provide probabilities, and are evaluated using some proper scoring rule, multiple-choice examinations serve both to improve the general ability of the population to assess probabilities, and to faithfully gauge their level of knowledge. Thus, probabilistic multiple-choice examinations serve society far better than their conventional counterpart, for they enhance the candidates abilities to assess probabilities, and they help to discriminate really good candidates from those merely lucky.

We have found that, even if the conventional form of examination is used, setting the penalty value to $c = (k + 1)/(k - 1)$ as suggested by the standardized quadratic score (in which case the optimal strategy for the candidate is to mark a mode if, and only if, its associated probability p^* is such that $p^* \geq (k+1)/(2k) > 1/2$ and guessing is not encouraged), does result in an appreciable improvement on the value of the multiple-choice examinations as a measure of the candidates' level of knowledge.

We have also found that, in practice, best results are obtained with $k = 2$, that is with 'multiple' choice examimations which simply consist of a sequence of statements, for each of which candidates are required to state their probability of the statement being true. Indeed, the use of a sequence of statements which are either true or false, rather than a sequence of questions with k alternative answers, has at least two obvious advantages: (i) it disposes of the need to provide alternative, often confusing answers, and (ii) it avoids a possible criticism of evaluation functions on the ground that, within each question, some wrong answers may be more nearly correct than others. In any case candidates should have immediate access to the behaviour of the evaluation function which will be used, that is to the information provided in Figure 1 if, as we are suggesting, the standardized quadratic score with $k = 2$ is actually used.

We have mentioned in Section 4 that the use of proper scoring rules is only guaranteed to encourage honesty if the candidate's preferences are to maximize her expected score. Thus, if the instructor is interested in faithful results, she should use a proper evaluation function *and* she should try to motivate the candidates into maximizing their score, rather than merely getting some minimum grade. Nevertheless, an interesting further development consists of determining whether there are conditions under which, using a proper evaluation function (so that the optimal strategy of a candidate interested in maximizing her score is to be honest), the optimal strategy of a candidate who wants to maximize the probability that her total score is larger or equal to some known minimum level,would *also* be to be honest.

It may also be interesting to study sequential decision problems within this context. Thus, depending on her preferences, a candidate may find it optimal to abandon an examination if, say, her expected score is not large, and she thus ensure another opportunity to take the examination.

Acknowledgements

This research was partially funded with grant PB96-0754 of the DGICYT, Madrid, Spain.

The author is grateful to Jim Berger, Dennis Lindley and Tony O'Hagan for their comments on an earlier draft of this paper.

References

Bernardo, J. M. (1979). Expected information as expected utility. *Ann. Statist.* **7**, 686–690.

Bernardo, J. M. and Smith, A. F. M. (1994). *Bayesian Theory*. Chichester: Wiley.

Brier, G. W. (1950). Verification of forecasts expressed in terms of probability. *Month. Weather Rev.* **78**, 1–3.

Chernoff, H. (1962). The scoring of multiple-choice questionnaires. *Ann. Math. Statist.* **33**, 375-393.

de Finetti, B. (1962). Does it make sense to speak of 'Good Probability Appraisers'?, *The Scientist Speculates: An Anthology of Partly-Baked Ideas* (I. J. Good, ed.). New York: Wiley, 257–364. Reprinted in 1972, *Probability, Induction and Statistics* New York: Wiley, 19–23.

de Finetti, B. (1965). Methods for discriminating levels of partial knowledge concerning a test item. *British J. Math. Statist. Psychol.* **18**, 87–123. Reprinted in 1972, *Probability, Induction and Statistics* New York: Wiley, 25–63.

Good, I. J. (1950). *Probability and the Weighing of Evidence*. London : Griffin; New York: Hafner Press.

Hsu, J. S. J., Leonard, T. and Tsui, K.-W. (1991). Statistical inference for multiple-choice tests. *Psychometrika* **56**, 327–348.

Hutchinson, T. P. (1991). *Ability, Partial Information, Guessing: Statistical Modelling Applied to Multiple-Choice Tests*. Adelaide, Australia: Rumsby.

Hutchinson, T. P. (1993). Second attempts at multiple-choice test items. *J. Statist. Computation and Simulation* **47**, 108–112.

Klein, S. P. (1992). Statistical evidence of cheating in multpiple-choice tests. *Chance* **5**, 23–27.

Lierly, S. B. (1951). A note for correcting for chance success in objective tests. *Psychometrika* **22**, 63–73.

Lindley, D. V. (1982). Scoring rules and the inevitability of probability. *Internat. Statist. Rev.* **50**, 1–26 (with discussion).

Martín, A. and Luna, J. D. (1989). Test and intervals in multiple-choice tests: A modification of the simplest classical model. *British J. Math. Statist. Philosophy* **42**, 251–264.

Martín, A. and Luna, J. D. (1990). Multiple-choice tests: Power, lengh and optimal number of choices per item. *British J. Math. Statist. Philosophy* **43**, 57–72.

Nogaki, A. (1984). Some remarks on multiple-choice questions in competitive examinations. *Behaviormetrika* **16**, 13–19.

Pollard, G. H. (1985). Scoring in multiple-choice examinations. *Math. Scientist* **10**, 93–97.

Post, G. V. (1994). A quantal choice model for the detection of copying on multiple-choice examinations. *Decision Sciences* **25**, 123–142.

Savage, L. J. (1971). Elicitation of personal probabilities and expectations. *J. Amer. Statist. Assoc.* **66**, 781–801. Reprinted in 1974 in *Studies in Bayesian Econometrics and Statistics: in Honor of Leonard J. Savage* (S. E. Fienberg and A. Zellner, eds.). Amsterdam: North-Holland, 111–156.

Solomon, H. (1955). Item analysis and classification techniques. *Proc. Third Berkeley Symp.* **5** (J. Neyman and E. L. Scott, eds.). Berkeley: Univ. California Press, 169–184.

Thissen, D. and Steinberg, L. (1984). A response model for multiple choice items. *Psychometrika* **49**, 501–519.

Equilibrium Policies among University Departments

R. Caballero[1], T. Gómez[1], M. González[1], L. Rey and F. Ruiz[1]

[1] Department of Applied Economics (Mathematics).
Campus El Ejido s/n. University of Málaga.
29071-Málaga. SPAIN

Abstract

A Dynamic Goal Programming model is proposed to determine the extra budget assignment to the departments of the University of Málaga, in order to ease an initial highly unbalanced situation.

Keywords. Dynamic goal programming, economy of education

1 Introduction

Multiple Criteria Decision Making has got an important range of applications in the field of the Economy of Education. In this sense, we can point out the works by Lee and Clayton (1972), Dinkelbach and Isermann (1980), Geoffrion, Dyer and Feinberg (1972) and Ghosh, Pal and Basu (1992), together with the great survey by Mustafa and Goh (1996).

In this paper a dynamic Goal Programming model is developed for the budget assignment among the University departments so that they can carry out their teaching duties. First, the inefficiencies of several departments are analyzed through a multiple objective model, and afterwards the best resource distribution to equilibrate the unbalances is studied in a medium range term (four academic years) within the global budget availabilities.

2 Initial situation

With the aim of getting a good formulation of our model, so that it represents as accurately as possible the problem that we are facing, that is, the budget assignment to each of the different departments that form the University of Malaga, Spain, it is necessary to carry out a thorough analysis of the initial situation, in such a way that it allows us study the features of the different teaching units that conform our

University. To this end, we have used a database which basically corresponds to one obtained in our University in January 1993, and which was developed with the aim of calculating the structure of the theoretical staff.

The data corresponding to the initial situation of our University are displayed in the appendix, and they express, column by column, the following variables:

The first column, *number assigned to the Department or Functional Unit*, determines the ordering of the variables and constants that correspond to the corresponding department. The second columns displays the *number of subjects* taught by the department.

The third and fourth columns make reference to the *number of students*. The former shows the total number of students, while the latter displays the number of students using their repeat option, who are not considered by the Junta de Andalucía in the same way that the new students, in what respects to the assignments to the departments of resources for their teaching tasks and for their internal organization.

The fifth column corresponds to the *number of groups* that are taught by the department, in a *number of theoretical hours* that is displayed in the next column, and which, multiplied by the last column, the so called *practicality*, gives as a results the number of real hours taught by the department. This practicality index must consider both the number of practical hours for each theoretical one and the possible necessary division of the theoretical groups in subgroups to teach the practical lessons.

The penultimate column corresponds to the *number of teachers* that belong to the department, which produces a *real cost* for the University displayed in the eight column. On the other hand, the seventh column shows the *theoretical cost*, which was given by the University assuming that the groups are formed by 125 students in the first cycle and 75 in the second, and assuming also an equilibrated staff of the department, formed by all kind of teachers in different proportions.

A quick glance at these data can easily lead us to the conclusion that there exist lots of initial unbalances among the different departments that form our University, specially referring to the number of students per department, the number of students per teacher, the number of teaching hours per department, and the difference between the theoretical cost and the real cost o each department.

Once the unbalances that we face in the initial moment have been analyzed, we will proceed to the formulation of our model, with which we will try to determine the budget assignment to each department with the aim of easing the above mentioned unbalances. In the following section, the description of such model will be given, noticing also the practical difficulties that we found for its elaboration. May be the main difficulty we faced was the lack of available data, which lead us in several occasions, given the impossibility to obtain the desired information on certain variables, to use approximate variables, having to adapt the available data and parameters to them.

3 Variables and relations

Next, the variables and parameters that are considered in the model are described. A planning period of 4 academic courses will be considered, which is equivalent to an University president's government period, and, thus, k will take the values 1, 2, 3, 4. For each value of k, a budget assignment to each department will be considered. Namely, in this model 64 departments or teaching units will be considered, indexed by i, $i = 1, \ldots, 64$.

Variables

State variables.

$RC_i(k)$: Real cost of the teachers staff, measured in millions of pesetas.
$S_i(k)$: Number of students, measured in thousands of persons.

Control variables.

$b_i(k)$: Budget assignment for the increase of the real staff, measured in millions of pesetas.

Intermediate variables.

$RS_i(k)$: Number of students that use the repeat option, measured in thousands of persons.
$NS_i(k)$: Number of newly enrolled students, measured in thousands of persons.
$NG_i(k)$: Estimated number of groups.
$H_i(k)$: Theoretical hours, according to the number of groups.
$TH_i(k)$: Total number of hours, taking the practicality into account.
$TC_i(k)$: Theoretical cost of the teachers staff, measured in millions of pesetas.
$RST_i(k)$: Ratio students per teacher.
$\alpha_i(k)$: Index of failed students in the department.
$\beta_i(k)$: Increase index on the number of students of the department.

Parameters

γ_i: Ratio theoretical cost/real cost in the starting instant.
THG_i: Mean number of theoretical hours per group.
PR_i: Practicality index.
NSU_i: Number of subjects.
NG_i: Number of groups in the initial moment.
SG: Mean number of students per group in the whole University, measured in thousands of persons.

Except for the control variables, the initial values of all the variables and constants, can be found, or derived from the data displayed in appendix I.

Relations

The following relations have been obtained between the intermediate variables and the state and control variables of our model:

$$
\begin{aligned}
NG_i(k) &= \frac{S_i(k)}{SG} \\
H_i(k) &= THG_i NG_i(k) = \frac{H_i(1)}{NG_i} NG_i(k) = \frac{H_i(1)}{NG_i}\frac{S_i(k)}{SG} \\
TH_i(k) &= H_i(k) PR_i = \frac{H_i(1)}{NG_i}\frac{PR_i}{SG} S_i(k) \\
RST_i(k) &= \frac{S_i(k)}{RC_i(k)} \\
TC_i(k) &= \gamma_i H_i(k) PR_i = \frac{TC_i(1)}{H_i(1)PR_i}\frac{H_i(1)}{NG_i}\frac{S_i(k)}{SG} PR_i = \\
&= \frac{TC_i(1)}{SG\, NG_i} S_i(k)
\end{aligned}
$$

Fig. 1. Relations between the intermediate variables and the state variables of the model

4 Constraints

Before defining the constraints of our model, the following important remark must be made. The model constraints must define the situation in which the system must necessarily evolve, but not the theoretical situation in which we would like it to evolve. Within a dynamic problem formulation, a constraint that is not satisfied by the initial values of the state variables of the system is not admissible. Therefore, a distinction must be made between the real factual constraints and our wishes, even in the case when the latter can be expressed as values for the bounds of the former. As a result, we will carry out the following procedure: the constraints functions will be defined, as functions of time, and their lower and upper bounds will be built according to our initial wishes, although in a parametric way. After that, an analysis will be carried out to show which departments fail to accomplish any of the constraints in the initial moment, and we will use this information to relax the original bounds, so as to assure that all the departments satisfy the constraints in the initial moment. This way, the constraints will just mean the exigency of not making the initial situation worse by any means. This procedure will yield three blocks of constraints, that will afterwards be joined in a single one. Later, in section 5, when a Goal Programming scheme is carried out on our model, the above mentioned constraints will be turned into goals, and their target values will be given by our initial wishes.

Apart from these three blocks of constraints, two budget constraints have been added to the model. The first of them is an upper bound on the budget assignment that a single department can receive in a single period while the second one limits the total budget that can be distributed among the departments in an academic year.

The first block of constraints that is defined implies a lower and upper bound on the ratio real cost per total number of hours in each department, which gives us a measure of the real cost of each teaching hour given by the department. Its expression is given by:

$$L1 \leq \frac{RC_i(k)}{TH_i(k)} \leq U1,$$

where $L1$ corresponds with the real cost of the worst possible staff, and $U1$ represents the cost of the best possible staff.

According to the relations given by Table 1, this constraint can be expressed in the following way:

$$\frac{H_i(1)PR_i}{SGNG_i}L1 \leq \frac{RC_i(k)}{S_i(k)} \leq \frac{H_i(1)PR_i}{SGNG_i}U1,$$

and, thus, it is given as a function of the ratio real cost per number of students.

The second block of constraints deals with the ratio number of students per teacher, on which lower and upper bounds are imposed, with global bound for the whole University. This ratio is directly expressed as a function of the two state variables of the model, resulting then into de following expression:

$$L2 \leq \frac{S_i(k)}{RC_i(k)} \leq U2,$$

where L2 y U2 are parameters that correspond to extreme cases where this value is small (the first one), and large (the last one). Namely, L2 corresponds to 15 students per teacher for the best possible staff, and U2 corresponds to 120 students per teacher for the worst possible staff. With the aim of expressing this constraint as a function of the same quotient that appears in the first one, its following equivalent form is considered:

$$\frac{1}{U2} \leq \frac{RC_i(k)}{S_i(k)} \leq \frac{1}{L2}.$$

The third constraint measures the ratio between the real and theoretical cost of each department, which gives us information about the extent to which the corresponding department is well provided. Its bounds are denoted by L3 y U3. This way, we have:

$$L3 \leq \frac{RC_i(k)}{TC_i(k)} \leq U3,$$

where, initially, the values, $L3 = 0.5$, $U3 = 1$ have been taken. Making use again of the relations given by Table 1, this constraint can be rewritten as:

$$\frac{TC_i(1)}{SGNG_i}L3 \leq \frac{RC_i(k)}{S_i(k)} \leq \frac{TC_i(1)}{SGNG_i}U3$$

Therefore, these three blocks of constraints can be joined into a single one, in the following way:

$$m_i \leq \frac{RC_i(k)}{S_i(k)} \leq M_i,$$

where:

$$m_i = \max\left\{\frac{H_i(1)PR_i}{SGNG_i}L1,\ \frac{1}{U2},\ \frac{TC_i(1)}{SGNG_i}L3\right\}$$

$$M_i = \min\left\{\frac{H_i(1)PR_i}{SGNG_i}U1,\ \frac{1}{L2},\ \frac{TC_i(1)}{SGNG_i}U3\right\}$$

As it was previously mentioned, these constraints are the desired ones, but are not valid for our dynamic model, because they are not verified by the initial state of the system. Given the values

$$A1 = \frac{H_i(1)PR_i}{SGNG_i}L1, \quad A2 = \frac{1}{U2}, \quad A3 = \frac{TC_i(1)}{SGNG_i}L3$$
$$A4 = \frac{H_i(1)PR_i}{SGNG_i}U1, \quad A5 = \frac{1}{L2}, \quad A6 = \frac{TC_i(1)}{SGNG_i}U3$$

there are a series of departments that fail to verify the corresponding constraints in the initial moment. Namely, approximately a 70% of them fail to accomplish one of the three lower bounds, that is, they teach too many hours and/or they have too many students per teacher and/or they are way under their theoretical staff. This fact is a proof of the difficult situation in which our University has to work nowadays, and the problem we face is even worse if we take into account the fact that around a 35% of the departments simultaneously fail to satisfy all the three lower constraints. But, on the other hand, nearly a 30% of the departments enjoy a real staff which is greater that their theoretical one, showing again a very deep unbalance problem.

Taking all the above into account, and going back to the formulation of our constraints, it seems obvious that the values $Ai, i = 1, \ldots, 6$, must be multiplied by different factors, so as to assure that all the departments will satisfy the constraints in the initial moment. Namely, the following values have had to be taken for the factors:

$$\omega_1 = 0.125, \quad \omega_2 = 0.125, \quad \omega_3 = 0.25 \quad \omega_4 = 2, \quad \omega_5 = 1, \quad \omega_6 = 5$$

so as to get feasibility for all the departments. Finally, the constraints have been linearized, and expressed in the following way:

$$RC_i(k) - M_{ri}S_i(k) \leq 0 \quad k = 1, \ldots, 5, \quad i = 1, \ldots, 64,$$
$$-RC_i(k) + m_{ri}S_i(k) \leq 0 \quad k = 1, \ldots, 5, \quad i = 1, \ldots, 64,$$

where m_{ri} and M_{ri} denote the relaxed values of the bounds, which have been obtained multiplying the original bound A_i by the corresponding factor ω_i. Finally, two budget constraints have been added to our model. The first block implies a budget constraint for each department in each period, that is,

$$0 \leq b_i(k) \leq U, \quad i = 1, \ldots, 64, \quad k = 1, \ldots, 4.$$

This constraint can be justified by two reasons. On the one hand, it was intended to get an adequate distribution of the available resources, trying to avoid cases when some departments get a very big assignment, not letting others to get budget to ease their situation. On the other hand, we tried to avoid situations in which a department would get in a single period more money than it could rationally spend.

The second budget constraint is given by:

$$\sum_{i=1}^{64} b_i(k) \leq UT, \quad k = 1, \ldots, 4,$$

and it is obviously justified by the limited budget availability of the University itself. As it will be later seen, different values will be used for these bounds along our study, and, thus, their particular values will be specified in each case.

In order to fully evaluate the extent of the initial unbalanced situation, and to have a better knowledge of the structure of the problem, a study has been carried out to determine the efficient solutions relative to four objective functionals. Namely, our objectives have been to minimize the difference between the real cost and the theoretical cost of each department; to minimize the distance between the number of weekly hours per teacher and a certain desired value equivalent to eight weekly hours per teacher; to minimize the difference between the number of students per teacher and a value equivalent to 15 students per teacher of an ideal staff; and to minimize the global expense of the operation. All these four functionals have been expressed as quadratic functions of the state and control variables, and the resulting problem has been solved using the algorithm described in Caballero et al. (1997b) which is based in the weighting method, and has been implemented in FORTRAN language on a VAX computer equipped with an ALPHA coprocesor.

The most outstanding feature of this analysis is the stability of the solutions obtained, because only when the fourth functional is highly weighted the solution substantially changes. In any other case, the solution clearly shows the structure of a set of departments with a highly deficit situation regarding any of the three first objective functionals, what makes necessary a strong budget assignment to make these departments come nearer to the ideal situation represented by the objectives.

As a matter of fact, if one observes the initial situation of such teaching units, it can be seen that we are speaking about those departments that have the highest number of students per teacher, some of them with over 350. Besides, their teachers teach an excessive number of hours, with quantities reaching 27 weekly hours and, of course, we are speaking about departments with a real staff way under their theoretical staff.

5 Calculation of satisfying solutions

As it was already mentioned in the previous section, our initial wish was the system to satisfy a set of constraints which were much more strict than those that were finally adopted as hard constraints. For this reason, it seems interesting to study, through a Goal Programming scheme based in the static approach described in Ruiz et al. (1997), the possibility to come near this situation, regarded as satisfactory. This is why, throughout this section, these constraints will appear as goals. Namely, let us remind that our initial wish was to establish constraints that took the form:

$$m_i \leq \frac{RC_i(k)}{S_i(k)} \leq M_i,$$

where, as it was stated in section 4,

$$m_i = \max\left\{\frac{H_i(1)PR_i}{SGNG_i}L1,\ \frac{1}{U2},\ \frac{TC_i(1)}{SGNG_i}L3\right\}$$

$$M_i = \min\left\{\frac{H_i(1)PR_i}{SGNG_i}U1,\ \frac{1}{L2},\ \frac{TC_i(1)}{SGNG_i}U3\right\}$$

So as to carry out a complete analysis, a study has been made, consisting of solving 18 Goal Programming models, in each one of which the above bounds are multiplied by different relaxation factors. This way, each model studies the possibility of eventually including all the departments in a band that ranges between m_i and M_i, which in turn depend on the relaxation factors ω_i in the following way:

$$m_i(\omega_1, \omega_2, \omega_3) = \max\left\{\omega_1\frac{H_i(1)PR_i}{SGNG_i}L1, \omega_2\frac{1}{U2}, \omega_3\frac{TC_i(1)}{SGNG_i}L3\right\}$$

$$M_i(\omega_4, \omega_5, \omega_6) = \min\left\{\omega_4\frac{H_i(1)PR_i}{SGNG_i}U1, \omega_5\frac{1}{L2}, \omega_6\frac{TC_i(1)}{SGNG_i}U3\right\}$$

Namely, the values that have been taken for each of these factors are the following ones: ω_1 and ω_2 take the values 0.25, 0.5 and 1; ω_3 takes the values 0.5 and 1, while the upper bounds take fixed values $\omega_4 = \omega_5 = 1$ and $\omega_6 = 1.5$.

In practice, this scheme yields two goals, one of them for the lower bound, and the other one for the upper bound. Besides, the minimization of the budget expense is kept as a goal, although it will be included in a priority level lower that the other two goals.

This way, the two first goals are given by our wish to satisfy the relations:

$$m_i \leq \frac{RC_i(k)}{S_i(k)} \leq M_i,$$

for the target values m_i y M_i given for each model as functions of the factors ω_j, as it was previously mentioned. With the aim of redefining the model as a linear one, a linearization of the goals is carried out, turning them into the following expressions:

$$RC_i(k) - M_iS_i(k) \leq 0 \quad k = 1, \ldots, 5, \quad i = 1, \ldots, 64,$$

$$-RC_i(k) + m_i S_i(k) \leq 0 \quad k = 1, \ldots, 5, \quad i = 1, \ldots, 64.$$

So as to practically solve this problem, it is convenient though to group these relations (which are, in practice 64×5 per each of them), into the least possible number of expressions, which will allow us a better and quicker resolution of the problem. Therefore, the following formulation has been used for the goal:

$$\sum_{k=1}^{5} \sum_{i=1}^{64} \max\{0,\ RC_i(k) - M_i S_i(k)\} \leq 0$$

As this formulation makes the goals initially lose their linear character, the auxiliary variable $z_i(k) = \max\{0,\ RC_i(k) - M_i S_i(k)\}$ is now introduced, and, thus, the goal can be written in the following way:

$$\sum_{k=1}^{5} \sum_{i=1}^{64} z_i(k) \leq 0$$

with:

$$z_i(k) \geq RC_i(k) - M_i S_i(k)$$
$$z_i(k) \geq 0$$

so that the new variable z_i is regarded as a control variable, and mixed constraints on the state and control variable appear as a result.

If an analogue reasoning is carried out for the second block of goals, the following expression is obtained:

$$\sum_{k=1}^{5} \sum_{i=1}^{64} y_i(k) \leq 0$$

with:

$$y_i(k) \geq -RC_i(k) + m_i S_i(k)$$
$$y_i(k) \geq 0.$$

Finally, the goal corresponding to the minimization of the total budget expense will take the form

$$\sum_{\kappa=1}^{k} \sum_{i=1}^{64} b_i(\kappa) \leq d(k), \quad k = 1, \ldots, 4,$$

where $d(k)$ is a target value on the accumulated value of the functional in each period, and takes the values 150, 300, 450 and 600.

So as not to allow the situation to become worse than the initial one in any moment, the hard constraints used in section 5 for the calculation of efficient solutions will be kept as hard constraints in this goal programming model.

The problem has been solved using the Lexicographic Goal Programming scheme with dynamic goals described in Caballero et al. (1997a), including the two goals corresponding to the original constraints in the first priority level, with the same weights, and the budget goal in the second priority level.

Taking all the above into account, the problem that has to be solved is:

$$\text{lexmin}\left\{\sum_{k=1}^{5}\pi_1(k)+\sum_{k=1}^{5}\pi_2(k),\ \sum_{k=1}^{4}\pi_3(k)\right\}$$

subject to

$$RC_i(k+1) = RC_i(k)+b_i(k) \quad k=1,\dots,4 \quad i=1,\dots,64$$
$$S_i(k+1) = \beta_i S_i(k) \quad k=1,\dots,4 \quad i=1,\dots,64$$

$$RC_i(k) - M_{ri}S_i(k) \leq 0 \quad k=1,\dots,5 \quad i=1,\dots,64$$
$$-RC_i(k) + m_{ri}S_i(k) \leq 0 \quad k=1,\dots,5 \quad i=1,\dots,64$$

$$z_i(k) \geq RC_i(k) - M_iS_i(k) \quad k=1,\dots,5 \quad i=1,\dots,64$$
$$z_i(k) \geq 0 \quad k=1,\dots,5 \quad i=1,\dots,64$$

$$y_i(k) \geq -RC_i(k) + m_iS_i(k) \quad k=1,\dots,5 \quad i=1,\dots,64$$
$$y_i(k) \geq 0 \quad k=1,\dots,5 \quad i=1,\dots,64$$

$$0 \leq b_i(k) \leq U \quad k=1,\dots,4 \quad i=1,\dots,64$$
$$\sum_{i=1}^{64} b_i(k) \leq UT \quad k=1,\dots,4$$

$$RC_i(k), S_i(k), \pi_1(k), \pi_2(k), \pi_3(k) \geq 0 \quad k=1,\dots,5 \quad i=1,\dots,64$$

$$\sum_{\kappa=1}^{k}\sum_{i=1}^{64} z_i(\kappa) - \pi_1(k) \leq 0 \quad k=1,\dots,5$$
$$\sum_{\kappa=1}^{k}\sum_{i=1}^{64} y_i(\kappa) - \pi_2(k) \leq 0 \quad k=1,\dots,5$$
$$\sum_{\kappa=1}^{k}\sum_{i=1}^{64} b_i(\kappa) - \pi_3(k) \leq d(k) \quad k=1,\dots,4$$

It is obvious, if the initial situation is taken into account, that it is impossible to find solutions which satisfy all the goals, for initially we had, on the one hand, departments that were already over their ideal levels and whose budget is impossible to shorten and, on the other hand, so many departments that are far under the required level that the amount of money needed to make them reach the ideal situation would be, from a realistic point of view, impossible to get during the planning period. As a summary, the aim of this goal programming scheme for our problem has been to analyze which is the minimum cost for the government so as to make all the departments get closer to a band of values considered as satisfactory, along the planning period. To this end, in this model, maximum assignment levels higher than in the weighting case have been allowed. Namely, the values $U = 10$ and $UT = 200$ have been taken, in an attempt to know the cost of the emergency plan that has to be carried out to reach our goals.

The results, for a sample department, corresponding to several problems can be found in the appendix. It must be noticed that, as the budget availability is greater, the number of teaching units that enter the desired band is greater than in the weighting method, for there are more departments that have their budget assignment increased, and in a greater quantity.

With respect to the differences between the solution of each model, it should be noticed that the first models, being more restrictive, yield the fact that more departments get extra budget assignments, because it is more difficult to achieve the goals. This way, for example, in the first three models, all the departments except those whose real staff was initially greater than the theoretical one, get extra assignment.

Finally, it can be seen that, as the target values are relaxed, the number of departments that get assignments is smaller, but the quantity they receive grows, for they are the ones that have a worse situation. Besides, it must be pointed out that the departments that receive the most assignment in these relaxed models, a maximum of 40 millions, are usually those that we mentioned as stable kernel in the weighting method, and this shows that they are the ones that need more help, for they are far from satisfying any of our original goals.

References

Caballero, R., Gómez, T., González, M., Rey, L. and Ruiz, F. (1997). Goal Programming with Dynamic Goals. Submitted to the *Journal of Multi-Criteria Decision Analysis*.

Caballero, Gómez, T., González, M., R., Rey, L. and Ruiz, F. (1997). An Algorithmic Package for the Resolution of Dynamic Multiple Objective Problems. In Caballero, R., Ruiz, F., Steuer, R. (Eds.) 1997. *Advances in Multiple Objective and Goal Programming*. Springer-Verlag, 265–273.

Dinkelbach, W. and Isermann, H. (1980). Resource Relocation of an Academic Department in the Presence of Multiple Criteria: some Experience with a Modified STEP Method. *Computers Operations Research* **7**, 99–106.

Geoffrion, A.M., Dyer, J.S. and Feinberg, A. (1972). An Interactive Approach for Multi-Criterion Optimization with Application to the Operation of an Academic Department. *Management Science* **19, 4**, 357–368.

Ghosh, D., Pal, B .B. and Basu, M. (1992). Implementation of Goal Programming in Long-Range Resource Planning in University Management. *Optimization* **24**, 373–383.

González, M. (1995). *Inter Temporal Decisions with Multiple Criteria. An Application to the Equilibrium Policies among University Departments (In Spanish).* PhD Dissertation. University of Málaga. Spain.

Lee, S. M. and Clayton, E. R. (1972). A Goal Programming Model for Academic Resource Allocation. *Management Science* **18**, 395–408.

Mustafa, A. and Goh, M. (1996). Multi-Criterion Models for Higher Education Administration. *Omega, Int. J. Mgmt. Sci.* **24, 2**, 167–178.

N.A.G. (Numerical Algorithms Group Limited). (1991). *The NAG Fortran Library Introductory Guide, Mark 15.*

Ruiz, F., Caballero, R., Gómez, T., González, M. and Rey, L. (1997). The Static Approach to Quadratic Dynamic Goal Programming. Presented at the *XIII International Conference MCDM*, held in Cape Town (South Africa) in January 1997. To appear in the Proceedings volume.

Appendix

Dpt. No.	Subjects	Students	Stud. Rep.	Groups	Th. Hours	Th. Cost	Real Cost	Faculties	Practic.
20	15	7685	2367	90	259	190749115	56077448	28	2
26	14	7607	2737	81	196	156131997	50052498	21	2.25
27	17	8050	3351	86	251	210583584	70062552	23	2.5
29	6	597	18	6	20	25309698	45404304	29	4.5
31	58	855	30	57	96	81933560	72240124	29	2.5
40	8	1156	391	15	42	58213982	70050126	34	3.5
56	37	4848	899	55	163	129604592	46519526	18	2.5
62	8	5616	2083	60	154	117091404	54918450	21	2.25

Table 1. Initial situation of some sample departments of the University of Málaga.

Parameters	Period 1	Period 2	Period 3	Period 4	Total assign.	Σ infeasibility	Becomes feasible in period:
1,1,1,1,1,1.5	0.9353	0.1554	0	1.3526	2.4433	282.7627	Not feasible
.25,.25,1,1,1,1.5	10	2.5396	1.9372	2.0292	16.5061	10.6902	3
.25,.25,.5,1,1,1.5	0	0	0		0	0	

Table 2. Results of the Goal Programming model for a sample department, and for different values of the relaxation parameters. The assignment received in each period and the total assignment are measured in millions of pesetas. Besides, the sum of infeasibilities and the period when the department becomes feasible are also displayed.

Part V

Miscellaneous Applications

Evaluation of Alternatives for the Disposition of Surplus Weapons-usable Plutonium

James S. Dyer[1], Thomas Edmunds[2], John Butler[1], Jianmin Jia[1]

[1] Management Science and Information Systems Department, University of Texas, Austin, TX 78712-1175, USA
[2] Lawrence Livermore National Laboratory, 7000 East Av. (L-195) Livermore, CA 94550, USA
[3] Department of Marketing, Chinese University of Hong Kong Shatin, N.T. Hong Kong, CHINA

Abstract

Multiattribute utility (MAU) theory provides a formal methodology which is used to evaluate alternatives for disposition of surplus plutonium to prevent the proliferation of nuclear weapons. Other concerns that were also addressed include economical, technical, environmental, and health and safety issues.

Keywords. Multiattribute utility theory, public policy decisions

1 Background

On January 14, 1997, The Department of Energy - Office of Fissile Materials Disposition (OFMD) announced a Record of Decision (ROD) selecting alternatives for disposition of surplus plutonium. A major objective of this decision was to further U.S. efforts to prevent the proliferation of nuclear weapons. Other concerns that were addressed include economic, technical, institutional, schedule, environmental, and health and safety issues. The technical, environmental, and nonproliferation analyses supporting the ROD are documented in three DOE reports [DOE-TSR 96, DOE-PEIS 96, and DOE-NN 97, respectively]. The disposition alternatives evaluated by DOE are shown in the Table 1.

The analysis reported here was conducted in parallel with these DOE technical, environmental, and nonproliferation analyses. It uses a logical and formal methodology, referred to as multiattribute utility (MAU) theory (Keeney and Raiffa, 1975), to provide a structure for combining these considerations to facilitate an integrated

REACTOR ALTERNATIVES

Existing Light Water Reactors, Existing Facilities

MOX fuel fabrication plant built in an existing building at a DOE site, MOX irradiated in existing privately-owned commercial reactors

Existing Light Water Reactors, Greenfield Facilities

A new co-located pit disassembly/conversion and MOX fabrication facility built at a DOE site, MOX irradiated in existing privately-owned commercial reactors

Partially Completed Light Water Reactors

Commercial LWRs on which construction had been halted would be completed and operated by DOE

Evolutionary Light Water Reactors

New LWRs would be built and operated by DOE

CANDU Reactors

MOX fuel fabricated at a U.S. facility would be transported to one or more Canadian commercial heavy water reactors and irradiated

IMMOBILIZATION ALTERNATIVES

Vitrification Greenfield

Surplus plutonium would be mixed with glass and radioactive materials at a new facility to form homogeneous borosilicate glass logs.

Vitrification Can-in-Canister

Surplus plutonium would be mixed with non-radioactive glass and poured into small cans. These small cans would be placed in larger canisters, which are then filled with radioactive waste glass.

Vitrification Adjunct Melter

Surplus plutonium would be mixed with glass and radioactive materials in a supplemental melter facility to form homogeneous borosilicate glass logs.

Ceramic Greenfield

Surplus plutonium would be mixed with ceramic and radioactive materials at a new facility to form homogeneous ceramic disks. These disks would be placed in a canister.

Ceramic Can-in-Canister

Surplus plutonium would be mixed with non-radioactive ceramic materials to form sintered ceramic pellets. These pellets would be placed in larger canisters filled with radioactive waste glass.

Electrometallurgical Treatment

Surplus plutonium would be immobilized with radioactive glass-bonded zeolite.

DIRECT DISPOSAL ALTERNATIVES

Deep Borehole (Immobilization)

Surplus plutonium would be immobilized with ceramic pellets and placed in a borehole.

Deep Borehole (Direct Emplacement)

Surplus plutonium would be converted to a suitable form and placed in a deep borehole.

Table 1. Disposition Alternatives

evaluation of the alternatives by decision makers. The data are a collection of system performance estimates and value or policy judgments that reconcile conflicting objectives through the use of explicit tradeoffs. This framework is used to identify critical information for the evaluation, and to help make the basis of decisions transparent to stakeholders. The framework is also used to evaluate the sensitivity of decisions to the individual value judgments and alternative performance estimates. This sensitivity analysis provides an assessment of the overall robustness of decisions. It is important to emphasize that the MAU process implemented here does not provide a computerized model that actually determines the decision for plutonium disposition. This analysis is intended to provide additional insights regarding the evaluation of the alternatives, and to assist in understanding the rationale for the choice of the alternatives that were recommended in the ROD.

2 The Objectives

The goals or objectives included in the MAU model are derived from criteria developed in the screening process [DOE-SCR 95]. In the MAU model, they are arranged in a hierarchy, as shown in the Figure 1. This hierarchical structure was chosen to facilitate the specification of a value model and the communication of insights from the model to the OFMD and other interested parties. This hierarchy emphasizes three major objectives for the plutonium disposition effort, which are labeled Non-proliferation; Operational Effectiveness; and Environment, Safety and Health (ES&H), respectively.

As shown in Figure 1, the Non-proliferation objective is further subdivided into five sub-objectives: Theft (minimize the opportunities for theft of the materials by unauthorized parties), Diversion (maximize the resistance of the disposition alternative to the diversion of the plutonium by the host nation during processing, and provide an internationally verifiable and acceptable process), Irreversibility (maximize the difficulty of recovering the material after disposition has been completed), International Cooperation (foster international cooperation with the U.S. disarmament and nuclear non-proliferation policy), and Timeliness (minimize the time required for the disposition effort to begin and to complete the disposition mission).

The second major objective shown in Figure 1, Operational Effectiveness, includes the Investment and Life-cycle costs associated with an alternative. The third objective; Environment, Safety, and Health; is made up of the following three sub-objectives: Human Health and Safety (minimize the incremental health impacts to the public and workers), Natural Environment (minimize the incremental impact on the natural habitat at the sites), and Socio-economic (minimize the incremental adverse impacts to the human environment).

Each sub-objective on the right-hand-side of Figure 1 is further specified in terms of one or more of thirty-seven measures that are included in the model (e.g., Life-cycle Costs, Time to Start, Material Form).

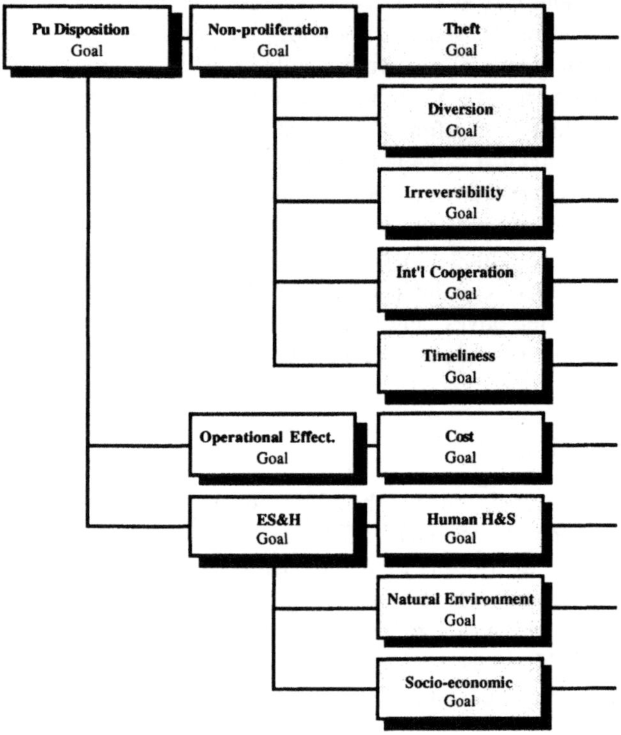

Fig. 1. Objectives Hierarchy for Plutonium Disposition Decision

3 Subjective Assessments

Once the objective hierarchy of Figure 1 was reviewed and accepted by decision makers, we conducted detailed assessment procedures to elicit value functions, weights, and in some cases, to provide performance estimates for the measures. In many cases, the value function for a measure was determined to be linear. Other value functions were developed using mid-value splitting (Keeney and Raiffa, 1976) and subjective evaluation. All weights for the model were determined by "tradeoffs"(e.g., Clemen, 1991).

All of the required information for the Theft, Diversion, and Irreversibility subobjectives were provided by a cross-cutting safeguards and security team at a series of three assessment meetings at Sandia Laboratories in Albuquerque, New Mexico. Specific team members were responsible for providing performance estimates for each technology group of alternatives, and worked together to ensure consistency. The performance estimates for International Cooperation were provided by personnel from the White Office of Science and Technology Policy, and the weights and value functions were assessed from OFMD decision makers.

A cross cutting cost and schedule group provided the both cost and schedule (Timeliness) estimates for all three technologies. Information about the relative importance and value functions associated with the measures within these sub-objectives were provided by OFMD.

All of the data concerning ES&H performance estimates were provided by an independent consulting firm contracted by OFMD. The ranges of these estimates were so narrow that OFMD felt that all value functions were linear, but did provide tradeoffs to determine relative importance.

After we had obtained performance estimates and value functions for each of the thirty seven measures, and had determined weights within each of the nine sub-objectives in Figure 1, we conducted an additional assessment with OFMD personnel to determine relative importance across these sub-objectives. We initially assumed an additive model for all levels of the objectives hierarchy. Some of our initial assessments and interviews with decision makers led us to test the implications of a multiplicative model at some levels of the hierarchy. As discussed in the next section, we found the results to be very robust to all of the sensitivity analyses performed. For more information about see Dyer et. al.(1997).

4 The Results

The MAU model was used to evaluate five reactor, six immobilization, and two borehole alternatives under a base case set of facts, assumptions, and value judgments, and for variations in assumptions and value judgments about this base case. The stacked bar graph shown in the Figure 2 provides a useful tool for summarizing the scores of these alternatives with respect to the measures. The overall score, labeled "Utility" in Figure 2, is a weighted sum of scores for the thirty-seven measures associated with the three objectives discussed previously.

The stacked bars shown in Figure 2 are segmented to show the relative contributions of these scores for each alternative. For example, the third segment for the existing LWR alternative is wider than the corresponding segment for the vitrification can-in-can alternative. This indicates that the Existing LWR scores higher than the Vitrification Can-in-Can alternative on the Russian cooperation measure. The weights used to generate the Figure 2 were established by OFMD personnel and by a review of previous DOE studies, and are presented as a base case.

Some key insights of the analysis are as follows:

1) both the vitrification and ceramic can-in-can alternatives achieve high overall scores based to a large extent on low cost and early start times
2) the existing LWR alternative scores higher than the CANDU alternative due to its lower life cycle cost and concerns regarding the civil use of plutonium in CANDU reactors
3) existing LWR and CANDU reactor alternatives score higher than new or partially complete reactor alternatives due to cost and schedule advantages
4) the boreholes and vitrification adjunct melter alternatives achieve moderate scores

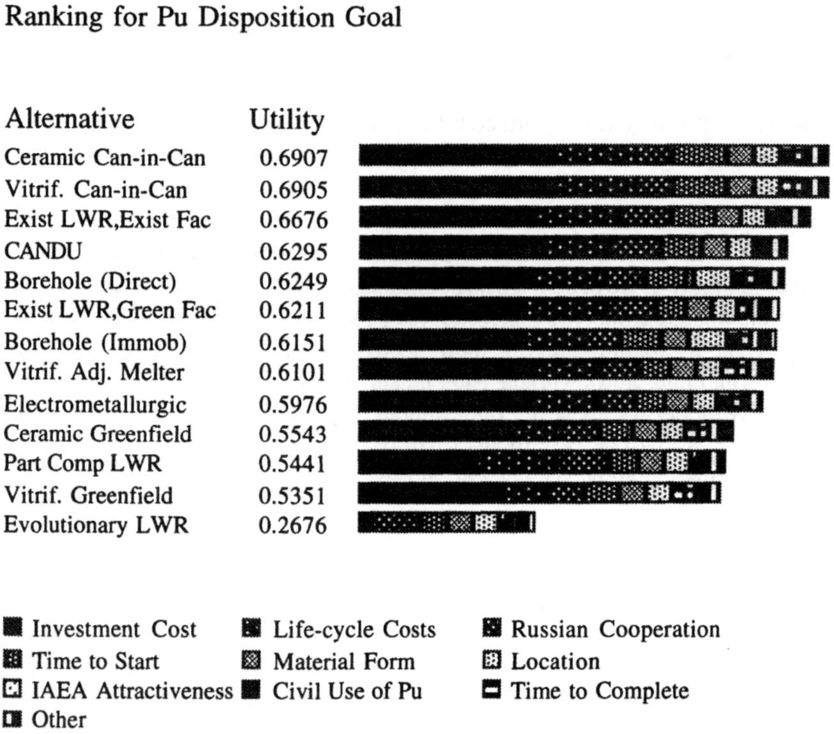

Fig. 2. Overall Ranking of Alternatives

5) the greenfield and electrometallurgical immobilization alternatives achieve low scores due to high life costs
6) reactor alternatives score high in terms of cooperation with Russia, but score low in terms of encouraging the civil use of plutonium æ the two effects tend to offset one another
7) a hybrid alternative that includes existing LWRs and can-in-can immobilization would score well on both Russian cooperation and time to start

This base case ranking of the alternatives was subjected to a series of sensitivity analyses. These analyses included the examination of the effects of varying the weights on the performance measures of the alternatives, and on the three major objectives of Non-proliferation; Operational Effectiveness; and Environment, Safety, and Health. Although some changes in the rankings were observed under extreme combinations of changes in the underlying MAU evaluation model, the general pattern of the rankings shown above proved to be extremely robust. In particular, the two can-in-can immobilization, existing LWR, and CANDU alternatives are generally ranked among the top four or five alternatives. Three of these four alternatives were recommended for further development and examination in the ROD. The fourth, CANDU, was recommended as a back-up alternative should negotiations with Russia lead to joint disposition activities in Canada.

Rankings are also presented with respect to each of the three major objectives. The stacked bar graph for the first of these objectives, Non-proliferation, is shown in the Figure 3. The overall Non-proliferation score is comprised of scores for measures associated with each of the five sub-objectives discussed previously. As indicated by the data in Figure 3, the borehole with immobilized material scores the highest due to its characteristics relative to Irreversibility. The deep geologic isolation and ceramic material form make the material difficult to recover relative to the other alternatives. However, the timeliness advantage of the can-in-can immobilization alternatives and the international cooperation advantage of the exiting LWR alternative almost compensate for the lower scores on Irreversibility, so that the composite scores of these alternatives are almost as high as that for the borehole with immobilized material. Theft and Diversion sub-objectives do not appear to be major discriminators among the alternatives.

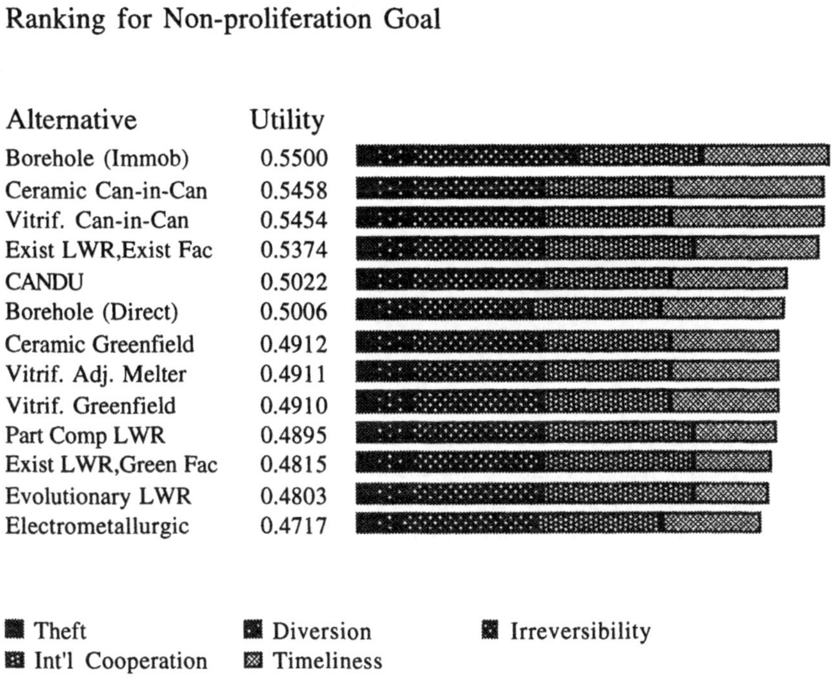

Fig. 3. Ranking of Alternatives on Non-proliferation Goal

The stacked bar graph for the Operational Effectiveness objective is shown in Figure 4. Investment Cost appears to be a major discriminator. The can-in-can immobilization alternatives and existing reactor alternatives, which save money by utilizing existing facilities, receive the highest utility scores. In addition, the high investment costs required to construct the Evolutionary LWR severely penalize this alternative.

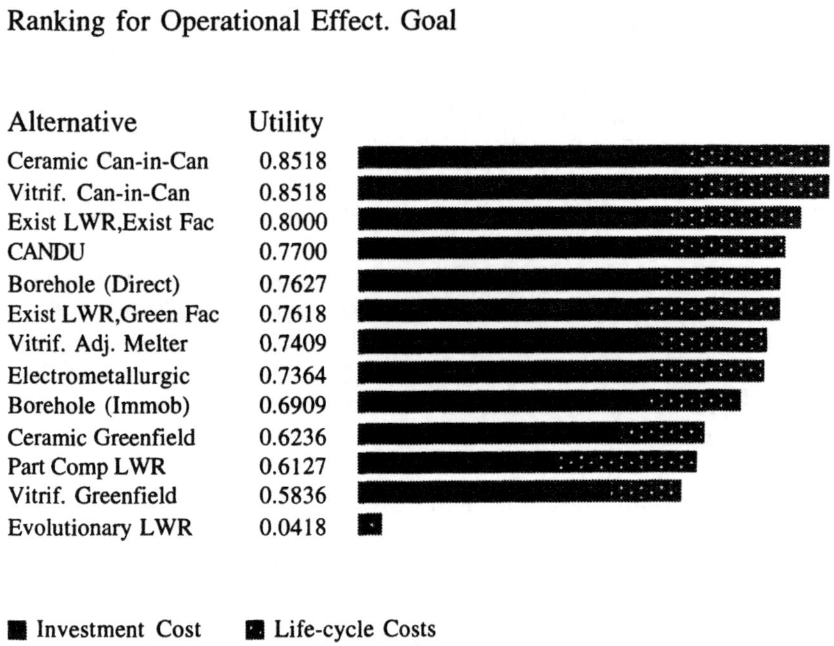

Fig. 4. Ranking of Alternatives on Operational Effectiveness Goal

A stacked bar graph for the Environment, Safety, and Health objective is shown in Figure 5. As indicated by the data in the figure, existing reactors outperform all other alternatives because switching from a uranium to a MOX fuel cycle would lower the expected number of fatalities to both workers and the public. This is because the use of MOX fuel would eliminate the need for the more hazardous operations required to mine and process the displaced uranium fuel [DOE-PEIS, pg. 4-978]. The Partially Complete LWR alternative and the Evolutionary LWR alternative are heavily penalized by a relatively large incremental health impact on workers and a relatively high volume of secondary waste generation, since they would represent new operating facilities.

5 "Hybrid" Alternatives

The seventh insight listed in Section 3 indicates that an immobilization-LWR "hybrid" – parallel development of several technologies – alternative may offer advantages based upon the analysis in this deterministic model. The technological and institutional uncertainties associated with all of the alternatives also suggest that a hybrid strategy may be advantageous. Intuitively, the reason for pursuing this hybrid strategy of multiple options is to hedge against the risks associated with such considerations as technology development, contract negotiations, and negotiations with Russia and other nations. One example of the advantage offered by this intuitively

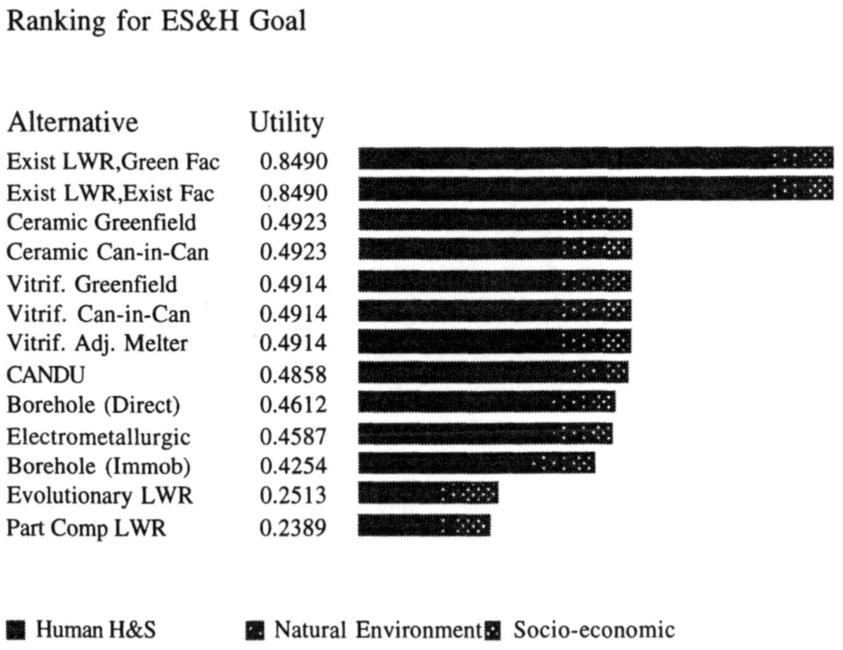

Fig. 5. Ranking of Alternatives on ES&H Goal

appealing notion is the flexibility a hybrid approach provides the U.S. in response to Russian degradation requirements.

At this point is it unclear whether Russia will state that it will only participate in a disposition program that renders weapons-grade plutonium in a "non-attractive" state. Immobilized forms would not meet this standard; only burning the material in a reactor would degrade the material sufficiently. By replacing the measure Russian Cooperation with a probability distribution over Russian degradation requirements, it is possible to recognize this uncertainty as illustrated in Figure 6. If the probability that Russia requires degradation is between 0.44 and 0.75, the hybrid alternative is preferred. This approach was the only successful attempt to quantify the flexibility provided by the hybrid.

6 Conclusion

In conclusion, the two can-in-can immobilization alternatives and the exiting LWR alternative are the most desirable alternatives under a broad range of value judgments regarding the importance of the individual measures. Further, a hybrid alternative consisting of parallel implementation of a reactor and immobilization technology provides significant benefits to the U.S. The findings of this report improved DOE's ability to identify discriminators among the alternatives and were consistent with DOE's final recommendation.

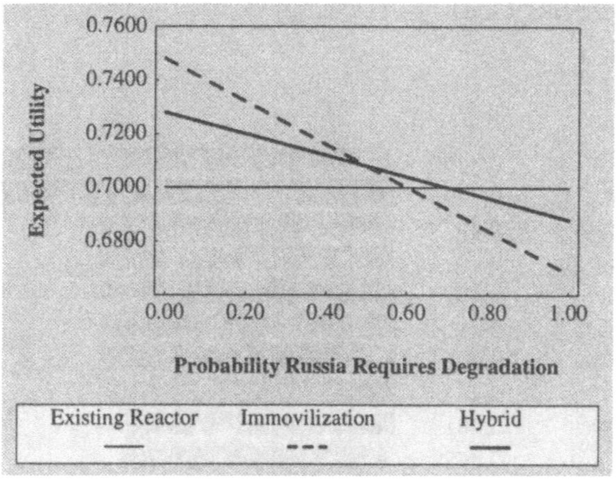

Fig. 6. Best Alternative as a Function of Probability Russia Requires Degradation of Plutonium

References

Clemen, R. T. (1991). *Making Hard Decisions*. Boston: PWS Kent Publishing.

Dyer, J., Edmunds, T., Butler, J. C., and Jia, J. (1997). Evaluation of Alternatives for the Disposition of Surplus Weapons-usable Plutonium. *Amarillo National Resource Center for Plutonium Technical Paper*. http://www.pu.org/main/reports/reports.html Pre-decisional Draft.

[DOE-NN] *Nonproliferation and Arms Control Assessment of Weapons-Usable Fissile Materials Storage and Plutonium Disposition Alternatives*, DOE/NN-0007. United States Department of Energy; Office of Fissile Materials Disposition, January 13, 1997.

[DOE-PEIS] *Storage and Disposition of Weapons-Usable Fissile Materials Final Programmatic Environmental Impact Statement*, DOE/EIS-0229. United States Department of Energy; Office of Fissile Materials Disposition, December 1996.

[[DOE-SCR] *Summary Report of the Screening Process to Determine Reasonable Alternatives for Storage and Disposition of Weapons-usable Fissile Materials*, DOE/MD-0002. United States Department of Energy; Office of Fissile Materials Disposition, March 17, 1995.

[DOE-TSR] *Technical Summary Report for Surplus Weapons-Usable Plutonium Disposition*, DOE/MD-0003 Rev. 1. United States Department of Energy; Office of Fissile Materials Disposition, October 31, 1996.

Keeney, R. L. and Raiffa, H. (1976). *Decisions with Multiple Objectives*. New York: Wiley.

A Graphical Model for Equipment Maintenance and Replacement Problems

Alberto Lekuona[1], Beatriz Lacruz[1] and Pilar Lasala[1]

[1] Departamento de Métodos Estadísticos. Universidad de Zaragoza, SPAIN

Abstract

From a statistical point of view, modelling stochastic temporal processes by graphical models turns out to be a suitable choice, specially when certain standard assumptions in classical modelling cannot be assumed.

Focusing the discussion on partially observed domains, it is also important to design algorithms which provide probability distributions over the current states of the unobservable components of the domain, using the information stored in the observed components.

In this paper, we consider an example based on *equipment maintenance and replacement problems*, included in the framework of partially observed markovian decision processes. For modelling it, we propose the use of a dynamic graphical model. This graphical model must be considered as a decision support system and allows to establish conditional inferences, both exact and approximate (using Monte Carlo techniques), about the state of the unobservable components of the system.

To study the goodness of the proposed model and validate the implemented algorithm, some numerical results are obtained.

Keywords. Graphical models, partially observed markovian decision processes, exact and approximate inference algorithms

1 Introduction

Generally speaking, a dynamic graphical model may be defined as a sequence of graphical submodels, each representing the state of a system at a parti-cular time slice, interconnected by temporal relationships. These temporal relationships stand for the dependencies between the state of the system in a certain time slice and its state in later time slices and capture the dynamic behaviour of the domain variables. Finally, the dynamic graphical model as a whole represents the evolution of a dynamic system over time.

Formally, let $\{X_t\}_{t\in\Gamma}$ be a stochastic process ($\Gamma \subseteq \mathbf{N}$ and $X_t = (X_t^1, \ldots, X_t^n)$), describing the changes in the state of a certain system over time. The definition of a *graphical structure associated with* $\{X_t\}_{t\in\Gamma}$, denoted by $G_{\{X_t\}_{t\in\Gamma}}$, is based on the union of a sequence of chain graphs $\{G_t\}_{t\in\Gamma}$, which describes relationships among the components of X_t in any time slice t, and a sequence of directed acyclic graphs $\{G_{kt}\}_{k,t\in\Gamma,k<t}$, which describes non contemporary relationships among any time slice t and previous time slices $k < t$. The former stands for the system state description in any time slice and the latter stands for the dynamic behaviour of the system. Fig. 1 shows an example of a graphical structure associated with a dynamic system, depicted in three consecutive time slices.

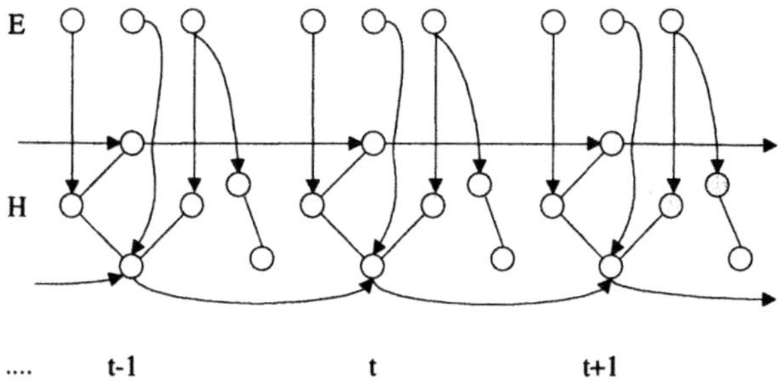

Fig. 1. Schema of dynamic graphical structure

Given a dynamic system described by a stochastic process $\{X_t\}_{t\in\Gamma}$, we define a *dynamic graphical model* as a tern $\left(\{X_t\}_{t\in\Gamma}, G_{\{X_t\}_{t\in\Gamma}}, \{P_t\}_{t\in\Gamma}\right)$ where $G_{\{X_t\}_{t\in\Gamma}}$ is a graphical structure associated with $\{X_t\}_{t\in\Gamma}$ and $\{P_t\}_{t\in\Gamma}$ is a sequence of probability distributions where P_t obeys the Markov property, relative to $\bigcup_{k\leq t}\left[G_k \cup \left(\bigcup_{k'<k} G_{k'k}\right)\right], \forall t \in \Gamma$.

If t is fixed, the graph $G_{0t} = \bigcup_{k\leq t}\left[G_k \cup \left(\bigcup_{k'<k} G_{k'k}\right)\right]$ turns out to be a chain graph and represents the whole qualitative structure of the model from the first time slice to the current time t. Therefore, it summarizes all possible influences of the past in the current time slice. This graph is associated with a probability measure P_t which is coherent with it, in the markovian sense. The previous definition generalizes in a natural way the concept of graphical model associated with a static domain.

If the system to be modelled is partially observed, variables $(X_t^1, \ldots, X_t^n)$ can be classified as *observable variables* $E_t = \{E_{it}, i = 1, \ldots, k\}$, and *non observable variables* $H_t = \{H_{jt}, j = 1, \ldots, m\}$, $k+m = n$. In what follows, we assume that observable variables will always be observed and their evidence will be instantaneously obtained.

The main goal in modelling these partially observed domains is to make inferences about the states of the non observable variables in a certain time slice, given a specific evidence accumulated up to that time slice. Furthermore, to build a conditional forecasting process of the future states can be useful.

We focus the discussion on a markovian behaviour of the process $\{H_t\}_{t\in\Gamma}$:

$$H_{t_n} \perp H_{t_0}, \ldots, H_{t_{n-2}} | H_{t_{n-1}} \quad [P] \qquad \forall t_0 < t_1 < \cdots < t_n$$

where P is a probability distribution properly defined in some product space and $X \perp Y | Z$ $[P]$ stands for *X is conditionally independent of Y given Z under P*. With this condition, non contemporary relationships between every two consecutive time slices have to be fixed and there will not simultaneously be relationships from two time slices to later time slices.

In Lekuona, Lacruz and Lasala (1996) we proposed a dynamic graphical model for modelling partially observed markovian dynamic systems and exact algorithms for inference and forecasting. Following with this model, in Lekuona, Lacruz and Lasala (1997) we presented an approximate algorithm for inference and forecasting using stochastic simulation.

In this paper, we apply both the model and the algorithms to an example based on equipment maintenance and replacement problems, wich can be included in the framework of partially observed markovian decision processes.

This paper is organized as follows: in section 2, we describe the equipment maintenance and replacement problem to be considered; in section 3, we propose its dynamic graphical modelization; in section 4, we present the exact and approximate algorithm to infer the real state of the system; finally, in section 5 we show some numerical results obtained applying the algorithm.

2 Description of the problem

The *equipment maintenance and replacement problem* is described, in general terms, as follows:

> *A decision maker periodically inspects the conditions of an equipment which produces an item. The equipment deteriorates with time and the decisor, after the inspection, decides on the extent of maintenance, if any, to carry out. Choices may vary from routine maintenance to equipment replacement.*

We will consider that the evolution of the *unknown* real state of a given equipment can be modelled by a Markov chain $\{X_t | t \in T \subseteq I\!N\}$ (*kernel process*) with both initial state of the system and non homogeneous transition probability matrix unknown.

In order to simplify the modelization, the assumptions of a finite set of working states and sequential deterioration of the equipment are imposed. Sequential deterioration means that, if the system is working in state j at time t, it will work in state j or $j-1$ at time $t+1$. State 1 stands for the absorbing state corresponding with the worst working state.

Therefore, a transition probability matrix $P_{t,t+1}$ in the form

$$P_{t,t+1} = \begin{bmatrix} 1 & 0 & \cdots & 0 & 0 \\ 1-\theta_2^t & \theta_2^t & \cdots & 0 & 0 \\ \cdots & \cdots & \cdots & \cdots & \cdots \\ 0 & 0 & \cdots & 1-\theta_M^t & \theta_M^t \end{bmatrix}$$

will be considered in each time, where θ_i^t is unknown $\forall i, t$ and stands for the probability of the system to remain in state i from t to $t+1$.

The equipment inspection will be sumarized by mean of the variables $\{Y_t | t \in T\}$ (*signal process*), where Y_t is, say, the percentage of non defective pieces by period of time, possibly categorized in a set of classes.

3 The dynamic graphical model

To model the described problem, we will use the signal process $\{Y_t | t \in T\}$ as observable variables and $\{X_t | t \in T\}$ as unobservable variables. More clearly, the kernel process will be represented in the model by the previous $\{\theta_i^t | i = 2 \ldots M, t \in T\}$ together with the initial state of the system, described by X_0 node.

Fig. 2 contains the dynamic graphical structure for the equipment inspection problem. Let us note that we do not necessarily consider cause-effects relationships among variables. Edges describing contemporary relationships mean that the evidence collected in the current time modifies our beliefs over the states of the unobservable variables. These relationships will cooperate with the directed non contemporary relationships.

The possible remaining relationships are not considered since we want a parsimonious model and are interested in making inferences for the unobservable variables. The considered relationships are enough to carry out this task.

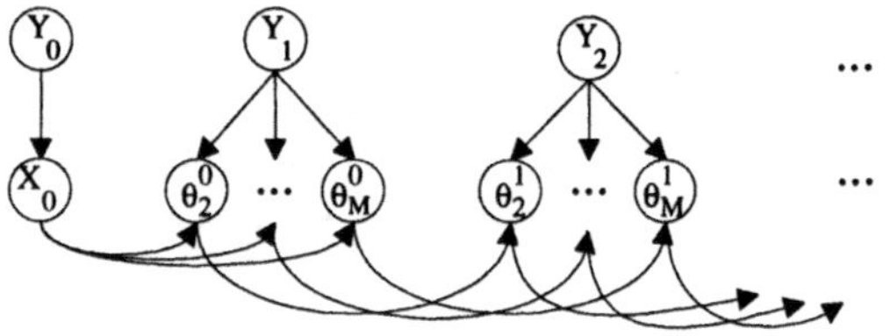

Fig. 2. Dynamic graphical structure for the equipment inspection problem

In order to build the dynamic graphical model, probabilities $P_0(X_0|Y_0)$ and densities $f_t(Y_t)$, $f_1(\theta_i^0|X_0, Y_1)$ and $f_t(\theta_i^{t-1}|\theta_i^{t-2}, Y_t)$ have to be known $\forall i, t$. The latter densities stand for the beliefs about the parameters based simultaneously on the previous state of these parameters *and* the evidence received.

The densities $f_t(Y_t)$ can be unknown in the inference algorithm described in section 4 but cannot be avoided in the graphical model building.

In these conditions, it is easy to see that

$$\left(\{V_t\}_{t\in T}, G_{\{V_t\}_{t\in T}}, \{P_t\}_{t\in T}\right)$$

is a dynamic graphical model where

$$V_0 = \{Y_0, X_0\} \qquad V_t = \{Y_t, \theta_2^t, \ldots, \theta_M^t\}$$

$$P_t(V_0, \ldots, V_t) = P_0(X_0|Y_0) \prod_{k=0}^{t} f_k(Y_k) \prod_{i=2}^{M} f_1(\theta_i^0|X_0, Y_1)$$
$$\times \prod_{k=1}^{t} \prod_{i=2}^{M} f_k(\theta_i^{k-1}|\theta_i^{k-2}, Y_k)$$

and $G_{\{V_t\}_{t\in T}}$ is the graphical structure partially depicted in Fig. 2.

This graphical model could include actions and rewards in each time slice, enlarging the dynamic graphical model to a decision dynamic graphical model. All this extension is depicted in Fig. 3.

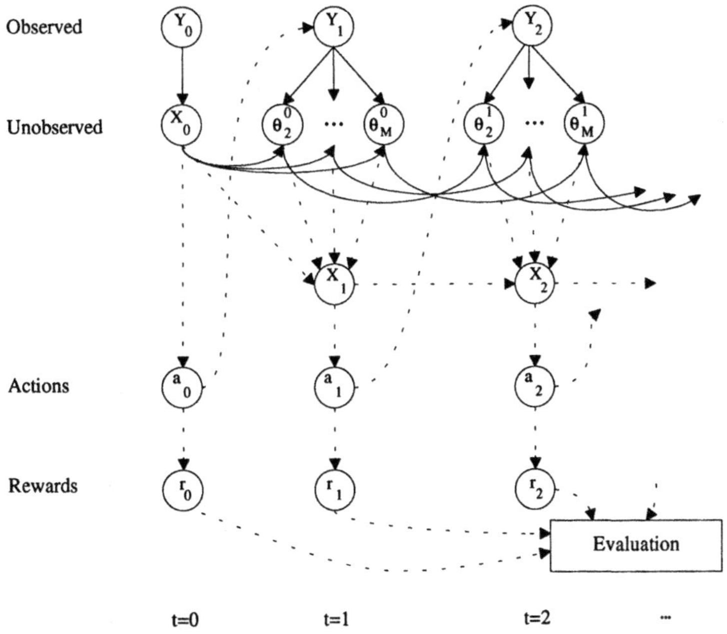

Fig. 3. Decision dynamic graphical structure for the equipment inspection problem

The purpose in the proposed graphical modelling is to estimate these θ_i^t in any time slice t, given the information stored in the observable variables. These will make the estimation of X_t possible.

4 An algorithm to infer the real state of the system

The sequential process to infer the real state of the system consists of the next six steps:

1.- Do $t = 0$ and consider $D_0 = \{Y_0\}$ (initial information). Infer X_0 through $P_0(X_0|D_0)$. Decide the action to be taken. If action= *Stop*, end.

2.- Do $t = 1$. Consider $D_1 = \{D_0, Y_1\}$. Build the conditional distributions $\theta_i^0|D_1$, $i = 2, \ldots, M$:

$$f\left(\theta_i^0|D_1\right) = \sum_{j=1}^{M} f_1\left(\theta_i^0|X_0 = j, Y_1\right) P_0\left(X_0 = j|D_0\right) \tag{1}$$

3.- Estimate $\theta_i^{t-1}, i = 2, \ldots, M$, obtaining $\hat{\theta}_i^{t-1}$. Infer X_t through the transition equation

$$P\left(X_t|D_t\right) = P\left(X_{t-1}|D_{t-1}\right) \hat{P}_{t-1t}$$

where $\hat{P}_{t-1t}$ stands for the estimated transition probability matrix from time $t-1$ to time t, associated with $\{X_t|t \in T\}$.

4.- Decide the action to be taken. If action= *Stop*, end.

5.- Do $t = t+1$. Consider $D_t = \{D_{t-1}, Y_t\}$ (information available at time t). Build the conditional distributions $\theta_2^{t-1}|D_t, \ldots, \theta_M^{t-1}|D_t$:

$$f\left(\theta_i^{t-1}|D_t\right) = \int f_t\left(\theta_i^{t-1}|\theta_i^{t-2}, Y_t\right) f\left(\theta_i^{t-2}|D_{t-1}\right) d\theta_i^{t-2} \quad i = 2, \ldots, M \tag{2}$$

6.- Go to step 3.

Formulas (1) and (2) are a consequence of the conditional independences derived from the graphical model.

Note that these expressions are iteratively built. In each inference step, beliefs over the states at time t are generated from beliefs at time $t-1$ and the new information received.

An alternative approach to (2) is based on stochastic simulation. The procedure to simulate $\theta_i^{t-1}|D_t$ can be as follows:

1.- Do $j = 1$.

2.- $\forall i$, instantiate $\theta_i^{t-2} = \theta_i^{t-2*}$ using $f\left(\theta_i^{t-2}|D_{t-1}\right)$.

3.- $\forall i$, instantiate $\theta_i^{t-1} = \theta_i^{t-1*}$ using $f_t\left(\theta_i^{t-1}|\theta_i^{t-2*}, Y_t\right)$.

4.- $\forall i$, add sample $\theta_i^{t-1} = \theta_i^{t-1*}$ in a frequency table.

5.- If $j \leq N$ do $j = j + 1$ and go to step 2.
Else, $\forall i$ assign

$$P\left(\theta_i^{t-1} \leq \theta_i^{t-1*} | D_t\right) := fr\left(\theta_i^{t-1} \leq \theta_i^{t-1*}\right)$$

5 An example

To study the goodness of the proposed model, let us consider $\{X_t\}$ as a homogeneus Markov chain with both initial distribution over $M = 10$ possible states, π_0, and transition probabilities matrix, P, known:

$$\pi_0 = [0, 0, 0, 0, 0, 0, 0, 0.3, 0.4, 0.3]$$

$$P = \begin{bmatrix} 1 & & & & & & & & & \\ 0.4 & 0.6 & & & & & & & & \\ & 0.3 & 0.7 & & & & & & & \\ & & 0.4 & 0.6 & & & & & & \\ & & & 0.3 & 0.7 & & & & & \\ & & & & 0.2 & 0.8 & & & & \\ & & & & & 0.2 & 0.8 & & & \\ & & & & & & 0.1 & 0.9 & & \\ & & & & & & & 0.1 & 0.9 & \\ & & & & & & & & 0.4 & 0.6 \end{bmatrix}$$

Using this process 400 paths were simulated. These paths were observed in 45 consecutive time slices. Each path was perturbated by a stochastic matrix $Q = (q_{ij})$. Thus, if $X_t = m$ then $Y_t = k$, $1 \leq k \leq 10$ is obtained with probability q_{mk}. These perturbated paths are the observable variables $\{Y_t\}$ to be used in the inference step. The algorithm has been implemented in C language.

Beta distributions and linear transformations of them have been used for modelling θ_i^t, $\forall i, t$ and the proposed Bayes estimator for each θ_i^{t-1} is the posterior mean

$$\hat{\theta}_i^{t-1} = E\left[\theta_i^{t-1} | D_t\right]$$

On the one hand, we comparc thc theoretical distribution of the real state of the equipment (given by $\pi_t = \pi_0 P^n$) in a set of time slices (specifically, in $t = 5$ and $t = 45$ which correspond with the system behaviour in the short and the long term) with the average bar diagram obtained by the algorithm over the 400 paths. On the other hand, we show the solution provided to a particular path, summarizing each posterior distribution in its mean.

First of all, we consider the identity matrix as the perturbation matrix, i.e., $Q = I_{10}$. Thus, the model receives the true system state and we study the goodness of the algorithm in ideal conditions. Fig. 4, 5 and 6 show up the results. The model correctly identifies the real behaviour of the system, even in the short term. Solid lines in Fig. 6 stand for a 95% probability band.

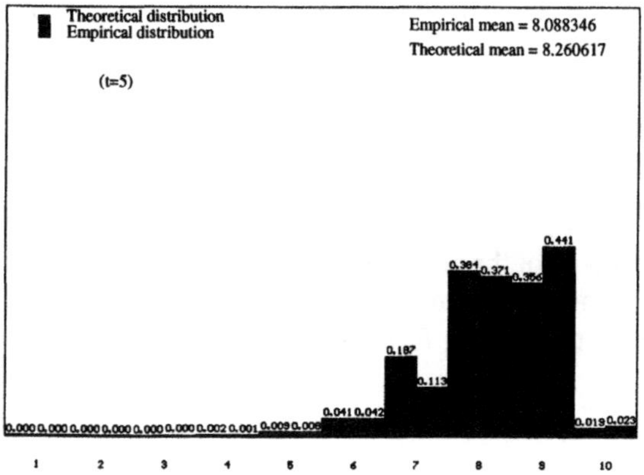

Fig. 4. Bar diagram for $t = 5$ and $Q = I_{10}$

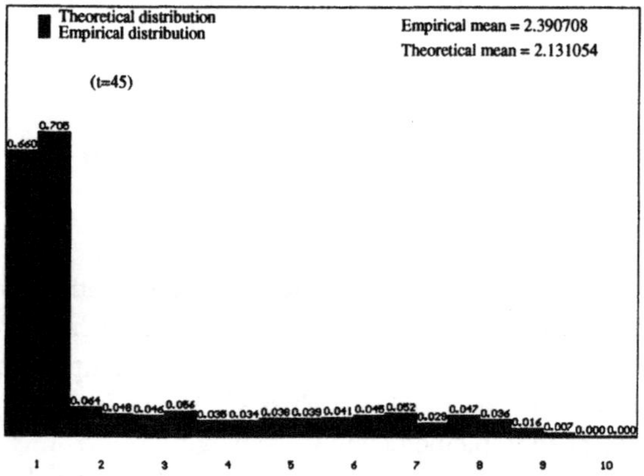

Fig. 5. Bar diagram for $t = 45$ and $Q = I_{10}$

Next, a sensibility study is proposed, using the perturbation matrix

$$Q_1 = \begin{bmatrix} 0.5 & 0.3 & 0.2 & & & & & & & \\ 0.2 & 0.5 & 0.2 & 0.1 & & & & & & \\ 0.1 & 0.2 & 0.4 & 0.2 & 0.1 & & & & & \\ & 0.1 & 0.2 & 0.4 & 0.2 & 0.1 & & & & \\ & & 0.1 & 0.2 & 0.4 & 0.2 & 0.1 & & & \\ & & & 0.1 & 0.2 & 0.4 & 0.2 & 0.1 & & \\ & & & & 0.1 & 0.2 & 0.4 & 0.2 & 0.1 & \\ & & & & & 0.1 & 0.2 & 0.4 & 0.2 & 0.1 \\ & & & & & & 0.1 & 0.2 & 0.5 & 0.2 \\ & & & & & & & 0.2 & 0.3 & 0.5 \end{bmatrix}$$

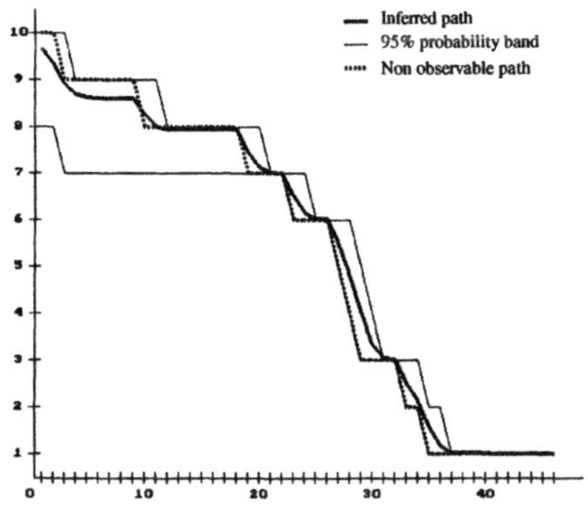

Fig. 6. Inference for a path

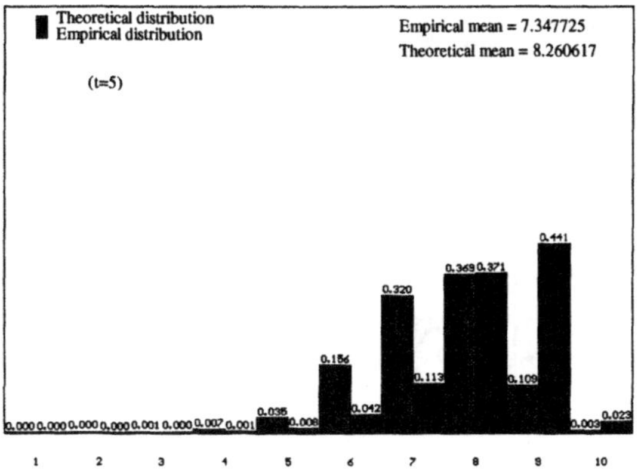

Fig. 7. Bar diagram for $t = 5$ and $Q = Q_1$

In the short term (Fig. 7), there is a difference in the probabilities. However, an effective filtration of the considered perturbation is observed in the long term (Fig. 8). In any case, Fig. 9 shows the closeness of the inferred path to the real path in periods of moderate perturbation.

6 Conclusions

We have proposed a dynamic graphical model for modelling a certain partially observed domain. Furthermore, we have presented an algorithm to build posterior distributions about the states of the unobservable components of the domain, using the information stored in the observed components.

Despite the increasing diffusion of graphical models in applications, they have rarely been used to model temporal processes, apart from a few exceptions (see references).

The development of this kind of models, which make use of detailed domain knowledge, traces a path from applied statistical techniques, to operations research methods, and finally to probabilistic reasoning.

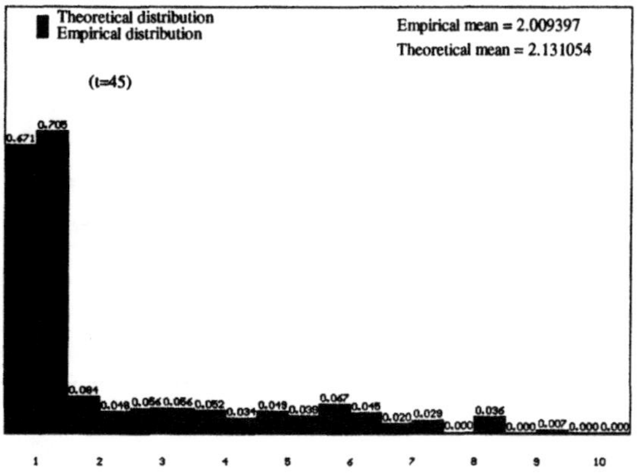

Fig. 8. Bar diagram for $t = 45$ and $Q = Q_1$

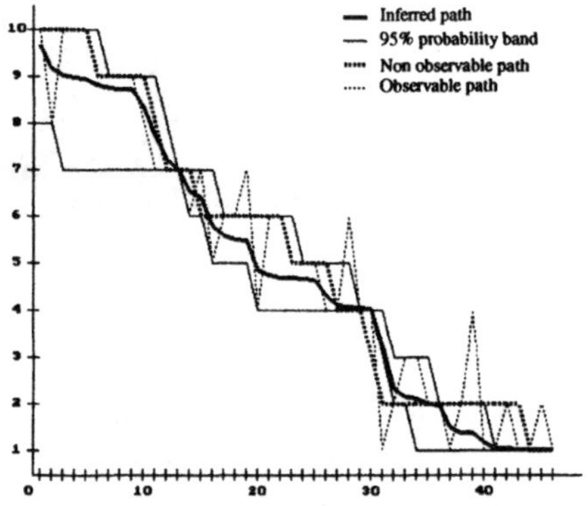

Fig. 9. Inference for a path

References

Berzuini, C. (1990). Modelling temporal processes via belief networks and Petri nets, with applications to expert systems. In *Annals of Mathematics and Artificial Intelligence* **2**, 39–64.

Dagum, P. and Galper, A. (1994). Time-series prediction using belief network models. Technical Report 522, Knowledge Systems Laboratory, Medical Computer Science, Standford University.

Kanazawa, K., Koller, D. and Russell, S. (1995). Stochastic simulation algorithms for dynamic probabilistic networks. In *Proceedings of the 11th Conference on Uncertainty in Artificial Intelligence (UAI-95)*, Montreal, Quebec, Canada.

Kjærulff, U. (1992). A computational scheme for reasoning in dynamic probabilistic networks. In *Proceedings of the 8th Conference on Uncertainty in Artificial Intelligence (UAI-92)*, Stanford University, 121–129.

Lekuona, A., Lacruz, B. and Lasala, P. (1996). Modeling and monitoring dynamic systems by chain graphs. In *Learning from Data: Artificial Intelligence and Statistics V*. Lecture Notes in Statistics **112**. D. Fisher and H.J. Lenz, Eds., 68–77, Springer-Verlag.

Lekuona, A., Lacruz, B. and Lasala, P. (1997). Approximate inference and forecast algorithms in graphical models for partially observed dynamic systems. In *Preliminary Papers of the 6th International Workshop on Artificial Intelligence and Statistics*. January 4–6, Ft. Lauderdale, Florida, 319–326.

Part VI

Epilog

Decision Analysis for Private and Public Sector Decisions

Rakesh K. Sarin[1]

[1] The Anderson School of Management, University of California, Los Angeles 110 Westwood Plaza/Box 952481 Los Angeles, CA 90095-1481, USA

Abstract

In this paper I provide insights into some similarities and some differences between private and public sector decisions. It is often asserted that in the private sector the decision maker deals with a single objective of profit maximization (or shareholder wealth maximization) whereas in the public sector often multiple conflicting objectives must be balanced. I will argue that in both cases the choice of a decision involves balancing multiple concerns and impact on multiple stakeholders.

Keywords. Decision analysis, multiple objectives, profit maximization, public sector

1 Introduction

If you ask a friend, a colleague, or a fellow traveler what does he think are some of the differences between private sector and public sector decisions, you are likely to encounter the following. In private sector, the pursuit of the profits is the objective and decisions must maximize shareholders' wealth. In Public sector decisions, managers are required to balance multiple conflicting objectives and decisions must attend to the concerns of multiple stakeholders. There is some truth to the above assertion though at the operational level where decisions are formulated and evaluated such a distinction is of little use. I will argue that decisions in both public and private sectors require balancing several competing objectives and are made towards an eye for satisfying the needs of several different stakeholders. The difference in decision making between two sectors lies in the *nature* of objectives and the *nature* of stakeholders that must be dealt with in private and public sector decisions.

Before I go on developing my thesis, I must confess that much of what I say is an opinion that is based on the experiences with several projects that I have been involved with over many years. The decision makers in these projects were usually senior managers but not the top managers (CEO's, heads of agencies). The conclusions drawn may therefore be valid only for certain types or levels of decisions. In this sense this is not a research study. The arguments presented here are observations and editorial opinions and not hypotheses supported by a scientific study.

2 Brief description of a case study

Several projects in private and public sectors that I have been associated with are listed in Table 1. Here I will draw upon from a project in private sector that involved selection of an R&D project requiring a commitment of $50 million of investment. The goal of the project was to develop a measurement while drilling product (MWD) for an oil service company. The product when completed was to provide geological and drilling information in a real time mode to facilitate decision making.

Private Sector	Public Sector
• Coal Power Plant Siting	• Proposal Evaluation
• Fuel Price and Availability	• Solar Enery Forecasting
• Electric Outage/Safety Analysis	• Electric Car/Storage Devices
• Capacity and Technology Planning	• Waste Disposal
• New Product Development	• Seismic Safety
	• Environmental Standards

Table 1. Applications

It was clear from the outset that different departments in the company did not agree on the most preferred design. The marketing group preferred Design A, which could be developed quickly and which caused the least interference with the way users (drilling operators) were accustomed to conduct their business. Since such a product was unavailable at the time to the industry, a quick entry into the market to gain first mover advantage was considered very important.

The R&D group preferred Design B, on which they had already made some progress. They also preferred a more sophisticated product which included a wider range of sensors, and a more patient approach to entry into the market to ensure a high degree of product reliability.

The manufacturing group favored a design configuration that was easy to manufacture. For example, one concern of the manufacturing group was to avoid the use of non-magnetic collars, as these tend to be harder to machine.

It was unclear, however, which of the several possible designs the company should pursue. Further, there was no agreement on which basic sensors must be included in the product first offered to the market.

To choose a preferred design which is in the best interest of a company, the various groups involved in the decision making process must first agree on the objectives or common success factors relevant to the decision. R&D groups often tend to place a greater emphasis on technical capabilities of the product. In contrast, marketing groups feel a greater pressure to generate sales and tend to emphasize quick entry into the market and product proliferation through market segmentation.

In this application we first interrogated R&D, marketing, and manufacturing people separately to identify the attributes that were most relevant from the perspective of their own group. The groups were then brought together and agreement was reached on the list of attributes that ought to be used in the evaluation process.

In Figure 1, the list of attributes that was finally agreed upon by various participants in the decision making process is shown. The four mid-level criteria shown in Figure 1 measure the concerns:

When will the product be ready to market?
(Timing)
What will the product do?
(Performance)
How well will it perform?
(Reliability)
How much will it cost?
(Cost)

The immediate decision facing the company was the choice of a Sonde or an Insert design and the sensors that must be included in the initial product. The design engineers had generated over one hundred possible alternatives. A careful screening based on development cost, development time, technical feasibility, etc., led to a reduction to nine contending design alternatives.

It is to be noted that several design alternatives that were not thought out in early investigation were created after the groups identified the relevant attributes. Additionally, something pleasant happened. The discussion that was focused on Sonde (the marketing group's favored design) versus Insert (the R&D group's favored design) shifted to which sensors would be in the Insert mode and which should be in the Sonde mode. At this stage the two groups were far from reaching a consensus on the preferred design but they began to appreciate the advantages of each design —a definite bit of progress.

Eventually, through the process of decision analysis, the relative weights for attributes and the relative desirability for alternative levels of outcomes on each attribute were quantified. The evaluation of alternatives and the final choice was based on how good each design alternative was with respect to the attributes in Figure 1 and through negotiation among the groups impacted by the decision. In this case, the groups finally agreed on a hybrid design that reflected a balance of concerns that the marketing and the design groups had raised.

Even when a formal decision analysis may not be carried out, the projects are evaluated by balancing concerns such as those depicted in Figure 1 and through a negotiation among parties impacted by the choice. Should an impasse occur, a senior executive has the decision authority to move the project along.

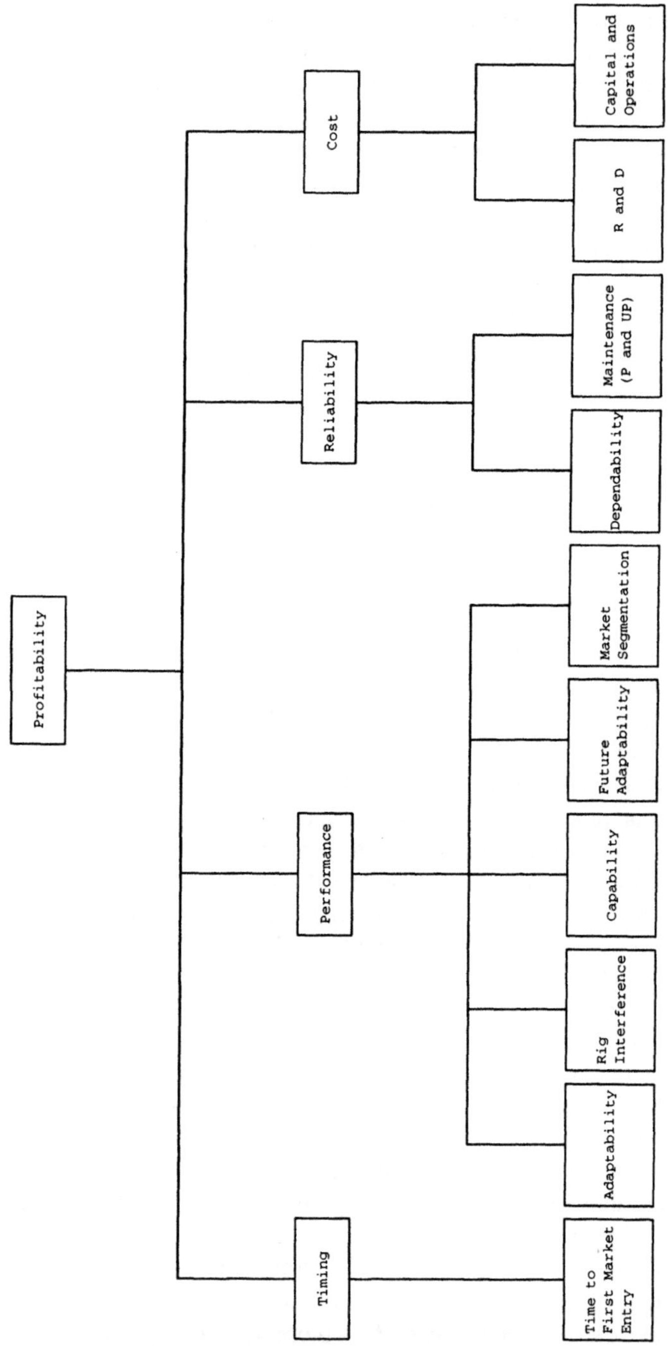

Fig. 1. Objectives and Attributes of the Decision Problem

This case study is typical of many private sector decisions at the project level. Even though the ultimate motive was to maximize shareholders' wealth, there was no mention of shareholders and no computation of profits associated with each design during the process of decision making. But, there was plenty of discussion about impact of chosen design on product performance, timing, reliability and cost. There was also a thorough discussion of the impact of chosen design on the ultimate users and on different departments in the company.

3 Myth: Maximization of Profits

In the R&D project selection decision described in Section 2 the problem was to choose a product design towards which research and development resources should be directed. Clearly, the senior managers are interested in choosing the product design that will ultimately lead to high profits and market share. In Figure 1, this intention is depicted as Profits sit atop the objectives hierarchy.

In the evaluation of alternative designs, however, it is often not feasible to compute profits (or Net Present Value of Cash Flows) associated with alternative designs that differ with one another in configuration and the number and the type of components included. It is easier and perhaps more useful if the decision process involves a consideration of the impact of a chosen design on criteria such as product performance, reliability, dependability, and cost. These criteria of course are further broken down in measurable attributes.

At the project level, the connection between a choice and its impact on profits is indirect. The impact of a new design of "head lights" in a car on profits is neither easy to quantify nor a useful starting point in deliberations that would lead to a sensible choice. Profit is too *aggregate* an objective to permit meaningful discrimination among alternative designs.

There are some decisions, such as buying a company, where financial measures (profits, earnings per share, etc.) are the dey drivers of decisions. Even in such cases the impact of a decision on long term profitability may be better assessed through non-financial criteria such as market share, fit with the existing business, growth potential, etc. There is no "meter" that would register the profit levels at future points in time associated with a decision. The choice of a decision often boils down to a pro and con analysis of several competing alternatives.

Profit in business decisions like happiness in personal decisions provides a motivation for action. Profits are the raison d'etre for the existence of businesses. The argument that I make here is that at the project level, where most decisions are made, profits often do not serve as a useful starting point for evaluating alternative decisions.

It is often necessary to break down the goal of the maximization of profits into relatively more directly measurable attributes such as product performance, reliability, sales growth, development and operational costs, etc.

Managers in private sector choose among myriad of options by balancing attributes that impact success of the project, organizational considerations such as impact on other departments and managers, and personal goals such as ego and relationship with others. Not all these attributes are explicitly acknowledged or stated and some may be deliberately hidden. But even for those attributes that are explicit in deliberations, managers may have little knowledge of how an improvement in one attribute at the expense of the other would influence ultimate profits. They hope that the choice they make will yield higher profits than the choices they forego but they know that this relationship of attractiveness of an alternative with eventual profits is ambiguous. The workings of a manager's decision process is similar to that of a doctor who manages a patient's health curing problems as they occur and hoping that his actions would lead to a healthier and a longer life for the patient.

So far we have argued that at the operational level, the private sector managers much like their counterparts in the public sector make tradeoffs among multiple conflicting concerns and their final choice reflects a balance among these concerns. There is however an important difference between managerial motivations and resulting decision processes between private and public sectors.

The managers in public sector (Internal Revenue Service, Passport Office, Police, Environmental Protection Agency) are often unsure of the purposes that their organizations serve. IRS must collect taxes but not pursue its task so zealously that taxpayers may perceive harassment. Passport office must renew or issue passports expediently but ward against these being handed out to improper hands (non-citizens). EPA takes action to protect the public health and environment but it should also listen to the businesses and avoid imposing undue economic costs on them.

Citizens require from the public sector managers that they be fair in their decisions and dealings and yet it is unclear how these fairness considerations are to be balanced against efficiency. For example, the managers of the UCLA housing project are required to select the contractor with the lowest bid, presumably to ensure fairness and avoid favoritism. The occupants of these homes are however concerned with the quality and timeliness of completion. There are numerous examples where a public sector manager must act without knowing the guidelines for balancing these multiple conflicting concerns. Further, the relative importance of different objectives keeps changing over time as public opinion sways back and forth. "Be tough on illegal immigrants" and "respect individuals' privacy" are both desires that public expresses but the strength of sentiments for each varies a great deal among various citizen groups and over time. The net result of these competing public demands is that the goals of many public agencies are ambiguous and often contradictory.

Managers in both private and public sectors must deal with multiple concerns. Profits provide a motive for action for private sector managers. In resolving conflicts among criteria (is it better to enter the market sooner with fewer features?), the intent to maximize profits is clear even when profit gains associated with each tradeoff may be unavailable. This clarity of purpose brings consistency to decisions made by private sector managers. In absence of a clearly defined purpose, the public sector managers often seem inconsistent in their decisions. It is this lack of clear purpose and the guideline for resolving conflicts among criteria and not merely the presence of multiple criteria that distinguishes managerial tasks in the public sector from those in the private sector.

4 Multiple Stakeholders

It is often presumed that managers in private sector are servant to the goals of the shareholders who in turn want maximum return on their capital. Few managers, at the project level, consciously think of shareholders let alone compute the impact of each decision on shareholders' wealth. Managers, however, actively consider the impact of their choices on their counterparts in other departments, their superiors and subordinates, customers and suppliers. The impacts on these stakeholders are often more vivid and more immediate than the eventual result of the decision on shareholders' wealth. There is a burgeoning literature in management that shows that the long term interest of a business are enhanced if it treats suppliers, customers, and other groups affected by the business as partners.

The motive is to maximize shareholders' wealth; after all they are the owners of the business. For operational decisions, however, managers need the cooperation of more immediate stakeholders to achieve desirable results for the ultimate owners. A decision to shorten lead time for a product may put pressure on suppliers and production department but may make marketing department and customers happier. Their interest must be balanced in arriving at a final decision. How does a shorter lead time impact shareholders is not the question a typical manager wrestles with; instead, he negotiates a solution that is acceptable to immediate stakeholders (suppliers, production, marketing in this example).

It is well recognized that public sector managers must balance the interests of several interest groups. Environmental Protection Agency, for example, evaluates its decisions with respect to the impact on the health of sensitive groups such as children, pregnant women, and people with medical conditions that may get worse if they are exposed to pollutants. EPA must also pay attention to the interests of businesses, environmental groups and general public who may not be directly impacted but still may have opinion about the policies and decisions of EPA.

Managers in both private and public sectors constantly balance the interests of multiple stakeholders when they face a choice among competing alternatives. Public sector decision tasks and decision processes differ from those in the private sector not because the former must satisfy multiple stakeholders but on who these stakeholders are and what are their ultimate motives. The nature of stakeholders differs a great deal for the two sectors.

In private sector, in spite of seemingly conflicting interests on a given issue (labor versus management on salary negotiations or production versus marketing on inventory decisions), they all ultimately want the business to succeed. A profitable business is the only way to ensure welfare of each group. Thus, all work towards increasing the size of the pie. Along the way they may differ in their opinions about the course of actions that may lead to a greater increase in the size of the pie. They may want a larger share of the pie or may believe that they deserve a larger share. Self-interest of a particular group may dominate in the way it negotiates business solutions.

In spite of all these differences, a level of cooperation and a common understanding exists that the success of business is paramount to their own group's welfare. This motivation is seen to induce high level of cooperation and self-sacrifice when the business is in danger. But even in good times different stakeholders often cooperate and recognize their mutual dependability.

The manager in private sector has the authority to choose a course of action even when it may not please all parties involved. His power in hiring and firing and determining the work content of his subordinates permits him to implement solution without the fear that the group that does not come out on top may thwart his decision. Actually, the employees in private sector understand the manager's role as an arbiter and go along with his decisions. This common understanding about the process of conflict resolution —the buck stops somewhere— creates a level of cooperation that keeps the businesses running smoothly.

In the public sector the story is quite different. The interests of General Motors and Sierra Club with regard to permissible levels of Carbon Monoxide emissions are inherently different. They are motivated by fundamentally conflicting goals. A public sector manager can not possibly please both groups and often can not avoid challenges in the court to whatever choice he makes. He hopes through public hearings and open participation of citizen groups a compromise may emerge but the presence of inherently conflicting goals make such compromises very difficult. The problem is actually even more serious.

A public sector manager must also watch out for the reactions of relatively less affected members of general public who may not have a direct interest in the decision. A news report, for example, could create a massive public reaction. An action to upgrade buildings for seismic safety is possibly driven more by its impact on general public (if in case of an earthquake an injury occurs) than by a cost-benefit consideration for the occupants of the building. A public sector manager thus operates in an uncertainty about how citizens are likely to react to his decisions.

Both private sector and public sector managers must seek the cooperation and acceptability from relevant stakeholders for their decisions to be effective. In private sector, an authority over the factors of production and a common motive of business success makes the balancing of these interests easier. In contrast, in public sector some of the stakeholders are driven by fundamentally conflicting motives and the managers lack authority in enforcing the choice. The result is often a slow decision process in the public sector and a more efficient one in the private sector.

It is my belief that in public sector, in spite of the presence of conflicting goals and stakeholders with motives that may be at cross purposes, a more rational and possibly a more efficient decision process would result if an attempt is made to quantify the importance weights and priorities. A decision analysis approach would be useful but other approaches may work as well. These priorities may change over time but having some guidelines on how conflicts may be resolved would take the blind guesswork out and make the decision process expedient.

5 Conclusions

A decision analyst approaches a problem in the private or the public sector with the intent to clarify issues and move the organization towards an acceptable solution. The basic building blocks of decision analysis —value hierarchy, strategy matrix, multi-attribute analysis and evaluation, stakeholder impact analysis— have been found to be useful in a variety of problems in both sectors.

A deeper understanding of decision processes and of reasons that explain evolution of these processes would facilitate the implementation of rational approaches for decision making. Rules and legislations constrain the decision process in the public sector. As a result, public sector managers have a lesser control over capital, labor, and organizational choices than their counterparts in private sector. These rules have evolved to preserve fairness that is demanded by the citizens. Justification of decisions is important and must withstand, in some cases, court challenges. This desire for fairness, that comes at first place from the citizens and not from the managers, slows down the decision process. To preserve some remnants of efficiency often deadlines are imposed and the process is forced to move along. It may be a clumsy way to expedite the decision process but it often works.

In spite of these difficulties, many public sector agencies carry out their tasks admirably. An explicit specification of goals even when these conflict and a clear guideline for resolving basic value tradeoffs would aid in achieving both fairness and efficiency in decisions. For example, a guidance on what value to use in reducing risks of mortality by a given magnitude would be useful to agencies that deal with public safety. Neither the goal of fairness nor of efficiency is helped by leaving such value tradeoffs ambiguous. I do not suggest that an agreement on such a guideline can be easily achieved. But, the interests of citizens are better served by an open debate on such value tradeoffs. Clarity of goals and purposes and a prioritization of these goals —quantitative or qualitative— would go a long way in reducing ambiguities that cloud public sector decision making.

<u>GPSR Compliance</u>

The European Union's (EU) General Product Safety Regulation (GPSR) is a set of rules that requires consumer products to be safe and our obligations to ensure this.

If you have any concerns about our products, you can contact us on ProductSafety@springernature.com

In case Publisher is established outside the EU, the EU authorized representative is:

Springer Nature Customer Service Center GmbH
Europaplatz 3
69115 Heidelberg, Germany

Batch number: 10823959

Printed by Printforce, the Netherlands